# Next to the
# Color Line

# CRITICAL AMERICAN STUDIES SERIES

*George Lipsitz*
UNIVERSITY OF CALIFORNIA–SANTA BARBARA
SERIES EDITOR

# Next to the Color Line

## Gender, Sexuality, and W. E. B. Du Bois

*Susan Gillman and*
*Alys Eve Weinbaum,* EDITORS

CRITICAL AMERICAN STUDIES SERIES

*University of Minnesota Press*
Minneapolis · London

Published by the University of Minnesota Press
111 Third Avenue South, Suite 290
Minneapolis, MN 55401-2520
http://www.upress.umn.edu

**Library of Congress Cataloging-in-Publication Data**

Next to the color line : gender, sexuality, and W. E. B. Du Bois / Susan Gillman and Alys Eve Weinbaum, editors.
    p. cm. (Critical American Studies series)
    Includes bibliographical references and index.
    ISBN-13: 978-0-8166-4722-4 (hardcover : alk. paper)
    ISBN-10: 0-8166-4722-4 (hardcover : alk. paper)
    ISBN-13: 978-0-8166-4723-1 (pbk. : alk. paper)
    ISBN-10: 0-8166-4723-2 (pbk. : alk. paper)
1. Du Bois, W. E. B. (William Edward Burghardt), 1868–1963—Political and social views. 2. Sex role—United States. 3. Feminism—United States. 4. African Americans—Politics and government. 5. African Americans—Social conditions. 6. Du Bois, W. E. B. (William Edward Burghardt), 1868–1963—Criticism and interpretation. 7. African American women in literature. 8. African Americans in literature. 9. Sex role in literature. 10. Sex in literature. I. Gillman, Susan Kay. II. Weinbaum, Alys Eve, 1967–
E185.97.D73N48 2007
305.48'896073—dc22
2006028297

# Contents

# Introduction:
# W. E. B. Du Bois and the
# Politics of Juxtaposition

■ *Susan Gillman and Alys Eve Weinbaum*

The uplift of women is, next to the problem of the color line and the peace movement, our greatest modern cause. When, now, two of these movements—women and color—combine in one, the combination has deep meaning.

W. E. B. Du Bois,
*Darkwater* (1920)

Gender and sexuality are rarely viewed as central analytical categories within Du Bois's substantial corpus. As is well known, Du Bois is most frequently touted as a modern theorist of the "race concept" and as a renowned scholar of "the problem of the color line," which he prophetically announced in 1900 "is the problem of this century," which was then not even one year old.[1] And yet, even as Du Bois's signature formulation activates in the insistent verb "is," the past, present, and future of race history as we in the twenty-first century know it, there could hardly be a more opportune time than the present to reengage his writings from the widest possible conceptual and historical vantage point. Indeed, it is precisely the long history of gender and

1

race's uncoupling within Du Bois studies that allows us, *per contra*, to excavate the implicit gender and sexual logics that form a part of the complex foundation of Du Bois's ideas about and figurations of race. For, as readers of Du Bois, we have finally arrived at a historical juncture when the daunting expansiveness of Du Bois's grammar—not to mention his life and work, spanning two centuries and straddling the globe—requires reinvigoration and renewal by scholarly and political concerns that have, over the past three decades, become inextricable from "the problem of the color line" that Du Bois formulated and against which he fought on multiple fronts.

The work of centering gender and sexual logics (broadly construed as thematics, threads, rhetoric, and discursive figurations) and of developing Du Bois's antiracism and anti-imperialism in feminist and sexually liberatory directions is undertaken by each of the contributors to this volume. This collection is enabled as much by Du Bois's own legacy as by feminist and queer studies scholarship, which has developed frameworks for theorizing the intersection of race, gender, and sexuality as identities, ideologies, and matrixes of power, which are all too often expressed in interwoven forms of racism, sexism, and homophobia. Thus we begin this introduction with the caveat, laid out forcefully by Joy James (see her essay in this volume), that Du Bois seldom pursued the express connections between the "Negro question" that defined so much of his intellectual and political life and the "woman question" that was being explored by the writers and feminist activists who surrounded him (including Pauline Hopkins, Ida B. Wells-Barnett, Anna Julia Cooper, Jessie Fauset, and Nella Larsen).[2] At the same time, we also argue that it is necessary to deepen our investigation to explore how Du Bois bequeathed to readers important, if often inchoate, traces of and speculations about the possibilities and difficulties of thinking gender, sexuality, and race side by side, as *juxtaposed*, if not fully interwoven or articulated. These gendered and sexualized traces and speculations are this volume's object of study; its objective is their excavation and reanimation for new theoretical, scholarly, and political ends.

### The Politics of Juxtaposition

What may be thought of as a dual, even contradictory positing that characterizes Du Bois's writings—the simultaneous juxtaposition of issues of race, gender, and sexuality and the submerging of their express connection—is instructively elaborated in our epigraph, drawn from Du Bois's second multigeneric, semiautobiographical text *Darkwater* (1920). Here he writes, "The uplift of women is, next to the problem of the color line and the peace movement, our greatest modern cause."[3] With his simple and straightforward phrase "next to," Du Bois sets out what we label a *politics of juxtaposition* that positions multiple political issues and related world historical movements for social justice as associated, as necessarily juxtaposed, if not fully interlinked, or self-consciously interwoven. After all, as our epigraph's syntax at once enacts and instructs, only when distinct movements are thought of as proximate—when juxtaposition renders apparent their necessary association—does "the uplift of women" emerge as "our greatest modern cause."

And yet, the same syntax that enables expression of desired political and analytical connection also tells the story of an elision that is, in its own right, characteristic of Du Bois's work. As the epigraph continues, the falling away of categories of concentration produces a semblance of connection among race, gender, and peace movements that is not in fact elaborated by Du Bois, and which *cannot* be elaborated precisely because the question of connection has been elided rather than integrated. Du Bois continues, "When, now, two of these movements—women and color—*combine in one,* the combination has *deep meaning*" (574, emphasis added). Just as "the peace movement" is readily added to Du Bois's equation, it drops out, leaving "women and color" to "combine in one" in a manner that posits a residual distinction between "women" and "color," even as the equation of gender and race simultaneously begs the question of the implied process of "combination." In other words, our epigraph leaves us—as do so many of Du Bois's writings—with a tantalizing if speculative political formulation and rhetorical strategy: a politics of juxtaposition grounded in a form of combination that acknowledges simultaneity and association, and yet elects not to work through how it is that connections among the movements for the "uplift of women," for racial justice, and for peace might be conceptualized or produced, or how black women might be included, as a group, within the analysis.

Another way to limn Du Bois's politics of juxtaposition is to underscore that his lexical constellation of "combine" and "combination" contains both political limits and possibilities. "Combine" according to the *Oxford English Dictionary* means to couple, or join two or more things, to associate, or ally. And yet, while the choice of the word "combine" clearly holds out the possibility of an ideal, even utopian union of conjoined parts, it resolutely retains a notion of difference. "Combine" is rooted in the Latin *com*, which means join, and *bini*, by twos, reminding us that the binary remains present in the idea of combination even as merger is beckoned. *Combine* holds in suspension the joining and the two, and thus reifies the idea of original separation. As a result, the ideal union is ultimately elusive and undefined, its only concrete manifestation a projected merger that is gestured toward but remains unachieved in the present moment of Du Bois's text. How, finally, to gauge the political efficacy of such futurity? This is a question to which we return shortly.

Given the double sidedness of "combination," it is perhaps unsurprising that two of the term's recent usages convey, respectively, its capitalist and its anticapitalist meanings. The former usage originates in the nineteenth-century United States and refers to groups formed in furtherance of special interests, as in bloc, cartel, syndicate, or to use a synonym that Du Bois would have frequently heard, trust. By contrast, the latter originates with the revolutions and insurgent social movement that galvanized Europe and the United States, including the labor unions and workingmen's associations that emerged in the early years of the twentieth century. For in the decade in which Du Bois wrote *Darkwater*, industrial capitalism burgeoned and gave birth to a popular front set on controlling, if not destroying, the capitalist expansion that took the form of the trust. In all of these opposing senses and contexts, "the uplift of women" is quite literally and perpetually "*next to* the problem of the color line and the peace movement": it is allied and associated with, if never directly linked or tied to, the antiracist and anti-imperialist movements in which Du Bois was more directly involved and of which he wrote far more often.

In sharp contrast to contemporary feminist theorists of "intersectionality" (Kimberlé Crenshaw's groundbreaking work immediately comes to mind), or to work on the concept of "articulation" associated with structuralist Marxism (especially that of Antonio Gramsci, Louis Althusser, Stuart Hall, and Ernesto Laclau), *combine* in Du Bois's usage is "fugitive."[4] It is persistently present, but elusive, covert in its operations, inconsistent, and hard to track in its appearance and function. It is infrequently named, foregrounded, or developed to show how domains of power work in and through each other to constitute identities and mechanisms of oppression. Rather, it is inserted into the text unannounced in order to create "blocs" of syndicated or associated meaning, and then removed from circulation after its moment of utility, after its use value has been realized as an exchange value, after it has been temporarily tapped out.

If the politics of juxtaposition, and the language, grammar, and syntax with which Du Bois develops it, lacks an entirely consistent application, it nonetheless has a decisive and repeated rhetorical and political outcome. Indeed, Du Bois's internationalist anti-imperialist politics, the object of much important contemporary scholarship on Du Bois, is enabled—even made possible by—the juxtaposition of questions of gender and sexuality with those of race and empire. This becomes evident when Du Bois's fictional and nonfictional writings are juxtaposed, as they are by nearly all of the contributors to this volume. This is also readily apparent in each of the multigenre, semiautobiographical texts for which Du Bois is famous. Beginning with *The Souls of Black Folk* (1903), and including *Darkwater* (1920), and *Dusk of Dawn* (1940), a politics of juxtaposition convenes stylistically incompatible textual parts and seemingly divergent political questions, and thus "combine[s] in one" the disparate elements that comprise the famous compendious texts that Paul Gilroy has eloquently dubbed as "polyphonic" in form.[5]

The political efficacy of a politics of juxtaposition (to make possible the anti-imperialist internationalism) might be readily excavated in any of the assembled texts or located among any grouping of fiction and nonfiction. For our theoretical and expository purposes, we have found it most succinctly and expansively elaborated in *Darkwater*. This text, commonly positioned as marking a turning point in Du Bois's thinking, heralds the heretofore incipient anti-imperialist themes (which, we have noted, emerge as early as 1900 when he first articulated the international dimensions of the "problem of the color line") that become Du Bois's enduring focus. Not coincidentally, *Darkwater*, our jumping-off point and the source of our epigraph about "combination," also includes Du Bois's signal statement on gender oppression: "The Damnation of Women." To borrow from Du Bois's own vocabulary, in *Darkwater* he "combine[s] in one" a group of stylistically incompatible textual genres, including autobiographical essay, poetry, allegory, science fiction, hymn, and polemic on diverse topics ranging from his childhood in Great Barrington, Massachusetts to expropriation of African resources and labor, from the "burden of black women" to the so-called burden of empire, from the ascent of black Christ to the ascent of "the darker peoples of the world" joined in anti-imperialist revolutionary alliance.[6]

Although scholars regard *Darkwater* as a highly crafted text, attention to its crafting has largely been confined to consideration of the text's aesthetics rather than to the political efficacy of Du Bois's art of assemblage. The outcome is a paucity of scholarship treating the political effects of Du Bois's craft: the politics of juxtaposition that is the end result of his choice to "combine in one" seemingly discrete, often unrelated, textual pieces.[7] The disparate parts that together comprise *Darkwater* are thus, with few exceptions, read separately, and analyzed as if they exist in isolation, as if meaning lodges discretely in each chapter, as if each polemic, poetic interlude, hymn, and allegorical tale stands alone, and is thus untransformed by the wider context of the other textual pieces Du Bois convenes. "The Damnation of Women," one of the only chapters written expressly for inclusion in *Darkwater,* is often excerpted and made to stand alone, rather than read "next to" the other chapters, especially "The Hands of Ethiopia," the famous anti-imperialist essay that preexisted *Darkwater,* and for which the volume is best known ("Hands" was first published in *The Atlantic Monthly* in 1915 as "The African Roots of War"). Consequently, the two most famous chapters of *Darkwater* are routinely treated as distinct (one celebrated for its treatment of black womanhood, the other as a signature statement of Du Bois's anticolonialism), rather than positioned in a mutual dialogue by which each is, in its turn, transformed.

Perhaps unsurprisingly, such critical isolationism is practiced by the vast majority of scholars, despite powerful evidence throughout *Darkwater* of Du Bois's use of juxtaposition as an aesthetic and a political tool linking the violent oppression of women and blacks. For example, in chapter VI, "Of the Ruling of Men" (notably the chapter that precedes

"The Damnation of Women"), Du Bois informs readers that denial of franchise to blacks and women—to both "persons and classes"—are related injustices, for "it is argued . . . that everything which women with the ballot might do for themselves can be done for them; . . . *So, too,* we are told that American Negroes can have done for them by other voters all that they could possibly do for themselves . . . *So, too,* we are continually told that the 'best' Negroes stay out of politics" (553–54, emphasis added). Here, the linking phrase "so, too" repeats and, in repeating, forges an alliance between "American Negroes" and "women," an alliance that emerges not through articulation (which might, by contrast, be expressed as an ability to think about women of color), but through juxtaposition. Significantly, the logic of the "so, too" extends outward beyond the question of the franchise to incorporate the injustice of imperial domination in an increasingly transnational world. Further on in the chapter, citing the paragon of imperialism, Rudyard Kipling, against himself, Du Bois rhetorically asks of the naysayers to whom his meditation is addressed, "what is this theory of benevolent guardianship for women, for the masses, for Negroes—for 'lesser breeds without the law'?" (553).[8]

With this example we wish to stress that Du Bois's concept of "combination" is put into practice as a politics of juxtaposition, the limits of which grant us insight directly keyed to the possibilities. For when we read "combination" against the Marxist theory of "articulation," the principal theoretical concept that it at once gestures toward and evades, the double-sided nature of the "combination" and its associated politics becomes apparent. Both "combination" and "articulation" refer to points or acts of separation and connection (as we note in our etymological discussion of "combine") but do so differently. "Articulation," as Stuart Hall notes, is necessarily ambiguous, shifting back and forth from the physical to the linguistic, thanks to its lexical history which includes the sense of anatomical "joint" and expressive modality. As Hall explains, articulation is about joining and "giving expression to" (1980, 328).[9] By contrast, Du Bois's "combination" works through an additive rather than expressive logic that places bodies (black and female) next to discourses (predominantly racial and ungendered), but nonetheless eschews the joining and expressive force of articulation. This difference is manifest in Hall's famous example of the "'articulated' lorry": a truck whose front cab and back trailer can, "but need not necessarily," be connected to each other through "a specific linkage that *can* make the unity of two different elements, under certain conditions" (1996, 141). Thus, an additive logic constitutes the limit of Du Bois's "combination" and reveals a refusal to link the distinct elements that articulation joins. For rather than asking how such elements do or do not cohere under certain historical conditions, or as Hall puts it, "at specific conjunctures [and] to certain political subjects" (141–42), Du Bois's "combination" posits this possibility without taking on the burden of materializing it. The net result, as we will further discuss, is a series of textual gaps, truncations, interruptions, and deferrals.

If the politics of juxtaposition is a practice of meaning making to which Du Bois made continuous recourse, it should be evident that it is also a politics of reading that we twenty-first century scholars of Du Bois must practice if we are to excavate the gender and sexual politics that "combine" in Du Bois's corpus and give it "deep meaning." Such a reading practice follows Du Bois's own textual strategy, but does so deconstructively, operating within his textual protocols to read against the grain of his text. Its goal is to displace what the text engages and, in the process, to produce new gendered and sexualized meanings. Taking our cue from Du Bois's language of combination, in other words, we push beyond the bounds of Du Bois's strictly associative or additive logic to animate the missing interrelations among available keywords, arguments, and textual parts. What is the shape of the whole, the collectivity, implied by the groups juxtaposed in Du Bois's list—"women," "the masses," "Negroes," and "lesser breeds without the law"? To answer this question, we turn to a politics of juxtaposition as a reading practice that deals with the unspoken, disrupted, or unfinished synergies that emerge among and between parts as often as with manifest content and stated import of the text.

A politics of juxtaposition would not be especially compelling if "The Damnation of Women" were the only essay in which gender and sexuality are figured, or if gender and sexuality did not reappear—as each contributor to this volume testifies—in so many of Du Bois's writings. Rather, *Darkwater*, like the other multigenre works, and the vast majority of fiction, poetry, and correspondence, contains numerous traces or fugitive figurations of gender and sexuality, and it is these that surround, and are surrounded by, the better known passages, essays, and chapters. In order to elaborate fully a politics of juxtaposition as a reading strategy, the next section offers a detailed analysis of a textual cluster, forming prominently around "Hands of Ethiopia," the chapter of *Darkwater* that most strongly expresses the volume's overarching anti-imperialism, and, notably, the chapter invariably read out of context, as if it had nothing to say about gender or sexuality. To recontextualize "Hands" within the larger work is to restore and accentuate Du Bois's politics of juxtaposition, and in doing so to reveal an array of gendered and sexualized connections that emerge not only between the signal anti-imperialist textual elements of *Darkwater,* but also among the political causes that the various essays and surrounding interludes that comprise the volume individually champion.

### Anti-Imperialism, Gendered Figuration, and Sexual Violence

In *Darkwater's* "Postscript", which Du Bois wryly and "perversely" places before the beginning of the main text, he reconsiders and self-consciously foregrounds the volume's peculiar organization. In marking what would otherwise be titled a "Preface" as a "Postscript," Du Bois announces, *avant la lettre,* Jacques Derrida's well-known analysis of the spatiotemporal paradoxes of the preface, which looks simultaneously in two directions of space and time: out into the text, a preview from a forward position, and backward temporally, from a future location, after both the writing and reading of the writing have been completed.[10] As Du Bois explains:

> Between the sterner flights of logic, I have sought to set some little alightings of what may be poetry. They are tributes to Beauty, unworthy to stand alone; yet perversely, in my mind, now at the end, I know not whether I mean the Thought for the Fancy—or the Fancy for the Thought, or why the book trails off to playing, rather than standing strong on unanswering fact. But this is alway [sic.]—is it not?—the Riddle of Life (483).

Here Du Bois instructs readers that his "little alightings" of poetry, hymn, and fiction should not be regarded as mere "Fancy" inserted "between" the "sterner" "Thought[s]." Rather, he muses, fantastical textual elements retroactively reveal themselves to be as significant to the overall meaning of *Darkwater* as the "flights of logic" with which they are juxtaposed. For the "Postscript" suggests that *not knowing* how the assembled textual elements articulate in and through each other ("whether I mean the Thought for the Fancy—or the Fancy for the Thought") is actually key to reading and making meaning of the text. Indeed, when "the book trails off to playing" rather than "standing on fact," the deepest level of meaning—the "Riddle of Life"—is revealed in all its opacity. Textual meaning is thus neither structured by nor aligned with a single genre (analytical essay or poetry, for instance), but rather resides in the nebulous space among genres and styles: it emerges in and through juxtaposition, or in and through what Du Bois characterizes as the "half-tone" he hopes to strike. (He uses this term in a kind of faux apology for *Darkwater,* which speaks to "themes on which great souls have already said greater words," leaving him, he says in mock self-derision, only the hope of striking "here and there a half-tone" [483]). In short, Du Bois's "Postscript" playfully warns readers by instructing them on how to read, on how to allow that which is caught between textual parts, that which is interstitial, "half-tone," to emerge "up from the heart of my problem and the problems of my people" (483).[11]

In the "Forethought" to *The Souls of Black Folk,* Du Bois famously draws back the "veil" so that readers might see within, and thus come to understand the "color line" from the perspective of one who is "bone of the bone and flesh of the flesh of them that live within the Veil" (100). By contrast, in the "Postscript" he updates his earlier formulation, noting that he has "seen the human drama from a veiled corner" (483). From the vantage point of the interwar years, persistent race riots, lynching, and Euro-American imperial aggression, he has come to realize that reason alone cannot fight and win the war against racism and empire; rather, the "little alightings" and other "tributes to Beauty," although "unworthy to stand alone," are central to his aesthetic and political agenda. Whereas in *Souls,* Du Bois, like other modern African American writers, reappropriates the framing apparatus of the text, reclaiming the preface formerly used by abolitionists to "authenticate" slave narratives, in *Darkwater* his "Postscript" clears space for "little alightings" and other "tributes to beauty" to exercise power over the text.[12] For the "Postscript" defiantly proclaims that self-authentication is no longer the sole purview of the black writer; rather, he who has liberated himself from such a narrow, reactive role can embrace the rich range of expressive modalities, styles, genres, and idioms. With his "Postscript," Du Bois's signals that his art of assemblage, his politics of juxtaposition, is iconoclastic and resistant—part of a long history of African American narrative innovation and political protest.

Du Bois's express attention to organizational strategy at *Darkwater*'s outset compels our attention to the series of textual juxtapositions that form the microstructure of the volume's chapters. As Du Bois suggests, the chapters are generically diverse, in that each is juxtaposed with a text of a different genre, a lyric interlude with which it duly appears coupled in the table of contents. Orthographically distinguishing the elements that comprise these pairs, the title of the main essay is capitalized, while its accompanying interlude is italicized. For our purposes, what is striking about Du Bois's pairings is their strong tendency to break down according to the presence or absence of explicit gender and sexual figuration. On the level of manifest content, Du Bois's polemical and analytical chapters (with the notable exception of "The Damnation of Women") treat, in a presumably gendered and sexually neutral fashion, the "sterner flights of logic" that arrest themselves, moment by moment, on a range of historical and political issues, including imperialism, lynching, racism in the labor movement, race riots, aesthetics and politics, and truth and beauty. Simultaneously, Du Bois's "little alightings," his poems, stories, and hymns, figure gender and sexuality directly, fancifully, and ultimately paradoxically: they are built upon the same range of historical and political issues as the prose chapters, but do not expressly announce this. Rather, the paired textual parts almost invariably bring gender and sexuality into the orbit of the "sterner" political logic of the volume through "play"—through innovative juxtaposition of genres, idioms, styles, and themes.

The key to understanding this division of rhetorical labor lies in analysis of the "figures" that people the "little alightings." These include an array of singular, often exceptional women scattered throughout, including several of Du Bois's own ancestors: Allegorical figures, such as the "Dark daughter of lotus leaves," who begins the poem "The Riddle of the Sphinx," and the "Black mother of the iron hills" who ends it (509–10); the eponymous princess of the allegorical tale "The Princess of the Hither Isles"; the white girl and the white farmer's wife who apprehend the black Christ figure in "Jesus Christ in Texas"; the black woman of the biblical allegory "The Call," who "quailed and trembled," yet summoned the courage to respond to the King, and, like Judith before her, goes into battle (564); the "I" who speaks as "a woman born" in the insurgent lyric "Children of the Moon" (577); the white woman who momentarily joins forces with the black savior in "The Comet," the science fiction tale that concludes the book; and, finally, the group of mythologized and unsung black women who comprise the pantheon dramatized in "The Damnation of Women." In contrast to these singular figures, seemingly gender-neutral groups and plurals make up the cast of characters in the volume's "sterner" chapters: the "Darker Peoples" and their other, the "White Folk" of the political call-to-arms, "The Souls of White Folk" (500); the "Africans" of the famous demand "Africa for Africans" that concludes "Hands of Ethiopia" (513, 517); and finally, the various groups, conjured in "Hands" and throughout the text, who are produced by capitalist imperialism in the United States and the colonized world, including "the imperial, commercial group of master capitalists," "the national middle classes," "the international laboring class," and "the backward, oppressed groups of nature-folk" (532).

In extending Du Bois's organizational impulses from a writing into a reading practice, we respond to the particular gendering and sexualization of his "alightings" by asking two interrelated sets of questions: How do race, gender, and sexuality combine and divide via these multi-genre textual clusters or constellations? How do mutually constituting parts associate in such a way that the "deep meaning" of Du Bois's anti-imperialism emerges from the juxtaposition of these gendered and sexualized elements? How might such organizational clusters be analytically employed to reveal the processes of combination that undergird the dynamic, if unstable and shifting, textual whole of Du Bois's anti-imperialist internationalism?

In order to resituate Du Bois's "alightings," we have found it useful to reorganize the textual clusters mapped in his table of contents. Even as we note that Du Bois's two-part, bigenre chapters formally embody his politics of juxtaposition, in reapproaching *Darkwater* we elect to construct our textual clusters—or better yet, *combinations*—so that they work against the grain of Du Bois's pairs. As a threesome, our combination (rather than his couple) ensures the proximity of gendered and sexual figuration to anti-imperialist content. Whereas in chapter III Du Bois pairs "The Hands of Ethiopia" with the previously unpublished allegory about a woman's quest for justice entitled, "The Princess of Hither Isles," we constellate these two texts with a third, the poem, "Riddle of the Sphinx," that immediately precedes "Hands" and is nominally paired with "The Souls of White Folk." In so creating a new tripartite text, we underscore the fact, obscured in the original table of contents, that the gender and sexual figuration of "Princess" echoes that of the poem, such that these two texts call forth the fugitive gender and sexual content of "Hands."[13] For when we flank the retitled 1915 essay, "The African Roots of War," by the black female seekers and wailing women that appear in the poem and the allegory, "Hands" metamorphoses and gives voice to new content. The result: our "perverse" textual threesome reveals that "Hands" is entirely surrounded by gendered and sexualized (con)texts, taking on full resonance only when these gendered and sexualized surroundings are foregrounded as its matrix, its condition of possibility.

To fully understand this interplay, greater familiarity with each part of the trio is needed. First, "Riddle," originally published in *Horizon* in 1907, with the openly gendered title "the Burden of Black Women," is a text recoded by Du Bois so that, ironically, gender *per se* appears to drop out. Indeed, Du Bois's change to a gender neutral title foreshadows and acknowledges the fate of the black female figures at the open and close of "Riddle." The poem begins with an apostrophe to the "dark daughter of the lotus leaves," a mythic figure, perhaps African, who has soothed the world into forgetfulness but whose prophetic voice blends with a cry "out of the South—the sad, black South," wailing a warning to the "ancient race" of "black men" and to "woman" that they must "awake" and "arise." This dark daughter of the "Southern Sea" links Africa to the violent history of slavery in the American South, recalling the famous formulation in *Souls* of the "darker . . . races of men in Asia and Africa, in America and the islands of the sea" (107). She reveals, as do so many of the figurations of Africa throughout *Darkwater*, that the struggle against the racist legacy of U.S. slavery and against imperialism in Africa, are two fronts of the same, larger battle. Moreover, the language of progress and uplift—"awake" and "arise"— used to warn and summon the "ancient race" is arrayed against the civilizational discourse to which it belongs, ringing a series of changes on, and producing an excoriating critique of, the imperial slogan (again Kipling's): "the white man's burden."

As the concept of "burden" is repeated throughout the poem, it, too, is redefined and regendered. The dark daughter's crying voice is stifled by "the burden of white men," "spoilers of women," "breeders of bastards" as well as "conquerors of unarmed men." However, if the dark daughter is initially depicted as a victim, bearing, "unthankfully," not simply white men's children, but also the whole complex of empire (the white man's burden "of liquor and lust and lies"), by the poem's end she is avenged by those who have heard her cry. In the last stanza, the dark daughter is supplanted by the "Black mother," who has been newly awakened alongside the other darker people who together constitute an insurgent, world-shaping mass. As the poet's voice takes over, it intones repeatedly, "I hate them," and in so doing prophesies worldwide revenge of "black men of Egypt and Ind,/Ethiopia's sons of the evening,/Indians and yellow Chinese,/Arabian children of morning,/ And mongrels of Rome and Greece." This internationalist cohort, the "darkwater" that Du Bois elsewhere labels "the darker peoples of the world," "shall," in the verb of biblical prophecy, drag "the boasters" "down/ down/ deep down."

The "downs," reiterated seven times, predict a movement through space and time, tracking a black genealogy through the mother-line that links the dark daughter at the poem's opening to the black mother at its end. And yet, even as a female genealogical thread invokes the past and predicts the future waking and rising of the darker peoples of the world, the black mass is expressly masculinized by the poem's end. And, significantly, it is in masculine form that it is deputized with a type of insurgent agency that the black female figures in the poem (daughter and mother) catalyze and witness, but in which they do not partake. When the "darker David" and "married maiden, mother of God,/Bid the Black Christ be born," then, and only then, Du Bois writes, shall the prophecy be fulfilled, and the "burden" lifted from off women's shoulders and transfigured one last time.[14] For once the male members of the larger insurgent anti-colonial mass have been restored to their proper role, the "burden" emerges, neither as that of sexual violation nor of white empire, but rather of "manhood," "Be it yellow or black or white."

The female agency that is summoned, instrumentalized, and ultimately eclipsed by black "manhood" in "Riddle," is conjured similarly in "The Princess of the Hither Isles," the chapter in *Darkwater* that appears to have so mystified critics that they are silent on the anti-imperialism it stridently, if uncomfortably, advocates, and thus on its rhetorical role within the context of the volume. The one exception is Eric Sundquist, who characterizes "Princess" as "a kind of iconographic condensation of the analytic essays that surround it," reading it as "crystallizing . . . historical forces into a tragic figuring of world conflict" (590–91). In this allegory, the princess, who sits on the silver throne of the drab Hither Isles, "well walled between the This and Now" (521), is trapped between the material power of the white King of Yonder Kingdom, the tropics of gold and sun, and the yearning of her "veiled" soul for the unnamed power that the sun represents: "the blackness of utter light," the "gleam" of "unfathomed understanding" (521). While the king claims the power of the sun as his own, just as he carelessly tosses gold pieces to the poor, the princess redirects her attraction to the "Empire of the Sun" onto a black beggar, whose "formless black and burning face" (522) echoes that of the Sun, but not the devastation and destruction over which the king presides. The stage is thus set for the inevitable tragic outcome of the conflict among the three players in what Sundquist unnecessarily labels an "opaque allegorical dialogue" (590).

If the king is the imperial conqueror and the princess a colonial prize to be taken, "the beggar man, was—was what?" (522). Ostentatiously silent on this question, the poem turns to the three figures who form the axis around which the allegory revolves; they march and struggle on, until the princess finally summons the courage to choose the beggar and his "retinue" of "squalid, sordid, parti-colored" souls, who "crouching underneath the scorpion lash . . . all walked as one" (522), over the King's Yonder Kingdom and the "golden entrails" of the earth that he violently mines, presumably by exploiting the retinue's labor. As in "Riddle," in which imperialism and American slavery, the colonized and the (formerly) enslaved, are joined, so, too, are they in this allegory. For the beggar's retinue recalls nothing so much as the "streams" of fugitive slaves and newly emancipated slaves that Du Bois depicts in *Souls* as, on the one hand, a "dark human cloud that clung like remorse on the rear of the swift columns" of Union troops, clamoring to follow them into battle, eager to fight and win the war for liberation (*Souls*, 110), and on the other, as "tired climbers" to whom "the horizon was ever dark, the mists were often cold, the Canaan was always dim and far away" (*Souls*, 105).

Prefiguring the struggle of the black beggar to redeem and liberate the retinue and the princess, Du Bois reanimates the former slaves whom he depicts in *Souls* as striving "to vote themselves into the kingdom" and to educate themselves, thus testing "the power of the cabalistic letters of the white man" to lead them up "the mountain path to Canaan" (104) as part of a larger internationalist mass. For it is the former slave, the "child of Emancipation" represented in *Souls*, whom we can imagine joining the insurgent, expectant group that follows the beggar's lead. In fact, as Du Bois expresses it, the plights of the former slave in the United States and the black beggar in some unnamed but all too recognizable colonial outpost are one and the same: both march and struggle "in those somber forests of . . . striving," each seeing himself "darkly, as through a veil," and even yet with "some faint revelation of his power, of his mission" (*Souls*, 105).

As powerful as is Du Bois's combination of national and international struggles, the limits of the politics of juxtaposition at work in "Princess" emerge (as in "Riddle") as distinctly gendered and sexualized. To mark her choice the princess violently pulls her heart out from her chest and offers it, bleeding, in her outstretched hand, to the beggar, while the king decrees that there shall be no interracial romantic alliances: "Never!", not to a "Negro . . . a nigger," and with his sword, strikes "down," "down," and "down," cutting off the princess's "little, white, heart-holding hand" (523). As Alys Eve Weinbaum argues (see her essay in this volume), anti-imperial protest is here cast in an explicitly romantic and interracial idiom. The princess's reply to the disciplinary violence of the king: "such a cry as only babe-raped mothers know," and then, poised at the edge of "great nothingness," summoned by the warmth of the sun, she "leapt" (523). Echoing the resistant movement of the "down," "down," "down" in "Riddle of the Sphinx," which predicts the rising of the darker peoples of the world in response to imperial plunder and the sexual defilement of black womanhood, the princess resists complicity in the king's brand of destruction and her own sexual exploitation, leaping "down," "down," "down" and choosing in death an alliance with the black beggar and his "parti-colored" retinue. And thus at the allegory's closing moment, the beggar's procession richly recalls not only fugitive and newly emancipated slaves represented in *Souls* but also the "black men of Egypt and Ind," "Ethiopia's sons," "yellow Chinese," "Arabian Children," and the "mongrels of Rome and Greece," who are conjured as the insurgent colonized mass awakened at the end of "Riddle." Having finally shouldered the revolutionary "burden of manhood," the international anti-imperialist masses point, yet again, to what is left behind once the worldwide struggle has coalesced: silently folded within, if never entirely excluded from the radicalized collectivity, woman as historical agent disappears from view, just as she did when Du Bois revised the title of the poem.

In "The Princess of Hither Isles," allegory (even one, like this, that ends in self-sacrifice and, like *Darkwater* as a whole, without immediate signs of liberation) holds together a story of interracial romance and anti-imperialism. This issue, of the racial and gendered utility for Du Bois of the genre of romance, is addressed in several essays in this volume. As Brent Edwards suggests, Du Bois uses romance in the fictional *Black Flame Trilogy* to "fill in the 'gaps' of historical action or 'unknown truth,' " for romance, as a genre allowed Du Bois to integrate, although not to unify or make continuous divergent threads of argument and political analysis (See Edwards's essay in this volume). Within the romantic idiom, as Weinbaum argues, female agents of interracial unions play a special role, often catalyzing black insurgent, internationalist, collectivities. Like the Indian Princess who leads the "darker peoples of the world" in revolutionary, anti-imperialist uprising in Du Bois's romantic novel *Dark Princess,* or the "black Mother" awakened in the final stanza of "Riddle," the princess in Du Bois's anti-imperial allegory conjures and stands in for a black mass whose form and ultimate mission Du Bois struggled to render fully in non-fiction prose. In Du Bois's "fanciful" "alightings" female figures are essential and expendable, wailing and silent—they clear space for the production of black revolutionary masses and agency even as they are subsumed within such masses. For when we juxtapose "The Princess of Hither Isles" with Du Bois's "sterner" polemic "Hands of Ethiopia," we can comprehend how gendered and sexualized figuration supplement and, in the process, highlight (even as they fail to entirely fill in or to suture), the unspoken, unfinished, unformulated "gaps" in Du Bois's anti-imperialist project.

One way to better comprehend the unfinished work of supplementation accomplished by Du Bois's gendered and sexualized figures is to return again to the Marxist theory of "articulation" and further explore how it differs from Du Bois's method of "combination." As we have already argued, "combination" refuses what Stuart Hall calls the "joining up," as in the anatomical structure of the joint, or, better yet, the structure of the "'articulated' lorry." Thus, when Du Bois speaks of combination—"woman and color"—it does not carry the "double meaning" that Hall underscores with the concept of "articulation": the discursive sense of "language-ing," as well as the material sense of physically joining—such that the distinct parts function together as a unity "under certain historical conditions" (1996, 141). For even as Du Bois asks, "what is today the message of . . . black women to America," in answering he finesses the question of the relationship among "movements" (in this instance, uplift of women and antiracism), strategically eliding discussion of the variegated and overlapping elements that politicize bodies and discourses, the multiple parts that together build—or, quite literally articulate—such movements. Put differently, by combining "woman and color," Du Bois subsumes the collective "message" of black women, and paradoxically uncouples black women's voices from the bodies that comprise the collective that speaks and acts. Whereas Hall defines articulation as a process that is bodily and discursive, Du Bois's politics of juxtaposition begs, and thereby raises, an important question not addressed by Hall—that of the nature of the articulation *between* bodies and discourses. Thus, in turning to Du Bois, we use his ideas to extend Hall's meditation, asking what *Darkwater* can reveal to us about how bodies and speech are severed in the effort to combine, rather than articulate, the unity of woman and color.

Not surprisingly, the election and elaboration of a politics based in combination have profound textual consequences. What Du Bois does not articulate conceptually reveals a chasm within his analysis between the *particular* (the list of exceptional black women, beginning with the four remembered from his boyhood, in "The Damnation of Women," to the Princess of Hither Isles, to the "dark daughter" and "Black mother" of "Riddle," and on to all the other individuated female figures in his "alightings") and the *universal* (the insurgent, international mass, the beggar's retinue, or most broadly, the "darker peoples of the world"). For in imagining a politics of combination but refusing to articulate bodies and discourses, it is not just that women disappear from view, but that "black" is uncoupled from "women"—understood as a vocal, plural category. In this uncoupling, the "language-ing" of collective voices, and the bodies that produce these voices, are violently severed from each other.

Given this twofold separation—bodies from discourses, and individuals from collectivities—the now well-known analysis offered by black feminists of the uneven structure of black political movements, from abolitionism through black power, emerges as germane to our critique of Du Bois's writings (as it has been in many other contexts).[15] In *Darkwater* all the insurgent masses are black and male, all the female collectivities white, and as for the mass of black women—those whose discursive agency enables, and whose individual bodies comprise the collectivity—they are mysteriously silent, nowhere to be found. In making the transition from representation of individual, often exceptional, women to representation of the supposedly gender-neutral (but implicitly, silently masculinized) mass, the exceptionality and individuality of black women that Du Bois sets forth emerge as an instructive stumbling block. For in the move from figuration of individual women to figuration of insurgent anti-imperialist masses, Du Bois forecloses the possibility that the individual women whom he has figured in poetry and prose might together comprise a larger collectivity, an *articulated* and *articulate* insurrectionary group.

Even as we mount such a critique, it is important to underscore that we do not do so in order to discount Du Bois's "profeminism," but rather to show how reading Du Bois against the grain can constitute a feminist politics. Building on the work of critics such as Hazel

Carby (whose essay is included in this volume), who have argued that Du Bois's writing is pervaded by a "gender bias" that silences the black women he represents and that mitigates against seeing black intellectual leadership as anything but masculinist, here we suggest that the problems of exclusion and silencing can also be conceptualized differently. At the very heart of *Darkwater,* the figuration of the international, anti-imperialist mass conjured by Du Bois obscures the constitutive presence of black female individuals as a *collectivity* that both enables and, in part, comprises it. In other words, because black women's singularity is central to his realization that, "in this veiled world of mine," it is "the five million women of my race who really count" (573), the notion of a plural aggregate, greater than the sum of its parts, that would articulate gender with race and discourse with bodies, remains at once a constitutive element within and an elusive dimension of Du Bois's thinking.

Nowhere is this supplementary function of gender and sexual figuration more visible than in the representations of rape that punctuate *Darkwater.* Of these, the most striking are the two that bracket the conclusions of "Hands" and "The Souls of White Folk" (the second deeply anti-imperialist essay in *Darkwater*). Not only does the female figure of "Black Africa—prostrated, raped, and shamed" that dominates the end of "Hands" (520) connect directly to the "despised and raped peoples" of the "Dark World" who appear at the end of "The Souls of White Folk" (507–8), but also it is these figures of rape that together link the anti-imperialism of the two essays with the gendered and sexualized lyricism of those "alightings" already discussed: "Riddle" and "Princess." In all four texts, racial, political, and economic exploitation—past, present, and future—coalesces around the figure of sexual violence, a figure that metaphorically, almost magically, embodies connections among distinct elements. And yet, even as rape figuratively pervades the text, constituting its connective tissue, the bodies of raped women recede into the distance. The price of universalizing the figure of rape is eclipse of the particular: the material bodies of those women who are swallowed up in the necessary abstraction of the metaphor.

In "Hands" this swallowing up and severing of voices from bodies can be suggestively excavated. "Hands" begins by focusing on Africa as ground zero of world imperialism and proceeds by working through the demand for an "Africa for Africans" that Du Bois conceptualizes as "a new African World State" (516). He explains, in the revealing form of a rhetorical question: "Does this sound like an impossible dream?" Perhaps not, given the fact that the impossible and the "unspeakable" have become commonplace. After all, readers have already witnessed the dethroning of the Czar of Russia, the extension of suffrage to women in England, and the advent of government control of the railroads in the United States (517). If such unprecedented events can transpire, then (by the associative logic of the "so, too" invoked in his meditation on suffrage) "is it really so far fetched to think of an Africa for the Africans?" (517). Significantly, although the self-evident answer to Du Bois's question goes initially unstated, later an urgent response is formulated. There is no other way out of the current global predicament, Du Bois prophesies: "either the white world gives up" its exploitation of the Dark World "or trouble is written in the stars!" (513). As he reasons, "this is not the end of world war,—it is but the beginning," "the prelude" to the uprising of the "despised and *raped* peoples" of the earth (507–8, emphasis added).[16] Here rape refers not only to the "new imperialism" ushered in by "World War" (which Du Bois defines broadly as "the jealous and avaricious struggle for the largest share in exploiting darker races"), but it also functions as a temporal mechanism, a marker of the future that foreshadows the beginning of and the prelude to a new era (507).

Clearly rape bears greater rhetorical and political burden than it can easily support. As a metaphor, it functions by connecting two different elements, in this case sexual violence and colonial exploitation. However, even as it does so, it gives way to an inherent structural weakness. Rape, as the violation of black women as a collectivity, becomes impossible to recognize from within the metaphor's associative confines. This is in part because, as Stuart Hall explains in another context, when the internal elements of any "structural combination" are left unchanged, this necessarily "weakens the historicity of the approach—contravening . . . the historical premise" of, in Hall's case, Marx's, and, in our case, Du Bois's work (1980, 329). In the deployment of rape as metaphor, neither the generalized female figure of

"Black Africa—prostrated, raped, and shamed" nor the universalized "despised and raped peoples" of the world, conveys the changing historical conditions of the rape of black women by both white and black men.[17] For when Du Bois casts rape as a broad figure for the violation of a continent, the historical specificity of rape as violence against colonized, enslaved, and newly emancipated women is lost.

Borrowing Hortense Spillers's terminology, we might say that Du Bois's work falls prey to what Spillers characterizes as an invidious and historically consequential distinction between "body" and "flesh." As she explains in her now classic essay, "Mama's Baby, Papa's Maybe," the "New-World diasporic plight" of middle passage and slavery marked a "theft" of the captive African body, amplified by the loss of gender difference, such that the female body and the male body become in the new world "a territory of cultural and political maneuver, not at all gender-related, gender-specific."[18] In a context in which the gendered body has been stolen, Spillers argues, it is only the "flesh" that may be said to escape as a "primary narrative" that precedes and exceeds the body. Working with a distinction so finely calibrated as that of body to flesh, Spillers conveys the manifold contradictions in the history of slavery in the sociopolitical order of the New World. The flesh is Spillers' term for the "zero degree of social conceptualization that does not escape concealment under the brush of discourse" (67); the flesh is "the concentration of 'ethnicity' that contemporary critical discourses neither acknowledge nor discourse away" (67). Thus the historic conditions of the African female subject under slavery produced both female bodies stripped of their gender specificity (and of the possibility of recognition of the particular forms of sexual violence to which they were subjected) and female flesh, a form of "lexical and living" evidence, part of the "primary narrative" of black women in culture and society (68). In creating a distinction between body and flesh, Spillers, of course, hopes to join together—or better yet, *articulate* these distinct elements.

Du Boisean figurations of rape clearly do not do the work that Spillers associates with the primary narrativity of the flesh, but rather obscure the black female body's particular, yet constitutive, membership within the wider collectivity. Indeed, while individual black women are certainly depicted in *Darkwater* as victims of rape, and colonized people, in general, as metaphorically raped, black women fail to be figured as a collectivity of narrative, historical, or material significance. Consequently, "Hands" is pervaded by their collective silence—a silence paradoxically audible to readers attentive to the politics of juxtaposition that structure the text. For it is precisely when this silence is juxtaposed with the loud cries of the individual female figures who punctuate Du Bois's lyrical and fanciful "alightings"—the "wailing" Black woman whose voice emerges out of "the sad black South" in "Riddle" and the Princess's "cry of dark despair" such as "only babe-raped mothers know" (509, 523)—that this silence reverberates and resonates, wordlessly and soundlessly.

### An Unfinished Revolution

If *Darkwater,* like "Hands of Ethiopia," ends on a note of prophetic warning, in an "unfinished revolution" (to borrow from the title of Eric Foner's magisterial history of Reconstruction),[19] this is precisely because of how the politics of juxtaposition work: the volume's anti-imperial analysis emerges piecemeal, not out of, or into, whole cloth but rather constructed from juxtapositions within and across textual parts. The outcome of such a method must therefore be provisional and open-ended. As such, Du Bois brings into view the question of how his conception of historical time undergirds his thinking on race, gender, and sexuality. We know that Du Bois's formulation of "the problem of the color line" relies on an uncanny prophetic mode that assumes the temporal recurrence of the past in the present, or what Walter Benjamin calls the "claim" of the past not yet redeemed by the present.[20] So, too, do we know how often Du Bois relies on the figure of the black mother—what he calls the "mother-idea" (*Darkwater,* 569, 567)—to provide a genealogical narrative of the global history of black peoples. Thus, not at all coincidentally, in concluding "Hands," Du Bois creates another voice, that of yet another fantastic female figure, who, although entirely ignored in the existing criticism, nonetheless dominates. Imagining the future via the past, in the closing sentences of his signal anti-imperialist chapter Du Bois writes, "Beyond the awful sea a black woman is weeping and waiting . . . What shall the end be?" Repeating Pliny's exclamatory, "*Semper novi quid ex Africa!*" [Something new always comes from Africa!], with the last words of his essay (which repeat the first), Du Bois summons forth, through the cries of a woman, the possibility of a place and time "beyond." Her singular wailing forms a wordless counter to the unspoken, collective narrative of *Darkwater*'s black women, or, in Toni Morrison's words near the end of *Beloved,* her wailing is like the "wave of sound" made by the thirty neighborhood women who come out to rid 124 of its ghost: "the sound that broke the back of words."[21]

Why is Du Bois's wailing woman the lightning rod both for narrating the injustices of the past and wordlessly summoning an image of a collectively claimed, redemptive future? Both Toni Morrison and Walter Benjamin provide insight into the nature of Du Boisean historical consciousness, which is "nourished by the image of enslaved ancestors rather than that of liberated grandchildren" (Benjamin, 260) and is thus attentive to the ostentatious absences, gaps, voids, and erasures that underwrite our "strategies of escape" (Morrison) from the repositories of "historical knowledge" in which we find ourselves imprisoned.[22] Indeed, Morrison reminds us that, contrary to the assumed victimization of the "silenced" in literary texts—and our supposed disciplinary need to reconstruct or rediscover their "lost" voices—unspeakability is not equivalent to silence.[23] As she explains, "invisible things are not necessarily 'not-there,' . . . a void may be empty, but . . . not a vacuum," so, too, with "unspeakable things, unspoken" (11). In short, the audible silences in Du Bois's writing call attention to their own absence—like the neighborhood women who come to rid 124 of its ghost, they "arrest us with intentionality and purpose" (11).

Morrison's term "arrest" resonates with Benjamin's use of the term, and then again with the Du Boisean project of *Darkwater.* For a materialist historiography, such as that which Du Bois produces, must involve not a causal narrative or a sequence of events, but rather a series of evocative stops in time that can "blast open the continuum of history" (262) and reveal "the 'state of emergency' in which we live" (257). From this vantage point it may be argued that Du Bois's figure of a black woman, weeping and waiting, forms a kind of dialectical flashpoint, a Benjaminian "monad," that is produced when "thinking suddenly stops in a configuration pregnant with tensions" and "crystallizes" (262–63), revealing the sign of "a revolutionary chance in the fight for the oppressed past" (263). The past is oppressed when it is seen as eternal, isolated for all time as a specific era in the "homogeneous course of history," rather than understood differently, as Du Bois suggests, as possessing a relationship to each succeeding present (263). For when a historical subject is encountered as a flashpoint, a monad, the historian is able to see "a past charged with the time of the now" (261).

In the context of *Darkwater,* understanding differently, apprehending the past in terms of the present, "the now," entails "seizing hold of a memory as it flashes up at a moment of danger" (255), for the moment of danger is, of course, also the revolutionary moment of prophecy, the moment when Du Bois employs gendered and sexualized figurations to caution that "trouble is written in the stars!" (513). Indeed, as we have seen, by the last paragraph of "Hands," framed by the figures of "Black Africa, prostrated, raped, and shamed" and a black woman "weeping and waiting" beyond the "awful sea" (520), Du Bois offers us a flashpoint, a monad, that at once leaves us in the waiting mode, with a pointed question rather than a call to arms: "What shall the end be?" Here, as elsewhere, Du Bois's female figures repeatedly exert the paradoxical political pressure of those who wait actively. The veiled threat of another world war, this time the possibility of impending race war that is everywhere present in *Darkwater,* is figured as a waiting, veiled woman.[24]

Finally, from the perspective of this waiting, veiled woman, it becomes possible to observe that the singular, individuated "veiled soul" of "The Princess of the Hither Isles" both looks forward and echoes back to the collective "Voices From Within the Veil" of *Darkwater*'s subtitle, and then again to Du Bois's own self-characterization in his prefacing "Postscript," in which he describes himself as seeing and speaking "from a veiled corner" (483). If, on the one hand, the singular female figure who closes "Hands" marks the limits of Du Boisean politics of juxtaposition in that she exposes his inability to think through black female participation in the collectivity, on the other hand she also represents Du Bois's principal creative outlet—the textual and rhetorical tool, the supplement that he creates in order both to fill and to expose the gap in his text where an insurgent, internationalist mass comprised of the darker peoples of the world might ideally stand. In *Darkwater*, the revolutionary cry, gendered female, is ultimately disrupted (by the apocalyptic end when the princess, her bleeding heart cut from her chest, leaps into the void), or displaced (when the woman as burden bearer drops out, replaced by the burden of manhood). And so, we conclude, gender and sexuality are simultaneously central to and outside of Du Bois's anti-imperialist internationalist imaginary. As the politics of juxtaposition reveals, gendered and sexualized figurations point to what's lacking /challenging /impossible in the activist politics of *Darkwater*'s Du Boisean moment, even as such figurations stand in the place of this lack /challenge/impossibility by exposing it to view and beckoning a response.

### Next to the Color Line

In many ways the essays collected in this volume constitute a response to the lack/challenge/impossibility of Du Bois's gendered and sexualized figurations. They range over a variety of texts, performances, and visuals that were produced by Du Bois throughout his life, and excavate gendered and sexualized elements in order to juxtapose them with those, defined largely by race and class, that are already familiar to readers. In so doing, these essays reveal the necessity of projects of excavation and juxtaposition to our fuller understanding of Du Bois's life and work. As a response, they carve out several new potentialities for Du Bois studies: an emerging Du Bois canon for feminist and queer readers, a revised understanding of the relationship between the writing and the life based on the juxtaposition of gender and anti-imperialist internationalism, a challenge to the conventional scholarly tendency to separate Du Bois's art, science, and activism from each other, and last but not least, these essays offer a reinvigorated approach to the multiplicity of genres and forms that Du Bois employed throughout his long and prolific career.

In exploring the gendered and sexualized content of Du Bois's work, all contributors to this volume build on the initial insights of those feminist scholars of Du Bois who first sought to treat questions of gender, sexuality, and eroticism. In particular, the groundbreaking scholarship by Hazel Carby, Joy James, and Claudia Tate (whose original contributions are collected here) has served as a shared touchstone. Their work has shown us where to begin our inquiries, and has indicated the many routes along which we might travel. Their work, published in the late 1990s, may also be taken as a historical guide to the different, if overlapping moments within feminist scholarship on Du Bois, and, as such, is suggestive of an alternative literary and critical history of Du Bois studies. In this view, James establishes the first feminist approach to Du Bois in which he is identified as a "profeminist," with all attendant limits and possibilities produced by that generative term. Carby's *Race Men* marks the other end of the conceptual spectrum; she places Du Bois within a framework that exposes his masculinism and posits a "gender bias" that (fatally) undermines his relations, textual and contextual, with black women. Finally, Tate, whose *Psychoanalysis and Black Novels* appeared the same year as *Race Men,* provides a landmark approach to the erotics of Du Bois's life and work that coalesces particularly around *Dark Princess,* and inaugurates Du Bois's Romantic novel (which Tate is responsible for reintroducing to contemporary readers through her reprint) as perhaps the single most important, newly canonized text for feminist studies of Du Bois.

The emerging feminist and queer studies canon is, in a variety of ways, both the object of study and subject of analysis in all the essays collected in this volume. While many of the authors return to the same clusters of passages in which gender and sexuality emerge most robustly in Du Bois's most familiar, often-read texts, others have sought to expand the discussion by taking it to newer terrain, including the late fictional works discussed by Brent Hayes Edwards, the pageants explored by Susan Gillman, and the science fiction and allegory engaged by Alys Eve Weinbaum. Others find in the Du Bois archive heretofore unmined sources: the early photographic collections that Du Bois assembled for display, examined by Shawn Michelle Smith, and the letters to Countee Cullen and daughter Yolande, discussed by Mason Stokes. Each approach to the question of the Du Bois archive has its merits. The repeated recourse made by several authors to the most well-known texts and passages in which gender and sexuality are discussed is, in our view, crucial in that it allows us, through repetition, to begin constituting a new set of canonical citations within Du Bois studies, a new set of passages and texts that necessarily bring in gender and sexuality. Such repetition paves the way for transformation not only of feminist and queer scholarship on Du Bois, but also of the larger field of Du Bois studies. In its turn, the new scholarship on the visual, discursive, and performative additions to the canon expands the archive upon which we build our arguments about gender and sexuality and, in so doing, transforms these arguments.

The return to the same textual moments—the lullaby of Du Bois's great-great-grandmother "Do bana coba" reiterated in the various autobiographies, the parade of so-called All-Mothers in *Darkwater,* and the messianic pageant at the finale of *Dark Princess* are three such examples—is also important in that it establishes the common ground essential to critical debate. Indeed, the different, sometimes radically divergent views expressed in the essays collected in this volume demonstrate that feminist and queer studies scholarship on Du Bois has moved to the stage of critical disagreement. It is also an exciting index of how far the study of gender and sexuality in the work of Du Bois has come in just over a decade. So, too, the different theoretical frameworks in which these signal moments and passages are read reveal the emergence of the new critical protocols generated by this set of textual materials. Here, for instance, the focus on music, and musical analysis, in the essays by Edwards and Fred Moten, stands out for extending the earlier critical interest in the sorrow songs to a broader, feminist-derived approach to "fugitive" sounds and voices. Likewise, the combined formal-historical mode that characterizes many of the essays in this volume at once resuscitates the categories of form and genre (most notably Romance, pageant, and allegory), and recontextualizes these categories within the social, cultural, and political history of Du Bois's long life.

The volume opens with Vilashini Cooppan's essay that serves, in its wide and long sweep, as an apt gateway to the essays that follow. Cooppan explores the manner in which Du Bois's writings draw on the "changing same of gender" to support his competing formulations of the "race concept" and "the color line" as biological and cultural phenomena. Beginning with *Souls,* moving through his sociological studies, and concluding with his multigenre collections of the 1920s,

Cooppan suggests that gender functions with fixity in Du Bois's work. Other essays argue, conversely, that gender and sexual logics are differently engaged by Du Bois at distinct historical moments of production and political intervention. This historical transformation of gendered and sexualized concepts is especially apparent in the essays by Weinbaum and Edwards. As they both demonstrate, ideas of romance and the generic conventions of Romance as form are employed by Du Bois at two different historical moments in his career: in the 1920s, in the fantastical and allegorical internationalist texts explored by Weinbaum, and in the late works, the romantic fictions collected as *The Black Flame Trilogy* and examined by Edwards. Weinbaum argues that in the 1920s, Du Bois's depictions of interracial romance express his anti-imperialist internationalism; in his late depictions of romance, Edwards suggests, they constitute an open-ended dialectic, a commentary on history.

Still other essays step back from the sexual allusions and figurations that are present in the manifest content of the text in order to reveal the erotics that subtend Du Bois's central political arguments and the heteronormative assumptions from which such erotics spring. In Elam and Taylor's essay, Du Bois's philosophy of self-realization is shown as permeated by what they label an "ethical erotica." As they argue, the long-perceived gap between Du Bois the moralist and Du Bois the "priapic" adulterer may be rethought by placing Du Bois among his contemporaries, within a philosophical context that they dub "Dionysian perfectionism." In Stokes's and Ferguson's essays, the biographical Du Bois is addressed through the lens of queer studies. Stokes explores the 1928 wedding of Du Bois's daughter Yolande to the gay poet Countee Cullen as the occasion of a spectacular and failed moment of black heterosexuality, arguing that this was also a moment of prophecy: the wedding, and Cullen, in "his queer way," heralded the racial-sexual logics of the new black nation, located between old and new, whiteness and blackness, art and politics, heterosexuality and homosexuality. By contrast, Ferguson takes the position that it is not Du Bois, the biographical subject, to whom we ought to turn in order to consider the internal contradictions of heteronormativity, but rather "W. E. B. Du Bois," the dominant discourse reproduced within Du Bois studies. All three of these essays respond, in different ways, to Tate's call for examination of Du Boisean sexuality, and Carby's call for a critique of Du Boisean masculinism.

In another cluster of essays, the paternalism and maternalism of Du Bois's texts that are an adjunct of the heterosexual norms (or, perhaps, their dialectical outcome) are read back through classical texts by Du Bois and lesser known pieces of the Du Bois archive to reveal anew the interrelationship of these archival parts. In Smith's essay, for instance, "double consciousness" as conceptualized in *Souls* remerges as "doublesight," a masculinist visual economy, when it is juxtaposed with the remarkable collection of photographs that Du Bois assembled for the American Negro Exhibit at the 1900 Paris Exhibition. As Smith suggests, Du Bois's visual and philosophical texts together provide a revisionist view of the Du Boisean gaze and its historical function in confirming the vision, at the dawn of the twentieth century, of black masculinity. In Moten's and Gillman's essays, the maternal matrix of Du Bois's thinking is foregrounded with reference to his ideas about uplift, criminality, and voice, on the one hand, and with reference to his elaborate pageantry on the other. While Moten engages with musical forms, and passages from less often read works such as *Black Reconstruction,* Gillman focuses on Du Bois's little known pageants by situating these in relationship to his writings on maternity. Together, Gillman's and Moten's essays historicize Du Bois's aesthetic and performative modes of political expression, and in so doing, meditate on the everchanging figure of the black mother, and the evolving role that she plays within Du Bois's political expression.

Overall, the essays collected in this volume demonstrate that gender and sexuality, often masculinist and heteronormative, are always present in Du Bois writings—underwriting in vexed and various ways the textual meaning and political expressions that scholars have come to regard as Du Bois's most important philosophical and historical contributions. This is so even though these gendered and sexualized issues, themes, and questions have until now been largely elided from view by scholarly approaches to Du Bois that refuse to examine his politics of juxtaposition—the manner in which he "combines in one" the political movements of his day, including antiracism, anti-imperialism, feminism, and an iconoclastic black internationalism.

## Notes

This introduction was presented to the Americanist Colloquium at Yale University in winter 2005; we are indebted to Hazel Carby and Michael Denning for their generous engagement. We have also benefited greatly from feedback on early drafts from Brent Hayes Edwards, George Lipsitz, and Nikhil Pal Singh.

1. Although Du Bois's formulation's most famous iteration is in the opening pages of his 1903 work, *The Souls of Black Folk,* it was first proffered in 1900 in London at the first Pan-African Conference in a speech entitled "To the Nations of the World," in *W. E. B Du Bois: A Reader,* ed. David Levering Lewis (New York: Henry Holt, 1995), 639. See also, *The Souls of Black Folk* in *The Oxford W. E. B. Du Bois Reader,* ed. Eric J. Sundquist (New York and Oxford: Oxford University Press, 1996), 97–240. Hereafter cited parenthetically in the text.

2. James focuses principally on Du Bois's relationships with and sidelining of Wells-Barnett and Cooper.

3. *Darkwater: Voices from Within the Veil* (1920), in Sundquist, *Du Bois Reader,* 574. Hereafter cited parenthetically in the text.

4. On the theory of articulation, see Louis Althusser, *For Marx* (London: Allan Lane, 1965) and with Etienne Balibar, *Reading Capital* (London: New Left Books, 1970); Ernesto Laclau, *Politics and Ideology in Marxist Theory* (London: New Left Books, 1977); Stuart Hall, "Race, Articulation, and Societies Structured in Dominance," in *Sociological Theories: Race and Colonialism* (Paris: UNESCO, 1980); repr. in Philomena Essed and David Theo Goldberg, eds., *Race Critical Theories: Text and Context* (Oxford: Blackwell, 2002), 38–68. On the wide influence of articulation in British cultural studies and beyond, see also Jennifer Daryl Slack, "Theory and Method of Articulation in Cultural Studies," in *Stuart Hall: Critical Dialogues in Cultural Studies,* ed. David Morley and Kuan-Hsing Chen (London: Routledge, 1996), 112–27; Ernesto Laclau and Chantal Mouffe, *Hegemony and Socialist Strategy: Towards a Radical Democratic Politics* (London: Verso, 1985); Bob Jessop, *The Capitalist State: Marxist Theories and Methods* (Oxford: Martin Robert, 1982), 213–20, and *State Theory: Putting Capitalist States in Their Place* (University Park: Pennsylvania State University Press, 1990), 193–272. More recently, Brent Edwards has offered an interpretation of articulation as a linking process that, in the context of black diaspora, allows us to think "difference in unity"; and David Kazanjian has offered an incisive exploration of articulation as figure and reading practice. See Edwards, *The Politics of Diaspora: Literature, Translation, and the Rise of Black Internationalism* (Cambridge, Mass.: Harvard University Press, 2003), 11–151; and Kazanjian, *The Colonizing Trick: National Culture and Imperial Citizenship in Early America* (Minneapolis: University of Minnesota Press, 2003), 7–17. On the idea of "fugitive" figuration, see Stephen M. Best, *The Fugitive's Properties: Law and the Poetics of Possession* (Chicago and London: University of Chicago Press, 2004), and Fred Moten's essay in this volume.

5. On the "self-consciously polyphonic form" of Du Bois's modernist writing, see Paul Gilroy, *The Black Atlantic: Modernity and Double Consciousness* (Cambridge, Mass.: Harvard University Press, 1993), 115.

6. In Du Bois's 1928 novel he refers to a fictional group of Middle Eastern and South and East Asian elites as "the council of the darker peoples of the world." Throughout this essay we adopt this terminology to designate the masses conjured as "darkwater" in Du Bois's 1920 multigenre text. See *Dark Princess: A Romance,* with an introduction by Claudia Tate (Jackson: University Press of Mississippi, 1995). On the problem of the fictional Council's elitism, see Alys Eve Weinbaum's essay in this volume and "The Sexual Politics of Black Internationalism: W. E. B. Du Bois and the Reproduction of Racial Globality," in *Wayward Reproductions: Genealogies of Race and Nation in Transatlantic Modern Thought* (Durham N.C.: Duke University Press, 2004), 208–9.

7. Some scholarship on both *Souls* and *Darkwater* constitutes an exception to this rule. See Sundquist (who focuses on "the antiphonal relationship" in *Souls* between the music of the "sorrow songs" and the text as characteristic of Du Bois's unique "blending of poetics and politics"), in *Du Bois Reader,* 459–60, 467–539; and Arnold Rampersad (who reads *Souls* as "a diverse mix of styles and genres" that raises the "problem of unity" in the "anthology"), *The Art and Imagination of W. E. B. Du Bois* (1976; repr. New York: Schocken, 1990), 69, 71. Although Sundquist and Rampersad examine the juxtaposition of the book's various parts, neither does so with an eye to how the anti-imperialist politics that is the product of juxtaposition is enabled by figurations of gender and sexuality.

8. Amy Kaplan also reads the "so, too," of this chapter as an internationalist gesture. See *The Anarchy of Empire in the Making of U.S. Culture* (Cambridge and London: Harvard University Press, 2002), 204. Chapter IX, "Of Beauty and Death," also elaborates the protocols for the politics of juxtaposition—in this instance among those things that Du Bois deems beautiful and finite and those he deems oppressive and infinite. As he suggests, the beautiful renders the oppressive tolerable through juxtaposition, for stark contrast breaks up harsh reality and reveals the possibility of struggle, even in the face of death.

9. On the double meaning of articulation, see also Hall, "On Postmodernism and Articulation," 141; on the genealogy of articulation, see also Kazanjian, *The Colonizing Trick,* 7–9, 14–17.

10. Derrida's formulation underscores the centrality of the verb tense in locating the Janus face, located both inside and outside, both before and after the text, of the preface. "The preface would announce in the future tense . . . the conceptual content or significance . . . of what will *already* have been *written* . . . The *pre* of the preface makes the future present, represents it, . . . and in going ahead of it puts it ahead. The *pre* reduces the future to the form of manifest presence." See *Dissemination,* trans., with Introduction, by Barbara Johnson (Chicago: University of Chicago Press, 1981).

11. The dialectic between fact and fiction, fantasy and logic that Du Bois sets up in this passage echoes that which he constructs in the postscript to *Dark Princess* where he invokes Shakespeare's *A Midsummer Night's Dream* to speak to the power of fantasy in constructing reality. As Brent Hayes Edwards argues, Du Bois's invocation of Shakespeare's multigenre play suggests his use of slippage, or play, among

genres to create meaning, and simultaneously parody meaning he has himself created. See Brent Hayes Edwards, *The Practice of Diaspora,* 234–37.

12. Robert Stepto was perhaps the first to argue for attention to African American writers' focus on questions of textual framing. See Stepto, *From Behind the Veil: A Study of Afro-American Narrative* (Urbana: University of Illinois Press, 1979), and Edwards, *The Practice of Diaspora,* 38–39, on the rhetorical function of the preface.

13. As Susan Gillman elsewhere argues, Du Bois's frequent reuse of textual bits constitutes a "practice of self-citation" and adaptation—both of which are additional dimensions of what we here theorize as a politics of juxtaposition. See Susan Gillman's essay in this volume and *Blood Talk: American Race Melodrama and the Culture of the Occult* (Chicago and London: The University of Chicago Press, 2003), 176–86.

14. Here our reading builds on Amy Kaplan's insight that in this poem Du Bois expresses "anxiety about [women's] . . . revolutionary agency and a need to control it through his assertion of militant manhood." See *The Anarchy of Empire,* 206.

15. See for instance, *All the Women are White, all the Blacks are Men, but some of Us Are Brave: Black Women's Studies,* Gloria T. Hull, Patricia Bell Scott, and Barbara Smith, eds. (Old Westbury, N.Y.: Feminist Press, 1982); Paula Giddings, *When and Where I Enter: The Impact of Black Women on Race and Sex in America* (New York: Morrow, 1984); and bell hooks, *Ain't I a Woman: Black Women and Feminism* (Boston, Mass.: South End Press, 1981). Roderick Ferguson's *Aberrations in Black: Toward a Queer of Color Critique* (Minneapolis: University of Minnesota Press, 2004) elaborates the insights of the earlier feminist work for examination of the heterosexism that subtends black liberationist thought.

16. As Amy Kaplan has put it, in this chapter, as in the rest of *Darkwater,* Du Bois turns the "accusation of rape against the accusers: he redirects the battle cry of the 'rape of Belgium' to the 'rape of Ethiopia'. " See *Anarchy of Empire,* 209. For further discussion of Du Bois's use of the idea of rape also see Vilashini Cooppan's essay in this volume.

17. By contrast, elsewhere in *Darkwater* (see "The Servant in the House" and its preceding paired tale, "The Second Coming"), Du Bois links sexual exploitation of women to the specific conditions of domestic labor, thus recognizing that women laboring in white homes are "naked to insult" (542), as individuals and as a class. In "The Servant," Du Bois writes of a young woman left alone with only one young white man to represent the family. Prefiguring her plight is the white-appearing young girl, with a black baby in her arms, who heralds the "second coming": " 'She's not really white,' " explains one of the bishops in the story, " 'you see, her mother worked for the governor—' " (537). By contrast with the raped figures represented in *Darkwater,* these women embody the raced and gendered history of service in slavery and freedom—a history to which Du Bois personally relates in his discussion of the "menial service" he performed one summer at a Lake Minnetonka resort.

18. See Hortense Spillers, "Mama's Baby, Papa's Maybe: An American Grammar Book," *Diacritics* (Summer 1987): 67. Hereafter cited parenthetically in the text.

19. Eric Foner, *Reconstruction: America's Unfinished Revolution, 1863–1877* (New York: Harper and Row, 1988).

20. Walter Benjamin, "Theses on the Philosophy of History," in *Illuminations: Essays and Reflections,* ed. and intro. Hannah Arendt, trans. Harry Zohn (New York: Schocken, 1968), 254. Hereafter cited parenthetically in the text.

21. Toni Morrison, *Beloved* (New York: Penguin, 1987), 261.

22. Toni Morrison, "Unspeakable Things Unspoken: the Afro-American Presence in American Literature," *Michigan Quarterly Review* 28 (Winter 1989): 1–34 (12). Hereafter cited parenthetically in the text.

23. Morrison's point resonates deeply with Gayatri Chakravorty Spivak's claim in *Can the Subaltern Speak? Marxism and the Interpretation of Culture,* ed. Cary Nelson and Lawrence Grossberg (Urbana: University of Illinois Press, 1988), 271–313.

24. On Benjamin's use of the figure of the veiled woman as a monad that reveals the gendered contractions of urbanization and industrial capitalism see Alys Eve Weinbaum, "Ways of Not Seeing: (En)gendered Optics in Benjamin, Baudelaire, and Freud," ed. David L. Eng and David Kazanjian, *Loss: The Politics of Mourning* (Berkeley: University of California Press, 2003), 402–3.

# 1

# Move On Down the Line: Domestic Science, Transnational Politics, and Gendered Allegory in Du Bois

■ *Vilashini Cooppan*

W. E. B. Du Bois's explosive formulation of the color line as "the problem of the twentieth century" was initially uttered at the first pan-African conference of 1900, famously repeated in the 1903 *The Souls of Black Folk,* and extended and expanded in the 1906 essay "The Color Line Belts the World." The figure of the color line would, in fact, return many times throughout Du Bois's long career, from his early sociological studies to his later historical, political, and literary writings, in works of nationalist bent as well as in those with internationalist, pan-Africanist, or socialist, allegiances. While Du Bois's later writings, like the essay and fiction combination *Darkwater* (1920), the political treatises "The Negro Mind Reaches Out" (1924) and "Worlds of Color" (1925), and the novel *Dark Princess* (1928), continued to present the color line as privileged signifier of the system of racial discrimination they so passionately denounced in their various generic registers, these works also began to redraw the color line, endowing it with an altogether different range of meanings. The color line was undoubtedly, as Eric Sundquist has claimed, a "fluid metaphor" capable of surviving different stages in Du Bois's thought and often serving as a catalytic figure and animating trope of each stage.[1] Beneath the shifting color line lie the traces of Du Bois's changing model of race, from his initial romantic nationalist understanding of races as distinct families of men with distinct historical tasks, to the more empirical tone of his social scientific effort to rethink race as culture, to his eventual imagining of a distinctly global model of race in the conjunctural unity of such proto–Third World alliances as the "darker races of the world." At each moment in his thought Du Bois imagined the color line differently, from the mythic line of racial descent and racial destiny that haunts "The Conservation of Races" (1897), to the differentiating line of discrimination that fires *The Souls of Black Folk,* and the sociological studies, in their effort to represent black America to its other, to the connecting line of pan-racial alignment that preoccupies Du Bois's later internationalist works.

We can find the beginnings of an explanation for the extraordinary reach of the rhetorical figure of the color line in the first sentence of chapter II of *Souls:* "The problem of the twentieth century is the problem of the color-line—the relation of the darker to the lighter races of men in Asia and Africa, in America and the islands of the sea."[2] Here the color line is both problem and answer, both that which has historically divided darker from lighter, and that which will eventually link darker peoples together in a global alliance that "belts the world." The color line performs its work precisely as the agent of double meanings: division *and* connection, differentiation *and* affiliation, historical sin *and* future salvation, spatial marker *and* temporal measure. Insofar as the color line forms a structuring component of all Du Bois's writings, it provides a site on which to chart not so much a unidirectional evolution of thought (from social science to politics, from nationalism to internationalism) as that thought's inherent duality and mobility.

At the same time that the color line provides an index to the genuinely protean quality of Du Bois's thought—its varying understandings of race, its changing models of community, its signal capacity to move back and forth across different discourses, genres, times, and spaces—it simultaneously attests to a strikingly constant deployment of gender. Gender provides the allegorical form for Du Bois's central concepts of racial history and racial mission. *Souls,* for example, invokes the black female body to represent the historical depredations of slavery and Jim Crow as "two centuries of systematic legal defilement of Negro women" (9), while it describes the emergent project of racial nationalism as the restoration of "manhood" to a race emasculated by the great compromiser Booker T. Washington (39, 45). Through recourse to a relatively unchanging set of gendered tropes—ravaged women, rising men—the color line manages to continually reinvent and redeploy itself within and across individual texts, from the story of slavery, segregation, and national division to that of colonialism, oppositional politics, and international, pan-racial connection. It is with this paradox that the concerns of this essay lie. "The uplift of women," writes Du Bois in *Darkwater,* "is next to the problem of the color line and the peace movement, our greatest modern cause. When, now, two of these movements—women and color—combine in one, the combination has deep meaning."[3] The color line's "movement" across the extraordinary breadth of Du Bois's career is in fact secured by remarkably fixed ideologies of gender. As the conceptual terrain over which the color line darts, gender plays the ground to the color line's endlessly mobile rhetorical and political figure. Because gender doesn't move, the color line can. It is in no small measure because of gender that Du Bois is able to sustain a consistent interplay between such apparently oppositional realms as race and nation, nation and globe, social science and politics.

This essay considers the shifting meanings of the color line and the stable meanings of gender as they intersect in several of Du Bois's major works over the first three decades of the twentieth century. This study is necessarily pointillist, focusing on a particular pair of entwined meanings that can be seen to punctuate many of his most well-known writings, and even to link them to one another outside the canonical chronology of a political progression.[4] This critical version of "connect-the-dots" emphasizes both the distinctiveness of individual works, and the larger pattern of a gendered color line that they collectively create. Faced with so resplendently diffuse a figure, the critic might well understand her task as that of thinking big; encompassing the full range of a prolific and protean career, with its various ideological transformations and many formal variations. But the critic might equally undertake to think in ways at once big and small: focusing on a series of textual nodes in which the color line and gender coalesce, and trying to uncover the simple logic of their connection. What, such an approach asks, does the color line engender in Du Bois's work and how is it itself gendered? The answer may be revealed by exploring the relationship between the historical structure of several of Du Bois's major arguments about race and their gendered form.

### "The Conservation of Races" and The Souls of Black Folk: Progress and the Color Line

Du Bois's 1897 address to Alexander Crummell's newly formed American Negro Academy, titled "The Conservation of Races," while not explicitly concerned with the color line, is nonetheless deeply structured by it. This messianic, romantic, profoundly nineteenth-century essay responds to a dominant body of social evolutionist racial science that placed whites and blacks at opposite ends of evolution and in separate realms of national life, effectively mapping the color line onto the time line. Against this model of civic inequality, uneven development, and temporal non-coevality, "The Conservation of Races" attempts to relocate blacks within national space and world-historical time.

> We are Americans, not only by birth and by citizenship, but by our political ideals, our language, our religion. Farther than that, our Americanism does not go. At that point we are Negroes, members of a vast historic race that from the very dawn of creation has slept, but half awakening in the dark forests of its African fatherland. We are the first fruits of this new nation, the harbinger of that black to-morrow which is yet destined to soften the whiteness of the Teutonic to-day.[5]

In contrast to prevailing narratives of racial progress (from black to white) and racial degeneration (from white to black), both of which propound a temporal color line on which blacks occupy the position of despised origin, Du Bois here imagines blacks as the future. Troubling the most fundamental premise of the color line—separation—Du Bois's vision of a black tomorrow tempering the whiteness of the Teutonic today replaces the specter of racial and temporal division with that of racial and temporal intermixture. Du Bois's response to the invidious temporalization of the color line in nineteenth-century thought is not to claim that color has no time, but rather to claim for it an altogether different kind of time, the messianic time of futurity. This resignifying of color's time depends on an underlying shift in the meaning of the color line, from social evolutionism's temporal plotting of racial difference to the more nationalist notion of line as historical lineage, reaching at once back into the past and forward into the future.

Nations, writes Benedict Anderson, "always loom out of an imme- morial past, and, still more important, glide into a limitless future."[6] The epic diachrony of history is of course subordinated to the syn- chronic axis of simultaneity in Anderson's general thesis, which understands the nation, like the novel and the newspaper which pro- vide the "technical means" for its representation, as "a complex gloss upon the word 'meanwhile,'" a radical break with earlier orders of prefigurative time (25). Though gender is by no means a central cate- gory in Anderson's notion of an imagined community born of print capitalism and transplanted from colony to metropole and back again, gender may nonetheless be seen to silently undergird the over- arching temporal logic of his theory. The simultaneously analeptic and proleptic time of the nation identified by Anderson and regularly deployed by Du Bois is enabled, like the simultaneously divisive and connective figure of the color line, by gender's continuum: the unchanging plot of reproduction. Reconceptualized and *gendered* as a line of descent ("a race is a family," observes "The Conservation of Races"), the color line becomes the basis for a new, protonational vision of black identity that seeks the promise of the future precisely through connection to the past. This vision is most fully realized in *Souls*' attempt to disprove the discriminatory version of the color line, with all its intimations of temporal division and raciocultural differences, and to redraw another, more connective color line through multiple references to an African past that must be actively proven, in the present, once to have existed. In this task, essentially a mapping and remaking of racial space, a marking and resetting of racial time, Du Bois repeatedly turns to a gendered iconography both to describe the old orders and to envision the new ones.

Like Du Bois's general sociological writings, *Souls* attempts a critique of dominant social evolutionism's guiding theory of progress. As efficiently condensed and popularized in 1857 by Herbert Spencer, the British father of sociology, progress referred to a cultural time line on which some races and nations advanced towards physical complexity, social differentiation, and ethical perfection while others stagnated as a kind of living fossil.[7] Chapter IV of *Souls* attempts to shift "the Meaning of Progress" from the status of, in Spencer's words, "a beneficent necessity" for all to that of a falsely extended, repeatedly broken promise for some. "Progress, I understand, is necessarily ugly," remarks Du Bois, describing his return to the rural Tennessee community where he had taught school for two summers, only to find his log schoolhouse replaced by a building with glass windows, his favorite student dead from overwork and despair, and the poverty of lives and dreams still unalleviated (59). The contrast between the forward march of progress and the wearying repetition of debt, death, and discrimination in Wilson County highlights the fundamental disjuncture between the governing paradigms of social science, and the pathos of black lives in white America. The chapter returns to this gap in its concluding lines.

> How shall man measure Progress there where the dark-faced Josie lies? How many heartfuls of sorrow shall balance a bushel of wheat? How hard a thing is life to the lowly, and yet how human and real! And all this life and love and strife and failure,—is it the twilight of nightfall or the flush of some faint-dawning day? Thus sadly musing, I rode to Nashville in the Jim Crow car (62).

What separates Josie from Du Bois is the distinction between folk woman and race man,[8] between an observed object bathed in nostalgia for a past (and progress) that never was and an observing subject all too conscious of the present. These differences find rhetorical expression in the tension between irony and allegory. As Paul de Man explains:

> [I]rony comes closer to the pattern of factual experience and recaptures some of the factitiousness of human existence as a succession of isolated moments lived by a divided self. Essentially the mode of the present, it knows neither memory nor prefigurative duration, whereas allegory exists entirely within an ideal time that is never here and now but always a past or an endless future. Irony is a synchronic structure, while allegory appears as a successive mode capable of engendering duration as the illusion of a continuity that it knows to be illusionary. Yet the two modes, for all their profound distinctions in mood and structure, are the two faces of the same fundamental experience of time.[9]

Reading de Man through Du Bois, we cannot help but wonder to what extent allegory's "engendering" of duration in fact depends on gender, or how irony's simulation of a divided self's temporal isolation connects to race. As the rhetorical mode that, in de Man's words, "takes us back to the predicament of the conscious subject,"[10] irony becomes *Souls'* preferred register for describing the travails of an explicitly racialized, implicitly masculinized double consciousness. Though *Souls* is punctuated, often piercingly, by an irony that details the sudden falling of the veil over one who imagines he has risen above it, the text is far more indebted to the diachronic sweep of allegory, in which it finds the mirror image of its unceasing temporal fluctuations between a distant racial history and a racial future to come. Allegory provides a vehicle through which opposites or, as Walter Benjamin puts it, "antinomies" can be sustained: both the "twilight of nightfall" into which those left behind by progress fall, and "the flush of some faint-dawning day" when racial subjects will have meaning beyond that temporalized color line.[11] It is women—reproductive women— who make possible through their production of the color line of descent, the creation of that always past, endlessly future, originary and prophetic time that de Man defines as allegorical and Du Bois imagines as racial. In the passage quoted here, allegory belongs to

Josie, irony to Du Bois. Yet for all their differences, these linked pairs are also, as de Man says, "two faces of the same fundamental experience of time"—*racial* time. If the temporalized color line of progress has no place for poor, rural, female, black Josie, its spatial corollary of the divisive color line of racial discrimination has only one place—the no place of the Jim Crow car—for the well educated, urban, male, black Du Bois. No less than Josie, Du Bois has been left behind on the time line of progress. To live in racial time is not to experience the dissolution of gender (and class) differences in the face of common blackness and collective racial discrimination, so much as it is to witness the constant mobility of gender as a figure for first one kind, then another, of marginality. Though voiced in the masculine register of irony, Du Bois's observation of his consignment to the Jim Crow car ultimately operates allegorically in order to denote a particularly feminized kind of second-class citizenship.

This is the version of citizenship that Du Bois seeks to counter in chapter II's famous attack on Booker T. Washington, where gendered allegory again does the work of racial critique. As the favored son of the white philanthropic and political establishment, Washington seemed to Du Bois to fulfill its racializing mission, buying into its temporal color line of darker and lighter, backwards and advanced races and fully accepting the social color line as a consequence of that difference. Although Du Bois also admitted the existence of intervals between what he himself called the "more advanced" and "less developed" races (43), what troubled him was the suspicion that those intervals were measured in arbitrary, unscientific, and often entirely subjective ways, with a profound disregard for the cultural and historical achievements of African and Asian peoples, and with little interest in seeing a racial group as anything other than a conglomerate of identical individuals. At this stage in his career it was thus possible for Du Bois to accept the social evolutionist notion of developmental racial time lines while disavowing the foregone conclusions about *collective* racial ability, aspiration, and place to which they so often seemed to lead in the hands of racists and racial "accommodationists."[12] For Du Bois, Washington's failure to differentiate among African Americans paved the way to acceptance of second-class status for the race as a whole—disenfranchised, legally inferior to the point of what Du Bois named "industrial slavery and civic death," and presumed educable only within vocational schools rather than the colleges and universities so dear to Du Bois's vision of racial advancement through elite leadership (46–47). To Du Bois higher education held out the promise of freedom, "the chance to soar in the dim blue air above the smoke," "to sit with Shakespeare and . . . [a]cross the color line [to] move arm in arm with Balzac and Dumas . . . to summon Aristotle and Aurelius and what soul I will" (90). Whereas Du Bois imagines the color line as something to be crossed, even transcended, in a transhistorical utopia of the great men of western letters, he understands Washington as choosing to remain within the divisive logic of the social, and temporal, color line. Such willful undergirding of racial discrimination could only for Du Bois be adequately condemned, as Hazel Carby has pointed out, through the wholesale feminization of Washington as a collaborator and compromiser, one whose counseling of "a silent submission" was "bound to sap the manhood of any race in the long run."[13] Feminized figures thus provide Du Bois with the means to critique both white and black corrupt ideologies of progress, both the abstract Progress of an industrial capitalism that cannot quantify Josie's death, and the Atlanta Compromiser's hallucinatory mirage of a progress "as separate as the five fingers, and yet one as the hand."

Du Bois's guiding effort in Souls to "make it possible for a man to be both a Negro and an American," that is, to imagine blacks precisely as full citizens, brought him into direct conflict with reigning ideologies of progress. To seek to close the schizoid gap between "Negro" and "American" was, in effect, to alter the temporal and spatial color line. In contrast to that dominant paradigm of two qualitatively different races situated at opposite ends of evolutionary time, Du Bois envisioned for blacks a racial identity that could not be temporally pinpointed any more than it could be geographically circumscribed. What Souls so eloquently chronicles is an African American culture that was their own, across time, from its African roots through slavery and diaspora to an undefined future. Du Bois's formulation of a racial identity that crossed time and space is thus one means by which the color line is transformed from the conceptual substructure of racist social evolutionism to the mythic possibility of a once and future racial glory.[14]

"Negro blood has a message for the world," concludes the description of double consciousness in a telling invocation of the rhetoric of inheritance and descent. The unified, Negro and American, "better and truer self" to which double consciousness aspires, and which it positions as an alternative to social evolutionism's temporalized color line, is a pointedly masculine self. We must look elsewhere to assess the place and purpose of racialized femininity in *Souls*.

## Gendered Bodies, Racial Histories, and National Allegory

Through a series of gendered figures and structures, *Souls* both indicts the social evolutionist color line and the hierarchical model of race it implies, and subsequently reimagines a protonationalist color line and an alternative, more lateral model of race as transgeographical kinship. If Josie emblematizes the former task, her dead body serving as the silent reproach of a Progress that moves forward only for some, Du Bois's deceased great-great-grandmother represents the latter, through the ghostly form of her lullaby "Do bana coba," a living retention passed over years and miles from parent to child, the west African coast to the Hudson valley. As described in *Souls'* final chapter, the ancestral "sorrow-song" enacts a space-time that is the very obverse of progress—lateral not linear, analeptic not proleptic— yet is nonetheless equally dependent on gender for its expressive medium. If *Souls* can be read as an attempt to break with the ideology of progress and to imagine a new spatiotemporal order for race, the text accomplishes that work by substituting allegories of reproduction for progress as the mark and measure of racial meaning.[15]

Reproduction comprises *Souls'* deepest, most structuring anxiety, a figurative site to which the text repeatedly returns as if to exorcise a series of historical specters: rape, miscegenation, illegitimacy. Scenes of coerced, illicit, or otherwise unlicensed black female sexuality punctuate the text, with the effect of warning cries issued in the face of racial destruction. Early on, Du Bois laments the "ancient African chastity" lost to "two centuries of the systematic legal defilement of Negro women" and "threatening almost the obliteration of the Negro home" (9). Chapter IV's catalogue of the many miseries that bring Josie to her death includes rural poverty, urban toil, thwarted romantic love, jailed and runaway brothers, and not least of all, the added burdens brought by her little sister Lizzie, who "bold and thoughtless, flushed with the passion of youth, bestowed herself on the tempter, and brought home a nameless child" (58). Chapter II, a historical overview of Emancipation, also connects social destruction and sexual license:

> [T]wo figures ever stand to typify that day to coming ages,—the one, a gray-haired gentleman, whose fathers had quit themselves like men, whose sons lay in nameless graves; who bowed to the evil of slavery because its abolition threatened untold ill to all; who stood at last, in the evening of life, a blighted, ruined form, with hate in his eyes;—and the other, a form hovering dark and mother-like, her awful face black with the mists of centuries, had aforetime quailed at that white master's command, had bent in love over the cradles of his sons and daughters, and closed in death the sunken eyes of his wife, aye, too, at his behest had laid herself low to his lust, and borne a tawny man-child to the world . . . (26)

Unnatural mother to all, black and white, the slave mother is an abstract canvas on which slavery's distortion and destruction of family life can be painted. Thanks to the curiously culpable phrase "laid herself low to his lust," in which she is positioned as both object and subject, both history's victim and its agent, she is also a kind of explanation for those wrongs. Like the thoughtless Lizzie who "bestowed herself on the tempter" (another instance of the syntactical guilt *Souls* accords women who reproduce outside social norms); like the classical figure of the fleet-footed Atalanta, whose surrender to a moment of "lawless lust" with her pursuer Hippomenes provides Du Bois with an analogy for the fatal desire animating the newly industrial, money-hungry city of Atlanta in chapter V (65); and like Washington whose emasculating compromise is attacked in chapter III, the slave mother who gives in to her master is positioned at the heart of those "ideologies of gender" that, as Carby has shown, structure *Souls* from beginning to end (11).

The ideological work of gender in *Souls* is the allegorization of an entire history of past and present dispossession. The female or feminized body is the metaphorical ground on which history can be written but not redeemed, for women are history's betrayers. Gendered reproduction thus becomes a site for the staging of the broader drama of racial destruction and regeneration. The cast of that drama is divided between those female or feminized persons like Washington, the slave mother, and Lizzie, who choose to weaken the race, and those men like Du Bois, his intellectual forefather Alexander Crummell, subject of chapter XII, and his literary alter-ego John Jones, subject of chapter XIII, who work to restore and uplift the race. It is in chapter V, "Of the Wings of Atalanta," that Du Bois most fully describes and, not incidentally, genders his vision of racial rebirth. The feminized city of Atlanta has forgotten her old ideals and lives now in enslavement to Mammonism. If the city is to end the profane habit of "interpreting the world in dollars," her citizens must once again seek the riches of the mind and the profits of the examined life (67). But even the black university whose classically patterned life of "knowledge and culture" will serve as Atlanta's wings and carry her, "virgin and undefiled," past the cotton and gold of materialism, is not immune from the imagery of destructive female desire. In Du Bois's imagined classrooms, future leaders of the race learn history and astronomy, and listen to the tales of Dido and Helen of Troy, women whose bodies, scorned or stolen, supposedly brought down empires (68–71). Menaced on all sides by voracious female appetites, the university must remain true to the higher calling of racial uplift: "Fly, my maiden, fly, for yonder comes Hippomenes!" concludes the chapter (73).

As a male intellectual, Du Bois is immune from such strictures of chastity. In a telling phrase that testifies to the persistence with which the tropes of racial regeneration thrust aside, even usurp, the terms of gendered generation in *Souls*, Du Bois endows the creative, racebuilding powers of the university with the aspect of sexual reproduction. The broad, passionately anti-Washington, liberal humanist educational schema that "will teach the workers to work and the thinkers to think" and that will found the common school on the university and the industrial school on the common school, is described by Du Bois as "weaving thus a system, not a distortion, and bringing a birth, not an abortion" (72). The arrogation of femininity to Du Bois's intellectually elite and embryonically nationalist project of educating the race finds its culmination in "The Afterthought," with its plea that "this my book fall not still-born into the world-wilderness" (217). Following upon chapter XI's elegiac lament for the difficulties of black fatherhood in white America as much as for Du Bois's dead infant son, the equation of book and baby in "The Afterthought" messianically converts Du Bois into a curious combination of race man and race mother, progenitor of his own version of the color line, stretching forward into the future of racial uplift and backward to his own ruptured maternal genealogy, in whose African origins lies the history of the race.[16]

It is possible to read *Souls* as effecting a consistent interpenetration of black and white, from the opening figure of double consciousness, to the national allegory of the plantation family, in which the slave owner's household is revealed to be as inextricably bound to his slaves as is America to the black sweat, song, and spirit woven into its "very warp and woof" (215), to the overarching textual strategy of the twin epigraphs that open each chapter with a few bars of the sorrow songs and a poetic fragment from the Judeo–Christian, European–American literary tradition. These interweavings ultimately reshape the meaning of race, from a system of hierarchized, temporalized, essentially biological differences plotted on the time line of progress, into a more diffuse category, at once historically deep and open to cultural syncretism and chronological synchronicity. This remaking of the space and time of race is as dependent on the figurative uses of gender as it is on the tropes of doubleness and hybridity for which the text is most famous.

Allegory, as a figure that seeks to connect distinct orders of time and space (earthly and divine, private and public, individual and national), offers a particularly appropriate method both for *Souls'* general project of racial and national redefinition and for the particular function of gender within it. As Jenny Sharpe observes, "allegory proceeds not only by metaphor (superimposed levels of meaning) but also by metonymy (a sequential relation of signs to anterior signs)."[17] In its "superimposed" or connective sense of space, and its simultaneously "sequential" and "anterior," proleptic and analeptic, sense of time, allegory has the very structure of Du Boisean space-time, which shuttles endlessly between nation and globe, racial histories and panracial futures.

In *Souls'* racialized version of the "national allegory" that Fredric Jameson has deemed characteristic of "third world" literature with its propensity to always narrate the story of public culture through that of private individuals, race is indeed subject to those "breaks and hetero-geneities," that "range of distinct meanings or messages," and the "chang[ing of] places," which Jameson defines as the characteristic structure of modern allegory, as opposed to the medieval typology of a fixed transposition of meaning from one register to another, by means of an interpretive key or code.[18] But in *Souls* the changing meaning of race (that category which the text precisely attempts to *modernize*) is enabled by the fixed figuration of the gendered body, as signifier both of the racial decay produced by the old regime and the racial uplift or liberation that will usher in the new one. If, as Jameson argues, the structure of national allegory is consciously present in "third world" texts and "unconscious" in "first world" texts, in *Souls* the structure of national allegory is subjected to a kind of "double consciousness," split between one order of meaning (race) and another (gender), ceaselessly striving to unite them yet never altogether sublating their differences. This allegorical work, so constitutive of the figural density and narra-tive complexity of *Souls* in all of its various generic registers, can also be seen to organize Du Bois's more exclusively empirical writings as well.

### Du Bois's Sociology and the Gendering of Racial Difference

Du Bois's early sociological studies took the color line as their adver-sary, seeking to dismantle its manichaean logic by portraying minute gradations of difference within black communities to which white America was only too content to assign an innately inferior, patho-logically criminal, sameness. *The Philadelphia Negro* (1899), commis-sioned by the University of Pennsylvania in conjunction with the philanthropic, Progressive, suffragist College Settlement Association, insisted upon a carefully delimited field of inquiry and an inductive method of data collection designed to chart the maximum differen-tiation in the city's black population. Against what Du Bois described as "a strong tendency on the part of the community to consider the Negroes as composing one practically homogenous mass," *The Philadelphia Negro* instead emphasized the "wide variations" within a racial group that was constantly changing.[19] Looking back in later years, Du Bois found *The Philadelphia Negro* "as complete a scientific answer as could have been given under the limitations of time and money; it showed the Negro group as a symptom and not a cause; as a striving, palpitating human group and not an inert, sick body of crime; it traced, analyzed, charted and counted."[20] *The Negro American Family* (1908), thirteenth of the eighteen *Atlanta University Publications* that Du Bois edited between 1896 and 1918, similarly sought to demonstrate the heterogeneity of African Americans.[21] Questions of racial advancement and moral health were paramount to the Atlanta Studies' attempt to create a comprehensive sociology of urban and rural black America, as the titles of the completed monographs in the series suggest: *Morality among Negroes in Cities; Social and Physical Conditions of Negroes in Cities; Some Efforts of Negroes for Social Betterment; The Negro in Business; The College-Bred Negro; The Negro Common School; The Negro Artisan; The Negro Church; Some Notes on Negro Crime, Particularly in Georgia; A Select Bibliography of the American Negro; Health and Physique of the Negro American; Economic Cooperation among Negro Americans; The Negro American Family; Efforts for Social Betterment among Negro Americans; The College-Bred Negro American; The Common School and the Negro American; The Negro American Artisan; Morals and Manners among Negro Americans.* Much broader in scope than *The Philadelphia Negro, The Negro American Family* assembled data, much of it paraphrased from secondary materials, on family life, living conditions, and marriage customs in pre-slavery West Africa, under Caribbean and American slavery, and in contemporary rural and urban Georgia. Like his portrait of the heterogeneous social microcosm contained within Philadelphia's black "city within a city" (5), *The Negro American Family*'s juxtaposition of varied times and geographies represented a conscious strategy in a larger battle. In contrast to the homogenizing vision of the social and temporal color lines, which assigned blackness one meaning (inferior) and one place (exterior or anterior) in relation to whiteness, Du Bois's sociological writings sought a more multiple and moving notion of blackness even as they continued to rely on a relatively solid idea, or ideal, of gender.

In the pursuit of what he famously called "my own sociology," Du Bois felt the need to turn away from the "vague statements," "vast

generalizations," and "fruitless word-twisting" of Spencerian method
and to consider instead "the facts, any and all facts, concerning the
American Negro and his plight."[22] These efforts, largely ignored by
mainstream American sociology, nonetheless constituted a penetrat-
ing critique of some of its most basic assumptions about race and culture. Beyond their empirical thrust and heterogenizing impulses, Du
Bois's sociological studies also seemed to map race onto quite different
spatiotemporal axes than the linear teleology of Spencerian progress,
with its guiding biological analogy between the development of the
human fetus from simple to complex structures, and the social evolution of some races and nations from primitive to civilized status.[23]

> Few modern groups show a greater internal differentiation of
> social conditions than the Negro American, and the failure to
> realize this is the cause of much confusion. In looking for differ-
> entiation from the past in Africa and slavery, few persons realize
> that this involves extreme differentiation in the present. The for-
> ward movement of a social group is not the compact march of an
> army, where the distance covered is practically the same for all,
> but is rather the straggling of a crowd, where some of whom has-
> ten, some linger, some turn back; some reach far-off goals before
> others even start, and yet the crowd moves on. (127)

In this passage from *The Negro American Family,* the "internal differentiation" of a sociological object depends on that particular combination of discontinuity and connection, fluctuation and constancy
which characterizes Du Boisean space-time more generally, from "The
Conservation of Races" description of a "black to-morrow which is
yet destined to soften the whiteness of the Teutonic to-day" to double
consciousness' model of warring two-ness and one-ness, Africanism
and Americanism. In the passage from *The Negro American Family,*
African American-ness, progressively located in "Africa," "slavery," and
"the present," is opened to ontological uncertainty precisely because
Du Bois refuses to fix the category in any one place or time.

Although the advancement described appears more Darwinian
than Spencerian in its random patterns, sharp variations, and slow
pace, the conclusion that differences aside, "yet the crowd moves on,"

is worthy of the most fervent believer in the universal law of progress. If Du Bois's image of differing rates of social advancement does not outright reject the vexed schemas of racial evolution, it does nevertheless expose those schemas to be less definitive in the place to which they assigned African Americans. In the image of some who "reach far-off goals before others even start," we can find not only a critique of the social scientific failure to capture the diversity of black experience, but also the traces of an environmental–cultural analysis of race and racial achievement, as well a burgeoning political analysis of the many restraints and obstacles—economic and educational, legal and social, structural and psychic—put in the path of black progress by white culture. Like the distinctly *un*progressing world that Du Bois found upon his return to his former Tennessee school district in *Souls*, *The Negro American Family*'s portrait of a straggling racial crowd emphasizes that sociological law, if such a thing exists outside the empire of Spencerian sociology's cosmic schemas, is not always compatible with social reality.

For Du Bois, the depiction of African American social reality entailed the marking of differing rates of racial progress—the heterogenizing of a group habitually homogenized as primitive and undeveloped, criminal and immoral. This in turn depended upon the cataloguing of differences in spaces that were at once emblematic of culture and deeply structured by gender. Despite the undisputed modernity of their attempt at racial resignification and the impressive originality of their creation of what Dan Green and Edwin Driver describe as "the most significant body of descriptive and empirically based information about black Americans in the early twentieth century,"[24] Du Bois's sociological studies can nonetheless be seen to rely for their racial newness upon a certain kind of gendered oldness, namely on such longstanding and deeply familiar analogues of the racial or national group as hearth and womb. Thus *The Philadelphia Negro*, the urban ethnography addressed to "outsiders who persist even now in confounding the good and bad, the risen and fallen in one mass," constructs its portrait of the distinct strata of a black professional aristocracy (11.5 percent), respectable working class (56 percent), honest, struggling poor (30.5 percent), and very poor, criminal minority or "submerged tenth" (5.8 percent) as much through accounts of family structure and sexual mores as through overarching empirical surveys of health, education, employment, income, politics, religion, and recreation, as they had evolved from slavery to the present.[25]

Du Bois cites a variety of causes for the "widespread and early breaking up of family life" in certain sectors, from economic stresses to the dangers of allowing male lodgers into private homes to the vestigial presence of the "lax moral habits of the slave régime," and proposes several solutions, including the "duty of the Negro to raise himself by every effort to the standards of modern civilization and not to lower those standards in any degree," a gospel of work, thrift, honesty, truth, and chastity within each African American home, and the leadership of the masses by "the better classes of the Negroes" (66–72, 388–93). Even as Du Bois diagnoses slavery, with its distorted sexual relations and communal ethos, as the root cause of sexual immorality, theft, and household extravagance among certain African Americans, he never fails to remind his readers of the ongoing legal and social inequality that prevents the great majority from triumphing over their past. In citing both a kind of Lamarckian inheritance of experience,[26] and a nascent historical materialist thesis of structural conditions as the causes of one class of black crime, while anatomizing the rise of an increasingly educated, "trained criminal class" (255) that perpetrates another set of more violent crimes, and distinguishing both classes from "the great mass" and the talented tenth (259), Du Bois effectively uncouples black identity from the innately criminal, biologically determined, collective racial character chronicled by late nineteenth-century American scientific, social, and literary writers.

As much as Du Bois sought in his "own sociology" to displace the field of racial analysis from a discourse of biological difference to one of cultural differentiation, culture could nonetheless lend itself to as rigid a calculus of racial character as biology ever did. *The Negro American Family* turns to the minute description of homes, ranging from the poverty of the slave quarter, to the one-room sharecropper's cabin, to the silver and china services of the urban professional, in order to evoke the heterogeneity that is for Du Bois constitutive of black being. An array of sociological tables and graphs, architectural plans, household budgets, and keenly observed sketches of individual homes and their inhabitants, produces a catalogue of domestic order and disorder across the spectrum of class. These descriptions of home life are never far from moral pronouncement: in one crowded and slovenly country household the sons are "rough" and the daughters "not wholesome," in contrast to the "neat and clean" persons and mores of the family of a city civil servant (135, 147). "Without doubt," proclaims *The Negro American Family*, "the point where the Negro American is furthest behind modern civilization is in his sexual *mores*" (37). Du Bois's comparison of white and black rates of economic independence (2/3 vs. 1/3) and of monogamy (9/10 vs. 1/2), and his conclusion with a statistical assessment of the rates of illiteracy, home ownership, and illegitimacy nationally (10.7 percent, 46.5 percent, and 2 percent, respectively) and among African Americans (44.5 percent, 20.3 percent, and 25 percent, respectively), all suggest the broader social discourses of both class and gender within which he felt his sociological studies needed to operate (151–52).

Du Bois is careful to distinguish "sexual immorality," for which the slave past and the Jim Crow present bear equal responsibility, from African Americans' "legitimate, beneficent appetite" for sex, an attitude "in many respects healthier and more reasonable" than that of other cultures.

> It seems to the writer that here the Negro race may teach the world something. Just as Olivier has pointed out that what is termed Negro 'laziness' may be a means of making modern workingmen demand more rational rest and enjoyment rather than permitting themselves to be made machines, so too the Negro woman, with her strong desire for motherhood, may teach modern civilization that virginity, save as a means of healthy motherhood, is an evil and not a divine attribute. (42)

The analogy between production and reproduction uncovers a series of oppositions between, on the one hand, the systems of capitalism and Christianity which perceive according to types (lazy/productive, magdalene/madonna), and, on the other, persons whose conditions of existence constitute a critique of those systems. Despite their comparison, the Negro worker and the Negro woman are nonetheless very differently positioned as the agents of critique. The workingmen's assumed laziness acquires the status of a planned tactic in the struggle of workers, alienated from their labor, to wrest for themselves some sense of self and dignity of employment, while the black woman's "strong desire for motherhood," her "Negro mother-love and family instinct" operate to place her within a less willed, more innate realm of action, albeit in heroic form. The tension in this passage between a nascent historical materialism, and a gendered essentialism in which "black woman" is rendered synonymous with "black mother" helps us to understand the contradictions in Du Bois's placing of women on the color line more generally. Like the spaces of hearth and womb that Du Bois traced across several strata of African American society, finding in their heterogeneity potential salvation from the unforgiving tape measure of collective racial stereotype, his analogy of black worker and black mother attempts to change the terms by which a race can be measured and assessed. But once unleashed, gendered allegories of racial progress cannot help but return Du Bois to the very bodied biologism that his culturalist sociology elsewhere strains to escape.

If Josie represents the conceptual limits of the ideology of progress, the end point beyond which it cannot or will not venture description ("How shall man measure Progress there where the dark-faced Josie lies?"), then the women and families, sexual bodies and domestic households of Du Bois's sociological studies are markers scattered along that temporal line. These gendered signs create the highly individualized spaces through which differentiation can be read, racial heterogeneity revealed, and progress in fact measured. Gendered signs do double duty, shoring up the temporal line of progress with their portrait of varying rates of advancement, yet thereby destroying its capacity to characterize *all* members of a racial group. Du Bois's sociological studies here reveal their contiguity with his other more political and poetic writings, for all can be seen to share a common reliance on what we might call the allegorical language of gender, in order to express the changing substance of race.

This phenomenon reveals itself most clearly through the gendered construct of the family. The family's operation as a trope for racial and national identity can be divided into two distinct yet overlapping realms: the first that of the evolutionary schema of "the family of man," with its greater and lesser, whiter and blacker, adult and infantile branches; and the second that of a diverse, often culturally specific, set of gendered relations and norms within the social institution of the family. Du Bois's efforts to counter the hierarchical logic and racist implications of social evolutionism's "family of man" model led him not only into a scientific empiricism that relied heavily on the family as a measure of racial progress, but also into a mystical messianism that sought to resignify and expand the concept of "racial family." The family of man thus represents one version of the color line, the racial family another. In the former, time is evolutionary and white, and black spaces are separated; in the latter, time is both recursive and progressive, just as racial spaces are both distinct and interconnected. Du Bois's reimagining of another kind of color line demanded a different articulation of the concept of race to the concept of family. Race had to be redefined as a form of historical kinship that actively traverses time and space to connect African Americans with Africa and the "darker world" more generally. This project in turn demanded a merging of expressive genres, interweaving historical science and literary creation, global political analysis and racial prophecy. But for all its generic diversity, Du Bois's reinvention of the color line as "spatiotemporal connection" remained, like his more narrowly sociological indictment of the color line as "spatiotemporal differentiation," consistently undergirded by a gendered sameness. In other words, the gendering of the color line survived the transformation of the color line, proving as crucial to the creation of an expansively internationalist notion of "racial family" as it had been to the dismantling of a narrowly social evolutionist notion of "families of races."

## The Gendered Form of the Global Color Line

Du Bois's later transnational texts, including the historical studies *The Negro* (1915), *The Gift of Black Folk* (1924), *Black Folk Then and Now* (1935), and *The World and Africa* (1946); the novel *Dark Princess* (1928); and the generically hybrid *Darkwater* (1920), all focus on the color line as a potent image for the harsh ways in which colonialism seeks to bisect the world into rulers and ruled. These texts, especially

*Dark Princess* with its romance plot between the budding African American revolutionary Matthew Townes, and the fervently socialist Indian princess Kautilya, also conceive of the color line as one that affiliates and joins the "darker races of the world" in political and sexual union. Kautilya describes the dual nature of this color line towards the end of the novel in one of the impassioned letters she writes to Matthew from her self-imposed exile in the American South.

> You are not free in Chicago nor New York. But here in Virginia you are at the edge of a black world. The black belt of the Congo, the Nile, and the Ganges reaches by way of Guiana, Haiti, and Jamaica, like a red arrow, up into the heart of white America.[27]

Color progresses in this passage from black to red to a white that can no longer be white, thanks to the black presence within it—a kind of visual condensation of the basic argument of *Souls*. Kautilya continues her description of the global black belt, telling Matthew of a "mighty synthesis: you can work in Africa and Asia right here in America if you work in the Black Belt." This transformation or domestication, we might even say nationalization, of the "darker world" into the American South finds its allegorical equivalent at the novel's end with the messianic birth of Matthew and Kautilya's son: Africa and Asia fused in rural Virginia. As the birthplace of a child heralded, in the final line of the novel, as "Messenger and Messiah to all the Darker Worlds," America ceases to be a nation and becomes something more like the globe or a dark swath of the globe. *Dark Princess*, like Du Bois's other works devoted to imagining a color line that belts the world, may be seen to move in both directions, both nationalizing the transnational (Africa and Asia right here in America) and transnationalizing the national (America as the darker world). What role does gender play in that shuttling movement, so constitutive of Du Bois's work as a whole, back and forth between the national and the transnational?[28]

If Du Bois's *pan-Africanism*, his *transnationalism* and *internationalism*, and his *diasporic consciousness* are each a web linking together the darker races generally, and African Americans and Africans particularly, then women are the connective tissue of those webs. *Dark*

*Princess*'s image of the black belt originating in Africa and India, reaching like a red arrow up through the Caribbean, and plunging into white America's heart, places blood at its center. As the discourse of reproduction repeatedly inscribed by Du Bois onto the black female body, it is blood that enables the color line to move from black to red to white, blood that undergirds the larger movements and connections between races which we have come to equate with the panracial, diasporic, proto-postcolonial Du Bois, blood that ironically enough reclaims the concept of race from the biologism of scientific racism. Women make possible Du Bois's vision of the color line as a continuum and congress of the darker peoples in two senses: first because women like Kautilya are themselves endowed with the capacity to produce an African-Asian panracial synthesis; and secondly because the explicitly feminized condition of rape serves a metaphorical conduit linking the experience of slavery to that of colonialism, the history of one set of darker peoples to another.

It is in this second, allegorical sense that women can be seen to organize the earlier pan-Africanist *Darkwater* (1920). By combining the registers of the essay and the literary fragment, alternating between competing visions of redemption, some in the guise of messianic birth, and others in that of socialist solidarity, *Darkwater* attempts to forge a series of generic, racial, spatial, and temporal connections through the figures of women. In a chapter entitled "The Souls of White Folk" (first published in 1910), Du Bois attacks European colonialism in terms that anticipate Fanon's *The Wretched of the Earth* (1961). "This is not Europe gone mad . . ." writes Du Bois, "this *is* Europe; this seeming Terrible is the real soul of white culture" (39). White culture, he continues, has as its basic theory the premise that dark peoples are "born beasts of burden for white folk" (41). A few pages earlier the colonial situation is described as "mutilation and rape masquerading as culture" (37). Europe is the rapist, colonial profits "the spoils of the rape" (47), and the colonies the raped.

In "The Riddle of the Sphinx," first published in 1907 as "The Burden of Black Women," the poem turns on the bodies of women, from its opening gesture to the "[d]ark daughter of the lotus leaves that watch the Southern Sea" to its closing vision of a liberation quaking "'neath the bloody finger-marks" on a black mother's "riven bosom."

The will of the world is a whistling wind, sweeping
   a cloud-swept sky,
And not from the East and not from the West knelled that
   soul-waking cry,
But out of the South,—the sad, black South—it screamed from
   the top of the sky,
Crying: "Awake, O ancient race!" Wailing, "O woman, arise!"
And crying and sighing and crying again as a voice in the
   midnight cries,—
But the burden of white men bore her back and the White
   world stifled her sighs. (*Du Bois Reader,* 509)

Seamlessly fusing the allegorical narrative of colonialism as rape with the historical narrative of the literal rape of black women, the poem proceeds to make women the vehicles both of history and historical change. This double function parallels the syntactical indeterminacy of the last two lines in the above passage. What is it that bears the black woman back to the historical past? The "white man's burden" to civilize darkness, the burden dryly defined by Du Bois as that of seeing dark peoples as "born beasts of burden," or the actual weight and burden of white men borne by a supine black woman? The difference is, in a sense, minor, a distinction between greater and lesser degrees of literalness. But the very redoubling of rape in these lines, and in the poem more broadly, attests to its signal importance as a figure of simultaneous division (white men's historical rape of black women as the brutal product of the bisected world of the color line) and connection (rape as the allegorical conduit linking African and Asian experiences of colonialism, and African American experiences of slavery and Jim Crow). The figure of the raped black woman connects the "sad, black South" to a darker world enumerated as "black men of Egypt and Ind/Ethiopia's sons of the evening/Indians and yellow Chinese/ Arabian children of morning,/And mongrels of Rome and Greece." This panracial group will drag down the white rulers until some dark couple "[b]id the black Christ be born" (*Du Bois Reader,* 510). The raped black woman thus comes to represent the liberation not only (perhaps not even) of her own body, but also of exploited territories, colonized minds, suppressed histories, and dehumanized persons. The historical change envisioned by the poem is not revolution but messianic birth: "Then shall our burden be manhood/Be it yellow or black or white" (*Du Bois Reader,* 510). The birth of the black Christ transforms the burden earlier connected with the rape of black women and the hollow imperial pretensions of white men into a redemptive, restorative, colorless "manhood."

A later chapter of *Darkwater* entitled "The Damnation of Women" meditates on the category of "free womanhood," meaning a woman's entitlement to economic independence born of work, knowledge, and "the right of motherhood at her own discretion" (*Darkwater,* 165). In the same chapter Du Bois alludes to "the primal black All-Mother," defines Africa as "the land of the mother" and credits it with "the mother-idea," and even positions Africa as mother in a peculiarly oedipal configuration of global politics: African mother, Asian father of tradition, and precocious, narcissistic European child (165–67). On the one hand, "The Damnation of Women" tries to distinguish women from obligatory motherhood, while on the other hand it concatenates, in a kind of rhetorical juggernaut, woman, Africa, mother. If, as Eric Sundquist has argued, *Darkwater* "repeat[s] the strategy of *The Souls of Black Folk* now on a global scale" (591), it necessarily returns to the earlier text's gendered lexicon in order to assert the material rights of oppressed persons (for which he finds the term "manhood" sufficient both in *Souls'* national context and *Darkwater*'s more global reach). The oscillating image of black women through the twin lenses of rape and motherhood enables Du Bois's particular brand of messianic transnationalism. It sutures African Americans to the "darker peoples," slavery to colonialism, the trauma of racialized histories to the prophetic imagining of a panracial future. This national pageant of racial history is presented through such iconic types as the "gentle" Phyllis Wheatley, the "crude Moses" Harriet Tubman, and the "sybil" Sojourner Truth, as well as through the various cryptic stories and poems that condense their concerns into such emblematic figures as a princess who tears out her own heart rather than accept African gold ("The Princess of the Hither Isles"), and a black Mary who ascends to find a black God ("The Call," and

"Children of the Moon").[29] *Darkwater* depends, like Du Bois's other writings, on this relentlessly allegorized black femininity as the expressive mode of a global racial politics.

### The Middle Ground of a Moving Line: Women in the Color Line

Du Bois consistently gendered his competing versions of the color line, both the line that divides, segregates, and leaves behind non-white people and the line that connects them to one another in a futuristic union or congress that is both political and sexual. Reproduction undoes the logic of the color line understood as separation while it simultaneously realizes and allegorizes the vision of the color line as affiliation. Labor, especially the question of a global proletariat, was critical to Du Bois's conceptualization of the color line in these two senses. Ultimately, Du Bois came to envision the relationship of white workers to black workers as a necessary factor in the achievement of worldwide equality. But what was the role of women within that relationship? Du Bois's notes for the preparation of his 1924 collection *The Gift of Black Folk* specifically mention African American women's "pioneer" status as laborers, employed at a rate twice that of white women and in many cases, economically self-supporting.[30] Yet in the final volume, the chapter devoted to black labor accords surprisingly little space to female work. In a sweeping catalogue of black agricultural and artisanal work and its central contributions to the rise of modern commerce and industrialism, black women are given a strangely detached paragraph of their own, detailing their domestic contributions as mammies, wet nurses, cooks, and maids. Though Du Bois does include some statistics on other occupations of black women, the nature and effects of that work go largely unmentioned in a chapter overwhelmingly devoted to the story of labor as the story of men.

An early sketch for *The Gift of Black Folk* provides a sense of the ways in which Du Bois would eventually abstract women out of the category of labor. The diagram constructs a pyramid of themes: a broad but thin base devoted to exploration and conquest; a full third of the structure given over to labor in the world, cultivating sugar, tobacco, rice, and cotton; a narrow band labeled "self-supporting women," and meant to be illustrated, as Du Bois's marginal notes explain, through portraits of "colored women types," including Harriet Tubman, Sojourner Truth, Mammy Pleasants, and other muses of black history; and then four progressively smaller bands devoted respectively to emancipation of democracy, defense, literature, and music, with notes for accompanying examples. If we compare this diagram's positioning of women, sandwiched between labor and democracy in a space that can only be described as that of historical allegory, with the actual chapter in *The Gift of Black Folk* devoted to "The Freedom of Womanhood," we find in both cases an insistence on women as what mediates between other categories, women precisely as the middle ground. In *Dark Princess* and "The Riddle of the Sphinx" the gendered allegories of rape and motherhood allow women to mediate between slavery and colonialism, America and the darker world. In "The Freedom of Womanhood" women are defined more as workers, "conspirator[s] urging forward emancipation" (273). But the primary portrait that the chapter paints, to which it returns more than once, is of the black woman, specifically "the colored slave woman" as "the medium through which two great races were united in America" (268).

Du Bois's conjuring of black women as the medium of race mixture resonates within a broader understanding of race that was itself indebted to the late nineteenth-century discourses of psychology, mysticism, and spiritualism, as imparted to the young Du Bois by his Harvard mentor William James. As Thomas Otten explains, James understood divided or, as he called them, "hidden" selves to "function as mediums . . . that part of the personality through which boundaries between individual consciousnesses can somehow dissolve." The divided or hidden self as, again in Otten's words, "a pathological condition, as the realm of the seer, as an unfathomable area of the psyche" would return in Du Bois's most famous model of racial identity.[31] With its depiction of the soul-shattering conflict of "two thoughts, two unreconciled strivings; two warring ideals in one dark body" and its desire "to attain self-conscious manhood, to merge [that] double self into a better and truer self," Du Boisean double consciousness is a pointedly masculine account of racial identity. "The

Freedom of Womanhood" very differently places black women at the
heart of the problem of racial identity, and in its figuration of black
women as "the medium" of racial mixture, finds a specifically gendered solution to that racially discriminatory logic which creates
double consciousness in the first place. "[N]ot even an extraordinary
drawing of the color line against all visible Negro blood has ever been
able to trace its [racial mingling's] limits," observes Du Bois (268).
Black women are here credited with a certain reproductive triumph
over the discriminatory version of the color line, which is rendered
not just "extraordinary" but illogical, impossible, and unthinkable,
thanks to the intermingling of blood in a new color line of descent for
which the black female body serves as medium.

The discourse of blood has posed a difficulty for scholars attempting to assess the political utility of Du Bois's theory of race. Sundquist
understands Du Bois's concept of race to expand from a scientific
category to a sociohistorical one, ultimately "reading race only as civilization or culture." For Kwame Anthony Appiah, on the other hand,
Du Bois's conceptual use of race as family, with its references to kinship, blood, inherited traces, visible resemblances and lineage, never
escapes the taint of biologism.[32]

Du Bois's various formulations of race-as-biology and race-as-
culture have spawned extensive critical debate over what exactly Du
Bois meant by "race" at various points in his career. What role does
gender play in his formulations? Gender, positioned by dominant
discourse between, but never irrefutably "of" the realms of nature
and culture, buttresses both versions of race, and indeed may prove a
significant factor in the oft-noted ability of Du Bois to sustain both
definitions simultaneously. In this regard, blood can perhaps be
understood as the figurative corollary to the rhetorical mode of allegory. Both are associated with women in Du Bois's work and both
enact that sustaining of contradictory meaning, that simultaneous
division and connection of distinct times and spaces, in which is
found the central function of the gendered color line.

Du Bois's vision in *Souls*, his early sociological writings, and later
writings from the 1920s is largely one of racial synthesis, national
incorporation, and transnational connection. Black women are the
grounds of those dual imperatives to move, join, mix, and hybridize.

The point has not been to ascertain just how feminist or not Du Bois's nationalism and transnationalism were. As Nellie MacKay points out in her comprehensive survey of black women in Du Bois's writings, he was a "staunch supporter of women's rights in all areas of life and work."[33] Rather, the point is to trace the fixed metaphor of gender against what Sundquist calls the color line's "fluid metaphor." The color line "belts the world" but it is undergirded by gender. If we take Du Bois's work as an invitation to read allegorically, perhaps we may do no better than to realize that there can be no definitive hierarchization of opposed orders of meaning, no final resolution of what Benjamin calls "the antinomies of the allegorical." However hard Du Bois may try at certain moments, race cannot definitively become gender, nor gender race, just as nation cannot become globe, nor past become future. Only in the shifting pattern of these categories' coalescence, on the uncertain terrain of allegorical representation, across the broad course of Du Bois's career, will we begin to find the real ends of the color line.

## Notes

An earlier version of this essay was presented at the 1999 American Studies Association meeting. I am grateful to Susan Gillman and Alys Weinbaum for the invitation to speak on that panel, for the insight and rigor with which they helped to shape the present essay, and for many years of friendship and conversation about Du Bois. Paul Gilroy's illuminating readings of Du Bois have long inspired and challenged me, as has his comradeship. Hazel Carby first opened the space for these investigations. For this, and for her example, encouragement, and friendship, I thank her.

1. Eric J. Sundquist, *To Wake the Nations: Race in the Making of American Literature* (Cambridge, Mass.: Harvard University Press, 1993), 547.

2. W. E. B. Du Bois, *The Souls of Black Folk* (New York: Penguin Books, 1989), 13. Hereafter abbreviated as *Souls*. Subsequent references appear parenthetically in the text.

3. W. E. B. Du Bois, *Darkwater: Voices from Behind the Veil* (1920; repr. Millwood, N.Y.: Kraus-Thomson Organization Ltd., 1975), 181. Subsequent references appear parenthetically in the text as *Darkwater*. *Darkwater* also appears reprinted in ed., Eric Sundquist, *The Oxford W. E. B. Du Bois Reader* (New York: Oxford University Press, 1996). References to this edition will appear parenthetically in the text as *Du Bois Reader*.

4. Critics who categorize Du Bois's career as a sequence of stages from sociologist to ideologist or poet to propagandist include: Charles U. Smith and Lewis Killian, "Black Sociologists and Social Protest," in James E. Blackwell and Morris Janowitz,

eds., *Black Sociologists: Historical and Contemporary Perspectives* (Chicago: The University of Chicago Press, 1974); Arnold Rampersad, *The Art and Imagination of W. E. B. Du Bois* (Cambridge, Mass.: Harvard University Press, 1976), 32–47; Elliot M. Rudwick, *W. E. B. Du Bois: Propagandist of the Negro Protest* (New York: Atheneum, 1968); and Manning Marable, *W. E. B. Du Bois: Black Radical Democrat* (Boston: G. K. Hall and Co., 1986). The relative absence of gendered analysis from these accounts is not, I suggest, coincidental to their chronological narratives of Du Bois's development or transformation.

5. W. E. B. Du Bois, "The Conservation of Races" (1897), reprinted in *W. E. B. Du Bois on Sociology and the Black Community,* eds. Dan S. Green and Edwin D. Driver (Chicago: The University of Chicago Press, 1978), 238–49, 245.

6. Benedict Anderson, *Imagined Communities: Reflections on the Origin and Spread of Nationalism,* revised edition (London and New York: Verso, 1991), 11–12.

7. Herbert Spencer, "Progress: Its Law and Cause," *Westminster Review* (April 1857), reprinted in *Essays on Education and Kindred Subjects by Herbert Spencer* (New York: E. P. Dutton, 1910), 153–97, 160.

8. For a foundational genealogy of these terms, see Hazel Carby, "The Souls of Black Men," in *Race Men* (Cambridge, Mass.: Harvard University Press, 1998), 9–41.

9. Paul de Man, "The Rhetoric of Temporality," in *Blindness and Insight: Essays in the Rhetoric of Contemporary Criticism,* revised edition (Minneapolis: University of Minnesota Press, 1983), 187–228, 226.

10. De Man, 222.

11. Walter Benjamin, *The Origins of German Tragic Drama,* trans. John Osborne (London: Verso, 1987), 174–75.

12. Recalling his initial encounters at Harvard with "scientific race dogma," Du Bois noted: "I could accept evolution and the survival of the fittest, provided the interval between advanced and backward races was not made too impossible." *Dusk of Dawn: An Essay Toward an Autobiography of a Race Concept* (1940) (New York: Schocken Books, 1968), 98–99.

13. Carby, 44–45.

14. Charles Lemert's rich reading of the forward and backward-moving structure of racial-historical time in *Black Reconstruction* (1935) similarly concludes that "[t]he appeal of the figure of the color line rests on its defiance of progress." My own reading of Du Bois's earlier writings attempts to connect that structure which Lemert so suggestively terms "the race of time" to what could be called the gender of race. Lemert, "The Race of Time: Du Bois and Reconstruction," *boundary 2* 27, no. 3, special issue on "Sociology Hesitant: Thinking with W. E. B. Du Bois," ed. Ronald A. T. Judy (2000): 215–48, 247.

15. For a related argument see David Krell's recent exploration of the interrelated discourses of African history, nature, and the racial (but not gendered) body in "The Bodies of Black Folk: From Kant and Hegel to Du Bois and Baldwin," *boundary 2* 27, no. 3 (2000): 103–34. For an extended discussion of the reproductive trope in *Souls* and other writings, see Alys Eve Weinbaum, *Wayward Reproductions: Genealogies of Race and Nation in Transatlantic Modern Thought* (Durham: Duke University Press, 2004), 187–226.

16. I agree with Weinbaum that Du Bois's eulogy (which leaves the race of his son's mother unmarked) "refuse[s] to make the black mother into the source of racial

identity in a context in which this same logic excluded blacks from the nation" (197). Here I have wished to emphasize, following Carby's argument (24–26), how Du Bois's maternalization of himself enables a bodily grounding of racial identity that *Souls'* occult thematics of racial consciousness otherwise seek to contest. Gendered figuration allows Du Bois to have race both ways, as body *and* mind.

17. Jenny Sharpe, *Allegories of Empire: The Figure of Woman in the Colonial Text* (Minneapolis: University of Minnesota Press, 1993), 140. De Man's "The Rhetoric of Temporality" formulates the schema somewhat differently, distinguishing between the world of the symbol, in which the coincidence of image and substance effects a "simultaneity, which, in truth, is spatial" and the world of allegory, in which "time is the originary constitutive category" and everything depends on the non-coincidence of difference. "The meaning constituted by the allegorical sign can then consist only in the *repetition* . . . of a previous sign with which it can never coincide, since it is of the essence of this previous sign to be pure anteriority" (207). For the purposes of this argument, I prefer Sharpe's formulation of an allegory that operates both temporally and spatially.

18. Fredric Jameson, "Third-World Literature in the Era of Multinational Capitalism," *Social Text* 15 (1986): 65–88, 73–74. On the notion of the pre-modern allegorical "master code" uniting earthly and divine, individual and collective history, and its interpretive alternative of the "political unconscious," within whose terms History is understood to be "inaccessible to us except in textual form," see Jameson, *The Political Unconscious: Narrative as a Socially Symbolic Act* (Ithaca: Cornell University Press, 1981), 29–35. For an extended discussion of the status of allegory in Du Bois's national and global thought, see Cooppan, "The Double Politics of Double Consciousness: Nationalism and Globalism in *The Souls of Black Folk*," *Public Culture* 17, no. 2 (2005): 299–318, special issue on W. E. B. Du Bois, ed. Robert Gooding-Williams and Dwight McBride; and chapter 3 of Cooppan, *Inner Territories: Fictions and Fantasms of the Nation in Postcolonial Writing* (Stanford University Press, forthcoming in 2007).

19. W. E. B. Du Bois, *The Philadelphia Negro; A Social Study . . . Together With A Special Report On Domestic Service By Isabel Eaton,* ed. Herbert Aptheker (Millwood, N.Y.: Kraus-Thomson Organization Ltd., 1973), 309. Subsequent references appear parenthetically in the text.

20. W. E. B. Du Bois, "A Pageant in Seven Decades: 1868–1938," reprinted in *Pamphlets and Leaflets by W. E. B. Du Bois,* ed. Herbert Aptheker (White Plains, N.Y.: Kraus-Thomson Organization Ltd., 1986), 244–74, 253.

21. *The Negro American Family: Report of a Social Study Made Principally by the College Classes of 1909 and 1910 of Atlanta University, under the Patronage of the Trustees of the John F. Slater Fund; Together with the Proceedings of the 13th Annual Conference for the Study of the Negro Problems, held at Atlanta University, May 26, 1908, The Atlanta University Publications, 13,* ed. W. E. B. Du Bois (Atlanta, Ga.: The Atlanta University Press, 1908). Subsequent references appear parenthetically in the text. On the general plan for the Atlanta Studies see: Du Bois, "The Laboratory in Sociology at Atlanta University," *Annals of the American Academy of Political and Social Science* 21 (May 1903); "The Atlanta Conferences," *Voice of the Negro* 1 (March 1904), reprinted in Green and Driver, eds., *W. E. B. Du Bois on Sociology and the Black Community,* 53–60; and *Dusk of Dawn,* 63–66.

22. Du Bois, *Dusk of Dawn*, 50–51. Du Bois expresses even stronger reservations about the project of social science and Spencer's "verbal jugglery" and "shadowy outline of the meaning and rhythm of human deed" in "Sociology Hesitant," an essay manuscript in the Du Bois Archives at the University of Massachusetts, Amherst, recently published in *boundary 2* 27, no. 3 (2000): 37–44, 39. Critics offer differing assessments of Du Bois's debt to Spencerian sociology. Most agree that Du Bois's graduate course work in ethics, history, and political science at Harvard between 1890 and 1892 and his introduction to the sociological methods of data collection and inductive analysis in Gustav von Schmoller's seminar at the University of Berlin from 1892–1894, prepared him for his own sociological studies of African Americans. For Rampersad, these studies showed an "acceptance of Spencer's basic beliefs" and a subsequent "faith in the power of empirical sociology" that lasted until he left academic sociology in 1910 to pursue a more literary and later, political, career (27). Adolph Reed points out a distinctly evolutionary, Spencerian cast to Du Bois's thinking in *W. E. B. Du Bois and American Political Thought: Fabianism and the Color Line* (New York and Oxford: Oxford University Press, 1997), 43–47. By contrast, Green, Driver, and Rudwick characterize Du Bois's relationship to Spencer and sociological doctrine as quite critical of "grand theoretical method" from very early in his career. Green and Driver, "Introduction," in *W. E. B. Du Bois on Sociology and the Black Community,* 25–35; Rudwick, "W. E. B. Du Bois as Sociologist," in *Black Sociologists: Historical and Contemporary Perspectives,* eds. James E. Blackwell and Morris Janowitz (Chicago: The University of Chicago Press, 1974), 25–55. Ronald A. T. Judy importantly observes that Du Bois's distancing of himself from positivist sociology and subsequent commitment to demonstrating the disjunctive, heterogeneous aspect of racial experience derived from his realization that grandiose observations and generalizations "were predicated on a typology of subjective meaning that was in no way ideologically neutral." Ronald A. T. Judy, "On W. E. B. Du Bois and Hyperbolic Thinking," *boundary 2* 27, no. 3 (2000): 1–36, 34.

23. In "On Progress" Spencer argues the measure of a race's progress lies in the heterogeneity of its biological structure: civilized races exhibit more developed limbs than "the Papuan" and a higher ratio of cranial bones to facial bones than "the savage." National progress is equally a function of differentiation: the "minute division of labour" in civilized nations contrasts with savage communities where "every man is warrior, hunter, fisherman, tool-maker, builder; every woman performs the same drudgeries" (160). Spencer's voluminous later writings further developed this influential analogy, borrowed from the work of the German embryologist Karl Ernst von Baer. On Spencerian social evolutionism, see George Stocking, *Race, Culture, and Evolution* (Chicago: The University of Chicago Press, 1968), 110–32 and 239–41; Robert L. Carneiro, *The Evolution of Society: Selections from Herbert Spencer's Principles of Sociology* (Chicago: The University of Chicago Press, 1967); J. D. Y. Peel, *Herbert Spencer: The Evolution of a Sociologist* (London: Heinemann, 1971); Stanislav Andreski, ed. *Herbert Spencer: Structure, Function and Evolution* (New York: Charles Scribner's Sons, 1971); Peter Bowler, "The Changing Meaning of 'Evolution,'" *Journal of the History of Ideas* xxxvi:1 (January-March 1975): 95–114; and Reba N. Soffer, *Ethics and Society in England: The Revolution in the Social Sciences, 1870–1914* (Berkeley: University of California Press, 1978). On Du Bois's "breaking ranks" with Spencerian sociology and its analogical method, see David Levering Lewis's

informative discussion of *The Philadelphia Negro* as a work of "interpretive radicalism" in his excellent biography, *W. E. B. Du Bois: Biography of a Race*, vol. I (New York: Henry Holt and Company, 1993), 186–210, 202, 189.

24. Green and Driver, "Introduction," in *W. E. B. Du Bois on Sociology and the Black Community*, 31. On the neglect of Du Bois by the American sociological establishment also see their "W. E. B. Du Bois: A Case in the Sociology of Sociological Negation," *Phylon Quarterly* 37.4 (1976): 308–33; and Elliot Rudwick, "Note on a Forgotten Black Sociologist: W. E. B. Du Bois and the Sociological Profession," reprinted in *The Bobbs-Merrill Series in Black Studies* (November 1969), 305.

25. *The Philadelphia Negro*, 171–78, 311–18, 393. See Rudwick's comprehensive discussion of *The Philadelphia Negro*, his summary of Du Bois's four classes, and his discussion of Du Bois's innovative emphasis on environmental factors rather than innate differences in "W. E. B. Du Bois as Sociologist," 29–39, especially 35–36. Also see Rampersad's discussion of *The Philadelphia Negro*'s presentation of "environmental rather than racial explanations" (48–67, 52); and, for a broad overview, *W. E. B. Du Bois, Race, and the City: The Philadelphia Negro and its Legacy*, ed. Michael B. Katz and Thomas J. Sugrue (Philadelphia: University of Pennsylvania Press, 2000).

26. Stocking argues that Lamarckianism, until its renunciation at the time of the first world war, offered an alternative to "a milieu of ascendant biological evolutionism," making it possible "to explain and to validate the cultural progress of mankind in biological terms, at the same time that it freed man from the conservative implications of biological evolutionism" (251, 256). A later statement of Du Bois's environmentalism which rejects any biological explanation of race in favor of a doctrine of "social heredity" and dismisses Lamarckianism as an "older and cruder doctrine of heredity" that has done much damage to the understanding of race, appears in "Heredity and the Public Schools: A Lecture Delivered under the Auspices of the Principals' Association of the Colored Schools of Washington, D.C." (1904) in Aptheker, ed., *Pamphlets and Leaflets by W. E. B. Du Bois*, 45–52, 48.

27. W. E. B. Du Bois, *Dark Princess: A Romance* (Jackson: University Press of Mississippi, 1995), 286. I have profited from Paul Gilroy's reading of the novel in "'Cheer the Weary Traveller': W. E. B. Du Bois, Germany, and the Politics of (Dis)placement," in *The Black Atlantic: Modernity and Double Consciousness* (Cambridge, Mass.: Harvard University Press, 1993), 111–46, 140–46; and Kenneth Warren's discussion in "An Inevitable Drift? Oligarchy, Du Bois and the Politics of Race Between the Wars," *boundary 2* 27, no. 3 (2000): 153–69.

28. For a searching analysis of how *Dark Princess* repeatedly "cast[s] reproduction as the motor of black belonging in the world," whether in national or international form, see Weinbaum, *Wayward Reproductions*, 199–215, 215.

29. Sundquist reads the allegorical structure of these and other literary fragments (590–91; 614–19). On the centrality of historical pageantry to the temporal and figural strategies of *Darkwater* and to its global thematics, see Susan Gillman, *Blood Talk: American Race Melodrama and the Culture of the Occult* (Chicago: The University of Chicago Press, 2003), 194–99.

30. W. E. B. Du Bois, "Memorandum on the Contributions of the Negro to American Life" (1922), in the Du Bois Papers at the University of Massachusetts at Amherst, reprinted in Herbert Aptheker's "Introduction" to Du Bois, *The Gift of Black Folk* (Millwood, N.Y.: Kraus-Thomson Organization Limited, 1974), 5–21, 9–12, 10.

31. Thomas J. Otten, "Pauline Hopkins and the Hidden Self of Race," *ELH* 59 (1992): 227–56, 243. Also see Cynthia D. Schrager, "Both Sides of the Veil: Race, Science, and Mysticism in W. E. B. Du Bois," *American Quarterly* 48, no. 4 (1996): 551–86. On James's influence on Du Bois also see Rampersad, 41, 73–74; Sundquist, 571–72; Dickson Bruce, "W. E. B. Du Bois and the Idea of Double Consciousness," *American Literature* 64:2 (June 1992): 299–309; and Shamoon Zamir, *Dark Voices: W. E. B. Du Bois and American Thought, 1888–1903* (Chicago and London: The University of Chicago Press, 1995), 153–68. For an argument that accords less influence to James and more to Du Bois's own identity as "a psychic purgatory fully capable by itself of nurturing a concept of divided consciousness," see Levering Lewis, (96, 282). Reed also surveys James's psychological theory of the divided self and argues against "a specific lineage" connecting James's ideas about consciousness to Du Bois's (99–105, 105). Useful background on James's psychological models of mental processes and human will as a revolutionary contradiction of Spencerian sociology's more deterministic laws of instinct, behavior, and heredity can be found in Soffer, 32–45, 135–61; Robert C. Fuller, *Americans and the Unconscious* (New York and Oxford: Oxford University Press, 1986), chapters 3 and 4; and Dorothy Ross, *The Origins of American Social Science* (New York and Cambridge: Cambridge University Press, 1991), especially 239–43.

32. Kwame Anthony Appiah, "The Uncompleted Argument: Du Bois and the Illusion of Race," in *"Race," Writing, and Difference,* ed. Henry Louis Gates, Jr. (Chicago: The University of Chicago Press, 1986), 21–37, 30–31; Sundquist, 569. For a detailed discussion of the tensions between biological and culturalist discourses of race in Du Bois's work see Nahum Dimitri Chandler, "The Economy of Desedimentation: W. E. B. Du Bois and the Discourses of the Negro," *Callaloo* 19, no. 1 (1996): 78–93.

33. Nellie McKay, "W. E. B. Du Bois: The Black Women in His Writings-Selected Fictional and Autobiographical Portraits," in William L. Andrews, ed., *Critical Essays on W. E. B. Du Bois* (Boston: G. K. Hall & Co., 1985), 230–53, 251, footnote 10. In the "bold," "brilliant," and fully realized black women of novels like *Dark Princess* and *The Quest of the Silver Fleece* (1911) and Du Bois's several autobiographical accounts, McKay finds a counter-narrative to his general tendency towards "a romantic idealization of women, particularly of the black mother" (251).

# Profeminism and Gender Elites: W. E. B. Du Bois, Anna Julia Cooper, and Ida B. Wells-Barnett

■ *Joy James*

$B$y expanding critical theoretical frameworks, W. E. B. Du Bois demystified racism and class elitism. Unfortunately, at the same time, he also mystified the agency of African American women. Du Bois's sexual politics suggest that he navigated between increasingly nonclassist and democratic ideologies, and a moribund gender progressivism, into a quagmire of contradictory progressive and paternalistic racial-sexual politics. Attempting to better understand the contradictions of Du Bois's profeminist ideology, we see an analogy with antiracism. Like some types of antiracism, certain forms of feminism and profeminism are disingenuous. Guided by a Eurocentrism that presents European (American) culture as normative, antiracist stances inadvertently reproduce white dominance; this reinscription of white privilege occurs despite avowed racial egalitarianism. Likewise, despite their gender progressivism, antisexists or profeminists whose politics unfold within a metaparadigm that establishes the male as normative, reinforce male dominance. For Du Bois, the African American male was the paradigmatic black intellectual.

Du Bois's profeminist politics clearly marks his opposition to patriarchy and misogyny. Still, a masculinist worldview influences his writing and diminishes his gender progressivism. Du Bois rejects patriarchal myths about female inferiority and male superiority. Yet he holds on to a masculinist framework that presents the male as normative. Since masculinism does not explicitly advocate male superiority or rigid gender social roles, it is not identical to patriarchal ideology. Masculinism can share patriarchy's presupposition of the male as normative without its antifemale politics and rhetoric. Men who support feminist politics, as profeminists, may advocate the equality or even superiority of women. For instance, Du Bois argues against sexism and occasionally for the superiority of women. However, even without patriarchal intent, certain works may replicate conventional gender roles.

Du Bois's fictional portraits of African American women emphasize and romanticize the strength of black women. They thus differ from his nonfiction writing regarding individual African American women. Although Du Bois makes no chauvinistic pronouncements like the aristocratic ones characterizing his early writings on the Talented Tenth, his nonfiction minimizes black female agency. Without misogynist dogma, his writings naturalize the dominance of black males in African American political discourse.

### Du Bois's Profeminism

The uplift of women is, next to the problem of the color line and the peace movement, our greatest modern cause. When, now, two of these movements—women and color—combine in one, the combination has deep meaning.

W. E. B. Du Bois

In the above quote from his 1920 essay "The Damnation of Women," Du Bois cites three "great causes": the struggles for racial justice, peace, and women's equality.[1] His use of the phrase "next to" does not refer to a sequential order of descending importance. Concerns for racial equality, international peace, and women's emancipation combine to form the complex, integrative character of Du Bois's analysis. With a politics remarkably progressive for his time (and ours), Du Bois confronted race, class, and gender oppression while maintaining conceptual and political linkages among the struggles to end racism, sexism, and war. He linked his primary concern, ending white supremacy—*The Souls of Black Folk* (1903) defines the color line as the twentieth century's central problem—to the attainment of international peace and justice. In his analysis integrating the various components of African American liberation and world peace, gender and later economic analyses were indispensable. Exploring Du Bois's relationship to that "deep meaning" embodied in women and color, we examine his representation of African American women and his selective memory of the agency of his contemporaries Anna Julia Cooper and Ida B. Wells-Barnett.

Du Bois's writings champion women's rights, denounce female exploitation, and extol women as heroic strugglers. But while condemning the oppression of African American women, Du Bois veiled the individual achievements of women such as Cooper and Wells-Barnett to the political landscape. In his profeminist politics, he obscured black women's radical agency and intellectualism. Here *feminist* refers to women's gender-progressive politics, and *profeminist* denotes male advocates of women's equality. In examining the contradictory aspects of Du Bois's profeminism, we should consider his political actions on behalf of women's rights, his representations of black women, and the place of African American women in his nonfiction essays and political autobiographies. In theory and practice Du Bois opposed women's subjugation. But his political representations of and relations with influential female leaders reflect a considerable ambivalence toward black women's political independence.

A vocal supporter of women's equality and a tireless critic of patriarchy, Du Bois provided important advocacy for ending women's oppression. He consistently emphasized the equality of females with the least rights—African American girls and women. Bettina Aptheker,

a pioneering feminist scholar and interpreter of Du Bois's profeminism, notes that Du Bois began his scientific studies of Africans and
African Americans "in an era when predominant scientific and theo-
logical opinion held the Negro to be an inferior, if not subhuman,
form."[2] As "a pivotal figure in the struggle for human rights," writes
Aptheker, Du Bois was also "strikingly advanced in his views on
women . . . a conspicuous theme in much of his work is the subjugation of women, especially Black women."[3]

The theme of women's subjugation is dominant in "The Damnation of Women." The essay argues for the liberation of females from
domestic exploitation: "Only at the sacrifice of intelligence and the
chance to do their best work can the majority of modern women bear
children. This is the damnation of women"(164). Such declarations
by Du Bois are often highlighted by those who note his profeminist
activism. Aptheker documents that through *The Crisis,* Du Bois celebrated women in the "Men of the Month" column popularizing race
leaders. (David Levering Lewis notes how white women were initially
privileged by Du Bois in this column.) He also condemned lynching,
violent attacks, and sexual assaults against black women as well as
white men's violence against white women. An advocate of women's
enfranchisement, Du Bois was invited to address the predominantly
white National American Woman Suffrage Association.[4] In January
1906, African American women in New York state formed a women's
Du Bois Circle. Charter members of this group, an auxiliary to the
male-dominated Niagara Movement, formed in 1905, gathered to
support and popularize the work of Du Bois. They also organized
around social issues and sex education.[5] Despite opposition from
some members of the original all-male organization, such as Monroe
Trotter, Du Bois successfully worked to ensure the inclusion of
women in this leadership group. He also organized, unilaterally, a
Massachusetts Niagara Women's Auxiliary.[6] These and other efforts
attest to his standing as a profeminist; however, as we shall see below,
Du Bois's profeminism proved problematic.

Holding exceptionally progressive positions on gender equality,
sexual violence, and the victimization of women and girls, Du Bois
condemned sexual assaults and endorsed initiatives waged by
the women's movement. His profeminist positions censured white

society's denigration of African Americans. In a strong denunciation of white males' sexual violence against black females, he wrote: "I shall never forgive, neither in this world nor the world to come . . . [the white South's] wanton and continued and persistent insulting of the black womanhood which it sought and seeks to prostitute to its lust."[7] Here, Du Bois eloquently condemns the hypocrisy of the prevailing sexual politics that legitimized violence against women: "All womanhood is hampered today because the world on which it is emerging is a world that tries to worship both virgins and mothers and in the end despises motherhood and despoils virgins."[8]

With references to Du Bois's essays on women's oppression, Lewis compares the familial patriarch with the public advocate of women's rights, describing Du Bois as a "theoretical feminist whose advocacy could erupt with the force of a volcano."[9] But Du Bois's condemnations of sexism and racial-sexual violence appear skewed by this "theoretical feminism" that simultaneously condemns social injustice and reproduces gender dominance. For Lewis, Du Bois's progressive sexual politics strongly emerge in his fiction, particularly his first novel, *The Quest of the Silver Fleece* (1911):

> *The Quest* reflected the force and sincerity of Du Bois's feminism, his credo that the degree of society's enlightenment and of the empowerment of disadvantaged classes and races was ultimately to be measured by its willingness to emancipate women—and, above all, black women. What he would later affirm with pistol-shot accuracy was found on virtually every page of the novel: that the race question is "at bottom simply a matter of the ownership of women; white men want the right to own and use all women, colored and white, and they resent any intrusion of colored men into this domain."[10]

Through Du Bois's writings, we easily ascertain that his response to the query "Should women be emancipated?" is an emphatic "Yes!" Answering the question "By whom?" is more difficult. His nonfiction presents vague and generalizing portraits of the agency of his female contemporaries. As Lewis notes, Du Bois largely reserves detailed depictions of specific black women leaders for fictive characters. In his

nonfiction essays and autobiographies, Du Bois withholds from his
female contemporaries the recognition given his invented women.[11]

## Feminist Assessments of Du Bois's Representations of Women

Rather than providing a critical analysis of Du Bois's profeminist
politics, accepting them at their face value seems to be the norm. A few
scholars analyze gender relations to offer a more critical assessment
of Du Bois's sexual politics. For example, Patricia Morton and
Nagueyalti Warren demystify Du Bois's symbolic treatment of black
women, analyzing the ways in which his contributions paradoxically
reproduced male elites or gendered black intellectualism. For Morton,
Du Bois "was a pioneer in the transformation" of antiblack woman
stereotypes "into empowering symbols of worth."[12] Through his literary representations of black women, Du Bois rewrote the place of
African American women in history. His representations obscured
women's political agency with symbolic imagery that undermined the
pragmatic politics of his profeminism. Consequently, Morton argues
that, given the black tradition of "idealized and ambivalent images of
black women"[13] that informed his work, Du Bois's challenges to denigrating stereotypes of African American females failed to "reconstruct
black women as full human beings in history."[14] In idealizing the
"black mother" as community and family caretaker, and linking
femininity to motherhood, Du Bois's "emphasis on the primacy of
women," and his "feminized symbolization of the virtues he attributed
to the Negro race," led him to employ the "all-mother" as "both the
controlling metaphor of his vision of black womanhood" and "his
mystique of race."[15] Morton contends Du Bois's reading of history
discerned a "legacy of survival and strength" rooted in the African
American woman "epitomizing and nurturing the ability of her race
to move ahead into the future."[16] His historical works praise women
such as Sojourner Truth and Harriet Tubman, but focus on male leaders. For Morton, his writings venerated "a not more worthy, but a
finer type of black woman" who embodied, in Du Bois's words, the
delicate "beauty and striving for self-realization which is as characteristic of the Negro soul as is its quaint strength and sweet laughter."[17]

Illustrating how his romanticization obscured political specificity and women's radical agency, Morton quotes Du Bois's description of Mary Shadd in *Darkwater*: "a refined, mulatto woman" of "ravishing dream-born beauty" whose "sympathy and sacrifice" were "characteristic of Negro womanhood." Morton points out that Shadd was also a confrontational abolitionist noted for independence, strength of character, and intelligence.

Du Bois's casting of black women as types transformed antiblack female stereotypes or caricatures such as the "mammy" into that of the black Christian martyr. However, the icon of black female martyr or noble sufferer, redeemed through crucifixion, cannot accurately depict the defiant militancy of race women such as Wells-Barnett. Nagueyalti Warren examines how Du Bois's fiction depicts African American women as victims and survivors. Surmising that his representations mythologize female victimization as well as agency, Warren argues that Du Bois's *Darkwater* uses "the Black Madonna or messianic symbol" as a "literary archetype" to project "a covert image of powerlessness"; this "canonizing of virginity and immaculate conception" strips the woman of "the power and control of her body."[18] For Warren, the "strength of the positive, strong African American woman" paints her as "invincible" as this strength is "mythicized to the almost total exclusion of her victimization."[19]

Both profound strength and deep suffering exist in Du Bois's depictions of African American women. In general, his writings present varied and contradictory relationships with them. He reveals a symbiosis with his fictional female protagonists and admiration for the generic, composite symbol of womanhood in African American women's suffering and strength. Du Bois's writings also show a reverence for his mother, familial women as well as personal friends and acquaintances, profeminist politics, and a censorious revisionism in obscuring the pioneering works of Cooper and Wells-Barnett. The diverse and conflictual nature of these relationships point to a "double consciousness" muddled with the contradictions of his gender politics.

Undoubtedly, the multiple oppressions and brutalities that women of African descent battled moved Du Bois to empathy and outrage. His 1907 poem "The Burden of Black Women" pays tribute to the trials of African American women:

> Dark daughters of the lotus leaves that watch the Southern sea.
> Wan spirit of a prisoned soul a-panting to be free
> The muttered music of thy streams, the whispers of the deep
> Have kissed each other in thy name and kissed a world to
>     sleep.[20]

This poem echoes the sensibilities of "The Damnation of Women": "To no modern race does its women mean so much as to the Negro nor come so near to the fulfillment of its meaning."[21] Despite the moral sentiment and political commitment, those women, including the ones informing his politics, largely remain nameless in Du Bois's nonfiction. African American women were an essential cause to be championed for Du Bois. Still, those black women leaders, whom Du Bois did not create as fictional characters, would have a difficult time finding themselves in his writings.

### Educational Elites: Anna Julia Cooper and Du Bois

Just as it is disingenuous to minimize Du Bois's significant contributions toward women's equality, it would also be deceptive to ignore his problematic representations of and political relationships with independent, influential African American women activists.

The writings and political works of Cooper and Wells-Barnett are so significant in the life struggles of their era that they compel juxtaposition with the work of Du Bois. Both Cooper and Wells-Barnett worked with, were influenced by, and influenced Du Bois. At times all three were members of the same organizations. Each struggled with and critiqued white supremacy and the conservative segments of African American leadership. Eventually each leader was isolated from mainstream African American leadership for his or her radical commitments. They were also alienated from one another. Du Bois rebuffed Cooper's and Wells-Barnett's independently made overtures to work with him. Neither woman left a record of having sought the other out as colleague and supporter.

Hazel Carby observes that black American history commonly perceives the turn of the century "as the Age of Washington and Du Bois." Such a view, writes Carby, marginalizes black women's political contributions during "a period of intense intellectual activity and productivity" marked by the development of black female-led institutions and organizations.[22] In the "Age of Washington and Du Bois," Cooper was a well-known figure among black leaders. One of three African American women invited to speak at the World's Congress of Representative Women in 1893, she later presented a paper, "The Negro Problem in America," at the 1900 Pan-African Congress Conference in London. Cooper had helped to organize that first Pan-African conference and served as a member of its Executive Committee, working alongside Du Bois, another prominent conference organizer. She co-founded the Colored Women's YWCA in 1905, the same year that Du Bois founded the Niagara Movement. Widowed as a young woman, and childless, she worked as a lifelong activist in black liberation. As principal of the prestigious M Street (later the Dunbar) High School in Washington, D.C., Cooper, who had a graduate degree from Oberlin, structured a curriculum enabling her students to be admitted to Harvard, Yale, and other prestigious universities. As a result of her successes, outraged European Americans and alarmed African Americans on the school board forced her out of the principalship. Racism and unsubstantiated rumors of sexual impropriety were the basis of the dismissal.[23] Continuing her activism as an educator, she obtained her Ph.D. from the Sorbonne in 1930 at the age of sixty-six. As an elder, Cooper assumed the presidency of Frelinghuysen University, an independent school known as the "College Extension for Working People" for employed working-class African Americans in Washington, D.C.[24]

In advocating liberal arts education for African Americans and criticizing Booker T. Washington's race-based ideology of vocational training, Cooper became an important ally of Du Bois. As a response to Cooper's urging, and her declaration of support for financing and distribution of such a publication, Du Bois embarked upon writing that led to *Black Reconstruction* (1935); however, he never acknowledged Cooper's request that *The Crisis* serialize her biographical sketch of Charlotte Grimke, the prominent activist-intellectual.[25]

He nevertheless drew upon Cooper's intellectual resources more than once. Paula Giddings writes that Cooper's 1892 political autobiography, *A Voice from the South,* provides a "treatise on race and feminism . . . [that] anticipated much of the later work of W. E. B. Du Bois."[26] Du Bois's later democratic revisions of the Talented Tenth adapt Cooper's gender critique and expand upon her assertion that elite African Americans were neither the panacea nor standard for black liberation.

In *A Voice from the South,* Cooper calls for a mass, female standard for evaluating the effectiveness of black praxis, a decade before Du Bois penned his concept of "The Talented Tenth." Cooper's standard to gauge the efficacy of African American praxis is defined by the mass of black people: "Is it not evident then that as individual workers for this race we must address ourselves with no half-hearted zeal to this feature of our mission [the lives of the masses and women]. The need is felt and must be recognized by all."[27] Rejecting the idealized "great leader" and the premise that the lives and (real and potential) contributions of elites were more consequential than those of laborers, she set new criteria for race leadership. Dispensing with black intellectual male elites as representative of black freedom, Cooper reasserted the whole, starting with the bottom, as the measure for liberation. Emphasizing the conditions of working-class and poor black women, she writes, "our present record of eminent men, when placed beside the actual status of the race in America today, proves that no man can represent the race." For Cooper, "Only the black woman can say, 'when and where I enter, in the quiet, undisputed dignity of my womanhood, without violence and without suing or special patronage, then and there the whole *Negro race enters with me.'* "[28]

Quoting Cooper's now-famous "When and where I enter" sentence in "The Damnation of Women," Du Bois fails to mention her by name, prefacing his remarks with the proprietary phrase: "As one of our women writes."[29] Du Bois's selective quotations curtail Cooper's full argument; the passage preceding the quote more accurately reflects the critical mandate for black leadership echoing throughout *A Voice from the South.* When Cooper argues "we must address ourselves with no halfhearted zeal to this feature of our mission,"[30] she refers to the uplift of the masses of black women. Du Bois's failure to name Cooper renders her anonymous. With no attributed source, his citation allows Cooper to disappear as her words appear. In her absence, readers were unlikely to juxtapose Du Bois with Cooper. Nor would they fully benefit from her own gender analyses. Her anonymity allows Du Bois to appear as a transgender representative for the entire vilified and oppressed race. Mary Helen Washington contextualizes this erasure of Cooper's name within masculinist and patriarchal thought. "The intellectual discourse of black women of the 1890s, and particularly Cooper's embryonic black feminist analysis," she writes, "was ignored because it was by and about women and therefore thought not to be as significantly about the race as writings by and about men."[31] This "embryonic black feminism" maintained that criteria for African American progress center on the emancipation of black women, who labor the longest for the least wages under the most numbing and exploitive conditions. Du Bois himself suggests this position by using her quote. Sharing Cooper's advocacy for the struggles of impoverished black women, he detaches from her depiction of leadership as the attribute of black female elites.

Cooper's gender politics revolved around poor black women's struggles and elite black women's agency. But Du Bois's evolving class politics allowed him to, theoretically, attribute greater agency to *poor* black women workers and laborers. Du Bois's later writings surpass Cooper's 1892 work in democratizing agency. Cooper repudiates masculine elites, or privileged black male intellectuals. However, her repudiations do not extend to feminine elites, or privileged black female intellectuals. Cooper countered the dominance of male elites with that of female elites and remained somewhat oblivious to the limitations of her caste and class-based ideology. Cooper's 1892 book failed to argue that the intellectual and leadership abilities of black women laborers equaled those of black women college graduates, whereas Du Bois's later revisions of the Talented Tenth included nonelite black women and men. In this respect, we see that Du Bois's maturing politics were less hampered by the cultural conservatism of bourgeois notions of respectability for (black) women. Black women elites such as Cooper "had a great stake in the prestige, the respectability, and the gentility guaranteed by the politics of true womanhood."[32] Conforming to standards of white, bourgeois respectability, black female elites sought a shield from racial-sexual denigration. The class-biased strictures placed upon middle-class African American women were partly self-imposed. Du Bois had written critically of this "cult of true womanhood" in bourgeois femininity and white society's racialized gender hypocrisy. Cooper's embrace of conventional femininity led her to minimize and evade the leadership that nonbourgeois black women could offer to their elite counterparts.

Not all middle-class race women were trapped by rigid social conventions. In the same year as the appearance of Cooper's *A Voice from the South,* Wells-Barnett's *Southern Horrors: Lynch Law in All Its Phases* was published. The antilynching crusader embodied race militancy and intellectualism. Her manifested responsible womanhood both reflected and rejected the cult of true womanhood. Wells-Barnett's treatment of the volatile racial-sexual politics of lynching deals with issues of race, sex, and violence unmentioned in *A Voice from the South*'s pioneering discussions of sexual violence. As the lioness of the antilynching crusades, Wells-Barnett endured death threats, the destruction of her Memphis press by a lynch mob, and decades of exile from the South. Transgressing the notions of feminine gentility and masculine courage, she traveled extensively, armed with a pistol, to document and organize against lynchings.

### Frayed Alliances: Ida B. Wells-Barnett and Du Bois

Lynchings had a tremendous impact on black intellectuals and academics during Du Bois's, Cooper's, and Wells-Barnett's era. Both Wells-Barnett and Mary Church Terrell lost friends in the 1892 Memphis lynching and were radicalized by the murders. Wells-Barnett's posthumously published memoir, *Crusade for Justice,* recalls how the lynchings of her associates and friends in Memphis brutally disabused her of her initial belief that lynching was a preventive measure to protect white female virtue from black male sexual savagery.

Du Bois's desire to respond effectively to the atrocities left him disaffected with academic life. Lynchings transfigured Du Bois, politicizing him into a militancy that left the Harvard Ph.D. ill-suited for academic society and liberal institutions. Du Bois's *Darkwater* short story about lynching, "Jesus Christ in Texas," speaks to his profound pessimism concerning racist violence. Two decades later, *Dusk of Dawn* describes how racial atrocities haunted and transformed his early adult life: "Lynching was a continuing and recurrent horror during my college days: from 1885 through 1894, seventeen hundred Negroes were lynched in America. Each death was a scar upon my soul, and led me on to conceive the plight of other minority groups."[33] The pressing need to confront racist violence furthered Du Bois's disaffection for and alienation in academic life.[34] Du Bois writes eloquently of his first encounter with lynching: "There cut across this plan which I had as a scientist, a red ray which could not be ignored, I remember when it first, as it were, startled me to my feet; a poor Negro in central Georgia, Sam Hose, had killed his landlord's wife." Having drafted "a careful and reasoned statement concerning the evident facts"[35] for publication in the Atlanta *Constitution* and en route to deliver his editorial to the newspaper, he recalls: "I did not get there. On the way news met me: Sam Hose had been lynched, and they said that his knuckles were on exhibition at a grocery store farther down on Mitchell Street, along which I was walking. I turned back to the University."[36] Shaken and galvanized by this close proximity to a lynching victim, Du Bois writes that thereafter he resolved that "one could not be a calm, cool, and detached scientist while Negroes were lynched, murdered and starved."[37]

The late nineteenth-century and early twentieth-century anti-lynching campaigns included and directly affected more African Americans than [did] the university education campaigns of Du Bois and Cooper. Only a small percentage of African Americans attained university educations. But all were susceptible to the violence of a lynch mob; poorer blacks tended to be more vulnerable to racial violence. Du Bois and Wells-Barnett, a former schoolteacher, participated in both the liberal arts education campaigns and the antilynching crusades. Advocating liberal arts education for African Americans, Wells-Barnett became a proponent of Du Bois's social thought. *Crusade for Justice* recounts how influential black and white leaders at a Chicago meeting debated the merits of *The Souls of Black Folk,* although most of those present, writes Wells-Barnett, were "united in condemning Mr. Du Bois's views."[38] Ida B. Wells-Barnett, and husband, Ferdinand,

championed Du Bois's critique of Booker T. Washington's promotion
of industrial education as a panacea. Wells-Barnett's stands in the
educational debates, which placed her in the line of Washington's fire,
were consistent with her outspoken opposition to lynching. Du Bois's
failure to mention her work in the educational campaigns is in tan-
dem with his silence about her extraordinary antilynching activism.
Despite Wells-Barnett's exemplary research and publications,[39] her
political courage and radical analysis of the sexual politics of lynching,
Du Bois's autobiographical writings on antilynching mostly ignore
Wells-Barnett.

As one of the most significant human rights campaigns in postbellum United States at the turn of the century, the antilynching crusades generated a black liberation movement in which black women
were prominent public leaders. Women initiated the first major
antilynching campaign in 1892. They embarked on this extremely
dangerous work without the backing of any influential, multiracial
organization such as the NAACP, which was not formed until 1909.
With uncompromising demands for justice, women such as Florida
Ruffin Ridley, Mary Church Terrell, and Wells-Barnett exposed and
challenged the U.S. "red record" of African Americans brutalized,
imprisoned, and murdered at the whim of whites. Skeptical that
media, court, or mob prosecution was motivated by the desire to end
sexual violence, black women created a legacy of investigative report-
ing and social analyses to ascertain facts distorted or denied by
the media or legal institutions. Wells-Barnett demystified the racial-
sexual politics of interracial sex and exposed the duplicity of the legal
system and its complicity in lynchings, in language few male or
female race leaders dared to use. Her writings discredited the apologists for lynchings by noting that the rape charge was used only in a
fraction of lynchings, and was generally used against men innocent of
sexual assault. Her arguments paraphrase Frederick Douglass's critique of postbellum rationalizations. (Like Du Bois, she did not
always credit her sources; *Crusade for Justice* does not fully acknowledge Douglass's influence on antilynching activism or the contributions of other activists.) Wells-Barnett's unique contribution to the
antilynching movement was her documentation and incendiary
rhetoric on the hypocrisy of American sexual politics in which white

men were the predominant assailants of white and black females, yet masked their violence, as well as their attempts to politically and economically dominate blacks, with racist terrorism.

Du Bois built on and benefited from the political and intellectual radicalism of Wells-Barnett without fully acknowledging his indebtedness. By refusing to name Wells-Barnett and her dynamic leadership, his writings erase her contribution much as he renders Cooper anonymous. Given their incendiary tone, Du Bois likely could not use Wells-Barnett's words, as he had Cooper's, without sharing her stigma and isolation as too combative in antiracist activism. Failing to document Wells-Barnett's antilynching agency, Du Bois obscures both her individual contributions and the range of antiracist militancy and radicalism. Consequently, Du Bois forgoes a critical examination of Wells-Barnett's political thought and so misses an opportunity to analyze the "deep meaning" of the lives of radical African American women activists.

Though neither as prolific a writer nor as formally educated as Du Bois, Wells-Barnett was widely influential in her day. With the decline in mob lynchings, her prominence waned while Du Bois's prestige increased in the first part of the twentieth century. As Du Bois's writings were increasingly "mainstreamed" through the NAACP, Wells-Barnett's work was marginalized. In part, this occurred because of her uncompromising politics and opposition to Booker T. Washington. In retaliation to the Barnetts's political independence and vocal critiques, Washington used his influence over the Afro-American press to cripple the publishing and journalistic careers of the Barnetts. Although Wells-Barnett and Du Bois were radicalized by lynchings, antilynching organizing unraveled rather than cemented the ties between them. In August 1908, white race riots and the lynchings of blacks in Springfield, Illinois, led progressive European Americans and African Americans to form what would become the NAACP. As founding members, Du Bois and Wells-Barnett were active in the first meetings at New York City's Cooper Union. From the floor, Wells-Barnett urged the assembly not to compromise its agenda with that of the Tuskegee machine.[40] Seated on the dais, Du Bois wielded influence behind doors in closed meetings of the nominating committee for the organization's initial leadership. Unlike Wells-Barnett, Du Bois was not isolated by white and black NAACP liberals for his radicalism and opposition to Washington as an accommodationist.

Du Bois's autobiographical record of the founding of the NAACP omits any reference to Wells-Barnett being ostracized at the NAACP founding conference. He writes in *Dusk of Dawn*: "The members of the Niagara Movement were invited into the new conference, but all save [William Monroe] Trotter and Ida Wells-Barnett came to form the backbone of the new organization."[41] Here he does not explain Wells-Barnett's absence from a key organization formed to fight a crusade she had pioneered. Nor does Du Bois refer to maneuvers to bar her from NAACP organizational leadership. One of two African American women signing the Call for the National Negro Conference in 1909 that led to the formation of the NAACP, Wells-Barnett's name was left off of the list of the Conference's Committee of Forty assigned to develop the NAACP. According to her memoir, in seeking a representative from the Niagara Movement, Du Bois substituted for her name that of an absent Dr. Charles E. Bentley. Wells-Barnett also speculates that Mary White Ovington's friendship and influence with Du Bois led to "the deliberate intention of Dr. Du Bois to ignore me and my work."[42] Ovington, who later chaired the NAACP, was on less than cordial terms with Wells-Barnett. Lewis minimizes Wells-Barnett's account to argue that philanthropist Oswald Garrison Villard's aversion to radicalism and anti-Tuskegee activists bears the primary culpability for Wells-Barnett's isolation. Yet Du Bois, also a radical and an outspoken critic of Washington, was not similarly censored. Lewis writes that Du Bois attempted to achieve moderate representation in leadership and so "was probably motivated far less by personal animus than by well-intentioned (though possibly sexist and perhaps mistaken) calculations."[43] Whatever the motivation, this slighting marginalized the era's most effective antilynching militant. After the restoration of her name to the Committee of Forty, following protests by herself and others, Wells-Barnett joined NAACP national leadership in name only. Thomas C. Holt notes: "The singular irony of her career is that Wells-Barnett, the most prominent voice opposing lynching over the preceding decade and the most persistent advocate of a national organization to combat racial oppression, was not among the leaders of the NAACP."[44] Wells-Barnett's bitterness must have been edged with a sense of betrayal. For years she had been an avid supporter of Du Bois and a critic of Washington, and, as a consequence, she suffered the backlash of the Tuskegee machine.[45] She consistently supported Du Bois until their break at the NAACP founding conference; her support was never reciprocated.

The most glaring omission by Du Bois regarding the significance of Wells-Barnett's antiviolence activism occurs in *Dusk of Dawn*. Here, in his depiction of the Steve Greene and Pink Franklin cases, he erases her unparalleled contributions to countering lynching. In 1910, Steve Greene arrived in Chicago, wounded from a shootout with a white Arkansas farmer who tried to indenture or enslave him on his farm. Greene was extradited to Arkansas, ostensibly to be lynched. However, Wells-Barnett's Negro Fellowship League raised money and organized a defense committee that safely spirited Greene to Canada. Lewis comments on Du Bois's selective recollection: "Curiously, Du Bois's coverage of the dramatic events behind Greene's removal from the clutches of his Arkansas warders omitted any mention of Wells-Barnett and her Negro Fellowship League."[46] Several months earlier, in a similar case, the NAACP had struggled and failed to save Pink Franklin from a legal lynching. Franklin had shot and killed a white farmer breaking into his house in order to return Franklin to sharecropping. Such "curious omissions" concerning Wells-Barnett are not aberrational in Du Bois's autobiographies.

After military service in World War I, black soldiers returned with raised expectations for racial equality, economic opportunity, and democratic politics. Instead, they were met with a white backlash. Lynchings increased, particularly in the South. *Dusk of Dawn* refers to the September 1917 military lynchings in Texas of soldiers in the Twenty-fourth Colored Infantry who participated in an armed rebellion against the repressive acts of local whites.[47] One hundred armed black troops, stationed in Houston, in response to racist assaults, marched on the city. The resulting confrontation left sixteen whites and four black soldiers dead. Following the revolt, the U.S. Army executed nineteen soldiers and court-martialed and imprisoned fifty. Du Bois makes no mention of Wells-Barnett's campaign to stop the executions and free imprisoned members of the Twenty-fourth Infantry. Wells-Barnett describes the soldiers as "martyred." Her agitation for the release and pardon of the Twenty-fourth Infantry was so noteworthy that Secret Service agents threatened her with charges of wartime sedition and imprisonment if she continued demonstrating on behalf of the prisoners. Despite government threats, she extended her organizing and remained free of incarceration.

*Dusk of Dawn* forgoes relaying information about Wells-Barnett's activism to detail the expansion of NAACP organizing against lynching. In 1919, notes Du Bois, the NAACP leadership was instrumental in two thousand antilynching public meetings and a government investigation of the Chicago riot; it also convened a national conference on lynching in New York City, which issued an address to the nation signed by prominent officials, including a former U.S. president and a then current chief justice. According to Du Bois, the NAACP organized African American political power to "make it influential and we started a campaign against lynching and mob law which was the most effective ever organized and eventually brought the end of the evil in sight."[48] Reconstructing NAACP activity as *the* antilynching movement, he writes that "Mary Talbert started the antilynching crusade, raising a defense fund of $12,000," and that NAACP Secretary James Weldon Johnson forcibly brought the Dyer Anti-Lynching Bill before Congress in 1921.[49] In his singular validation of NAACP antilynching activism, Du Bois deflects from the work of the Negro Women's Club Movement, Wells-Barnett, and other antilynching activists whose radicalism and analyses laid the foundations for later NAACP campaigns.

While describing or embellishing upon NAACP antilynching activism, Du Bois refers to the organization's internal contradictions, inefficiency, and its ideological liberalism. In "Revolution," the final chapter of *Dusk of Dawn*, Du Bois closes his memoir by expressing disappointment over the increasing ineffectiveness of the NAACP, an organization to which he had devoted decades of his lifework. His regrets echo those of Wells-Barnett.[50] This antilynching crusader reflects in her own autobiography that had she been more active in its national leadership, the NAACP would have been more responsive to the dire conditions of African Americans. Lacking allies for radicalizing organizational leadership (it would seem, allies with the tenacity and militancy of Wells-Barnett), Du Bois recalls that by 1930 he had increasing doubts about the viability of NAACP liberalism. For him the organization's ideology advocated "a continued agitation which had for its object simply free entrance into the present economy of the world, that looked at political rights as an end in itself rather than as a method of reorganizing the state; and that expected through civil rights and legal judgments to reestablish freedom on a broader and firmer basis."[51] This ideology, wrote Du Bois, "was not so much wrong as short-sighted." He argued that liberalism, legalism, and an inadequate economic program led the NAACP to miss an essential opportunity "to guard and better the chances of Negroes" to earn an adequate income.[52] In 1934 Du Bois resigned as editor of *The Crisis* and from the NAACP national board. It is uncertain if a successful Du Bois/Wells-Barnett alliance might have influenced NAACP national leadership towards civil rights radicalism and a program for economic justice. In any case, such an alliance was apparently undesirable on Du Bois's part.

Despite his distance from Cooper and Wells-Barnett, Du Bois's increasing radicalism led him to develop a structural analysis of black oppression. The later writings of Du Bois, who worked until his nineties, address economic exploitation, capitalism, and state oppression, issues that Cooper's and Wells-Barnett's analyses largely ignore.

## Nonspecificity and Erasure in Du Bois's Profeminism

Specificity entails detailed accounts of agency and includes identification of subjects or political actors in accord with their deeds. The lack of specificity contextualizes Du Bois's profeminist and (later) proworker stances. This absence inadvertently highlights the black vanguardism that he eventually repudiates. Perhaps Du Bois's early, progressive views on women shielded him (in his own self-reflections) from criticism. This shield may blind us to the fact that his writings about African American women noticeably erase women's political agency. Specificity and erasure inform Du Bois's gender politics. In their lack of documentation, his autobiographical records choose a generic rather than an empirical study regarding the achievements of his female and working-class contemporaries. We need not suggest that Du Bois should have written his memoirs with the impressive detail found in *Black Reconstruction*. We should only note that he reserves specificity in his memoirs and essays for fellow elites. His autobiographies privilege activists who were personal friends or acquaintances: African American men such as Monroe Trotter and James Weldon Johnson, as well as European Americans Joel Spingarn and Mary White Ovington. In the process of democratizing black leadership, Du Bois inadvertently reinscribed the primacy of elites through his representations of political agency. Nonelite blacks and black women appear largely without specifics or names. Du Bois frequently withheld the attribute of political agency from those who had earned a place in political history.

If we address black women as a generic topic without their specificity, we obscure the radical dimensions of black politics and history. If we portray African American women in an aggregate as victims, icons, or the embodiment of a cause, we project the notion that political change transpires without black female independence and leadership. If we assert black women's leadership in theory, but minimize the empirical record of African American women leaders, we masculinize black agency and implicitly elevate men to a superior status as intellectuals.

In studying Du Bois's treatment of women activists, we see that nonspecificity and erasure overlap to some degree. Nonspecificity promotes the disappearance of the detailed historical or empirical record. In some respects, it erases subjects, deeds, and events, while simultaneously discussing them. Nonspecificity promotes erasure. With the solo appearance of the generic, the category becomes surrogate for the individual: The "black woman" replaces Wells-Barnett. The generic also supplants historical or empirical data in representation: Black women's victimization stands in place for the uniqueness of their political praxes in the suffragette movement or antilynching crusades. The documentary writer controls representation and memory in his or her use of nonspecificity and generic representations. With specificity in representation, the historical subject appears to put forth her own ideas; at times, she may interrupt the chronicler with her own voice. That intervention or corrective is no longer possible if her words are appropriated and her identity obscured (as happened with Du Bois's use of Cooper's intellectualism). If we understand "erasure" as the complete absence of representation, the refusal of agency and identity altogether, it seems obvious that representations that fail to reference marginalized groups promote the erasure of those groups in political discourse. Erasure and exclusionary bias also appear when we discuss disenfranchised peoples without the specifics of their historical and contemporary political leadership.

Some contend that Du Bois's nonspecificity regarding black women in his political writings implies no bias or attempt to elide the significant contributions of a marginalized group. To be consistent, those who argue this position must also maintain that the use of generalizing and vague discourse concerning the achievements of males and elites is a common and acceptable practice. Engaging in nonspecificity and erasure misrepresents intellectual ability and political agency, and detracts from comprehensive and progressive political analyses. Gender erasure reconstructs politics as the purview of male elites. Whether the elites are determined by race, gender, or education and wealth, dominance is reasserted when racially, sexually, and economically marginalized groups are presented as categories or characterized in symbolic and abstract terms. The distance between attentiveness to black women as a category and disinterest in their political praxes creates a void in which progressivism disassembles itself.

### The Heirs of Du Bois

Building upon the gift of sight that Du Bois bequeathed to progressives, we better comprehend the deep meaning that manifests when two movements for justice—women and color—combine. Evaluating our inheritance from Du Bois, as well as our own antiracist sexual politics, we can strategize for a gender progressivism that unpacks this legacy to transcend the limits of Du Bois's profeminism. Doing so requires addressing the profeminist politics in the writings of present-day progressive intellectuals.

Given the racial and sexual biases that inform our concepts of political, intellectual, and moral ability, it is unsurprising that black male intellectuals intentionally or inadvertently reproduce sexist thought. Du Bois, his profeminism notwithstanding, proved no exception to the norm. Profeminism permitted Du Bois to include women in democratic struggles; paternalism allowed him to naturalize the male intellectual. Like their predecessor(s), today's male thinkers infrequently cite or analyze African American women's intellectual and political productivity. Contemporary African American political thought reflects both Du Bois's profeminist politics and his gender amnesia. Gender conservatives resist while gender progressives embrace and expand upon his profeminist politics. The trickster in Du Bois's legacy, though, suggests that his profeminism, both its advocacy for gender equality and its erasure of radical black women's agency, might be a cornerstone in the construction of the contemporary black intellectual as male elite. In current works by black males, we encounter writings on black politics and history in which black women disappear or have only token inclusion; we also find writings that extol black women's political and intellectual power while excising the details of their radicalisms.

Regarding the erasure of radical women from black history, both feminist and profeminist writers seem to have inherited Du Bois's penchant for selective memory. Contemporary writers diminish the significance of black women activists and intellectuals, with various objectives in mind. For example, both profeminists and feminists may elide women's agency in order to reify black women's status as victims of black male dominance. Minimizing the presence and impact of black women's radicalism on [the] black liberation struggle promotes generalizations about black patriarchy. Some writers condemn patriarchal political history that ignores women, only to highlight women's contributions in ways that further ignorance of African American women's radical agency. In this sense, their progressive works are wedded to male elitism and sexist censorship.

Some contemporary profeminist writings, while reductively universalizing black male leadership in African American politics, offer a subtle erasure of black radicalism in their generally progressive sexual politics. The privileging of males in black intellectualism produces male elites. Hence, male leadership is naturalized as universal and normative in the history of black thought and politics. Patriarchal myopia deradicalizes, as does a profeminism that obscures the roles of women in political and intellectual movements. Deleting the contributions of black women from African American political thought and radicalism is a fairly common practice that produces flawed historiography and political analysis. Consider how Paul Gilroy's *The Black Atlantic* fails to discuss the prominent African American women activist-intellectuals who also crossed the Atlantic: Jessie Fauset, Anna Julia Cooper, Ida B. Wells, and Mary Church Terrell.[53] These female contemporaries and colleagues of Du Bois either studied or organized in Europe. Their histories, and with them much of black history, disappear in Gilroy's depiction of cultural hybridity and migratory intellectualism. (This male-biased account of Afro-American intellectualism is compatible with the larger antiradicalism of his project, which decontextualizes Du Bois and African American culture from radical politics to argue for the primacy of European influence on Du Bois's thought and African American culture.)[54] Gilroy's academic scholarship on blacks renders black women invisible. (David Roediger's *Wages of Whiteness* also provides an example of the erasure of women; citing Du Bois as a major influence on his understanding of race in class formations, Roediger fails to reference women workers in his study of Irish American workers.)[55]

Contrary to Gilroy, other black male writers draw attention to the masculinist, historical erasure of black women. Manning Marable's commentary offers one example. Given the pervasiveness of male elites, it is unusual for African American male intellectuals to discuss black paternalism or sexual opportunism vis-à-vis black females. Counter to the norm, Marable's essay "Grounding with My Sisters" denounces the erasure of black women from political texts and memory. Although increasingly we find similar writings by black male profeminists, Marable's 1983 text was one of the earliest statements of such politics. Describing "Black social history" as "profoundly patriarchal" and shaped by male bias, Marable writes: "The sexist critical framework of American white history has been accepted by Black male scholars; the reconstruction of our past, the reclamation of our history from the ruins, has been an enterprise wherein women have been too long segregated."[56] A decade before the 1990s explosion in literature published on black Americans, Marable flagged a critical weakness that led not only to gender-distorted notions of political agency but also to skewed scholarship.

Marable's own profeminist contributions offer an interesting corrective. "Groundings With My Sisters" describes patriarchy in the black liberation movements and the limits of some feminisms. Marable quotes Michelle Wallace's observation that: "Every black male leader of the 1960's accepted and perpetuated the idea of Black Macho, the notion that all political and social power was somehow sexual, and that the possession of a penis was the symbol of revolution."[57] He notes that this statement is accurate concerning tendencies; patriarchy and misogyny existed within the black movement, yet, machismo politics cannot be generalized to all male leaders. Former Student Nonviolent Coordinating Committee leader James Forman's autobiography, *The Making of Black Revolutionaries,* praises Ruby D. Robinson and acknowledges Ella Baker's pivotal leadership role in the civil rights movement. Radical women active in the movement do not use such a broad brush to paint the gender politics of movement organizers. Assata Shakur describes how sexism and elitism led her to leave the Black Panther Party, yet writes of her coactivist Zayd Shakur: "I also respected him because he refused to become part of the macho cult that was official in the BPP. He never voted on issues or took a position just to be one of the boys."[58] The Montgomery Women's Political Caucus organized the 1955 bus boycott with E. D. Nixon and chose the politically inexperienced Martin Luther King, Jr. as its titular leader for appearances of respectability and authority tied to middle-class male clergy. Although women constituted a good part of the civil rights leadership, Wallace depicts black civil rights leadership as uniformly sexist. Profeminists may follow this feminist message that diverges from women activists' own accounts of the complexity of gender struggles within movements and promotes erasure of women's leadership. Yet, African American women activists cannot be reduced to mere gender victims or subordinates in a movement they designed and waged.

Interventions that call attention to black male abuses in political leadership and male privilege in historiography are essential. Interventions that diminish the significance of black female activism in order to project images of black female victimization offer problematic profeminist politics. While eliding black female militant leadership to characterize black women as politically paralyzed by black male dominance makes a point about black patriarchy, it also rein-scribes male elitism into black intellectualism and radical politics. Furthering the elision of black female militants, truncating notions of black agency and intellectualism, some black feminist writings offer ahistorical deconstructions of black women radicals that prove compatible with the erasures of profeminist writers.

## Notes

1. W. E. B. Du Bois, "The Damnation of Women," (1920) in *Darkwater: Voices from Within the Veil* (New York: Schocken Books, 1969), 181.

2. Bettina Aptheker, "On 'The Damnation of Women': W. E. B. Du Bois and a Theory of Woman's Emancipation," *Woman's Legacy: Essays on Race, Sex, and Class in American History* (Amherst: University of Massachusetts Press, 1982), 78.

3. Ibid.

4. Ibid., 77–88.

5. Carolyn J. Hardnett, "The Unbroken Du Bois Circle: The Women Behind the Noted Historian," *Emerge* (October 1993), 66.

6. David Levering Lewis, *W. E. B. Du Bois: Biography of a Race, 1868–1919* (New York: Henry Holt Company, 1993), 328.

7. Du Bois, "The Damnation of Women," 172.

8. Ibid., 164.

9. Lewis, 451.

10. Ibid., 449–50.

11. According to Lewis, after Du Bois's mother, Jessie Fauset and Mary Church Terrell figure peripherally in his political autobiographies.

12. Patricia Morton, "The All-Mother Vision of W. E. B. Du Bois," *Disfigured Images: the Historical Assault on Afro-American Women* (New York: Praeger, 1991), 65.

13. Ibid., 57.

14. Ibid., 64.

15. Ibid.

16. Ibid.

17. Ibid., 61.

18. Nagueyalti Warren, "Deconstructing, Reconstructing, and Focusing our Literary Image," in *Spirit, Space and Survival: African American Women in (White) Academe,* eds. Joy James and Ruth Farmer (New York: Routledge, 1993), 111. Warren uses Catherine Stark's definition of "archetype."

19. Ibid.

20. W. E. B. Du Bois, "The Burden of Black Women," in *W. E. B. Du Bois: A Reader,* ed. David Levering Lewis (New York: Henry Holt and Company, 1995), p. 291. "The Burden of Black Women" was first published in *The Horizon* 2 (November 1907): 3–5, then reprinted in *The Crisis* 31 (November 1914): 31, and, finally, republished under the title "The Riddle of the Sphinx," in *Darkwater: Voices from Within the Veil* (1920).

21. Du Bois, "The Damnation of Women," 173.

22. Hazel V. Carby, *Reconstructing Womanhood: The Emergence of the Afro-American Woman Novelist* (New York and Oxford: Oxford University Press, 1987), 6–7.

23. For a discussion of Cooper's dismissal, see: Mary Helen Washington's Introduction to *A Voice from the South* by Anna Julia Cooper (New York: Oxford University Press, 1988), and Kevin Gaines's "The Woman and Labor Questions in Racial Uplift Ideology: Anna Julia Cooper's Voices from the South," *Uplifting the Race: Black Leadership, Politics and Culture in the Twentieth Century* (Chapel Hill: University of North Carolina Press, 1996).

24. See Washington, Introduction to Cooper, *A Voice from the South,* and Leona C. Gabel, *From Slavery to the Sorbonne and Beyond: The Life and Writings of Anna J. Cooper* (Northampton, Mass: Smith College Studies in History, 1982), Vol. XLIS.

25. See: Washington, Introduction to *A Voice from the South.*

26. Paula Giddings, "The Last Taboo," in *Race-ing Justice, En-gendering Power: Essays on Anita Hill, Clarence Thomas, and the Construction of Social Reality,* ed. Toni Morrison (New York: Pantheon Books, 1992), 447.

27. Cooper, 31.

28. Ibid., 30–31.

29. Du Bois, "The Damnation of Women," 173. Washington also points this out in her introduction to Cooper's work.

30. Cooper, 31.

31. Washington, xxviii.

32. Ibid., xlvii.

33. W. E. B. Du Bois, *Dusk of Dawn: An Essay Toward an Autobiography of a Race* (1940; New York: Schocken Books, 1968), 29–30.

34. Du Bois would later sit with a shotgun on the front steps of his home during the Atlanta race riots by white mobs.

35. Du Bois, *Dusk of Dawn,* 67.

36. Ibid.

37. Ibid.

38. Ida B. Wells-Barnett, *Crusade for Justice: The Autobiography of Ida B. Wells* (Chicago: The University of Chicago Press, 1970), 280–81.

39. In 1889, revolutionizing journalism as an effective medium for antiracist organizing, Wells-Barnett became the first woman secretary of the Afro-American Press Association. In addition to *Southern Horrors* (1892), numerous newspaper articles, editorials, and the posthumously published memoir *Crusade for Justice: The Autobiography of Ida B. Wells,* her written legacy includes *A Red Record: Lynchings in the U.S., 1892, 1893, 1894* (1895) and *Mob Rule in New Orleans* (1900).

40. Lewis, 393–94.

41. Du Bois, *Dusk of Dawn,* 224.

42. Wells, *Crusade for Justice,* 326.

43. Lewis, 397.

44. Thomas C. Holt, "The Lonely Warrior: Ida B. Wells-Barnett and the Struggle for Black Leadership," in *Black Leaders of the Twentieth Century,* eds. John Hope Franklin and August Meier (Urbana: University of Illinois Press, 1982), 50.

45. Holt observes that Wells-Barnett claimed to have elevated Du Bois to national leadership in 1899 by advocating that the Afro-American Council board of

directors, whose antilynching bureau she headed, appoint him as director of its business bureau. This claim is likely overstated. Du Bois seemed destined for national prominence.

46. Lewis, 413.

47. Du Bois, *Dusk of Dawn,* 252.

48. Ibid., 228.

49. Ibid., 265.

50. Ibid., 295–96.

51. Ibid., 289.

52. Ibid., 289.

53. Paul Gilroy, *The Black Atlantic: Modernity and Double Consciousness* (Cambridge, Mass.: Harvard University Press, 1993).

54. For reviews of this work, see: *Social Identities* vol. 1, no. 1 (1995).

55. David Roediger, *The Wages of Whiteness: Race and the Making of the American Working Class* (New York: Verso, 1991).

56. Manning Marable, *How Capitalism Underdeveloped Black America* (Boston: South End Press, 1983), 70.

57. Ibid., 100.

58. Assata Shakur, *Assata: An Autobiography* (London: Zed Press, 1987), 223.

# 3

# Interracial Romance and Black Internationalism

■ *Alys Eve Weinbaum*

In late June 1926, at the annual NAACP conference convened in Chicago, Du Bois delivered an address that announced what has subsequently been enshrined as his mandate: "all art is propaganda." He published "The Criteria of Negro Art" later that same year in *The Crisis,* presenting it as the final contribution to an ongoing "Symposium" prompted by a short questionnaire on representations of "the Negro in Art." Over a period of eight months (beginning in March), responses by a number of contemporary race leaders, artists, and cultural pundits including Countee Cullen, Jessie Fauset, Langston Hughes, Alfred A. Knopf, Sinclair Lewis, Joel Spingarn, Carl Van Vechten, and Walter White duly appeared.[1] As David Levering Lewis attests, Du Bois understood the "Symposium" as a referendum on the so-called New Negro Renaissance that had at stake nothing less than the question of the role of art in promoting and maintaining group identity in a context of racist onslaught.[2] Du Bois's own capstone contribution to this debate was cast by him as both further provocation and last word. Then, as now, the passage from "Criteria" invariably cited by readers declares:

> [a]ll art is propaganda and ever must be, despite the wailing of purists. I stand in utter shamelessness and say that whatever art I have for writing has been used always for propaganda for gaining the right of black folk to love and enjoy. I do not care a damn for any art that is not used for propaganda. But I do care when propaganda is confined to one side while the other is stripped and silent.[3]

The scholarly attention paid to Du Bois's strident declaration is understandable—it defines all art as ideological and simultaneously enters the fray to advocate this position. And yet, our understanding of Du Bois's oft-cited gambit is deepened and ultimately transformed when we not only engage with its self-evident claims, but also with its heretofore unacknowledged rhetorical detail. For what is all too often unrecognized about Du Bois's call for propaganda is its elaboration in and through a discourse on interracial romance—a call, albeit subtle, for the centrality of romance, as both form and content, to the production of propaganda. Building on the work of Claudia Tate (see her essay in this volume), who argues for deep connections among Du Boisean "eroticism," "racial radicalism," and "propaganda," this essay suggests how a Du Boisean obsession with interracial romance became constitutive to the substance and success of his antiracist, anti-imperialist, internationalist politics in the 1920s. For, as we shall see, Du Bois produced a steady stream of representations of interracial romances over the course of the decade in which his politics took its most decisively internationalist turn.

The discourse on interracial romance submerged in "Criteria" can be recovered by restoring the oft-cited passage reproduced above to the context from which it is excerpted. In so doing, it becomes possible to locate it as the culminating idea in a longer argument, developed in large part through three vignettes about romance and Romance (more on the distinction shortly), which incrementally move outward from the domestic space, to the national, and then to the international. The first vignette portrays a mixed marriage and its fallout. "I once knew a man and a woman," Du Bois begins,

[t]hey had two children, a daughter who was white and a daughter who was brown; the daughter who was white married a white man; and when her wedding was preparing the daughter who was brown prepared to go and celebrate. But the mother said, "No!" and the brown Daughter went into her room and turned on the gas and died. (292)

Here, Du Bois presents interracial romance as evidence that "the romance of the world did not die and lie forgotten in the Middle Age" (292), but that black life in the twentieth century furnishes the stuff of "romance," however tragic. As he observes, "if you want romance to deal with you must have it here and now and in your own hands" (292). The details of black life in the context of racism are monumental and monumentally moving, the natural foundation for black artistic production. Du Bois further admonishes, although previously it had been thought that "nothing could come out of . . . [our] past that we wanted to remember . . . suddenly, this same past is taking on form, color and reality and in a half shamefaced way we are beginning to be proud of it" (292). The existence of the Renaissance, and of "Negro Art" more generally, reveals the existence "within us as a race . . . [of] new stirrings . . . a new appreciation of joy, of a desire to create, of a new will to be" (292).

Although "Criteria" initially appears to suggest that all forms of racist oppression can be metamorphosed into "Negro Art," Du Bois argues that the most efficacious art emerges specifically from those forms of violence linked to the injustices expressed in and through interracial intimacy, and into propaganda that takes the form of "Romance." Continuing his meditation on the inspirational reservoir that constitutes the "here and now" of black life in the twentieth century, Du Bois proffers a second vignette, as sexually charged as the first, if differently so. "Or again," he writes,

here is a little Southern town and you are in the public square. One side of the square is the office of a colored lawyer and on all the other sides are men who do not like colored lawyers. A white woman goes into the black man's office and points to the white-filled square and says, "I want five hundred dollars now and if I do not get it I am going to scream." (292)

In the first vignette, romance emerges in the form of a private, hidden interracial marriage predicated on a black daughter passing as white, whereas in the second, it takes on the sinister form of a black man cheated out of his livelihood by white "men who do not like colored lawyers" and who threaten him by setting him up as an alleged rapist. In its second iteration, romance moves out of the domestic sphere and appears on the national stage. While "romance" in the context of the first vignette explicitly references the tragedy of interracial intimacy, in the second, "romance" is implicitly dragged into the vignette in such a way that it grotesquely contorts itself, and comes to reference not only a domestic tragedy, but also the entire sexualized drama of American racism in an age of Jim Crow. As in other writings from the 1910s and 20s, in this vignette, lynching is exposed as the white nation's routine response to the specter of black equality, and "the charge of rape" as the all too transparent alibi, "invented by the white South after Reconstruction to excuse mob violence" and legitimate "re-enslaving blacks."[4] In this sense, Du Bois's first two vignettes constitute antiracist propaganda—contrapuntal representations that expose the hypocrisy of the dominant racist mythology subtending lynch law.

Even as we note the particularly American anxiety about interracial sex that "Criteria" counters, we must remember that the idea of romance that it develops is not solely calibrated to American racial terror, but also to the racial violence that emerges within the wider field of imperialism and colonialism. In a third vignette, immediately following that depicting the black lawyer in the "Southern Town," Du Bois invokes romance one last time, effectively linking domestic and national interracial dramas to the international drama of imperial race war. Supplying as his example the heroic struggle of an insurgent mass of black men against colonialism and imperialism, Du Bois juxtaposes racism in the U.S. South with colonial and imperial racism. As he explains, "the story of the conquest of German East Africa" by white men "who talked German" and violently put down the insurrection of "thousands of black men from East, West, and South Africa, from Nigeria and the Valley of the Nile, and from West Indies," constitutes the "true and stirring stuff of which *Romance* is born" (294, emphasis added). From "this stuff" comes the "stirrings of men who are beginning to remember that this kind of material is theirs" and that "this vital life of their own kind is beckoning them on" (294).

In his first invocations of "romance," Du Bois leaves the term uncapitalized and thus colloquial; in his third internationalist vignette, he conspicuously capitalizes "Romance," elevating it to the status of a literary genre with roots in narratives of heroic conquest, and back further still in the chivalric tradition. In the United States, Romance is a genre most often employed by Hawthorne and Melville, in their dark contributions to what F. O. Mathiessen called the American Renaissance. In this way Du Bois transforms "romance"—understood broadly as a love story, however tragic—into "Romance"—understood as narrative form and convention, as well as political protest. Consequently, across Du Bois's three vignettes the two meanings of romance/Romance become imbricated; indeed, the elements of the three examples, when taken together, merge to such an extent that the political emerges as romantic, and Romance as political. As others have observed (Doris Sommer perhaps most influentially in the context of Latin America), Romance in the modern period may be distinguished from other genres by its capacity to depict and resolve social, historical, and political conflict through resolution of narrative tensions. Romances tend to function allegorically and/or symbolically to express an "erotics of politics" in which naturalized heterosexual love can be used to express, and often diffuse, tensions among antagonistic forces.[5] Whereas Sommer argues that Romance is principally a pacifying project in the service of national consolidation, which works to rearticulate conflict as mutual interest or love rather than coercion, Du Bois regards Romance (whether resolved or indefinitely attenuated) as galvanizing not only of national politics, but also of international solidarities. Of all the generic forms that he might have elected as his principal vehicle for propaganda, Romance is the logical and natural choice. Romantic themes and Romantic forms are germane to expression of black life in the United States *and* black insurgent activity in the world. Romance is the idiom and romance the content in which black life is expressed and lived in rebellion against Jim Crow and imperialism the world over.

Even though scholars frequently argue that Du Bois wrote "Criteria" in large part to urge black artists to produce creative work that would contest denigrating, salacious, or voyeuristic images of blackness by offering "uplifting" representations of black sexuality,[6] there has been scant attention to the romantic content and sexualized figuration embedded within Du Bois's many critical writings on "Negro Art" (including "Criteria"), or, for that matter, within those artistic writings that are patently propagandistic. In fact, with few exceptions, critics have been unwilling to read Du Bois's creative works as what Tate labels "eroticized revolutionary art," reliant on conventions of the Romantic genre and romantic content to facilitate "the expression of propaganda."[7] The aim of this essay is thus twofold: first, to demonstrate the centrality of representations of interracial romance to Du Bois's political project during the1920s; second, to demonstrate Du Bois's repeated deployment of "the stuff of Romance" as a form of propaganda that conjures a black internationalist response to both U.S. racism and Euro-American imperialism. For it appears that it was precisely when Du Bois was at a conceptual impasse, unable to concretely map his political aspirations, or to set out detailed plans for their achievement, that he produced representations of interracial unions (sometimes consummated, sometimes not) that effectively supply readers with propaganda capable of filling the gaps in his thinking about praxis.[8]

There was also an unintended negative consequence of this formal experimentation: each time Du Bois turned to romance/Romance, he made recourse to a highly troubling heterosexual logic of narrative resolution particular to the genre. As a result, he all too often created unanalyzed, racially essentialist representations of reproductive heterosexuality as the motor of black belonging in both the nation and the world.

### *Empire's Romance:* Darkwater

Du Bois's multigenre, semiautobiographical 1920 assemblage, *Darkwater,* is frequently interpreted by scholars as marking a turn in Du Bois's thinking toward the linkages between American racism and Euro-American imperialism.[9] It is also routinely interpreted as a turn away from an analysis of racism framed principally in terms of the failures of Reconstruction in the United States (as it is, for instance, in *Souls*), and toward a broader analysis of racism as the foundation for a modern world system based on white domination of the "darker peoples of the world," including African Americans.[10] To this assessment I would add that by 1920, influenced by the rise of popular-front politics and his forays into Marxism, Du Bois had begun to robustly configure whiteness as a concept signifying class as well as race, and thus to think about race as the modality in which class is lived within the United States and around the world.[11]

Du Bois's imbrication of race and class is evident in *Darkwater*'s critique of imperialism and colonialism as forms of international capital expansion directly connected to U.S. racism and the racial segmentation of the domestic labor force. As he suggests, the whiteness produced in the context of U.S. racial nationalism is part and parcel of a world straddling imperial whiteness that seeks to establish itself as a world economic power. Like European Empires, the United States produces itself as an avatar of white civilization, and thus of *Darkwater*'s readers he asks, "Are we not coming more and more, day by day, to making the statement 'I am white' the one fundamental tenet of our morality?" Are not Americans "shoulder to shoulder" with Europeans in their quest for the accumulation of wealth through imperial escapades and racialized exploitation? Encapsulating the hypocrisy of the U.S. position in the world in the new American century, and in so doing, building an analytical connection among foreign and domestic contexts, Du Bois rhetorically queries, "How could America condemn in Germany that which she commits, just as brutally, within her own borders?" After all, "what is the black man but America's Belgium"? (500).

Among the chapters of *Darkwater* frequently discussed in analyses of the text's anti-imperialism are those in which Du Bois attributes the first world war not to the immediate Balkan conflict (which, he argues, is a mask), but rather to European blood lust in Africa ("The Souls of White Folk" and "The Hands of Ethiopia"); and those in which he analyzes the race riots pervasive in the United States during and after the war as the necessary fallout of the European conflict and the scramble for Africa. As he argues, this combination of events produced, among other catastrophes, intensified racial antagonism within the U.S. labor force ("Of Work and Wealth"). In particular, through an account of a cleverly fictionalized race riot fomented by racist union activity, Du Bois explains that during the war, the United

States failed to protect blacks migrating from the South to take jobs in the industrial war economy of the North from white mobs of unionized workers; while, after the war, the U.S. government failed to support returning black soldiers seeking jobs in the postwar economy, effectively transforming black veterans into objects of white hatred.[12] As significant as the forceful linkage of domestic and imperial racism is in these famous anti-imperialist chapters, so, too, is the manner in which each chapter is coupled with and/or surrounded by a range of more stylistically adventurous, expressly romantic "alightings" (including memoir, poetry, allegory, and science fiction) that are gendered and sexualized in both content and form.[13]

As Susan Gillman and I discuss at length in this volume's introduction, what might be thought of as Du Bois's "politics of juxtaposition," the political heuristic and formal literary strategy he employs in *Darkwater,* is used to position his explicitly anti-imperialist chapters "next to" a range of more stylistically adventurous texts, which consequently emerge as the necessary supplement, sexualized and gendered, to his anti-imperialist political argument. For this reason, Du Bois's "alightings" deserve special attention. For it is these too often unstudied or at best understudied textual elements that subtend Du Bois's political agenda, constituting the gendered and sexualized textual matrix out of which his anti-imperialist imagination springs.[14]

In *Darkwater* there are two "alightings" that are especially germane to the present argument about Du Bois's use of interracial romance as propaganda. In the first, "The Comet," the unusual science fiction story with which he closes *Darkwater,* a romance between a black man and white woman is held out as a utopian promise, a symbolic (if unrealized, because unconsummated) solution to racial antagonism—national and international—that pervades the book as a whole. The story's conceit is that a comet has swept across New York City, producing in its wake a deadly gas that instantly exterminates all those who breath it in, save for a lone black laborer (a messenger for a Manhattan bank sent down into "the lower vaults" deeply buried beneath Broadway to retrieve old records, a task both thankless and far "too dangerous for a more valuable" employee to undertake [611]), and a white woman described as "rarely beautiful and richly gowned, with darkly-golden hair and jewels" (614).

As Amy Kaplan (the only critic to write at length on "The Comet") argues, here, as in the rest of *Darkwater,* domestic racism and international imperial racism are condensed, in this particular instance through externalization of the conflagration of World War I as natural or cosmic disaster, and through the implicit connection of the labor performed in the bowels of the earth by the black messenger (who discovers in the bank vaults a chest of gold) to the labor performed in the colonies, especially in African gold mines. As Kaplan details, the light in the sky and the noxious gas the comet emits invoke European battlefields, while the comet's explosion represents the inner combustion of Empire, the coming to pieces of the imperial project under the pressure of its internal contradictions, or what Kaplan (following Du Bois), elsewhere denotes as "the anarchy of empire." In this sense, the comet brings home the World War sparked by imperial plunder, so that it is experienced first hand in the modern metropolis of New York (207). What is equally significant about "The Comet" is that it renders imperialism intimate and immediate precisely in and through the portrayal of interracial romance, a relationship between a black man and a white woman that Du Bois offers as an answer (albeit disturbing and foreclosed) to the question of how to build a new world in the face of the imperial destruction of the present one.

Although Du Bois initially describes the white woman as unable to see the black man as fully human ("he did not look like men, as she had always pictured men" [616]), she is subsequently won over by his transcendent "manhood." Likewise, although the messenger realizes that but "yesterday [she] would scarcely have looked at him twice" (614), he too comes to regard the woman differently. Of course, beneath this superficial dream of colorblindness lurks a less sanguine argument: this romance would formerly have been held in check by racism and by mutual fear, by the conventions of Jim Crow, by laws criminalizing miscegenation, and not least by differences in class.

In concluding his tale, Du Bois does not shy away from depicting interracial sexuality, but rather represents it as a deep longing, a wish, the realization of which will enable civilization to continue in the face of imperial destruction. Significantly, when the messenger deferentially asks the woman if he may end his grief in suicide, she responds to his query with a "clear and calm 'No'" (620). In a skillful inversion, Du Bois casts the white woman's desire for the black man (rather than his supposedly predatory desire for her) as the romantic catalyst, the liberating spark that, in Du Bois's words, allows "the ghastly glare of reality . . . [to be replaced] with the dream of some vast *romance*" (618, emphasis added) in which it becomes clear "how foolish [are the] . . . human distinctions" (619) by which his protagonists have formerly been guided. Lapsing into saccharine prose, Du Bois writes first of the woman's revelation and then of the man's:

> A vision of the world had risen before her. Slowly the mighty prophecy of her destiny overwhelmed her . . . she was no mere woman. She was neither high nor low, white nor black, rich nor poor. She was primal woman; mighty mother of all men to come and Bride of Life. She looked upon the man beside her and forgot all else but his manhood, his strong, vigorous manhood—his sorrow and sacrifice. She saw him glorified. He was no longer a thing apart, a creature below . . . but her Brother Humanity incarnate . . . great All-Father of the race to be. (619)

> The shackles seemed to rattle and fall from his soul. Up from the crass and crushing and cringing of his caste leaped the lone majesty of kings long dead. He arose within the shadows, tall, straight, and stern, and with power in his eyes and ghostly scepters hovering to his grasp. It was as though some mighty Pharaoh lived again . . . He turned and looked upon the lady, and found her gazing straight at him. (620)

In this dream, resolution of world war and the global racial conflict that ignited it is presented as at once the foundation of romance and romantically allegorical. Race is transcended and common humanity embraced through the idiom of heterosexual union and interracial reproduction, inextricable processes that join two lost souls and give birth to "the race to be." Indeed, the woman's maternal fantasy expressly situates interracial reproduction as the motor of world salvation, while the man's predicates attainment of "vigorous manhood" on interracial union, and, not coincidentally, on his installment within an august genealogy (already familiar from Du Bois's "Star of Ethiopia" pageant) in which he inherits the earth as a "Pharaoh lived again."[15] In sum, Du Bois's protagonists transcend racism, albeit differently, through an imagined interracial, heterosexual union that is cast as symbolic rejoinder and concrete answer to imperialism.

And yet, even as Du Bois explores the utopian promise of interracialism he simultaneously reminds us of the impossibility of such a dream's realization in the "here and now." In the story's last pages, the romance with the potential to save the world by repopulating it with a racially mixed population is arrested by the "Honk! Honk!" of the motorcar carrying the white woman's father and fiancé to the building on the roof of which she and the black messenger have "moved toward each other" (620) and, it can be inferred, are about to consummate their sexual and spiritual union.[16] Again employing the conventions of Romance, Du Bois exploits, even as he forestalls, the narrative expectations that generic allegiance entails. For he patently resists resolving the conflict with the lover's embrace, using instead the "stuff of romance" to create Romantic propaganda that underscores racial strife through the failure of the couple to come together. This is made plain in the story's portentous conclusion: Upon finding her in the arms of a black man, the woman's fiancé blurts out: "It's—a—nigger—Julia! Has he—has he dared—" (621). And even as the woman answers, "he has dared—all, to rescue me," the crowd ignores her, and instead strikes up the rallying cry of the mob: " . . . lynch the damned—" (621).

As the fiancé and father reestablish white paternal authority over the romantic and reproductive life of the woman (Du Bois makes clear that "the [white] couple" are instantly reunited), the black messenger reconnects with his "properly" raced partner, his "brown, small, and toilworn" wife who carries to him the corpse of their baby (621). By the end of "The Comet," which for one significant moment allows readers to envision the new world that might arise from the destruction of the old, a harmonious future is foreclosed by the decimation of interracial romance and the reestablishment of intraracial reproductive imperatives. From this perspective, the death of the black baby represents the corollary of the white couple's promised fecundity. Du Bois understood well the eugenicist reproductive politics that organized ideas of national belonging in the United States in the early part of the century, and recognized too the denigration and destruction of black maternity so central to the nativist and restrictionist concerns with white reproductive power and "purity."[17] Without the promise of interracial romance as catalyst and *reproducer* of global interracial unity, the consolidation of white racial nationalism and the related decimation of black reproductivity together hold sway.

The unresolved interracial romance of "The Comet" repeats elsewhere in *Darkwater*. In a second romantic allegory, a surreally abstract "alighting" to which Du Bois gives the antique sounding title "The Princess of Hither Isle," a white princess violently tears her bleeding heart from her chest and gives it to a "black beggar" and his "parti-colored retinue," rather than sacrifice it to a corrupt white king who presides over "Yonder Kingdom." The Kingdom, a vast empire of gold, has been violently mined by exploited laborers (metonymically linked to the messenger of "Comet" through their toil under the earth), those who follow the lead of the beggar whom the Princess desires. In "Princess," as in "Comet," imperial conflict is presented as racial conflict that is in turn subtended by sexualized racial violence such that the consummation of interracial romance amounts to the symbolic resolution of global race war. As in "Comet," so, too, in "Princess," the internationalist dream of anti-imperialist solidarity is catalyzed by a white woman's desire across the color line, and destroyed by white masculinist racism. Indeed, the comments of the King to the princess resonate audibly with those of the fiancé to the white woman, and with the violent sentiments of the lynch mob. For upon realizing the princess's choice of the black beggar and the meaning of her commitment to his anti-imperialist cause, the king exclaims: "It's a Nigger! . . . It's neither God nor man, but a nigger!" To seek love and fulfillment in the beggar's subhuman form is, in the king's eyes, "blasphemy and defilement and the making of all evil" (523). With these fighting words, the king of "Yonder Kingdom" conflates anti-imperialism and interracial romance, ringing changes on the same association that Du Bois would several years later set forth in "Criteria," through the juxtaposition of his three vignettes exploring the tragedy of interracial intimacy in Jim Crow America and the Romance of anti-imperial insurgency.

If in "Comet" and "Princess" Du Bois employs unconsummated romance to express utopian anti-imperialist longings, eight years later he uses romance to new effect. The final section of this essay, thus turns to Du Bois's 1928 novel *Dark Princess: A Romance,* in order to revisit the unconsummated interracial romances that punctuate *Darkwater.*[18] For as we shall see, *Dark Princess* radically revises the initial argument about the necessary connection between romance/Romance and propaganda both by refusing to arrest sexual consummation, and by strategically renovating the idea of interracialism itself. In *Dark Princess*—which Du Bois regarded as his "favorite book"—he explores global racial conflict neither through depictions of suicide nor lynching, but rather through representation of interracial sex and the birth of a biracial child expressly positioned as the symbolic embodiment of an emergent international, anti-imperialist uprising.[19]

## Internationalism's Reproduction: Dark Princess

As in *Darkwater,* in *Dark Princess* Du Bois couples excoriating critique of U.S. racial nationalism with analysis of white Euro-American imperialism. Once again, he gazes outwards toward emerging struggles for decolonization, while simultaneously working to position African Americans as participants in such historical world events. And yet, despite the similar political orientation of the two texts, *Dark Princess* distinguishes itself from *Darkwater* in that it recalibrates interracialism to a more robust black internationalism. Instead of turning upon a romance cast in black and white, *Dark Princess* narrates a tale of the bond forged between Matthew Townes, a self-identified "American Negroe" and the Indian Princess of the novel's title, Kautilya, The Maharanee of Bwodpur. In so doing it shifts focus from the most glaring dimensions of the U.S. color line, to the color-line that exists within the color line—that which prevents one part of the colonized world from comprehending its necessary connection to all others. In *Darkwater,* interracial romance exposes the coincidence of national and global racial formations, whereas in *Dark Princess,* Asian and African American interracialism critiques, catalyzes, and finally cements black internationalist anti-imperialism.

The romance between Matthew and Kautilya is related in four parts that simultaneously detail Matthew's growing internationalist sensibility and describe the political movement to which he and the Princess belong. In Part I, Matthew meets the Princess when he rescues her from the advances of a white American in a Berlin café. Impressed by his actions, she invites him to join "The Council of the Darker Peoples of the World." Although the Council is uncertain about whether African Americans should be included amongst them, the Princess overrides dissent and discharges Matthew to report on the activities of Manuel Perigua, a figure reminiscent of Marcus Garvey, who is devoted to the overthrow of white supremacy through terrorism. In Part II, grief-stricken over the lynching of a fellow Pullman porter, Matthew joins Perigua in dynamiting a train transporting Klan members to an international conference. In Part III, having been saved from serving out a prison sentence by the conniving and ambitious political assistant Sara Andrews, Matthew begins a new life, and at Sara's behest, makes a bid for control over the political machine controlling black Chicago. Just when it appears that Matthew will lose himself in Sara's narrow and corrupt world, the Princess reclaims him. Thus it comes as no surprise when, in the last section of the novel, the long awaited romance is consummated in sex, marriage, and the birth of a baby cast as the "Messenger and Messiah" of a new world order in which Pan-Asia and Pan-Africa are united against white world domination.

As in the earlier Romances, in *Dark Princess,* the events that catalyze and resolve the drama pivot around interracial desire and its teleological resolution through interracial reproductive sexuality. Matthew has left for Berlin because he has been dismissed from medical school for failing to complete obstetrics, a course that would place him in intimate contact with the bodies of white women. As the Dean of the medical school explains, "What did you expect? . . . [Do] you think white women patients are going to have a Nigger doctor delivering their babies?" (4). In rescuing the white maternal bodies that regenerate the nation from the contamination of black hands, the Dean exposes Matthew's "exile" from "his own native land" (7) as an exclusion from the reproductive order of things. Thus, when Matthew arrives in Berlin, his burning rage channels itself into an action that avenges the particular wrong done him: a chivalric attack on a white man who has attempted to defile a woman of color. As Matthew first envisions the Princess, she appears to him as "a glow of golden brown . . . darker than sunlight and gold . . . a living, glowing crimson," who, in contrast with the white bodies that persecute and haunt him, brightens "the absence or negation of color" in which he exists in Europe (8).

From one perspective the lovers' encounter allows Du Bois to expose a racialized American sexual dynamic; from another perspective, that of the Princess, it allows him to propose a global rather than a nationally exceptionalist consciousness of racism, one already familiar from *Darkwater*. Although the male actors within the scene set in Berlin operate within a U.S. racial and sexual economy, the Princess comprehends Matthew's rescue through an internationalist lens. As she acknowledges, although she is "colored," she is "not at all colored in [Matthew's] intimate sense" (14). For her, his action holds within it not so much a critique of the charge of rape leveled against black men, but rather "a curious sense of some great inner meaning . . . some *world movement*" (17, emphasis added). As the romance unfolds, this "world movement," cast as an alliance between Pan-Africa and Pan-Asia, is literally borne out in the international and interracial reproductive romance that serves as the novel's symbolic culmination. Before turning to the narrative's resolution, however, it is necessary to limn the conflict. In order for the internationalist interracialism that dynamizes this novel to flower—for the Princess to emerge as Matthew's "proper" match—the non-reproductive, frigid, and whitened body of Sara Andrews must first be uncoupled from Matthew's.

A barrage of textual details forecast the troubling castigation of Sara's pale form. The "new and shining" (142) house, furnished in anticipation of her marriage, boasts an "electric log" in a fireplace that Matthew longed to fill with real ones. From her symbolically hearth-less home, Sara banishes all Matthew's personal effects that in any way connote sensuality, pleasure, or by extension, his emergent worldliness. These include his "long coveted . . . copy of a master painter's female nude," a reproduction of an eroticized modernist image that spoke to him of "endless strife, of finer beauty and never dying flesh" (142–43), and an oriental rug whose golden color scheme ecalls for him the shades of the Princess's skin, and is thus expressive of his (notably, orientalist) desire for foreign intimacy. Additional depictions of Sara as an unfeeling check to her full-blooded, amorous mate are unrelenting. On their wedding day, as Matthew gazes on her "roll of silken hair" and the "single pearl shining at the parting of her" noticeably "little breasts," Sara's "metallic voice" reminds him to straighten his tie. After the nuptials, as the pair drive off in a new car, Matthew is moved to tenderness by his "immaculate," "slim white bride" (144); and yet, Sara's ominous response comes in the form of a command, "be careful of the veil" (144).

Predictably, "the veil" that Du Bois depicts in *Souls* not as a wedding garment but rather as the symbolic divide between the white and black world, segregates the light skinned Sara from Matthew. And, although their relationship is never expressly cast as interracial (Sara can pass as white but does not do so in the context of her marriage), Du Bois renders it unseemly and politically inefficacious. The union in which Sara ensnares Matthew works against the antiracist, anti-imperialist cause that Du Bois believes interracial romance (as propaganda) has the power to symbolize and cement. Given Du Bois's heavy-handed contempt for Sara, it follows that when the Princess returns to seduce him away from Sara's sterile whiteness, her fecund brownness proves irresistible. In contrast to Sara, who is depicted as adorned in a "flesh colored even frock" and described as "white to the lips" in Du Bois's estimation, Kautilya's body is racialized by adjectives ("dark," "strong," "long") that eroticize and mark it as visibly molded by sexy hardships experienced as a maid, waitress, tobacco worker, and official of the box makers union. As Matthew observes, "The Princess that [he] worshipped is become the working-woman whom [he] loves" (209), a laborer whose darkened and toil-worn "body is beauty" and whose soul is "freedom to [his] tortured groping life" (210).

Although the international interracialism of the novel dictates that the Princess be cast as Indian, as racially distinct from Matthew—after all, she must bring the entire continent of Asia into their union—it is also important that she be associated with the fecundity and spiritually transcendent blackness represented by Matthew's formerly enslaved mother, an "All-Mother" of the type familiar to us from "The Comet."[20] Within the logic of the novel, this is achieved through the creation of a black maternal genealogical thread that stretches between the two women. As Kautilya explains in a letter to Matthew, she regards his mother as none other than "Kali, the Black One; wife of Siva, Mother of the World" (220), "one of the ancient prophets of India," a direct descendant of Gotama the Buddha, who will lead her "out of the depths . . . and up to the atonement" (221).[21] Through identification with Matthew's mother, Kautilya's own imminent maternity becomes global and ancient, racially specific and transcendent. Indeed, she is so compelled by these connections that she depicts her beloved India as a black mother source metonymically linked to Matthew's mother: "India! India! Out of black India the world is born. Into the black womb of India the world shall creep to die. All that the world has done, India did, and that more marvelously, more magnificently" (227).

When Kautilya asks Matthew whether he comprehends this global maternalist connection, his deceptively simple reply encapsulates the affective logic of Kautilya's conception of black internationalism: "No I can not understand," he concedes, "but I feel your meaning" (227). In refusing a strict analogy between black India and black America, Pan-Africa and Pan-Asia, Matthew and the Princess conjure the darker world and clear space for a form of interracial internationalism unprecedented in Du Bois's writing. Through a shared "structure of feeling" (to borrow a formulation from Raymond Williams), they together reveal the lineaments of a form of consciousness that connects all the world's darker peoples into a single, world shaping force.[22] And, it is in this sense that Matthew's concession that he "feel[s] . . . meaning," resonates with the Princess's earlier "sense of . . . some world movement": "Black America" and "Black India" are affectively joined, and kinship between them animated through construction of a shared sense of primordial origination in a "black womb" capable of gestating revolutionary alliance.

If "the Council of the Darker Peoples of the World" is initially reluctant to grant membership to African Americans, the novel moves inexorably toward its enlightenment, and the Council's subsequent embrace of the unity of the colonized world. Hence, while the Japanese, Indian, Chinese, Egyptian, and Arab elites who comprise the Council initially believe that there is a necessary "color line within a color line" (22) separating the worthy and the rabble, by the novel's end their insistence on an internal division dissolves.[23] As they finally realize, and as Matthew and Kautilya concur, "the mission of the darker peoples . . . of black, brown, and yellow is to raise out of their pain, slavery, and humiliation, a beacon to guide manhood to health and happiness and life and away from the morass of hate, poverty, crime and sickness, monopoly, and the mass-murder called war" (257).

Although these lofty sentiments conspicuously fail to materialize revolutionary masses as agents of historical change within the novel's pages, it is important to recognize that the Marxist proclivities expressed here emerge out of actual historical circumstances. As Du Bois was acutely aware, especially after his trip to the Soviet Union in 1926, Communist debate over the so-called "Negro question," like that sparked within the Council, was linked from the outset to the so-called "colonial question." In the early twenties Lenin introduced the "Negro Question" at the Second Congress of the Communist International by way of his famous "Draft Theses on the National and Colonial Question" in which he advanced the idea that African Americans constitute an oppressed nation whose struggle is necessarily connected to all other national struggles arrayed against imperialism and capitalism.[24] After the Second Congress, Lenin pressed on, writing to the Communist Party U.S.A. to express concern that reports to Moscow did not discuss party work among "American Negros." After all, he reasoned, "American Negros" occupy the most oppressed sector of the nation and therefore ought to be central to communist activity. Though Lenin, like Kautilya, had detractors (in Lenin's case, John Reed, the outspoken leader of the Communist Labor Party,[25] in Kautilya's case, the elite members of the Council), by 1922 a more realistic basis for discussion of the connection between the "National Question" and the "Negro Question" was established. At the Fourth Congress, the first attended by blacks (the unofficial and non-communist Jamaican-born poet, Claude McKay, and an official communist delegate, Otto E. Huiswood)[26], formal declaration of Comintern policy on blacks was finally announced: the "history of the Negro in America fits him for an important role in the liberation of the entire African race" whose "international struggle . . . is a struggle against Capitalism and Imperialism and . . . its further penetration."[27]

Comintern debate helps historicize the debate within the Council, and, equally important, it provides a source for the conceptual language with which Du Bois expresses Kautilya's internationalism. As Kautilya argues in a letter to Matthew, the black world of Virginia is closer to the black world of the Council

> . . . than I had thought. This brook dances on to a river fifty miles away . . . And the river winds in stately curve down to Jamestown of the slaves . . . [T]ake your geography and trace it: from Hampton Roads to Guiana is a world of colored folk . . . a world . . . physically beautiful beyond conception; socially enslaved, industrially ruined, spiritually dead; but ready for the breath of Life and Resurrection. South is Latin America, East is Africa, and east of east lies my own Asia. (278)

Here, Kautilya closely follows the official Comintern language, situating black America as part of a larger insurgent black world to be organized by a central party, in this case the Council of the Darker Peoples of the World.[28] It is, however, Kautilya's invocation of the so-called "black belt" thesis that consolidates the historical resonance between her fictional discourse and that which Du Bois would have read in the pages of *The Worker*. Kautilya repeatedly invokes the idea of black America as a "nation within a nation" (a formulation officially announced at the Sixth Party Congress in 1928, the year *Dark Princess* was published), to rescript black America as a black nation that is part and parcel of a "black belt" that girds the world.[29] As she observes, although Asia and Africa are the dark world's center, African Americans must be regarded as part of a world swaddling swatch of color and consciousness:

> here in Virginia you are at the edge of a black world. The black belt of the Congo, the Nile, and the Ganges reaches by way of

Guiana, Haiti, and Jamaica, like a red arrow up into the heart of white America. Thus I see a mighty synthesis: You can work in Africa and Asia right here in America if you work in the Black Belt. . . . You may stand here . . . halfway between Maine and Florida, between the Atlantic and the Pacific, with Europe in your face and China at your back . . . and yet be in the *Land of the Blacks*. (286)

Significantly, Kautilya's vision of "the Land of the Blacks" comes to her while she is pregnant. As the "Black Belt" wraps itself around the world, the black world develops, enveloped in Kautilya's womb. Indeed, Kautilya's epic reproductive process powers Du Bois's Romance to resolution by effectively intertwining biological conception, Kautilya's transformation into an "All-Mother," and the birth of a robustly global form of black consciousness. In this consummated (as opposed to unconsummated) Romance, Kautilya's womb emerges as the repository of a form of black internationalism that symbolically encompasses people of color the world over.

Whereas hegemonic white racial nationalism and its demand for white reproductive purity triumph in the interracial romances of *Darkwater,* in *Dark Princess* the romance between Pan-Asia and Pan-Africa prophesies transformation of the global racial formation. On returning to Kautilya for the last time, Matthew is beckoned to her side for their wedding and the inextricably connected coronation of their newborn son.[30] In the logic of *Dark Princess,* interracial heterosexuality, interracial reproduction, and interracial (and thus internationalist) anti-imperialism are interlinked. No sooner are Kautilya and Matthew married than a mysterious pageant emerges from the gloom of the Virginia woods. In this ritual, Matthew's mother hands the baby, the manifest join of black America and black India, over to the Brahmin leader of ceremonies, while the Princess makes plain the meaning of this birth: "Brahma, Vishnu, and Siva! Lords of Sky and Light and Love! Receive from me, daughter of my fathers . . . his Majesty, Madhu Chandragupta Singh . . . Maharajah of Bwodpur . . . Protector of Ganga the Holy! Incarnate Son of the Buddha! Grand Mughal of Utter India! Messenger and Messiah to all the Darker Worlds" (311).

In *Dark Princess,* interracial romance reproduces a child capable of inheriting the world. In contrast to *Darkwater*'s foreclosed romances, *Dark Princess*'s consummated interracial union counters national and international tensions, producing instead antiracist, anti-imperialist internationalism. There is, however, a high price paid for this generically recognizable narrative resolution. For alongside its utopian conclusion, *Dark Princess* proffers a highly troubling vision, one that even Du Bois's early critics recognized as the musing of a "romantic racist."[31] Through consummation of Matthew and Kautilya's romance in marriage and childbirth, Du Bois glosses over historic Brahmin caste prejudice against blacks, shrugs off criticism of the unrelenting elitism of his imagery, and, posits heterosexuality and reproductivity as twinned motors of black internationalist anti-imperialist politics. In short, with its hallucination of Brahmin royalty, its suggestion of the organic transferability of racially marked royal blood, and its portrait of the "golden" child as the biological incarnation of a black internationalism, *Dark Princess* reinscribes the elitism and Orientalism we might expect it to challenge, while simultaneously making what can be called a *racial origin mistake.*

Such a mistake involves conflation of biological and/or cultural essences and symbols, and the production of essentialist ideas about the reproducibility of racial belonging within the crucible of heterosexual romance. For the success of this Romance as propaganda rests upon its representation of insurgent worlds of color as reproducible. On a structural level, this Romance also constitutes a form of legitimation by reversal—a mere revamping of the racial nationalism that undergirds an array of propagandistic works of art produced in the interwar period by nativists, restrictionists, eugenicists, and white supremacists—by those who regarded reproduction of "purified," "racially superior" whiteness as the principal requirement for national belonging and continued well-being in the world.[32] Such a racial origin mistake, of course, also depends on Du Bois's apparently uncritical naturalization of the heterosexual matrix out of which spring "properly" gendered and sexed reproductive subjects.[33] The disturbing consequence: Du Bois's "favorite book" emerges as racially essentialist in the way in which it conjures black internationalism, and heterosexist in the manner in which it (re)produces antiracist, anti-imperialist alliances.

## All Romance is Propaganda, Despite the Wailings of Purists

Perhaps the fictional and fanciful nature of Du Bois's various Romances of the 1920s allowed them to evade the tough scrutiny he might otherwise have subjected them to had they been expressed in another idiom or genre. And then again, it is also possible that Du Bois elected to express his deepest internationalist, anti-imperialist, and antiracist longings in and through his Romantic "alightings," precisely in order to evade such tough scrutiny. For Du Bois's Romantic fictions provided space for ongoing artistic experimentation with the type of "Negro Art" that he felt ought not be judged by the same standards as nonfiction. And yet, even though Du Bois sidestepped self criticism of his formal innovation, as contemporary readers we are in a position to scrutinize Du Bois's generic and formal choices. When we turn from Du Bois's fiction to his nonfiction, from his romantic fictions to his polemical prose on interracial intimacy, instructive differences rapidly surface.

Although Du Bois wrote a number of critical essays on interracialism beginning in the 1910s and 1920s, three in particular reveal the development in his thinking. In the first, "Marrying of Black Folk" (1910), he focuses on whether "black folk" should marry outside the group. In language redolent with nineteenth-century racial science, he concludes that although it is clear "that in general the best results follow when persons marry in their own social group," and that "so-called 'laws against intermarriage' are simply wicked devices to make the seduction of [black] women easy and without penalty."[34] For this reason, Du Bois proposes, such laws must be opposed and the consequences of occasional "intermarriage" risked. Only three years later, in an essay published in *The Crisis* and simply titled "Intermarriage," Du Bois schematizes the insights of the 1910 essay and develops them into a full-fledged call to arms.[35] Once again arguing that "colored folk [should] marry colored folk and white marry white" (180), this time he offers three carefully outlined "exceptions." The first, denoted as "physical," is that prohibition of intermarriage amounts to public acknowledgement that "black blood is a physical taint" (180). The second, denoted as "social," is that prohibition of intermarriage leads to forced indecency among people who, if given the opportunity, would prefer to be "decent" (his example is boxing champion Jack Johnson, who sought to marry his white lover but was forced to leave the United States in order to do so). And finally, the already familiar exception, denoted as "moral," is that "laws against intermarriage leave the colored girl absolutely helpless before the lust of white men" (180). Du Bois concludes this second essay on interracialism with a strategic command: "Note these arguments, my brothers and sisters, and watch your state legislatures. This winter will see a determined attempt to insult and degrade us by . . . non-intermarriage laws. We must kill them, not because we are anxious to marry white men's sisters, but because we are determined that white men shall let our sisters alone" (181).

If the first two essays on interracialism focus paternalistically on the protection of black women's virtue, moralistically on normalization of heterosexual coupling through legal sanction, and strategically on opposing anti-miscegenation legislation, in a third essay, "Social Equality and Racial Intermarriage" (1922), Du Bois fully elaborates the stakes of his argument for the creation of democracy: "At the bottom of the race problem is the question of 'Social Equality': And the *kernel of the 'Social Equality' question is the question of intermarriage.*"[36] In order for true "democracy" to exist, he continues, so too must the legal possibility of interracial marriage. Although "group solidarity," "cultural efficiency," and differences in "human taste and beauty," should and will dissuade "the great mass of individuals" from intermarrying, "democracy and human culture demand social contact." Without protection of the freedom to intermingle, and in the process to validate the equality of all individuals within the nation, "modern culture" becomes "impossible" to achieve (84).

While Du Bois's Romantic fictions and his nonfiction writings clearly share a dream of "social equality," of modern democratic culture grounded in legitimation of interracial romance, the striking difference between the treatment of interracialism in his fiction and nonfiction is that the former actually represents interracial romances that the latter can do no more than posit as hypothetically necessary to the realization of social justice. Whereas in Du Bois's polemical prose writings interracial romance is deemed an undesirable strategic necessity, in his Romantic fictions interracial romance is represented as realized. Put differently, when "art is propaganda" Du Bois realizes forms of interracial intimacy impossible to express otherwise. Thus, while his polemical essays discuss interracialism in "cold phrase," as potentially "hateful and hurtful," and as scientifically inadvisable, Du Bois's interracial Romances effectively concretize a democratic dream that his nonfiction could do no more than advocate. Du Bois's Romantic propaganda is often uncomfortably sentimental, disturbingly normative, and essentializing. And, yet, as argued in this essay, when we expand the context within which we assess it, we recognize it as a union of political advocacy and representation unachievable in another idiom or form. To conclude thus is not to excuse Du Bois's "racial origin mistake"—after all, much of this essay is devoted to its exposure. Rather, it is to acknowledge the function of interracial romance/Romance within Du Bois's larger political project. For Du Bois did not begin and end his meditation on interracialism with his signature prose essay on "Negro Art" and propaganda, rather, he devoted himself to production of a continuous stream of interracial romances/Romances that together elaborate his antiracist and anti-imperialist politics over the course of the decade in which this politics took its most decisively and radically internationalist turn.

## Notes

This essay has benefited greatly from ongoing dialogue with Susan Gillman and Brent Hayes Edwards; I thank them for their insights and questions.

1. Additional responses to the questionnaire by the following were also published in *The Crisis* from March through October 1926: H. L. Mencken, DuBose Heyward, Mary White Ovington, John Farrar, William Lyon Phelps, Vachel Lindsay, Sherwood Anderson, Benjamin Brawley, Robert T. Kerlin, Haldane MacFall, Georgia Douglas Johnson, J. Herbert Engbeck, Julia Peterkin, and Otto F. Mack. Several key essays contribute to the debate on which the "Symposium" directly builds, or indirectly respond to it. See George Schuyler, "The Negro Art Hokum," *The Nation* 122, no. 3180 (June 16, 1926): 662–63; Langston Hughes, "the Negro Artist and the Racial Mountain," *The Nation* 122, no. 3181 (June 23, 1926): 692–94; Wallace Thurman, "Negro Artists and the Negro," *The New Republic* 52, no. 665 (August 31, 1927): 37–39; and Carl Van Vechten, "'Moanin' Wid A Sword In Ma Han': A Discussion of the Negro's Reluctance to Develop and Exploit his Racial Gifts," *Vanity Fair* 25, no. 6 (February 1926): 61, 100, 102.

2. David Levering Lewis, *W. E. B. Du Bois: The Fight for Equality and The American Century*, 1919–1963 (New York: Henry Holt & Co., 2000): quote 175; on the "Symposium," 175–78.

3. "The Criteria for Negro Art," *The Crisis* 32, no. 6 (October 1926): 290–97, quote 296. All subsequent citations will be given parenthetically in the text.

4. See W. E. B. Du Bois, "Rape," *The Crisis* 18 (May 1919): 12–13, quote 12, reprinted in Herbert Aptheker ed., *Writing in Periodicals Edited by W. E. B. Du Bois, Volume 1:1911–1925* (Millwood, NY: Kraus-Thomson Limited, 1983), 193–95. In his critique of the myth of the black rapist, Du Bois is indebted to Ida B. Wells—a debt, as Joy James argues, he never frankly or fully acknowledged. See Joy James's essay in this volume.

5. The term "romance," derived from the Latin or "Roman" to distinguish it from Latin itself, was originally used to label works written in French, Spanish, or other romance languages. Starting in the eighteenth century, romance became a synonym for novel. Although critics agree that so-called "Romances" differ from novels in that they are more allegorical and symbolic, there is considerable flexibility in contemporary usage. Today, "Romance" refers to a range of texts and forms, from legends of the Saints to tales of Knightly errantry, from the texts of courtly love to pulp Romances. Here my use of Romance most closely follows that developed by Sommer, who argues that Romance combines erotics with politics, and stages political commentary through romantic encounters. Whereas Sommer reads Romances as expressive of modern nationalism, I suggest that Du Bois used Romance to contest the hegemonic form of U.S. racial nationalism and to catalyze internationalist thinking. See Doris Sommer, *Foundational Fictions: The National Romances of Latin America* (Berkeley: University of California Press, 1991). Sommer draws on the earlier insights of Leslie Fiedler, *Love and Death in the American Novel* (New York: Stein and Day, rev. ed. 1966), which explores the role of Romantic novels in national consolidation; and Benedict Anderson, *Imagined Communities: Reflections on the Origin and Spread of Nationalism* (London: Verso, 1983), which famously argues for the centrality of print culture to the production of nationalism.

6. For instance, in his critique of *Home to Harlem,* Du Bois writes that Claude McKay "has set out to cater for the prurient demand on the part of white folk for portrayal in Negroes of that utter licentiousness which conventional civilization holds white folks back from enjoying . . . he has used every art and emphasis to paint . . . lascivious sexual promiscuity and utter absence of restraint in as bold and as bright colors as he can." See "Home to Harlem" and "Quicksand," *The Crisis* (June 1928), reprinted in Theodore G. Vincent and Robert Chrisman eds., *Voices of a Black Nation: Political Journalism in the Harlem Renaissance* (Trenton, NJ: Africa World Press, 1990), 359–60. Notably, Du Bois's views on McKay's novel resonate with those on Carl Van Vechten's *Nigger Heaven,* in which, he argues "love is degraded" and "cheap melodrama" elevated as art. See "Critiques of Carl Van Vechten's *Nigger Heaven,*" David Levering Lewis, ed., *The Portable Harlem Renaissance Reader* (New York: Penguin Group, 1994), quote 107; and Levering Lewis, *W. E. B. Du Bois,* 180–82, 214.

7. Tate focuses on *Dark Princess* and argues that in it Du Bois substituted erotic pleasure for racial justice, creating a text that failed politically but succeeded erotically (see Tate's essay in this volume). By contrast, I suggest that Du Bois figured racial justice in and through romance and its attendant pleasures. Michele Elam and Paul Taylor also explore Tate's watershed claims. See their essay in this volume.

8. For a fascinating discussion of Du Bois's use of Romance as a dialectical term—as that which allows him to shuttle between historical action and unknown truth—see Brent Hayes Edwards's essay in this volume.

9. W. E. B. Du Bois, *Darkwater* [1920], reprinted in Eric J. Sundquist, ed., *The Oxford W. E. B. Du Bois Reader* (New York and Oxford: Oxford University Press, 1996), 483–623. Hereafter all citations will be made parenthetically in the text.

10. Amy Kaplan argues that the Du Bois of *Darkwater* is simultaneously at his most national and international, and thus that this assemblage is a "hybrid text." See Amy Kaplan, *Anarchy of Empire in the Making of U.S. Culture* (Cambridge, Mass.: Harvard University Press, 2002), 182.

11. See Stuart Hall, "Race Articulation and Society Structured in Dominance," in *Sociological Theories: Race and Colonialism* (Paris: UNESCO, 1980), 55.

12. Although the riots described in "Of Work and Wealth" have been interpreted as those that transpired in 1917 in East St. Louis, Du Bois links this violence, through allegory, to riots of the Red Summer of 1919, thus condensing the issues surrounding racialized labor conflict during and after the Great War.

13. Du Bois distinguished between the "sterner flights of logic" and his "little alightings" in the "Postscript" to *Darkwater.* On the logic of this "Postscript" see the introduction to this volume.

14. We argue in the introduction to this volume that this is so, despite the dominant critical tendency to argue (wrongly) that Du Bois had little to say about gender or sexuality, save for his frequently cited observations in "The Damnation of Women." Of course, the present volume constitutes an exception to this claim.

15. On "Star of Ethiopia" see Susan Gillman's essay in this volume.

16. It may be objected that Du Bois casts this relationship as platonic: "it was not lust; it was not love—it was some vaster, mightier thing that needed neither touch or body nor thrill of soul. It was a thought divine, splendid" (620). To overemphasize this statement is to mistakenly downplay the powerful sexual tension that structures the story and constitutes its radical edge. Notably the princess's "longing . . . and love" for the beggar are most starkly rendered in the story's first version. See "The Princess of Hither Isles," *The Crisis* 6 (October 1913): 285, 288–89.

17. See Alys Eve Weinbaum, *Wayward Reproductions: Genealogies of Race and Nation in Transatlantic Modern Thought* (Durham, N.C.: Duke University Press, 2004) 187–226.

18. W. E. B. Du Bois, *Dark Princess: A Romance,* Claudia Tate intro. (Jackson, Mississippi: Banner Books, 1995). All further references will be made parenthetically in the text.

19. See Du Bois, *The Autobiography of W. E. B. Du Bois* (New York: International Publishers, 1968).

20. The term "All-Mother" is fully developed in "The Damnation of Woman," where Du Bois paints an unapologetically orientalist portrait of the black mother as the lifegiving goddess of the entire world capable of rescuing black women from historical occlusion, scorn, and racist stereotype.

21. Rampersad argues that Du Bois's portrait of India drew upon Whitman, Emerson, Thoreau, and Eliot, and that his portrait of Matthew's mother was indebted to Radhakrishnan's, *The Hindu View of Life* (1927), a popular racist tract in which Kali is cast as a black, non-Aryan goddess. See Rampersad, "Du Bois's Passage

to India," *W. E. B. Du Bois: On Race and Culture,* edited by Bernard W. Bell, Emily R. Grosholz, and James B. Steward, 163–64. Dorha Ahmed, "'More than Romance': Genre and Geography in *Dark Princess,*" *ELH* 69 (2002): 775–803, builds on Rampersad's insights to caution against easy embrace of the idea of "the Global South."

22. Raymond Williams uses the concept to denote forms of consciousness that emerge from historical conflicts that are not fully understood, and thus correspond to residual rather hegemonic tendencies. See *Marxism and Literature* (London: Oxford University Press, 1977), 128–35.

23. Isaacs explains that this coalition was made possible by Du Bois's erasure of the hostilities between Japan and China, and his naïve understanding of Japan's attacks on China as a prelude to a Japanese–Chinese block against the white world. See Harold Isaacs, "Du Bois and Africa," *Race* 2, no. 1 (November, 1960): 14–15.

24. See Lenin, "Draft Theses on the National and Colonial Question" (1920) in *V. I. Lenin, Selected Works, Vol. 3* (New York: International Publishers, 1967), 422–27; Bill Mullen, "Du Bois, *Dark Princess,* and the Afro-Asian International," *Positions* 11, no. 1 (2003): 217–40; Cedric J. Robinson, *Black Marxism: The Making of the Black Radical Tradition* (Chapel Hill: The University of North Carolina Press, 1983), 302–25; Roger E. Kanet, "The Comintern and the 'Negro Question': Communist Policy in the United States and Africa 1921–1941," *Survey* 19, no. 4 (Autumn, 1973): 86–122; Philip Foner and James Allen, eds., *American Communism and Black Americans: A Documentary History, 1919–1929* (Philadelphia: Temple University Press, 1987), vii–xvi; and Harry Haywood, *Black Bolshevik: Autobiography of an Afro-American Communist* (Chicago: Liberator Press, 1978), 81–176, 223–27. Notably, Congress debates on the Negro Question were directly linked to those about Indian Communism, as expressed in the writings of the founder of the Indian Communist Party, M. N. Roy. See John Patrick Haithcox, *Communism and Nationalism in India: M. N. Roy and Comintern Policy 1920–1939* (Princeton: Princeton University Press, 1971), 11–19; M. N. Roy, "Original Draft of Supplementary Theses on the National and Colonial Question" reprinted in Ray Sibnarayan ed., *Selected Works of M. N. Roy Vol. I, 1917–1922* (Oxford: Oxford University Press, 1987), 165–68; and M. N. Roy, "On the National and Colonial Question," reprinted in *Selected Works of M. N. Roy Vol. 2, 1923–1927* (Oxford: Oxford University Press, 1988), 291–306.

25. Reed argued that Garveyism failed because blacks wanted to be part of the nation, and because separatist movements were divisive to working class solidarity. See "Speech by John Reed at IInd Congress of Communist International on Negro Question" reprinted in Philip Foner and James Allen eds., *American Communism and Black Americans* (Philadelphia: Temple University Press, 1987), 5–8.

26. On McKay's and Huiswood's participation in the 1922 Comintern see Mullen, "Du Bois, *Dark Princess,* and the Afro-Asian International," 228–29; and William J. Maxwell, *New Negro, Old Left: African-American Writing and Communism Between the Wars* (New York: Columbia University Press, 1999), 63–93.

27. The Declaration is reprinted in Philip Foner and James Allen eds., *American Communism and Black Americans,* 28–30.

28. Compare, for example, Kautilya's remarks to those of comrade Rose Pastor Stokes, as expressed in the pages of *The Worker.* Stokes, "The Communist International and the Negro" reprinted in Philip Foner and James Allen eds., *American Communism and Black Americans,* 29–31.

29. On the Sixth World Congress and the "Negro Question" see Harry Haywood, *Black Bolshevik,* 227–35, especially 232, and 259–80; and Philip Foner and James Allen eds., *American Communism and Black Americans,* 163–200.

30. Elsewhere I argue that the portrait of this child must be coupled with that of Du Bois's deceased son, Burghardt, who is "torn from beneath the heart" of his mother, an act signaling intimate violence. In contrast, the son born to Matthew and Kautilya is described as "leap[ing] [from] beneath [the] heart" of his mother, an act signaling joy and possibility. Whereas Burghardt, when separated from the protective maternal body, is literally and metaphorically consumed by racism, the golden child thrives in the world's warm embrace. See Alys Eve Weinbaum, *Wayward Reproductions,* 213–14.

31. The term is Harold Isaacs'. See "Du Bois and Africa," 17.

32. See Nancy Ordover, *American Eugenics: Race, Queer Anatomy, and the Science of Nationalism* (Minneapolis: University of Minnesota Press, 2003).

33. On Du Bois's commitment to regimes of governmentality that produce sexually normative subjects, see Roderick Ferguson's essay in this volume.

34. See W. E. B. Du Bois, "Marrying of Black Folk," *The Independent* 69 (October 13, 1910): 812–13, quotes 812 and 813. In this essay Du Bois concedes that "there are human stocks with whom it is physically unwise to intermarry," and simultaneously insists that "to think that these stocks are all colored . . . is unscientific and false" (812). As in other essays on interracialism, he here uses the language of racial science and eugenics against itself. Daylanne English argues that Du Bois's promotion of superior black families in the pages of *The Crisis* evinces his commitment to an uplift project undergirded by eugenics. Unfortunately, English does not treat the writings (such as those discussed above) that might caution against unqualified acceptance of her conclusion. See "W. E. B. Du Bois's Family Crisis," *American Literature* 72, no. 2 (June 2000): 292–319.

35. W. E. B. Du Bois, "Intermarriage," *The Crisis* 5 (February 1913): 180–81. Hereafter cited parenthetically in the text.

36. W. E. B. Du Bois, "Social Equality and Racial Intermarriage," *World Tomorrow* (New York) 5 (March 1922): 83–84, quote 83. Hereafter cited parenthetically in the text.

# 4

# Late Romance

■ *Brent Hayes Edwards*

In reflecting upon the hundredth anniversary of the publication of *The Souls of Black Folk,* it is worth noting that W. E. B. Du Bois might justifiably be described as the paradigmatic black proponent of centennial logic: the compartmentalization of history into regular units of *longue durée,* and the theorization of history's shifts and conundrums using the abstract outer limit of an individual human lifespan as a basic measure of evaluation. This predilection was integral to Du Bois's intellectual orientation, not simply a function of his longevity as a public figure who lived long enough to grumble sardonically on the eve of his ninetieth birthday that he had "lived to an age which is increasingly distasteful to this nation."[1] How many other young Victorians, studying abroad in the early 1890s, would have not only planned out a twenty-fifth birthday celebration (to the half-hour), but also recorded in his journal with bluster that "I will in this second quarter century of my life, enter the dark forest of the unknown world for which I have so many years served my apprenticeship"?[2] One might be tempted to ascribe such rhetoric to the hyperbolic effects of youthful ambition. When Du Bois, as a new faculty member at Atlanta University, assumed the directorship of the Atlanta Conference of Negro Problems in 1897, he "laid down an ambitious program for a hundred years of study," proposing to "take up annually in each decade the main aspects of the group life of Negroes with as thorough study and measurement as possible, and repeat the same program in the succeeding decade with additions, changes, and better methods."[3] Yet this tendency toward the long view is equally apparent in Du Bois's late works. How many other magisterial nonagenarians, embarking on their third autobiographical effort, would be tempted to employ the subtitle *A Soliloquy on Viewing My Life from the last Decade of its First Century,* as though there might well be a "second century" to contemplate? Du Bois wrote an article called "Negro History Centenaries" in the *National Guardian* in January 1957, announcing that he was "venturing to write several leading men and organizations within the Negro race to remind them that the year 1957 will usher in a series of centenaries which deeply affect the history of the Negro race and of this country," including the anniversary of the Dred Scott decision, the death of John Brown, the Emancipation Proclamation, the Civil War, the Freedman's Bureau, and the birth of Paul Laurence Dunbar.[4] If this centennial logic might be read as one way Du Bois defied the prevailing pretensions of an ascendant "American Century," it might also be considered the mark of an intellectual at odds with his time, intransigent, out of joint, "surviving beyond what is generally acceptable."[5]

To come to terms with Du Bois's legacy, it is indispensable to come to terms with the effects of this predilection, particularly in Du Bois's later works, which are too often overlooked or dismissed as overly dogmatic screeds, bitter broadsides, or grandiose failures. This is to ask at another level of echo—much more distant than is common—about the function of dialectical thought in Du Bois's work across more than sixty years of writing. A number of critics have remarked on Du Bois's recourse to dialectics, most often pursued through a singular formalist practice of texts framed and structured through a layering of prefaces and postscripts.[6] In November 1934, undertaking yet another revision of the manuscript of his groundbreaking historical study *Black Reconstruction,* Du Bois wrote to his publisher Alfred Harcourt that "My method of writing is a method of 'after-thoughts.' I mean that after all the details of commas, periods, spelling . . . there comes the final and to me the most important work of polishing and resetting and even re-stating. This is the crowning achievement of my creative process." (The increasingly impatient Harcourt shot back, "I must say I wish you had had your afterthoughts first.")[7]

This dialectical formalism is one of the most striking features of the 1903 *The Souls of Black Folk*, not just in terms of its own variants of preface and postscript ("Forethought" and "After-Thought")— bookends conducting the reader within and without the Veil, in a means to stage the authorial first-person as the privileged keeper of that crossing—but also within the internal dynamics of the book's chapters, both in relation to one another and internally. The most illuminating instance may be the opening of Chapter Six, "Of the Training of Black Men," in which Du Bois invokes a vision of modernity inaugurated within and through the slave trade, "many thoughts ago." From that origin, there "have flowed down to our day three streams of thinking," multiply linked doublets of thesis and antithesis, thought and afterthought. First, the imperative of internationalism on the basis of a idealist universalism (the thought that "the multiplying of human wants in culture-lands calls for the world-wide coöperation of men in satisfying them, pulling the ends of earth nearer, and all men, black, yellow, and white"), met by an afterthought that critiques that idealism by noting that the history of the world is a record less of universalism than of inequity, exploitation, "force and domination." Second, the thesis of racism—that "somewhere between men and cattle, God created a *tertium quid,* and called it a Negro"—countered by a reformist humanist argument that "some of them with favoring might become men." And third, the "thought of the things themselves," the demand of civil rights emerging from what Nikhil Pal Singh has termed the black counter-public sphere, then undermined by self-doubt and internalized racism: "suppose, after all, the World is right and we are less than men?"[8] These "streams" leave us, Du Bois writes, with a "tangle of thought and afterthought wherein we are called to solve the problem of training men for life."[9] If such a problematic "tangle" vibrates through the remainder of the chapter, as Du Bois considers the politics of higher education in the post-Reconstruction era, it also reverberates at greater levels of remove in *The Souls of Black Folk* as a whole, particularly in the concluding "After-Thought," in which Du Bois offers the book to the reader with the hope that "infinite reason" may "turn the tangle straight."[10]

The question here is whether we can hear such a dialectics staged not only within a single work such as *The Souls of Black Folk,* but also between entire texts, and even among different periods of Du Bois's intellectual production. Perhaps the most obvious way to approach this question would be to consider Du Bois's four main books that engage the mode of autobiography in one manner or another, since these texts appear with such regularity: *The Souls of Black Folk* at the turn of the century, and then—at twenty year intervals—*Darkwater* (written when Du Bois was fifty years old), *Dusk of Dawn* (written in his seventieth year), and the *Autobiography* (written as he turned ninety). But the stakes of Du Bois's dialectical formalism may be most evident in those of his works that, like *The Souls of Black Folk,* are generically hybrid articulations of autobiography, history, sociology, and fiction. Among his last works, this formalism may be less apparent in the posthumously published *Autobiography* than in what is perhaps the most neglected of his most ambitious undertakings: *The Black Flame,* the trilogy of historical novels published in the last years of his life. He began writing the first book in the trilogy, *The Ordeal of Mansart,* at the sprightly age of 81 in May 1949 during a vacation in the French resort town of Hyères with his colleague, lover, and future second wife, Shirley Graham, after they had attended the World Congress of the Partisans of Peace conference in Paris. In 1955, he asked the historian Herbert Aptheker to read a completed draft manuscript of more than 1,200 typed pages.[11] The three novels of the trilogy—*The Ordeal of Mansart* (1957), *Mansart Builds a School* (1959), and *Worlds of Color* (1961)—have been out of print for nearly three decades, and have received almost no critical attention. The handful of critics who have slogged through them have not demonstrated a great deal of gratitude for the opportunity. Arthur P. Davis's review of *The Ordeal of Mansart* concludes that it is "definitely not a good historical novel."[12] Considering the trilogy as a whole, Julius Lester puts it even more bluntly: "As novels, they fail completely. As fictionalized history, they are interesting, sometimes absorbing, and often boring."[13] They garner a scant two sentences in David Levering Lewis's exhaustive two-volume biography of Du Bois, and the most elaborate description offered of the trilogy is "sprawling."[14] Even Arnold Rampersad, the only scholar to give the novels sustained and relatively sympathetic attention, sighs that "the historical novel is one of the more torpid genres," and calls *The Black Flame* "sluggish."[15]

Herbert Aptheker, who was instrumental in publishing the trilogy through the leftist journal *Masses and Mainstream,* has noted that some of Du Bois's conception of *The Black Flame* originated decades earlier, in the form of two abandoned novel projects. In 1935, Du Bois wrote to Edwin R. Embree of the Rosenwald Fund that he had thought of using the novel form "to dramatize and put in the form of a romance the development of a group." Eight years later, after his traumatic dismissal from Atlanta University, he wrote to the editor-in-chief at the publishing house Reynal and Hitchcock, saying that he had begun a novel "stressing and illustrating the leadership of the presidents of Negro Land [Grant] Colleges."[16] I am especially interested in Du Bois's initial designation of *The Black Flame* as a "romance," reminiscent of his characterization of his 1928 novel *Dark Princess,* although with a peculiar twist.[17] As in *Dusk of Dawn,* which Du Bois subtitled "An Essay Toward an Autobiography of the Race Concept," manuscript drafts of *The Black Flame* propose an odd generic mix (or clash), as the trilogy is subtitled "A Romance of the History of the American Negro."[18] The third book in the trilogy, *Worlds of Color,* follows the life and career of Manuel Mansart, a black college president in Georgia, from 1936 until his death in 1956.[19] The book is intriguing, not only as Du Bois's final foray into fiction writing, but also as what one might term his last "romance" with internationalism.[20]

The novel's title is itself provocative, as it is also the title of one of Du Bois's most incisive attempts to offer a vision of anti-imperialist internationalism in the 1920s. The 1925 essay "Worlds of Color," which first appeared in *Foreign Affairs,* is most familiar in the revised version that Du Bois provided for Alain Locke's seminal anthology *The New Negro,* where the essay is retitled "The Negro Mind Reaches Out."[21] There, Du Bois patiently tracks the history of European colonialism through an optical metaphor of "shadows," yet another dialectical formalization ("here is a field of inquiry, of likening and contrasting each land and its far-off shadow"), moving through sections on "The Shadow of Portugal," "The Shadow of Belgium,"

"The Shadow of France," "The Shadow of England," "Labor in the Shadows," and "The Shadow of Shadows" (investigating efforts at internationalist organizing among what Du Bois terms "the darker peoples of the world").[22]

It is crucial to recognize that if the article is thus constructed through contrast, through "after-thought," Du Bois's revision for *The New Negro* is itself an "after-thought" or shadow of the *Foreign Affairs* essay, reformulating its terms in subtle but significant ways. In the initial published version, Du Bois frames the problem of understanding colonialism as a global force as the task of looking outside, attending to the plight of the world's others: "is it not possible," he questions, "that our research is not directed to the right geographical spots and our good-will too often confined to that labor which we see and feel and exercise right around us rather than to the periphery of the vast circle and to the unseen and inarticulate workers within the World Shadow?"[23] In *The New Negro*, though, these sentences are transformed: the task is not to look outside the center of Western capitalism, paying attention to the "periphery," but instead to recognize that the so-called margins *are* the foundation—the "determining factors"—of global capitalist accumulation. "Our good will is too often confined to that labor which we see and feel and exercise around us," Du Bois now counsels, "rather than directed to the periphery of the vast circle, where unseen and inarticulate, the determining factors are at work."[24] The tone is no longer special pleading, the original essay's call to consider the labor problem in Europe and America "from this external vantage ground—or, better, ground of disadvantage."[25] Du Bois shifts in *The New Negro* to a much more pointed call to view the issue of labor in general "from this wide perspective, remembering always that empire is the heavy hand of capital abroad."[26]

If the novel *Worlds of Color* extends or responds to or "thinks after" the essay "Worlds of Color," in other words, it follows in the wake of this previous revision of the piece, which pushes towards a "planetary" perspective on labor and imperialism rather than accepting the hierarchy of a center-periphery model.[27] In this light, the novel *Worlds of Color* might be said to approach its "fore-thought" essays in something like the way that, in 1953, Du Bois revises the "color line" in terms of global imperialism and class dynamics, in a fascinating preface to a fiftieth anniversary edition of *The Souls of Black Folk:*

> I still think today as yesterday that the color line is a great problem of this century. But today I see more clearly than yesterday that back of the problem of race and color, lies a greater problem which both obscures and implements it: and that is the fact that so many civilized persons are willing to live in comfort even if the price of this is poverty, ignorance and disease of the majority of their fellowmen; that to maintain this privilege men have waged war until today war tends to become universal and continuous, and the excuse for this war continues largely to be color and race.[28]

*The Black Flame* is organized around the family saga of the Mansarts, and its scope is the exact scope of Manuel Mansart's life from birth to death. As *Worlds of Color* opens, Manuel is sixty years old, a successful and established college president, and yet one whose life-long focus on the "Negro problem" and higher education in the U.S. South has been torn asunder by a series of national and global events. "The First World War, the Depression and the New Deal had shaken Mansart to the depths of his being," we are told on the first page. "All the old certainties were gone—all that neat little world with its good God, bad men and hovering angels" (9). The novel commences with a conference in the spring of 1936, gathering the presidents of the Negro Land Grant colleges in the south, a project that Du Bois himself had pursued in the late 1930s and early 1940s. In April 1941, with funding from the Carnegie Foundation, Du Bois convened the First Phylon Conference of black educators; there he proposed a concentrated effort to agitate for an increased share of federal funding for black colleges in the south, with the goal of producing a collaborative and systematic series of sociological studies of black life in each state— what *Worlds of Color* terms "a controlled laboratory test on a grand scale unequaled in history" (18).[29] In the novel, it is decided that the project headquarters will be at Georgia State, under the direction of Mansart; at the same time, the group of educators comes to the conclusion that Mansart needs to take a sabbatical and travel around the world since "his education has been narrow," and he has little or no understanding of labor on a broader scale, or of the "problem of colonies in the world" (18).

Du Bois himself was unable to pursue the Land Grant studies since he was forced to retire from Atlanta University in 1944, just after the project had been approved by a wide range of black colleges. He considered his ouster from Atlanta, and the lost opportunity for a revival of sociological inquiry, to be a "catastrophe."[30] In other words, the first third of *Worlds of Color*—in which Mansart travels through England, France, Switzerland, Germany, Russia, China, and Japan, slowly gaining a sense of global politics and colonialism (in chapters titled "The American Negro's World," "The Color of England," "The Color of Europe," and "The Color of Asia")—can be read as an attempt to imagine the formation of the kind of black southern educator who might have been able to pursue Du Bois's collaborative studies in sociology (the project in fact had collapsed as soon as Du Bois was not able to lead it). Mansart, by the end of these chapters, after much reading and long discussions about class and color with a variety of Europeans and Asians, "began to have a conception of the world as one unified dwelling place. He was escaping from his racial provincialism. He began to think of himself as part of humanity and not simply as an American Negro over against a white world" (85).

Herbert Aptheker claims that Du Bois "appears in the person of Mansart,"[31] and yet there are clear divergences between the author and the character, who is somewhat timid and constrained by the limitations of his ability and circumstances during much of the trilogy. As Mansart himself puts it in the first volume, he "burns slow," lamenting that "always behind my firm decisions lurks doubt; numbing, paralyzing doubt. I am not ever absolutely certain."[32] Arnold Rampersad comments that in *Worlds of Color*, "Manuel Mansart stands at the center of the book yet paradoxically is almost peripheral to its historical action."[33] On the one hand, the trilogy constantly shifts its focalization among a dizzying variety of characters, black and white, in a wide variety of locales. Whole chapters are given to the upbringing and adult lives of Mansart's four children (Bruce, Sojourner, Douglass, and Revels) and to an enormous number of other families in multiple generations: the Breckinridges, Southern white aristocrats clinging to the last trappings of privilege; the Scroggs, leaders of the labor movement in the South fearful of the influence of black workers; the Baldwins, educators and emerging business leaders; the Sheldons, the family of the President of Atlanta University; the Coypels, modest and enlightened educators from North Carolina; the Pierces, headed by the rapacious capitalist John Pierce; and the Du Bignons, an old, upper-crust New Orleans family with both white and black lines of descent.

On the other hand, *The Black Flame* tosses its dozens of characters among a mindboggling host of historical figures and events. While in Paris, Manuel Mansart comes across a "colored man from the West Indies," a writer named James, who tells him about the Haitian Revolution, arguing that "the slave trade and slavery were the economic basis of the French Revolution" (40–41). Even if the reader does not recognize the portrait in passing of the Trinidadian Marxist C. L. R. James, who was in Paris researching *The Black Jacobins* in 1936, the novels are populated with a large number of identified historical personages, many with extensive speaking roles: Booker T. Washington, Marcus Garvey, Huey Long, Woodrow Wilson, Madame C. J. Walker, Theodore Roosevelt, Harry Hopkins, Franklin D. Roosevelt, Hitler, Stalin, Félix Eboué, Félix Houphouët-Boigny, Paul Robeson, and Shirley Graham (to whom the first two volumes of the trilogy are dedicated). Du Bois himself appears in the hardly concealed guise of a radical intellectual named Burghardt, who in the novels is an organizer of the Niagara Movement and the Pan-African Congress, and the editor of *The Crisis,* from which editorials and articles are quoted regularly throughout the trilogy. A number of key historical events are depicted in some detail, including the Atlanta riots, the 1911 Universal Races Congress in London, the 1936 Olympic Games in Berlin, the Second World War, the 1943 riots in Detroit, the 1945 Manchester Pan-African Congress, and the United Nations Conference in San Francisco.

Rampersad contends that if "in depicting Manuel Mansart, Du Bois was to some extent writing vicarious autobiography," there are other characters who share "the task of speaking—and living" for the author.[34] Aside from Burghardt, the most important is Jean Du Bignon, a light-skinned woman who identifies as African American and works for many years at Georgia State, first as Mansart's secretary, then as a sociology professor (she earns a Ph.D. from the University of Chicago), and finally as Mansart's wife. It is Jean Du Bignon, not Mansart, who is the driving force in the Negro Land Grant College sociology study initiative, working behind the scenes to lay out "a tentative plan for cooperative, continuous sociological investigation in each state as a scientific beginning" (18). It is Du Bignon who is harassed by the Federal authorities during the Cold War and eventually prosecuted (and acquitted, like Du Bois himself in 1951) for the trumped-up charge of failing to register as an "agent" of a "foreign power" (261). It is she who is ousted from the college in the wake of the scandal over her trial, just as Du Bois had been removed from Atlanta University. She tells Mansart she's written a novel which no publisher will accept (the initial fate of *The Black Flame* itself) and reads him a passage from it (322). She, not Mansart, pursues a sort of underground activism, taking advantage of her ability to pass in order to enter an all-white Textile Union in the South to combat its racism from within. She does so only with great regret at having to leave the world of the African American South, in a passage that explicitly invokes the "Forethought" of Du Bois's *Souls:* "She had lived too long with her own black folk. She felt completely bone of their bone and flesh of their flesh" (267).

What does it mean to describe *The Black Flame* as a "romance"? What difference does it make that Jean Du Bignon—rather than the novels' titular protagonist, Mansart—is so clearly the parallel to Du Bois's political sensibility in the trilogy? One way to make sense of the trilogy as a "romance" is to read it in the wake of the understanding and critique of that genre in the 1925 essay "Worlds of Color," where it is linked to an understanding of the implications of race for labor organizing, precisely the issue that concerns Jean Du Bignon as she infiltrates the textile union. Du Bois argues in the essay that "the attitude of the white laborer toward colored folk is largely a matter of long continued propaganda and gossip." He adds that racist propaganda is "buttressed" through a range of discursive practices: "the propaganda of poet and novelist, the uncanny welter of romance, the half knowledge of scientists, the pseudo-science of statesmen—all these, united in the myth of mass inferiority of most men, have built a wall which many centuries will not break down."[35] Therefore, *The Black Flame* is a "romance" in its ambitions to track the complex and many-sided connections between capitalism and the modalities of race, in the aim of countering the "attitude" of the laborer with an explicitly antiracist propaganda fiction.[36] This is to say that, although thus framed in the interest of a radical internationalism, Du Bois's recourse to the term "romance" can also be understood to signal an engagement with one of the foundational tensions in the novel as a genre: its "categorical instability" as the record of an epistemological crisis around the relations of narrative and truth.[37]

At the same time, *Worlds of Color* is also expressly a "romance" in the more common sense of a fiction that stages an erotic union. After the death of Mansart's wife, Jean Du Bignon and Manuel Mansart do indeed marry, albeit late in life and with nothing like the lusty self-indulgence and purple prose of the coupling in Du Bois's *Dark Princess*. One thinks immediately of Du Bois's own second marriage in 1951, at the age of eighty-three, to Shirley Graham. In the novel, "late romance" has everything to do with an erotics of deferral, duty, and long term devotion. The trilogy strikes this note especially in its melodramatic paeans to Jean Du Bignon as the perfect secretary, somehow at once self-effacing and highly intellectually engaged:

> She was indefatigable and uncomplaining. She kept herself in the background, asked no recognition and yet foresaw every contingency. . . . The newspapers and magazines were marked and placed before him, and now and then books of interest appeared on his desk. Facts and figures were found for him miraculously and, above all, whenever he had time or wish, Jean Du Bignon was ready to talk, to advise and to encourage, and she showed the result of study, wide reading and clear thinking.[38]

It is perhaps the appropriate commemoration of the May–December wedding of the great intellectual and a woman more than two decades younger to whom he had been, in his own words, "a sort of father confessor in literary affairs and difficulties of life for many years."[39] In the same passage of the *Autobiography*, Du Bois comments, with an odd tone that seems simultaneously shamefaced and patronizing, on the "beautiful martyr complex" of his wife. (Graham herself had fewer qualms: alluding slyly to the night in 1951, which she tactfully claims—against the evidence of their longstanding affair—was the first time they consummated their relationship. She wrote later: "He reiterated that he was 'selfish' and 'too old,' but he didn't *act* old!")[40]

Is romance, here, then a mode that strives for mastery, for a level of totalizing authorial control in its shuttling between these two generic impulses (propaganda and erotics)? Rampersad claims that Du Bois "telescopes repeatedly between the more minute figures of his fictional world, especially those in the Mansart family, and the epic sweep of historical continuity."[41] Du Bois himself writes, in the Postscript to the first novel in *The Black Flame*, that "the basis of this book is documented and verifiable fact," but that he "used fiction to interpret those historical facts which otherwise would not be clear."[42] Despite this claim that what Du Bois terms "the fiction of interpretation" is an integrative force, that romance thereby fills in the "gaps" of historical action or "unknown truth,"[43] one might argue that the most prominent characteristic of Du Bois's late style is not at all the sweeping continuity of a unifying intelligence—telescoping among registers of historical generality and imagined specificity, as it were, to offer the masterful interpretation of a world's century. On the contrary, the late style is marked above all by discontinuity, a pervasive failure of mastery—disjunction and parataxis rather than smooth transitions among registers and context.

How does one account, that is, for the slips and apparent narrative flaws in *Worlds of Color:* the passages that break off clumsily, the innumerable digressions, the pedantic historical overviews? Over the space of two pages in Chapter Six, at one of the conferences of Land Grant College officials, a man named Aba Aziz (also known as Alexander Abraham), a "chance visitor" from Yemen, is allowed to address the gathering, and gives a bizarre speech about quantum physics that none of the college presidents understand; he is subsequently pursued by the FBI and charged with being "either a spy or a saboteur" as well as a Communist. In a short summary paragraph, he is detained by the authorities, and then he disappears with only the explanation that "he had apparently been accidentally killed by falling from the walls of Alcatraz" (90). In another instance, directly after we read at the end of a chapter that Jean Du Bignon "must now study" the "inner development" of the Negro in relation to the labor movement (104), we are wrenched somewhere entirely different, into a lengthy section devoted to Jack Carmichel, the husband of a niece of Mansart's wife, and his efforts to run a grocery store in Springfield, Massachusetts (105–30).

Another such moment occurs on a train ride that Mansart takes to visit his son Revels in New York. Eating his lunch alone in his compartment, he is overtaken by a terrifying vision: after the meal, he

> settled back again to rest and stare out on the darkening landscape. The world swept by—the dark loafers at the stations—the white girls in the factories—the burdened wagons staggering along dusty roads. Then, suddenly, with startling clearness, out there in the night he seemed to see a great green Spider nestling in Hell, weaving an impenetrable Web. It sat in a pool of blood, which had gushed down from China, flowed in from Spain and seeped through from Mississippi. The Spider seemed to be spinning out thin tendrils of American gold, linking strand to strand. To the drying, stinking mess, the Spider added clods of British dirt and moistened all with the slime of France, until the spreading Web grew wide as the Earth and high as Heaven. It was too horrible. It seemed to divide the Darkness from the Light and the White World fought the Dark World and both faced Death. (163)

Instead of reflection, instead of elaboration of this figure—"interpretation," indeed—we are jerked out of this hallucination and back into an evocation of the everyday that seems impossibly placid. A new paragraph opens: "Here, the porter shook Mansart gently and suggested he make up his berth so that he could sleep more easily. Mansart slept soundly the rest of the night and next day breakfasted with his son Judge Revels Mansart and his wife, sitting on Washington Heights opposite the Jersey Palisades" (163). He never thinks of or mentions the vision, and its vivid symbolism is abandoned in the singularity of this passage. Thinking back to *The Souls of Black Folk*, though, one might suggest that it is possible to read an "afterthought" in this perplexing lack of fit: rather than charging the reader with "setting straight" a "tangle" through the instrumental use of reason (as in *The Souls of Black Folk*), here the text would seem to confront the reader with a "Web"—stark, apocalyptic, and yet quickly passed over without a trace—that is precisely insusceptible to integration, to any response that wants to gauge its subsequent import. As they erupt in the narrative time and again, these kind of unintegrated moments haunt the reader, not only because they are melodramatic and "horrible" but also because they seem to run so thoroughly contrary to the trilogy's progressive historical framing.

The reason to highlight the problematic formal discontinuities in *The Black Flame* is not to echo the critics who have described the novels as "failures," but instead to raise the question of the function of disjuncture and discontinuity in Du Bois's late style. As Edward Said and others have noted, any consideration of the politics of late style must grapple with the writings of Theodor Adorno.[44] In his well-known 1937 essay on the final works of Beethoven, Adorno contends that the "maturity of the late works of significant artists" is difficult, "furrowed, even ravaged [*zerrissen*]," in that the works "lack all the harmony that the classicist aesthetic is in the habit of demanding from works of art, and they show more traces of history than of growth."[45] The "usual view" of a great artist's late work tends to see them as "products of an uninhibited subjectivity, or, better yet, 'personality,' which breaks through the envelope of form to better express itself, transforming harmony into the dissonance of its suffering." From this vantage point, late works are relegated beyond their particular aesthetic contours, beyond the peculiarity of their form, to mere expressions of the great individual—that is, to "the vicinity of document." But for Adorno, "the formal law of late works . . . is, at the least, incapable of being subsumed under the concept of expression [*Ausdruck*]." In them subjectivity is in no way a unifying force, marshaling the artwork's form into a construction that allegorizes totality. Instead, Adorno continues,

> the power of subjectivity in the late works of art is the irascible gesture with which it takes leave of the works themselves. . . . Of

the works themselves it leaves only fragments behind, and communicates itself, like a cipher, only through the blank spaces from which it has disengaged itself.[46]

Perhaps this characterization offers insight into the unusual difficulty of Du Bois's last novels. It would be one way of coming to terms with the discontinuities, the awkward unwieldiness, of *The Black Flame*, in which, as Arnold Rampersad puts it, Du Bois abandons "that combination of liberal idealism and piety which had given *The Souls of Black Folk* its remarkable flavor. And he strove to erase from his writing the confabulation of the self, the deliberate design of the ego as hero, which had been a principal source of dramatic power in his propagandistic literature from the dawn of the century."[47]

To take on such a parallel would necessitate a consideration of the differences between music and literature. In Adorno's reading, Beethoven is the "inborn son" of the European bourgeois class: his music, he writes, "is structured like the society to which—with doubtful justification—we give the name of 'rising bourgeoisie,' or at least like its self-consciousness and its conflicts."[48] If Beethoven's middle period music exemplifies the ascendancy of that class with its structures of seamless compositional control, his later works bespeak the dissolution of the bourgeois articulation of totality under the conditions of modernity. Clearly, such a historically specific description does not fit Du Bois, who nonetheless might be identified with a rising class (the upwardly mobile black petty bourgeoisie emerging out of the Victorian era). If there is a dissolution of, a pulling away from that subjectivity in his work, it is oriented towards the possibility of a radical black internationalism—a Pan-Africanist socialism bursting the husk of the Talented Tenth.

One should hesitate before making any hasty analogies between musical form and literary form. There are moments where *Worlds of Color* adopts musical metaphors in proposing its transnational realms of coverage, the layering of its "worlds." At one point early on, for example, we are told that "like an obbligato running above the development of a nation becoming socialistic, and at the same time being drawn into defense of colonial imperialism, went the apparently unheeded and untouched line of development among the groups into which the nation was divided" (131). But this adoption of a formal metaphor from music is evidence of precisely the ways that literature is *not* akin to music; the narration describes its structural contours with reference to another artistic medium of syntax and counterpoint.

In Beethoven's late work, Adorno is particularly fascinated by the role of musical conventions: he locates a buzzing horde of clichéd gestures (formulas, phrases, "decorative trill sequences, cadences, and *fiorituras*") in the late string quartets and piano sonatas, intact but scattered about, unconnected—discrete gestures rather than ornaments of a progressing harmonic trajectory. What would the equivalent be in late Du Bois? Rose Subotnik reminds us that in Adorno's aesthetics, for the artwork to resist "neutralization" within the confines of the culture industry, it must "express itself through surface means that are not obviously expressive and that can be apprehended only by a few highly individualized listeners. . . . In a representational art, this can be done most easily by obscuring the correspondence of content, in the traditional sense, to external reality."[49] But this seems exactly wrong with regard to the representational art of Du Bois's historical fiction—indeed, part of the difficulty of the work is its excessive referentiality, its insistent ties to the "facts" of history. It seems to me that if there is resistance in the late Du Bois, it is apprehended on a level that approximates the *formal* effect of difficulty in music: as Subotnik glosses it, a practice that "requires interfering with the perception of coherence in structural and syntactical elements." That interference is registered in the episodic and shifting qualities of the novel, its "apparent carelessness about its own continuity."[50] It is on that level, in the absent or failing connective tissue of the book—in the lack of articulation, syntax, and transition between its sections (all quite conventional within themselves, both in terms of style and in terms of reference)—that *Worlds of Color* might be said to strive for a set of effects that are not unrelated to the structuring of Beethoven's late music.

Like Du Bois's *Dark Princess* in 1928, *Worlds of Color* culminates with a secret internationalist gathering of the darker peoples of the world.[51] Mansart is invited by a mysterious European princess, Zegue de Laurinberg, to attend a midnight conclave in New York with an impressive gathering of African, Caribbean, and African American dignitaries, political leaders, and intellectuals (334–35). But in contrast to the mystical and messianic essentialism of the wedding that concludes *Dark Princess,* uniting the Indian princess Kautilya and the African American intellectual Matthew Towns and crowning their infant son the "golden" incarnation of their revolutionary internationalist alliance,[52] the bejeweled royal hostess at the end of *Worlds of Color* lays down a gauntlet:

> I am not here alone, your highnesses, excellencies, gentlemen and ladies; nor am I your host. Some of the sixty men who own America and are the real rulers of one world are behind me, sitting back of this great mirror and seeing you clearly although you do not see them. . . . The point I bring you is this—they are the powerful of the earth. They rule. What I want you to do in the time that you are with us is to think of your own future under them. Will you join with the white European race to help crush and beat back the crazy Chinese and Russian Communists, help bring that world back to its normal procedures; or will you join this rebellion against established authority—this revolt against civilization? (337–38)

One African American businessman responds in obsequious tones until Mansart cuts him off brusquely, finally speaking up to reject her white supremacy in unsparing terms: "I hate, I detest the pretensions of the white race. They shall not continue to rule—their end is near, Socialism is not creeping, it is marching, and in its triumphant march I see the end of all war. . . . Black Brothers, let us never sell our high heritage for a mess of such White Folks' pottage!" (338)

This speech should mark the explosion, the long-awaited upheaval of radical internationalism. But there is no reaction. The princess says nothing, and there is no description of the other luminaries of African descent in the wake of Mansart's outburst. Instead, a curtain opens onto a sumptuous buffet of food, and out emerge a number of white men and women "to welcome the dark guests," leading them to seats "carefully mixed by race and color." We are informed that "a lively buzz of conversation soon ensued." "Hardly anyone noticed," the passage continues, when Mansart was escorted out of the hall by two footmen, "moving unobtrusively" (341). Such an anticlimax undermines any readerly investment in the promise of a unifying vision, a staging of internationalism at the book's close that might articulate its disparate worlds of color. The trilogy ends on a very different note; as Mansart says to Jean: "God is no playwright. His lives end dimly, and without drama; they pile on no climax on tragedy nor triumph on defeat. They end quietly or helplessly—they just end" (343).

On his deathbed, Mansart has two visions: a global apocalypse on the one hand, and a revolutionary utopia on the other. He does not resolve them or choose between them, but dies lying back in Jean's arms. As his voice falters, his daughter Sojourner plays "a dissonant flame of protest" on her violin (349). This harsh music is not a symbol of reconciliation, much less transcendence, but instead—in Adorno's terms—the sounding of "a catching fire [*Zündung*] between the extremes, which no longer allow for any secure middle ground or harmony of spontaneity."[53]

In a memoir of her years with Du Bois, Shirley Graham notes that in his final days, he was "completing the last book of his trilogy, which he was calling *Worlds of Color,* and I am sure that his own feelings were expressed in the laments made near the bedside of the dying patriarch, whose life had been traced through the three books."[54] Yet Du Bois was also working at the same time on the text that would be published as the *Autobiography,* and one might wonder why he would choose to put "his own feelings" in the feeble, confused deathbed visions of his fictional character, rather than in his own voice. Indeed, although the trilogy concludes with Mansart's death, I am suggesting on the contrary that *Worlds of Color* must not be read as an expression of Du Bois's subjective feelings about his own impending death—as though one could read the characterization of Mansart as nothing more than a kind of covert autobiography.[55] Recalling the novel's constant parallels between Du Bois and Jean Du Bignon makes it impossible to read *Worlds of Color* as "autobiographical fiction." When Mansart passes, we read that "gently Jean closed the lifeless eyes" (349).

The title of the trilogy, *The Black Flame,* remains cryptic even in the final pages of *Worlds of Color.* In its various iterations in the novels, the "black flame" seems to suggest by turns an apocalyptic figure of annihilation, a more conventional figure for human progress, and a messianic figure of deliverance. Before the final "dissonant flame" of Sojourner's musical outpouring in the last lines of the novel, the title is evoked most vividly in the penultimate chapter, when Jean Du Bignon undergoes a sort of breakdown while teaching a summer sociology class. Suddenly delirious, she "los[es] sense of time and place" and speaks to her uneasy students about a "Black Flame" (314–15). It is another disjunctive moment in *Worlds of Color:* a prophetic dream in which a figure of redemption can only be articulated as ecstatic, dislodged from any social impact or historical ramification.[56] When she stops speaking and collapses at her desk, her students wonder whether she has "gone crazy," or "seen a vision," or even died. One wonders out loud, "Do you think we ought to let the Dean know?" (315) In the next paragraph, Jean wakes up in a hospital bed, two weeks later.

There is a fragment in Adorno's unfinished book on Beethoven that considers music as a representational medium by comparing it with the form of dreams. He gives as an example the first movement of Schubert's Symphony in C major, where

> at the beginning of the development, we feel for a few moments as if we were at a rustic wedding; an action seems to begin unfolding, but then is gone at once, swept away in the rushing music which, once imbued with that image, moves onwards to a quite different measure. Images of the objective world appear in music only in scattered, eccentric flashes, vanishing at once; but they are *essential* to it precisely in their decaying, consumed state.[57]

We are *in* the music, Adorno claims, in the same way that we are in dreams: "We are at the rustic wedding, then are carried away in the musical flood, heaven knows where (it may be similar with death—perhaps the affinity between music and death has its locus here)."[58] This is to say that the closest art can come to the representation of death is not some majestic summing-up or bird's-eye contemplation, some subjective expression of looming demise, but instead a formal undoing, a leavetaking manifested in a structural collapse.

Although it is not constructed with the disjunctive formalism of *The Black Flame,* parts of the posthumously published *Autobiography* (which Du Bois was writing during the same period) offer an intermittent, rhetorical contemplation of impending death. Near the end of the *Autobiography,* the exiled intellectual, writing in Ghana, meditates once more on the significance of history. "I just live," he rumbles:

> I expect snatches of pain and discomfort to come and go. And then reaching back to my archives, I whisper to the great Majority: To the Almighty Dead, into whose pale approaching faces, I stand and stare: you whose thoughts, deeds and dreams have made men wise with all wisdom and stupid with utter evil.[59]

One might pause at the unusual appropriation of "archives," a term that Du Bois very rarely uses, and that he here twists into a new range of connotation: less public and singular than personal and plural, less documentary and positivist than imagined, less a locus of power and intelligibility than a place of "whispering," of an intimacy with the eternal. The "Almighty Dead"—or as he later rephrases it, the "Forever Dead"—are figured not as the dearly departed, much less the bypassed or outmoded, but as an active force ("You are not and yet you are: your thoughts, your deeds, above all your dreams still live"), a "majority" standing for eternal justice in the face of present "Evil."[60]

This is perhaps as close as Du Bois comes to eschatology, but what would it mean to read this invocation of the archives as historiography? It would mean an entirely different posture, an entirely different understanding of what we mean by a phrase like the "romance of history," to return to Du Bois's subtitle for *The Black Flame.* The passage announces what might be termed a romance of the remnant. Yet, here, the remnant is not at all the stuff on the side of the road, everything lost in the corners of the library. We are the remnants. Thus the Dead are asked to "overwhelm, outvote, and coerce this remnant of human life which lingers on, imaging themselves wisest of all who have lived just because they still survive." The Dead are enjoined to "teach living man to jeer at this last civilization which seeks to build heaven on Want and Ill of most men and vainly builds on color and hair rather than on decency of hand and heart."[61] This is to redefine "remnant" in a rather different manner than, say, Giorgio Agamben's appropriation of the term, which reads the remnants as "witnesses" speaking from the aporia of testimony, "neither the dead nor the survivors, neither the drowned nor the saved" but "what remain between them."[62] Twenty years earlier, in *The World and Africa,* Du Bois recounts an anecdote that offers the same redefinition, bracketing the present as the remnant of a historical absolute:

> I remember once offering to an editor an article which began with a reference to the experience of last century. "Oh," he said, "leave out the history and come to the present." I felt like going to him over a thousand miles and taking him by the lapels and saying, "Dear, dear jackass! Don't you understand that the past *is* the present; that without what *was,* nothing *is?* That, of the infinite dead, the living are but unimportant bits?"[63]

This is to suggest a historical posture, a mode of address, as Du Bois puts it in his apostrophe to the Dead: "Reveal, Ancient of Days, the Present in the Past and prophesy the End in the Beginning." It is also to hold on to "dream" and "romance," to the work of the imagination, as the means to operate this inversion, even if dream is never simply fancy or pure invention but an orientation towards reading the past differently: "there is no Dream but Deed, there is no Deed but Memory." What Adorno calls the "catching fire" in this inversion would be but the tiniest ignition: not the hallucination of a triumphant revolution, but the chance that in the gap as it withdraws, "reaching back," the locally residual might spark the generally emergent.[64]

This orientation makes the late style of autobiography, like the late romance of fiction, something unexpected: not "indisputable authority," but a text that is "always incomplete" and "often unreliable," as Du Bois himself phrases it—a mode of addressing a past that both authorizes and ever exceeds the grasp of any single speaking subject.[65] Thus the subtitle of the *Autobiography,* which announces not mastery but instead (as it is glossed in the first pages of the book) the "Soliloquy of an old man on what he dreams his life has been as he sees it slowly drifting away."[66] If the century's accumulation of those solitary speakings can function, as Du Bois still hopes here—in yet another striking dialectical formulation—as "contradictions to truth,"[67] then the revelation comes elsewhere, out of grasp. It is heard in what's left.

## Notes

Early versions of this essay were presented as lectures at Duke University in November 2003 and Brown University in December 2003. I would like to thank those audiences for their many useful suggestions for revision. I would also like to thank Alys Weinbaum, with whom I discussed many of the theoretical issues at stake in this essay. The essay greatly benefited from her insights and comments.

1. W. E. B. Du Bois, "A Vista of Ninety Fruitful Years," *National Guardian* (February 17, 1958) in *Writings*, ed. Nathan Huggins (New York: Library of America, 1986), 1110. This passage also appears in Du Bois's posthumously published autobiography, where he writes, "I have lived to an age of life which is increasingly distasteful to this nation. . . . I would have been hailed with approval if I had died at 50. At 75 my death was practically requested." *The Autobiography of W.E.B. Du Bois: A Soliloquy on Viewing my Life from the last Decade of its First Century* (New York: International Publishers, 1968), 414.

2. Du Bois, "Celebrating His Twenty-Fifth Birthday," in *Against Racism: Unpublished Essays, Papers, Addresses, 1887–1961*, ed. Herbert Aptheker (Amherst: University of Massachusetts Press, 1985).

3. Du Bois, *Dusk of Dawn: An Essay toward an Autobiography of a Race Concept* (1940), in *Writings*, 600. On the Atlanta Conferences (which Du Bois directed until his departure from Atlanta University in 1910), see *The Autobiography of W. E. B. Du Bois*, 209–19, and David Levering Lewis, *W. E. B. Du Bois: Biography of a Race, 1868–1919* (New York: Henry Holt, 1993), 217–20.

4. Du Bois, "Negro History Centenaries," *National Guardian* (January 14, 1957), collected in *The Seventh Son: The Thought and Writings of W. E. B. Du Bois*, vol. 2, ed. Julius Lester (New York: Vintage, 1971), 643. Three years later he opened an article on what he considered to be the poor state of history teaching in the U.S. by reminding his readers that "one hundred years ago next year this nation began a war more horrible than most wars, and all wars stink." See Du Bois, "The Lie of History as It Is Taught Today," *National Guardian* (February 15, 1960), collected in *The Seventh Son*, 666.

5. Edward Said, "Adorno as Lateness Itself," *Adorno: A Critical Reader,* ed. Nigel Gibson and Andrew Rubin (New York: Blackwell, 2002), 202.

6. See Vilashini Cooppan's discussion of Du Bois's "dialectical formalism" in "The Double Politics of Double Consciousness: Nationalism and Globalism in *Souls*," *Public Culture* 17, no. 2 (spring 2005): 308; and Brent Hayes Edwards, *The Practice of Diaspora: Literature, Translation, and the Rise of Black Internationalism* (Cambridge: Harvard University Press, 2003), 39–40.

7. Du Bois, letter to Alfred Harcourt, November 17, 1934, quoted in David Levering Lewis, *W. E. B. Du Bois: the Fight for Equality and the American Century, 1919–1963* (New York: Henry Holt and Company, 2000), 364.

8. Du Bois, *The Souls of Black Folk* (1903), collected in *Writings,* 424–25. See Nikhil Pal Singh, *Black Is a Country: Race and the Unfinished Struggle for Democracy* (Cambridge, Mass.: Harvard University Press, 2004).

9. Du Bois, *Souls,* 425.

10. Ibid., 547.

11. David Levering Lewis, *W. E. B. Du Bois: the Fight for Equality and the American Century, 1919–1963* (New York: Henry Holt and Company, 2000), 545.

12. Arthur P. Davis, review of *The Ordeal of Mansart, The Journal of Negro History* 42 (July 1957): 214–15, quoted in Hebert Aptheker, "Introduction," *The Ordeal of Mansart* (1957; reprint Millwood, NY: Kraus-Thomson, 1976), 8.

13. Julius Lester, "Introduction," *The Seventh Son: The Thought and Writings of W. E. B. Du Bois,* vol. 1, ed. Lester (New York: Vintage, 1971), 136.

14. Lewis, *W. E. B. Du Bois: the Fight for Equality and the American Century,* 545.

15. Arnold Rampersad, *The Art and Imagination of W. E. B. Du Bois* (Cambridge: Harvard University Press, 1976), 270.

16. Du Bois, letter to Edwin R. Embree (1935), letter to Frank E. Taylor (1943), quoted in Aptheker, "Introduction," *The Ordeal of Mansart,* 5.

17. Du Bois, *Dark Princess: A Romance* (1928; reprint Jackson: University Press of Mississippi, 1995).

18. W. E. B. Du Bois, *The Black Flame,* fragments and notes, Du Bois Papers, University of Massachusetts-Amherst, Series: Novels, Reel 87.

19. Du Bois, *Worlds of Color* (New York: Mainstream, 1961). Subsequent references will be indicated parenthetically in the text.

20. He was putting the finishing touches on the book in 1958 as he turned ninety, ostracized and hounded by the U.S. State Department, but still attuned to the currents of Cold War politics in the years before his final departure from the United States. See Shirley Graham Du Bois, *His Day is Marching On: A Memoir of W. E. B. Du Bois* (Philadelphia: J. B. Lippincott, 1971), 230.

21. Du Bois, "Worlds of Color," *Foreign Affairs* 3, no. 3 (April 1925): 423–44; Du Bois, "The Negro Mind Reaches Out," in *The New Negro,* ed. Alain Locke (1925; reprint New York: Atheneum, 1989), 385–414.

22. Du Bois, "The Negro Mind Reaches Out," 386. On the figure of the "shadow" in this essay, see my essay "The Shadow of Shadows," *Positions* 11, no. 1 (spring 2003): 41–42.

23. Du Bois, "Worlds of Color," 422.

24. Du Bois, "The Negro Mind Reaches Out," 385.

25. Du Bois, "Worlds of Color," 422.

26. Du Bois, "The Negro Mind Reaches Out," 385.

27. I am thinking of Gayatri Chakravorty Spivak's brilliant proposition of "planetarity" in Spivak, *Death of a Discipline* (New York: Columbia University Press, 2003). She discusses "The Negro Mind Reaches Out" on pages 97–100.

28. Du Bois, "Fifty Years After," *The Souls of Black Folk: Essays and Sketches* (1903; reprint New York: Blue Heron, 1953), xi.

29. Du Bois, *Autobiography,* 309–10, 316–17, 321.

30. Ibid., 321.

31. Hebert Aptheker, "Introduction," *The Ordeal of Mansart* (1957; reprint Millwood, NY: Kraus-Thomson, 1976), 7.

32. Du Bois, *The Ordeal of Mansart* (New York: Mainstream, 1957), 313.

33. Rampersad, *The Art and Imagination of W. E. B. Du Bois*, 269–70.

34. Ibid., 280, 281.

35. W. E. B. Du Bois, "The Negro Mind Reaches Out," 407.

36. In other words, the trilogy is a "romance of history" in the rather unusual sense espoused by Du Bois in his infamous article on the "Criteria of Negro Art," where he enumerates a number of transnational examples from the post-World War I period (the struggle against racist violence in the U.S. South, the conquest of German East Africa for the Allies, in large part through the sacrifice of black African troops) and comments, "Such is the true and stirring stuff of which Romance is born and from this stuff come the stirrings of men who are beginning to remember that this kind of material is theirs; and this vital life of their own kind is beckoning them on." See Du Bois, "Criteria of Negro Art," *The Crisis* (October 1926): 292.

37. See Michael McKeon's comments on the rise of the novel in relation to the romance in the early modern period in *The Origins of the English Novel, 1600–1740* (Baltimore: Johns Hopkins University Press, 1987), 20. With regard to the internationalism of Du Bois's vision, Alys Weinbaum has pointed out the divergence of Du Bois's model of romance from the common scholarly assumption that romance is a matter of "foundational fictions" integrally linked to the nation. See Weinbaum, *Wayward Reproductions: Genealogies of Race and Nation in Transatlantic Modern Thought* (Durham: Duke University Press, 2004), 299, no. 35.

38. W. E. B. Du Bois, *Mansart Builds a School* (New York: Mainstream, 1959), 159. In this regard, one might suggest that although dedicated to Graham, the novels are also somewhat disturbingly a "romance" of a long list of women that Du Bois knew intimately in long term parallel affairs (including Jessie Fauset, Georgia Douglas Johnson, Virginia Alexander, Mildred Bryant Jones, Louie Shivery, Eileen Diggs, and Ethel Ray Nance), many of whom served him in one way or another as secretaries or assistants.

39. Du Bois, *The Autobiography of W. E. B. Du Bois*, 367.

40. Shirley Graham Du Bois, *His Day is Marching On: A Memoir of W. E. B. Du Bois* (Philadelphia: J. B. Lippincott, 1971), 135.

41. Rampersad, *The Art and Imagination of W. E. B. Du Bois*, 269.

42. Du Bois, *The Ordeal of Mansart*, 315.

43. Ibid., 316.

44. See Edward Said, *On Late Style: Music and Literature against the Grain*, ed. Michael Wood (New York: Pantheon, 2006).

45. Theodor W. Adorno, "Late Style in Beethoven," in *Essays on Music*, ed. Richard Leppert, trans. Susan H. Gillespie (Berkeley: University of California Press, 2002), 564.

46. Ibid., 564.

47. Rampersad, *The Art and Imagination of W. E. B. Du Bois*, 263.

48. Theodor W. Adorno, *Introduction to the Sociology of Music* trans. E. B. Ashton (New York: Seabury Press, 1976), 212.

49. Rose Rosengard Subotnik, "Adorno's Diagnosis of Beethoven's Late Style: Early Symptom of a Fatal Condition," in *Developing Variations: Style and Ideology in Western Music* (Minneapolis: University of Minnesota, 1991), 32.

50. Edward Said, "Adorno as Lateness Itself," 198.

51. There is a prior gathering of "a group of colored leaders" organized in the early 1940s by an African American Masonic organization and held at the Cloisters in Manhattan. Mansart attends "a meeting of about one hundred delegates representing the Colored Peoples of the world, 'to take council as to their situation in this war and its aftermath'" (165). In addition to the African American contingent, there are delegates from Africa, India, China, South America, and Japan, among other places. One unnamed man, "small and thin and white turbaned," his eyes "caverns of gloom," gives a speech that makes Mansart's son Revels suspect that he might be Gandhi himself, traveling incognito. The man calls for resistance both to fascism and to colonial imperialism, and concludes that "it should be our bounden duty to seek Peace through Non-resistance" (166). Interestingly, though, the potential of this organization is immediately tempered: we are told that "certain Negro Americans" took reports of the meeting to a committee on Wall Street comprised of representatives from "most of the chief international cartels which controlled the production and distribution of goods the world over." The committee is reassured by the reports of the secret meeting of the darker peoples: "There was as yet no conspiracy and the mirage of peace and non-violence still guided them" (168).

52. Du Bois, *Dark Princess: A Romance*, 307.

53. Adorno, "Late Style in Beethoven," 567.

54. Shirley Graham Du Bois, *His Day is Marching On*, 230.

55. On the issue of "subjective" expression, see Shierry Weber Nicholsen, *Exact Imagination, Late Work: On Adorno's Aesthetics* (Cambridge, Mass.: MIT, 1997), 41.

56. Jean proclaims to her students that "this world must reach into a world beyond—with its flames and leaders" (314). She describes a "white flame lighting up the North" with an odd assortment of European cultural and political figures (leaders?): Hitler, Bismarck, Wagner and Freud; the "flaming tri-color of the boastful West" incarnated in Napoleon, Mussolini, Washington, and Churchill; and a "red flame" "rising in the East to light up the sky," with Lenin, Pushkin, Buddha, and Sun Yat-sen; and finally the "dazzling Black Flame of the South—the Black Flame of Tarharqua and Askia, Toussaint and Lobengula" (315). The flames of the North and West, she says, will "fail" and "decline," but "that of the East, as we can see, is growing, growing. Oh, few of you know as I know what the Black Flame of the South will bring." The bizarre prophecy that follows can only be termed a vision of revindicationist, apocalyptic blackness:

> Away down there in the Antarctic, at the end of the world, we have been building an ice palace. Nothing the world has seen is of such size. The inches of the pyramids have been yards in this massive and gigantic building; the Empire State Building is a mere pilaster. The building already looms so that at the end of the globe the earth soon will lurch, and swinging outward into the barriers of the stars lay open a universe with no assumptions of Space nor hypotheses of Time. . . . And then between the pillars of the universe, looming from highest Heaven to lowest Hell, will appear again the Black Flame (315).

There is not space here to offer a reading of the various invocations of the titular phrase in the trilogy as a whole. They include Mansart's tragic birth, when his grandmother dramatically anoints him "the Black Flame" (*The Ordeal of Mansart,* 72); the conclusion of the first book, where Mansart interprets the phrase to mean that he should work in education as a force of reform, a "flame" used "for cleaning, not destroying" (*The Ordeal of Mansart,* 313); and the striking triptych of visions at the end of the second novel, which juxtapose a "White Flame," a "Red Flame," and a "Black Flame" as vaguely racialized symbols of Europe, Asia, and Africa, respectively (*Mansart Builds a School* [New York: Mainstream, 1959], 366–67).

57. Adorno, *Beethoven: The Philosophy of Music, Fragments and Texts,* ed. Rolf Tiedemann, trans. Edmund Jephcott (Stanford: Stanford University Press, 1998), 7–8. This passage is discussed at some length in Stephen Hinton, "Adorno's Unfinished *Beethoven,*" *Beethoven Forum* 5 (1996): 146.

58. Adorno, 8.

59. Du Bois, *The Autobiography of W. E. B. Du Bois,* 422–23.

60. For a fine reading of this figure, see Jodi Melamed, "Killing Sympathies: U. S. Literature and the Limits of Racial Liberalism, 1940–1960" (Ph.D. dissertation, Columbia University, 2003).

61. Du Bois, *The Autobiography of W. E. B. Du Bois,* 423.

62. Georgio Agamben, *Remnants of Auschwitz: The Witness and the Archive,* trans. Daniel Heller-Roazen (New York: Zone Books, 2002), 163–64.

63. Du Bois, *The World and Africa: An Inquiry into the Part which Africa Has Played in World History* (1946; reprint New York: International Publishers, 1965), 80.

64. With this shift in terminology I am thinking of one of the more suggestive ancillary propositions in Raymond Williams's theorization of historical change and "structures of feeling." Discussing the issue of the emergence of "new meanings and values, new practices, new relationships and kinds of relationship," he considers the ways that the dominant strives to "incorporate" any emergent that threatens to become "substantially alternative or oppositional" to the existing social structure (rather than simply a "new phase" of it, or a "residual" element of its past). One of the difficulties in analyzing the dynamics of emergence, he adds, is that there is "regular confusion between the locally residual (as a form of resistance to incorporation) and the generally emergent." See Williams, *Marxism and Literature* (Oxford: Oxford University Press, 1977), 123, 125.

65. Du Bois, *The Autobiography of W. E. B. Du Bois,* 12.

66. Du Bois, *The Autobiography of W. E. B. Du Bois,* 12. As I mentioned at the opening of this essay, the book's subtitle is *A Soliloquy on Viewing my Life from the last Decade of its First Century.*

67. He writes: "Forty years ago when at the age of 50, I first essayed a brief autobiography, my memories furnished many details and conclusions which now disappear or return as quite strange. . . . In *Dusk of Dawn* I wrote much about my life as I saw it at the age of 70, which differs much from what I think at the age of 91. One must then see these varying views as contradictions to truth, and not as final and complete authority. This book then is the Soliloquy of an old man on what he dreams his life has been as he sees it slowly drifting away; and what he would like others to believe." Du Bois, *Autobiography,* 12–13.

# 5

# Race and Desire: *Dark Princess: A Romance*

■ *Claudia Tate*

Mother was dark shining bronze, with smooth skin and lovely eyes; there was a tiny ripple in her black hair, and she had a heavy, kind face. She gave one the impression of infinite patience, but a curious determination was concealed in her softness.

W. E. B. Du Bois,
*The Autobiography of W. E. B. Du Bois* (1963)

The tale is done and night is come. Now may all the sprites who, with curled wing and starry eyes, have clustered around my hands and helped me weave this story, lift with deft delicacy from out the crevice where it lines my heavy flesh of fact, that rich and colored gossamer of dreams which the Queen of Faerie lent to me for a season. Pleat it to a shining bundle and return it, sweet elves, beneath the moon, to her Mauve Majesty with my low and fond obeisance. Beg her, sometime, somewhere, of her abundant leisure, to tell to us hard humans: Which is really Truth—Fact or Fancy? the Dream of the Spirit or the Pain of the Bone?

W. E. B. Du Bois,
"Envoy," *Dark Princess* (1928)

The greatest and fullest life is by definition beautiful, beautiful—
beautiful as a dark passionate woman, beautiful as a golden-
hearted school girl, beautiful as a grey haired hero.

> William E. B. Du Bois,
> "Celebration of My Twenty-Fifth Birthday"
> (Journal, February 23, 1893)

## *Du Bois,* Crisis *Propaganda, and Desire*

On December 15, 1927, Du Bois sent the final version of the manuscript of *Dark Princess: A Romance,* his second novel, to Harcourt,
Brace and Company. In the attached letter, he asked whether his prior
statements about the work's social purpose were adequate for the
publisher's promotional plans for the novel, which would appear in
the spring of 1928. The marketing staff at Harcourt, Brace evidently
requested no additional information but drew on these statements
to prepare the newspaper notices about the novel (Aptheker,
Introduction, 18). This publishing firm was well aware of Du Bois's
prominence and was confident that the book would demand wide
attention.

Du Bois's activist strategy in *Dark Princess* was like that in his other
works. He had been agitating for racial equality by combining his
rather impassioned creative compositions with social analysis since
1903, when he published *The Souls of Black Folk.* In *The Crisis,* the
official publication of the National Association for the Advancement
of Colored People (NAACP), which was under his editorial control
from its inception in 1910, he also repeatedly referred to what he
thought to be an intrinsic relationship between art and propaganda.
This position, as Keith Byerman notes, "is consistent with emerging
Marxist aesthetics and anticipates the black arts movement of the
1960s in its recognition of the ideological nature of art."[1] In the
October 1926 issue of *The Crisis,* Du Bois published a definitive statement on this subject—"The Criteria of Negro Art." This work reveals
a terse example of Du Bois's use of eroticism for representing
racial protest that appears throughout his writings and especially in
*Dark Princess.*

In "The Criteria of Negro Art," Du Bois confronts his readers' reluctance to recognize the utility of art for political activism by asking,

> How is it that an organization like this [the NAACP], a group of radicals trying to bring new things into the world, a fighting organization which has come up out of *the blood and dust of battle*, struggling for *the right of black men to be ordinary human beings*—how is it that an organization of this kind can turn aside to talk about art? (279; [author's] emphasis)

Du Bois answers this question here by contending that "all art is propaganda and ever must be, despite the wailing of the purist" (288).

Although this excerpt has been very prominent in the scholarship on Du Bois, scholars seldom mention the three sentences, immediately following it, that bring the paragraph to closure. In them, Du Bois attests,

> I stand in *utter shamelessness* and say that whatever art I have for writing has been used always for propaganda for gaining *the right of black folk to love and enjoy.* I do not care a damn for any art that is not used for propaganda. But I do care when propaganda is confined to one side while *the other is stripped and silent.* (288; [author's] emphasis)

Here Du Bois not only proclaims the persuasive potential of art for securing racial justice—"the right of black men to be ordinary human beings" (288). He also characterizes this objective by abandoning the public arena of social protest for the private domain of erotic pleasure. "[I]n utter shamelessness," he proclaims racial justice as "the right of black folk to love and enjoy" (288). Thus, rather than invoking the conventional and no doubt expected rhetoric of civil rights to define the objective of his social mission, he refers instead to libidinal prerogatives—indeed, to desire and gratification—to describe the goals of racial activism. Du Bois underscores this position at the end of the extract by disavowing the efficacy of any propaganda "stripped" of art and "silent" on desire and pleasure.

The complex association of propaganda with erotic delight in "The Criteria of Negro Art" illustrates a paradoxical pattern of representation that Du Bois would regularly employ in his creative writings and especially in *Dark Princess*. This pattern suggests that the public satisfaction of racial equality is connected and somewhat analogous to the private pleasure of eroticism, for eros and polity are mutually signifying. By unconsciously instilling eroticism within his understanding of propaganda, Du Bois complicates his initial equation between art and propaganda by including passion and its gratification. This conceptual framework allows him to idealize the members of the NAACP as dusty, blood-stained crusaders in a chivalric campaign of high moral significance, as the extract implies. Fighting in this crusade on the behalf of an ideal, traditionally figured as feminine, would convert the desire for freedom into liberatory action.

Du Bois's use of chivalric imagery would have been particularly meaningful for his black and white contemporaries who would have recalled D. W. Griffith's representation of the Ku Klux Klan's appropriation of chivalric zeal, codes, and images in *The Birth of a Nation* (1915).[2] Based on *The Clansman, an Historic Romance of the Ku Klux Klan* (1905) by Thomas Dixon Jr., this film championed southern, native-born, Anglo-Saxon Protestant males by depicting their violent reprisal of black(faced, white) male desire for white women and in doing so stimulated the rebirth of the "Invisible Empire" of the Ku Klux Klan.[3] Griffith appealed to white male anxiety during the years immediately after World War I by staging the mythic attack on the idealized symbol of white supremacy—the white woman. Defending white honor was the rallying cry of the Klan, just as it had been for the Confederacy. What had been a white male, nineteenth-century contest about capital and nation was, at the turn of the twentieth century, a more mystified struggle about white political privilege now executed as sexual authority. Hence, white male supremacists not only used white female sexuality to objectify their persecutory fantasies and to justify (or condone) the lynchings of thousands of African Americans and a few Jews and Catholics as well; many white men also exercised the presumption of their racial/sexual privilege by raping black women.

Chivalric idealization of female sexuality was the means for inciting and representing both the Klan's racist propaganda for white supremacy and Du Bois's counterpropaganda for racial equality in *The Crisis*. The Klan enhanced the esteem and political power of the working-class whites who largely comprised its membership, by relying on displaced persecutory fantasies to police white female sexuality and to denigrate as well as exploit black people in general. Du Bois retaliated by using *The Crisis* to (re)appropriate chivalric imagery so as to idealize himself and others fighting for racial equality.

While Du Bois's *Crisis* readers eagerly identified with his liberational objective, they often found the eroticized expression in his writings peculiar and, as we will see, even problematic. Scholars would generally deal with this curious feature by either disregarding it or castigating Du Bois for his surplus passion. Their critical reproach was undoubtedly met with his bewilderment, because Du Bois repeatedly insisted that "my writing of fiction, as well as other forms of literature, is for propaganda and reform. I make no bone on saying that art that isn't propaganda doesn't interest me."[4] Yet as "The Criteria of Negro Art" entreats us to see, Du Bois seems unconsciously to associate propaganda for social reform with erotic desire. The eroticism is not depicted as mere sensuality; on the contrary, it is personified as a heroic ideal much like the noble and unobtainable queen of courtly romance to whom a knight would dedicate his chivalric zeal. This feminine figure is implicit in Du Bois's representation of the NAACP in "The Criteria of Negro Art," for she bids the "radicals" of this "fighting organization" to "come up out of the blood and dust of battle" and claim "the right of black men to be ordinary human beings" which is, according to Du Bois, equivalent to demanding "the right of black folk to love and enjoy" ("Criteria" 279, 288).

The erotic relationship between art and propaganda in "The Criteria of Negro Art" is emphatic in *Dark Princess*. Here, Du Bois's chivalric tropes and passionate dedication to racial propaganda come to life to stage a romance. The "dark princess" of the title commands the protagonist's valiant fight against racism. As his reward, though, he does not triumph over racism; rather, he wins the princess and the assurance that their son will free all the dark races of the world from

Western imperialism. Like "The Criteria of Negro Art," *Dark Princess* also substitutes erotic pleasure for the achievement of racial justice. This exchange suggests that the majestic female figure commanding Du Bois's activist devotion is an integral part of his imaginative process or what Roland Barthes might call Du Bois's personal "hermeneutic code."[5] This code structures his conceptual framework . . . [and may be] represent[ed] with the following equations: propaganda = art = erotic desire; the goal of propaganda = freedom = erotic consummation. *Dark Princess* relies on such figurative analogies to express racial propaganda; they appear again and again in Du Bois's writings.

To explain, analyze, and appreciate the deep meaning of these hermeneutic equations in *Dark Princess,* it is useful to engage the psychoanalytic model of the "fantasmatic." A fantasmatic is a "structuring action" or a recurring pattern of an individual's fantasies that "lie[s] behind such products of the unconscious dreams, symptoms, acting out, [and] repetitive behavior."[6] The fantasmatic is not only an internal or masked thematic that determines a subject's unconscious associations; it is also a dynamic formation that seeks conscious expression by converting experience into action. For as the subject attaches unconscious fantasies to new experiences, she or he reproduces pleasure by copying "the patterns of previous pleasure."[7] In "The Criteria of Negro Art," Du Bois discloses a brief illustration of what I suspect is his fantasmatic template for encoding racial activism—that is, his unconscious pattern of consolidating the libidinal economies of desire and freedom. This mental pattern would allow him not only to reproduce pleasure in his writings but to produce an extraordinary amount of work and to dedicate his life to laboring for racial progress as well, for he seems to have experienced the emotional effect of laboring for racial uplift like the pleasure of libidinal satisfaction. As we shall see, *Dark Princess* allows its protagonist to recover aspects of what psychoanalysis calls the "lost mother" (which I explain later) as an effect of black political engagement.

The symbolic function of the princess in *Dark Princess* is clearly to represent the desire to achieve racial justice. But the princess becomes detached from this objective and evolves into an autonomous and enigmatic signifier of a beloved woman. How does this signifier structure Du Bois's hermeneutic code? Recognizing the importance of this question is instructive for understanding Du Bois's unswerving devotion to racial activism. Answering this question will help us to understand the deep emotional and intellectual investments that Du Bois placed in his activist writings. Although *Dark Princess* is unquestionably a flawed novel, it provides a provocative venue for "taking a more exact measure of the range of Du Bois's interests and concerns, and of his extraordinary intellect and imagination"[8] (Rampersad, "Du Bois's Passage," 1).

While Du Bois was apparently unaware of his tendency to eroticize racial justice in his writings, he was probably at least familiar with Sigmund Freud's basic hypotheses about unconscious desire by 1910, and certainly by the 1920s, when Freud's works were in wide circulation in the United States.[9] In spite of Du Bois's continued interest in psychology, ever since his undergraduate study with Harvard professor William James, Du Bois was reluctant to question his staunchly held conviction about the power of knowledge to eradicate social oppression.[10] He wanted to believe (to use his own words) "that race prejudice was based on widespread ignorance." Therefore, he insisted that the "long-term remedy was Truth" which he understood as "carefully gathered scientific proof that neither color nor race determined the limits of a man's capacity or desert [*sic*]." For most of his life, Du Bois studied black America "with the honest hope of alleviating—through the therapy of reason and truth—the vast race hatred in America."[11] By the early 1940s, though, he was ready to recognize "the unconscious factor," inherent not simply in all human activity but his own as well.[12] Prior to that time, as he confessed, he was not "sufficiently Freudian to understand how little human action is based on reason" ("My Evolving Program," 9). This is the observation of an elderly Du Bois.

Whether by the early 1940s Du Bois was also ready to acknowledge his chronic fixation on eros is difficult to determine, despite his admission in *The Autobiography* (written some twenty years later) that he "was a lusty man with all normal appetites" and that he "loved 'Wine, Women and Song'" (283). We do know, however, that by the mid-1910s his depictions of eroticism in *The Crisis* often confused his readers and annoyed the executive board of the NAACP. The matter first became public in 1915 when the provocative cover of the November *Crisis*, featuring the sultry portrait of a light-skinned woman, "scandalized the Boston branch of the NAACP"[13] (See Figure 5.1).

Given Du Bois's fantasmatic formula, it is not difficult for us to see how he could regard this cover as an expression of his racial vision and therefore appropriate for *The Crisis*. It is easier, though, to see how his readers might fail to associate a lovely mulatta with racial uplift, for they had no means of connecting Du Bois's pattern of erotic representation to his political ambitions.

Even when Du Bois's portrayals of the erotic objective of propaganda were less tangible and confined to the rhetorical fancy of his creative writings, they undoubtedly mystified his *Crisis* readers. For were it not for the figure of a black Christ, allusions to oppression, and the personification of freedom, respectively in "The Riddle of the Sphinx," "The Princess of the Hither Isles," and "Children of the Moon," for example, his readers probably would not have been able to connect the passion in these works to racial propaganda. Despite the formidable display of eroticism in these and other creative works, Du Bois was probably unaware of the degree to which this feature controlled their development. When he wrote *Dark Princess*, the most extreme case in point, he claimed propaganda as his motivation. In explaining *Dark Princess* to his publisher, Du Bois described the novel as "a romance with a message":

> Its first aim is to tell a story: the story of a colored medical student whom race prejudice forces out of his course of study. He tries to run away from America and then learns of a union of darker peoples [led by a young, beautiful Indian Princess, the "Dark Princess"] against white imperialism. It is not a union of hatred or of offense, but of defense and self-development of the best in all races. But the problem is how such a movement can be set going. (Aptheker, Introduction, 19)

Given the nature of this declaration, Du Bois's editors at Harcourt, Brace had to have been at least a bit surprised when they encountered more romance than message. No doubt, they hoped the passion would sell the book.

**The CRISIS**

Vol. 11—No. 1  NOVEMBER, 1915  Whole No. 61

FIGURE 5.1 *Cover of* The Crisis, *November 1915. Courtesy of The Crisis Publishing Co., Inc., the magazine of the National Association for the Advancement of Colored People.*

Du Bois's first readers expected *Dark Princess* to be a work by the man with whom they were familiar: Du Bois the polemicist; Du Bois the unyielding proponent for the advancement of the race. They were aware of his challenge to Booker T. Washington for the leadership of black America during the first years of the twentieth century and his central role in founding the NAACP in 1909. However, when they looked for analysis of the race problem in *Dark Princess* and for practical ways to attack Western imperialism, they were rather disappointed, for what they found was a love story that functions as a melodramatic deterrent to the novel's polemical objective. The aims of *Dark Princess* and its effects, as Arnold Rampersad notes, "do not always succeed, and occasionally a failure is ludicrous."[14] Still, as Rampersad adds elsewhere, Du Bois intended the novel to be "a corrective" for "the growing trend among the younger artists" who asserted "their artistic independence" by sacrificing the radical politics that defined Du Bois's own life and work ("Du Bois's Passage," 2).

Du Bois's intentions notwithstanding, the numerous reviews of *Dark Princess* characterize it as "bewildering," "an amazing mixture of fact and fancy," "a sentimental melodrama," and "the queerest sort of mixture: clear sharp observation, thoughtfully considered and carefully written, helter-skelter with Graustarkian romance" (Reitell, *Annals,* 347; see also T. S., Review, 9, and M. P. L., Review, 27).[15] Literary scholars have shared this opinion, which explains why the first printing of the novel sold poorly, rapidly went out of print, and received marginal notice in the annals of U.S. literary history.[16] For example, two scholars describe the novel as "an opera in prose," "a strange book, a strange compound of revolutionary doctrine and futilistic philosophy, refuting, it seems, Dr. Du Bois's own text of aggressive independence." Another insists that "it is the only novel by an American Negro which makes an exhaustive study of the place of black folk among the darker races of the earth." And yet another summarizes the critical consensus by writing, "*Dark Princess,* although a poor novel, is socially, psychologically, and politically significant."[17]

*Dark Princess* fictionalizes the Indian resistance to British imperialism, the rise of what would later be called the Third World, and Du Bois's actual efforts to understand "the interplay between race and politics on a global scale" (Rampersad, "Du Bois's Passage," 3).

Yet the novel's focus on an emphatically sexualized messianic plot makes it deviate from the popular trends of social realism that dominated African American fiction during the New Negro Renaissance and defined the novelistic standards of Du Bois's predecessors of the post-Reconstruction period, like Sutton Griggs, Frances Harper, Charles Chesnutt, and Pauline Hopkins. While these writers emphasize the public plot of collective black polity and efface practically all references to explicit eroticism in their works, the Renaissance writers frequently address sexuality. Here, however, sexuality is presented as a repressed and frequently destructive force—for example, in Jean Toomer's *Cane* (1924) and Nella Larsen's *Quicksand* (1928) and as a pleasant complication in Jessie Fauset's *There's Confusion* (1924), all of which Du Bois admired. By contrast, the representation of black sexuality in Claude McKay's *Home to Harlem* (1928) clearly provoked Du Bois's ire. In an often cited remark, Du Bois claimed that the novel "for the most part nauseates me, and after the dirtier parts of its filth I feel distinctly like taking a bath." As far as he was concerned, *Home to Harlem* was "padded" with "utter licentiousness" to cater to the white marketplace.[18] While *Dark Princess* is clearly a steamy novel, its propaganda, sartorial eroticism, and urbane consumption of art, music, and food as well as its focus on one extraordinary love object evidently made the novel's refined depiction of adultery appear less distasteful to Du Bois than the crass promiscuity of McKay's raunchy novel.

The reception of *Dark Princess* also reveals a historic preference for representing collective social arguments rather than personal desire in black literature. U.S. reviewers, scholars, and readers have routinely understood black novels as expressions of racial politics even when such a formulation earns reproach. Yet this audience has celebrated the highly individualistic portraits of desire in white literature (such as Edgar Allan Poe's necrophilia, Vladimir Nabokov's pedophilia, and Ernest Hemingway's infatuation with bullfighting, as well as the unique forms of eroticized passive resistance in the works of Charlotte Perkins Gilman, Kate Chopin, Edith Wharton, Virginia Woolf, and on and on the list could go) while expecting desire in black textual production to be defined by and subsumed within the political ambitions of the black masses.

Projections of Du Bois's personal desire and pleasure are certainly dominant features of *Dark Princess*—so much so that in spite of its mixed reviews, in 1940 Du Bois proclaimed it to be his "favorite book" (*Dusk of Dawn,* 270).[19] What makes this remark particularly meaningful is that at the time of its pronouncement he had been a prominent social scientist of U.S. race relations for nearly thirty years, with a spate of impressive books to his credit.[20] His prolific writings endorsed his faith in education, work, and protest as the best defenses against racial oppression. Still, he did not declare *The Souls of Black Folk* to be his favorite book, even though it endorsed such faith and "made him a leader of black Americans."[21] Instead, this distinction he gave to his unpopular *Dark Princess,* in which the protagonist is hardly a model of success. He quits school, works at an assortment of meaningless jobs, and even fails to execute effective racial protest. Arnold Rampersad contends that *Dark Princess* "was Du Bois' favorite book because it said much of what he regarded to be essential and true [about racial politics], at a time when his effectiveness as a political and cultural leader of black America first appeared to be under serious threat" (*Art,* 204). No doubt Du Bois thought the novel would present his unfailing devotion to social activism with such passion that he could secure his role as the quintessential proponent of the race. Yet I suspect the real source of pleasure in this text for Du Bois is its emphatic manifestation of his unconscious fantasmatic processes that encode the novel's impassioned representation of racial activism.

While passion may enhance polemicism, it is a most subjective and therefore contestable form of evidence. For passion to be convincing, it needs to be attached to a rational core of information. In this regard Du Bois draws on his considerable knowledge, experience, and observations about Western imperialism to construct *Dark Princess*'s polemicism. However, he invokes a lot more passion than rational detail. Indeed, as he bolsters the justification of his argument for the inevitability of racial equality with the messianic plot, a distinct desire seizes control of the novel and especially the character of the dark princess. This type of desire has much in common with the subject's primary desire for the lost mother.

. . . The lost mother . . . [is the psychoanalytic term for] . . . the imaginary object that is the young child's—here the son's—earliest, principal, and most enduring attachment, one that develops over the first few years of the child's interactions with her. The feelings that bond her to him cohere into his gratifying, libidinal fantasies about her and define what Freud called the pre-oedipal stage. During the later oedipal stage,[22] Freud theorizes, the young boy becomes socialized as he represses and displaces both his strong, sexual feelings for the mother and his wishes to kill the father. In *Totem and Taboo* (1913–14) and *Civilization and Its Discontents* (1930), Freud further claims that civilization is a product of the guilty reparations of sons to their fathers.[23] The lost mother, then, is an imaginary construction of the historical mother whom the child believes is omnipotent. This, like all imagoes, is generated more by the subjective dynamics of an individual's personality than actual experience. The maternal imago has two extreme forms—the idealized good mother and the persecutory bad one. Whereas fantasies of the good mother are predominant in Du Bois's writing, those of the bad mother dominate the textual unconscious of Richard Wright's fictions . . . .

*Dark Princess* depicts an oedipalized story; it is a messianic narrative about a black son's conflict with the white patriarchy. But instead of idealizing the paternal imago and making reparations to it, as discussed in Freud's *Totem and Taboo, Dark Princess* idealizes the maternal imago and makes the lost mother the object of the son's reparations. The emphasis that *Dark Princess* places on the protagonist's repeated acts of reparation for failed activism complicates the novel's plot and makes . . . [the reader] . . . wonder whether Du Bois was unconsciously associating his endeavors at working for racial uplift with reparation to one person in particular—his mother. Du Bois's mother not only helped him to define his character, genius, and social commitment; she also made it possible for him to enhance these aspects of his personality by dying at a most propitious time in his life.

As David Levering Lewis explains in his prize-winning biography on Du Bois, *W. E. B. Du Bois: Biography of a Race* (1993), his knowledge that his mother, Mary Silvina, "lived almost entirely to see him prosper in the world, that she would die for him if need be," did not lessen the fact that she became a burden to him (52). His father Alfred's desertion of them before Du Bois was two condemned the mother and son to certain poverty. As her health rapidly failed during his senior year in high school, Willie (as Du Bois was then called) knew that his intellect would not prevent his having to work at menial jobs to support her. "But if his mother were to die," Lewis speculates, "then it surely followed that his life would make sense only if he repaid [*sic*] her sacrifice with extraordinary success" (52). Her death in the spring of 1885, the year after his graduation, opened the way for him to go to college: the townspeople of Great Barrington, Massachusetts, who had long marveled at his genius, took up a collection and sent him to Fisk University, thereby launching him in his career of racial uplift.

The circumstances of Du Bois's early life had to have produced his ambivalent feelings toward his mother, which would define the unique sexual constitution of his fantasmatic pattern for structuring his political attachments. Mary Silvina Burghardt Du Bois was a member of an old Great Barrington black family that, Du Bois claimed, could trace its freedom back to the late eighteenth century. Such a background allowed Du Bois to aggrandize his maternal family as "part of a great clan" (Lewis, *W. E. B. Du Bois,* 19). Yet his mother's sexual transgression, which produced an illegitimate son five years before Du Bois's birth, embarrassed the youngster and made him silently question the legitimacy of his own birth.[24] In addition, his mother's identity as a poor dark-skinned woman, more so than his mulatto father of middle-class origins, placed Du Bois decidedly behind what he would later call the "veil" of racial difference, for his father's absence exacerbated Du Bois's insecurity, poverty, and humiliating confrontations with racial prejudice. Young Du Bois blamed his mother for his father's absence. The youngster believed that "she had deserted his father and was largely responsible for their demeaning material predicament in Great Barrington" (Lewis, *W. E. B. Du Bois,* 52). Thus, the pain caused by the absent father, "the stigma of bastardy" (already associated with his half-brother and, therefore, with himself as well), his mother's extreme poverty, and subjugation to racial prejudice had to have made his efforts to idealize his mother extremely conflicted (Lewis, *W. E. B. Du Bois,* 27; Allison Davis, *Love,* 107). Under these circumstances, we can readily imagine this very bright, ambitious, and somewhat egotistical youngster wishing for a different mother even while deeply loving the one he had.

While sociologist Allison Davis[25] does not actually use the word "hatred" to describe Du Bois's contradictory feelings for his mother, Davis suggests that Du Bois resented his mother and hid this from himself with "compensatory fantasies" (*Love*, 112). According to Davis, "Du Bois was relieved when his mother suddenly died. He felt 'free.'" She had driven him to excel. Before her death, Davis continues, Du Bois had "felt sorry" for his mother. He had "nursed her and he expressed his concern and solicitude for her. But these [responses] are not love. In fact, they might have been defensive expressions of guilt from resenting her for having disgraced him" (*Love*, 116). . . . Davis's speculation [leads] to [the] suggest[ion] that when her death made it possible for Du Bois to accomplish what her continued existence could not, all of his prior guilty wishes to be rid of her assailed him and probably complicated his already ambivalent feelings for her. . . . Du Bois [may have] unconsciously transformed his guilty grief into a lifelong process of mourning and reparation in the only emotional economy that had given him sustained pleasure—the satisfaction of work. Du Bois's labor for the race would be like an act of reparation to his internalized, idealized mother and to his heroic image of himself. His writings would unconsciously inscribe his devotion to the memory of his mother and repair his assaulted ego. For these reasons his energy for accomplishment was virtually inexhaustible.

Du Bois's figurative "veil" of color is especially provocative in light of . . . [the] extension of Davis's discussion of Du Bois's "compensatory fantasies" (*Love*, 112). By associating Davis's observations with what Mary Ann Doane calls "the iconography of the veil," we can understand Du Bois's veil as an overdetermined symbol for the lost mother, the racial and sexual differences she embodies, and his ambivalence toward her.[26] For Du Bois, the veil locates an arbitrary and, indeed, diaphanous social barrier that represents the trivial basis of racial hierarchies. Hence, the veil of racial difference "acts as a trope that allows one [in this case Du Bois] to evade the superficial, to complicate the surface by disallowing its self-sufficiency," and to make skin color into "a secondary or surplus surface," to borrow

Doane's words (*Femmes,* 55–56). Du Bois's veil also acts as a trope of ambivalent feelings for the lost mother because the veil "incarnates contradictory desires" to see and not to see her racial and sexual difference (Doane, *Femmes,* 54). Thus, Du Bois's veil marks a contested site where conscious, secondary, social ambition is superimposed upon the primary desire for the mother. The veil then consolidates the libidinal economies of desire and freedom by conceptualizing the pleasure of both, lifting the racial obstruction that made Du Bois see himself as a social problem and lowering the blind that shields him from his guilty feelings about the lost mother. In representing race and filial desire, the veil locates a symbolic embodiment, indeed a fetishistic form of "control over what might otherwise be terrifying ambiguities."[27]

*Dark Princess* lavishly inscribes the lost mother's absence as presence and eroticizes the site of racial difference. For these reasons, I suspect, this novel delighted Du Bois but estranged his critics. They identified an "unwholesome sanity" and "poisonous power" in the novel (Redding, *To Make,* 8), undoubtedly ensuing from the collapse of its exorbitant eroticism into maternal allusions. As a result, they were unable to appreciate the novel's attempt to bond "sentimental melodrama" and "poetic intensity" with Du Bois's political goals ("Day Letters" and "Throb of Dark Drums").

My objective is not to be an apologist for *Dark Princess.* Neither is it my intention to psychoanalyze Du Bois, though as a work that undeniably appears to be an extensive undertaking in sexual sublimation, *Dark Princess* invites such an endeavor.[28] Rather, my objective is to demonstrate how psychoanalysis assists me in disclosing Du Bois's conscious superimposition of propaganda onto unconscious primary desire. For the pleasure of *Dark Princess* is not simply the product of an eroticized polemic; pleasure is also inscribed in the language of the text that reproduces desire and its gratification. My psychoanalytic approach thus means that rather than depreciating, disregarding, or disparaging *Dark Princess*'s implausible plot, messianic love story, maternal allusions, and intense eroticism, to name just a few of its amazing aspects, I regard them as manifestations, indeed signifiers of Du Bois's unconscious fantasmatic template that generates the novel's imaginary discourses. These discourses play out Du Bois's deep emotional story about primary attachment, loss, and reparation.

By regarding "the structure of literature," here *Dark Princess,* as similar to "the structure of mind"—not a specific mind, but what the translators of the *Standard Edition of the Complete Works of Sigmund Freud* call "the mental apparatus" or "the dynamic organization of the psyche," again to borrow the words of Peter Brooks—I hope to demonstrate that this novel possesses what could be called a psychic structure of subjectivity.[29] According to such a framework, the subjectivity of *Dark Princess* (like that of any novel) is structured by conscious, preconscious, and unconscious discourses of desire. By conscious discourses, I mean the explicit social discourses in the text. By the novel's unconscious, which I also call textual unconscious or unconscious textual desire, I mean prohibited infantile desire for primeval unity with the mother inscribed in the stylistic language and structural elements of the text.[30] Finally, by preconscious discourses, I mean those implicit (and often figurative) discourses that, unlike the deeply obscured discourses of the unconscious, are readily accessible by means of interpretation. Even though a novel's closure is both tenuous and arbitrary, the end nevertheless claims a "final plenitude of meanings" that ensues from Du Bois's and our own determination to make even fictive experience bear meaning (Brooks, *Reading,* 314, 323). Hence, *Dark Princess's* ending, . . . gratifies and terminates its conscious desire in agitation for racial justice and its unconscious desire in a fantasy for the lost mother. Because the novel dramatizes the protagonist's political development in what resembles a series of pre-oedipal and oedipal narratives, Freudian tenets about psychosexual development complement [this] Lacanian rhetorical analysis of the novel's subjectivity.

To psychoanalysis I add cultural criticism to determine the social currency of the novel's discourses about decor, landscape, and fashion that are a part of the novel's preconscious textual desire. Together these stages of the discussion explain why *Dark Princess* is a work of extraordinary passion and yet unconvincing as propaganda. The power of these discourses in *Dark Princess* make it a virtually unobstructed site for revealing Du Bois's fantasmatic pattern for inscribing unconscious desire that is better concealed but also operative in his more successful works, like *The Souls of Black Folk* and his first novel—*The Quest of the Silver Fleece* (1911). By analyzing *Dark Princess*'s unconscious and preconscious discourses, I hope to recuperate Du Bois's eroticized protocol of racial propaganda. I want to emphasize that the interplay between desire and race in *Dark Princess* is not simply a unique feature of this novel, but a fundamental principle of black textuality that we must appreciate in conjunction with conscious expressions of politicized social desire if we want to increase our general understanding of the signifying structures of black expressive cultures.

## *Eroticizing Propaganda in* Dark Princess

Du Bois clearly intended for *Dark Princess* to be a work of black heroic art and underscored that purpose by subtitling the work "a romance." The novel tells the story of "a creative spirit in [its] painful growth toward maturity and poetic power" by means of a struggle between good and evil, to borrow the words of M. H. Abrams.[31] The plot repeats "the familiar Romantic model of a self-formative educational journey, which moves through division, exile, and solitariness toward the goal of a recovered home and restored familial relationship" (225). Narrative resolution adheres to the romantic belief that love is "the only available solution to the problem of the good and evil of our mortal state" (305). Du Bois, of course, racializes this basic story of moral development in *Dark Princess* so as to construct family (re)formation as the means by which to unify the dark people of the world and to recover an apocalyptic kingdom on Earth as home. As this chapter's second epigraph, from the "Envoy" of *Dark Princess,* makes clear, Du Bois fabricates the novel out of a veritable Hegelian dialectic of fancy and fact, dream and reality, spirit and bone to reveal his deep and abiding faith in the providential nature of human history, a belief that his student years at Harvard and the University of Berlin had reinforced.[32]

As a late-nineteenth-century man educated to believe in divine providence and historical progress, the genre of romance gave Du Bois the means for adapting the Hegelian model of human progress to his propaganda. Hegel furnished Du Bois with a philosophical framework for understanding black people's oppression as a part of the workings of divine providence. According to this framework, human progress evolves "through the successive histories of six world historical peoples: Chinese, Indians, Persians (culminating with the Egyptians), Greeks, Romans, and Germans" (Williamson, *Crucible*, 404). To these nationalities, Du Bois added the American Negro as "a sort of seventh son, born with a veil and gifted with second-sight in this American world."[33] In this racialization of Hegel's model, Du Bois invested his own frustrated ambition to be "one of Hegel's world-historical-men, a dark Messiah" to redeem black America (Williamson, *Crucible*, 408).

Within *Dark Princess*, Du Bois transforms the Hegelian model of history into his passionate belief in the potential of racial propaganda to serve as the catalyst for the redemption of black people from racial oppression, and the reformation of capitalism. These two objectives fulfill the novel's conscious providential design. Thus "the concept of Providence," to borrow the words of Fredric Jameson, "provides [Du Bois with] an adequate theoretical mediation between the salvational logic of the romance narrative and the nascent sense of historicity imposed by the social dynamic of capitalism."[34] The providential nature of the romance thus not only allows Du Bois to explain the historical relationship between racist ideology and capitalist labor exploitation but also facilitates Du Bois's conscious endeavor to preserve his faith in the inevitability of racial justice.

Despite the heroic idealism of *Dark Princess*, we should not underestimate the sheer force of conviction necessary for Du Bois to maintain his activist position, for he was not a detached observer of this battle of "two warring ideals—an American, a Negro" (*Souls*, in Sundquist, *Oxford*, 102). He was one of its most valiant warriors. Nevertheless, he possessed not only this cultural duality but complex historical, professional, and personal identities as, respectively, a Victorian and a modern, a scientist and a poet, a pragmatist and a visionary. Allison Davis provides a provocative analysis of Du Bois's complex and divided personality. Davis explains that Du Bois

> realized early that his own emotions were ambivalent and that his identity was split with regard to "race." At times he was

ashamed of his color and his "race"; at other times he was proud of his "Negro blood" and aggressive in defense of the rights and abilities of his "people." In his books, he is pulled apart before our very eyes, like a man twisted on a rack. (*Love*, 119–20)[35]

Davis contends that white America's repeated refusal to recognize Du Bois's superior ability, training,[36] and herculean effort, and black America's failure to grant him its steadfast support, accentuated his already deeply conflicted personality. Davis further explains that Du Bois was "vain but shy, pompous but uncertain of himself, defiant but anxious to be accepted. Ambitious to lead," Davis adds, "he was essentially retiring and withdrawn. Longing to be admired and worshipped, he often was rude and scornful" (*Love*, 146). Arnold Rampersad provides a similar analysis of the powerful but conflicted sides of Du Bois's character in *The Art and the Imagination of W. E. B. Du Bois*. According to Rampersad, Du Bois was partly the empirical, practical, and tough-minded proletarian who compiled and interpreted evidence on the material conditions of black Americans. He was also the romantic, idealistic, imaginative, high-strung aristocrat who marked his writings with mythic longing and messianic prophesy. Du Bois's personality, as Davis and Rampersad explain, reveals contradictory motivations and their effects. *Dark Princess* novelizes these contradictions by relying on his penchant for combining romantic conventions with activist prose.

Such a venture in *Dark Princess* was not new for Du Bois, for he had also projected the duality of his character onto the coprotagonists—Blessed (Bles) Alwyn and Zora Cresswell—of his first novel, *The Quest of the Silver Fleece*, published in 1911. However, Matthew Townes, the protagonist of *Dark Princess*, is the most comprehensive representation of Du Bois's complex temperament, and this novel presents the most intense rendition of his fantasmatic equation for eroticized social activism. The Hegelian synthesis provided Du Bois with a model to attempt to unite not only these disparate parts of his personality but his own social alienation—his "double consciousness"—as well. This perspective also facilitated his effort to argue that black people have an essential role in human destiny and to define an important one for himself in this process.[37]

No incident in *Dark Princess* departs more extravagantly from formulating a pragmatic response to racism than the spectacular messianic masque that closes the work. This scene, reminiscent of the Magi's adoration of the Christ child, salutes the infant son of Matthew and Kautilya and consecrates the novel's conviction in its prophetic racial mission:

> There fell a silence, and then out of the gloom of the wood moved a pageant. A score of men clothed in white with shining swords walked slowly forward a space, and from their midst came three old men: one black and shaven and magnificent in raiment; one yellow and turbaned, with a white beard that swept his burning flesh; and the last naked save for a scarf about his loins. . . . They gave rice to Matthew and Kautilya. . . . Then the Brahmin took the baby from his grandmother and wound a silken turban on its little protesting head. . . . Slowly Kautilya stepped forward and turned her face eastward. She raised her son toward heaven and cried:

> "Brahma, Vishnu, and Siva! Lords of Sky and Light and Love! Receive from me, daughter of my fathers back to the hundredth name, his Majesty, Madhu Chandragupta Singh, by the will of God, of Bwodpur and Maharajah-dhiraja of Sindrabad."
> Then from the forest, with faint and silver applause of trumpets:
> "King of the Snows of Gaurisankar!"
> "Protector of Ganga the Holy!"
> "Incarnate Son of the Buddha!"
> "Grand Mughal of Utter India!"
> "Messenger and Messiah to all the Darker Worlds!"[38]

This scene is a grandiose repetition of Du Bois's prophetic aspirations and wistful yearning for his infant son Burghardt, eulogized in "The Passing of the First Born" in *The Souls of Black Folk* (1903). Here, the narrator

> mused above [Burghardt's] little white bed; saw the strength of my own arm stretched onward through the ages through the

newer strength of his; saw the dream of my black fathers stagger a step onward in the wild phantasm of the world; heard in his baby voice the voice of the Prophet that was to rise within the Veil. (Sundquist, *Oxford*, 209)

Whereas the narrator of *The Souls of Black Folk* is the lone listener to the "baby voice [that was to be] the voice of the Prophet," the narrator of *Dark Princess* assembles a majestic audience for the later infant that obliterates this novel's fragile construction of social realism. No wonder Du Bois's readers have failed to appreciate the novel's polemical message, for it is effaced by the spectacular masque at the novel's ending, a masque also reminiscent of the grand finale of Du Bois's pageant *The Star of Ethiopia*.

Like *The Star of Ethiopia*, which was staged before 35,000 people in New York, Washington, and Philadelphia in 1915 and 1916,[39] the masque at the end of *Dark Princess* opts for fancy rather than fact. The spectacle of pageantry seems a curious choice for a man whose prodigious scholarship was devoted to scrupulous factual detail, yet it is remarkably consistent with the pronouncement in "The Criteria of Negro Art" that equates propaganda and eroticism. For the closing spectacles of the pageant and the novel are manifestations of Du Bois's fantasmatic template and thus reflect Du Bois's deep and steadfast devotion to the transformative power of the romantic imagination.

*Dark Princess* is set during the middle years of the 1920s and begins with racism frustrating Matthew Townes's dream to be an obstetrician. No longer believing that hard work and talent will enable him to achieve his ambition, Matthew leaves New York for life as an exile abroad. While in Berlin, he forestalls a white man's sexual insult of a woman of color, whom he learns is Princess Kautilya of India.[40] She is a member of an international team of dark-skinned people who are forming an organization to resist Western imperialism. Matthew immediately falls in love with the beautiful princess, who charges him, much like a knight, with the task of providing her with information in order to determine whether black Americans should be included in this organization. Kautilya departs, presumably for India, and Matthew returns to the United States and secures a job as a railway porter in order to survey the social progress of African Americans for the princess. Upon completion of this task, he is unable to contact her. When a porter is lynched, Matthew plans a porter strike to relieve his frustration, but it is unsuccessful. In another attempt to express his outrage, Matthew joins a suicidal plot to dynamite the train transporting the top officials of the Ku Klux Klan, on which he is assigned to work. When he learns that Kautilya is also on the train, he prevents the train's destruction but refuses to disclose his knowledge of the conspiracy. Kautilya tries to protect him from prosecution by telling the authorities that she informed him of the scheme, but to no avail. He is sentenced to prison for ten years, and she is deported.

Matthew's conviction attracts the attention of Sara Andrews, the secretary to a leading black politician of Chicago, the Honorable Sammy Smith (who is reminiscent of Oscar De Priest). Through a complicated exchange, they secure Matthew's speedy release from prison and make him into a local hero. Matthew deplores leading a life of unscrupulous political exchanges, but he reluctantly participates, believing that he can effect meaningful social change as an elected public servant. It is not long before Matthew marries Sara, and she manages his campaign for state legislature. After their marriage, though, he learns that her efficiency is the product of a life devoid of sexual passion. Rather than sharing the tastefully decorated house Sara has purchased for them, Matthew spends more and more time in the apartment of his bachelor days.

At the moment of his nomination to Congress, Kautilya miraculously reappears to rescue Matthew from political corruption. He abandons Sara. After Matthew and Kautilya live together for several weeks, they realize they must return to their original quest for racial justice. She departs, presumably for India. Sara sues Matthew for a divorce, and he seeks penance for his passionate excesses in the arduous labor of digging a tunnel for the new subway. However, Kautilya has not returned to India. She has gone to visit Matthew's mother on her Virginia farm. Once before, when Kautilya was deported, she returned illegally to visit Matthew's mother in order to learn about the nobility of his people. At the end of the novel Kautilya again rescues Matthew. She summons him to join her at the Virginia farm, where, after an extraordinary flight and train ride, he finds that Kautilya has given birth to his son, who is heir to her throne. In the masque, described earlier, he is proclaimed the "Messenger and Messiah to all the Darker Worlds" (*Dark Princess*, 311).

Several plots of frustration motivate the plot. The first is racial, and it concerns Matthew's expulsion from medical school. He must leave the University of Manhattan because he cannot register for his third-year classes in obstetrical medicine. Despite his high class rank and honors, the school will not permit him to fulfill its clinical requirement by delivering white women's babies, a prohibition hurled at Matthew in the dean's insulting words: "Do you think white women patients are going to have a nigger doctor delivering their babies?" (*Dark Princess*, 4). The novel recalls this story five times: three times in the early pages of Part 1, once in Part 2, and again in Part 4. This repetition not only underscores the severity of the racist assault on Matthew but also motivates the entire story by identifying the principal sites of Matthew's trauma and textual desire.[41] Thus, each instance of his medical school history indicates the resurgence of a conflict with prohibition consciously depicted as racism and figured, as I argue later, in the novel's textual unconscious as desire for the lost mother.

Freudian pre-oedipal and oedipal paradigms, respectively, for attachment and loss are very useful for analyzing Matthew's social aspirations and confrontations with racism and unconscious textual desire.[42] Much like the delight that Du Bois himself describes when he writes in *The Souls of Black Folk*, "I beat my mates at examination-time, or beat them at a foot-race, or even beat their stringy heads" (Sundquist, *Oxford*, 102), Matthew experiences hard-won pleasure at a northern white medical school, which supports his self-esteem. But his success comes to an abrupt end when the racist white patriarchy forbids his advancement. Racism thus presents an oedipalized assault on Matthew's ego, and he must find a way to obliterate this new threat (which Freud conceptualized as castration, the very punishment inflicted on black men who were accused of challenging racist hegemony during most of Du Bois's lifetime). What is important to see here is that the text amplifies Matthew's conscious awareness of his racial trauma with a corresponding, unconscious sexual trauma, symbolized by his aspiration to be an obstetrician.

The novel's choice of obstetrical medicine as the site for enforcing racist prohibition suggests unconscious textual desire. Given the pervasiveness of racism, Du Bois could have selected any number of situations to invoke racist proscription. But obstetrics here is particularly meaningful. By means of a displacement, the text inscribes Matthew's concealed fantasy about the mother behind his frustrated effort to enroll in a required course which dictates intimate contact with pregnant women. These women constitute an overdetermined symbol for the lost mother and a site of intense textual desire that magnify both incest and racial prohibitions. By making the women white, the text displaces the incest prohibition onto race and the specter of miscegenation. Under these circumstances Matthew's means for sublimating his primary desire—literally laying therapeutic hands on mothers—vanishes until he meets Kautilya, who is another displacement for the unobtainable mother. Prior to meeting Kautilya, though, Matthew attempts to escape the castrating effect of racism by seeking exile in Germany. The trip provides the text with another opportunity to inscribe the lost mother.

During the trans-Atlantic voyage, Matthew succumbs to the imaginary embrace of the ocean much like the infant in the arms of the omnipotent mother. Matthew is "soothed by the sea—the rhythm and song of the old, old sea. He slept and read and slept; stared at the water; lived his life again to its wild climax; put down repeatedly the cold, hard memory about the dean's insult; and drifting, slept again" (*Dark Princess*, 6). This episode has much in common with the pre-oedipal bond linking the omnipotent mother and child that Freud named the *oceanic feeling*.[43] However, Matthew's pre-oedipal merger is only temporary. Just as the ship must dock, Matthew, to remain a viable character, must recover his memory of racial trauma and reenter the oedipalized plot of desire for this story to preserve its polemical objective.

At the moment he again becomes aware of his racial frustration, Kautilya enters the story. The text exchanges one form of frustration for another as Matthew now experiences surging desire for the princess whom the text describes as a "wildly beautiful phantasy," a veritable reincarnation of Scheherazade of the legendary *Tales from the Thousand and One Nights* (*Dark Princess*, 8). When she enters the story, the pain of racism becomes contiguous with the agony of sexual longing as the text becomes hypnotized by desire.

The novel invigorates Kautilya's presence with erotic and political discourses. Her immediacy allows Matthew to reaffirm his racial longing for "that soft, brown world," a longing that the text constructs as a heterosexual fantasy incarnate, reminiscent of the *Crisis* cover mentioned earlier:

> First and above all came that sense of color: into this world of pale yellowish and pinkish parchment, that absence or negation of color, came, suddenly, a glow of golden brown skin . . . It was a living, glowing crimson, *veiled* beneath brown flesh. It called for no light and suffered no shadow, but glowed softly of its own inner radiance. *(Dark Princess*, 8; author's emphasis)

The text goes on to describe Kautilya as a "radiantly beautiful woman" who "was colored":

> There was a hint of something foreign and exotic in her simply *draped* gown of rich, creamlike silken stuff and in the graceful coil of her hand-fashioned turban. Her gloves were hung carelessly over her arm, and he caught a glimpse of slender-heeled slippers and sheer clinging hosiery. There was a flash of jewels on her hands and a murmur of beads in half-hidden necklaces. His young enthusiasm might overpaint and idealize her, but to the *dullest and the oldest* she was *beautiful, beautiful. (Dark Princess*, 8; author's emphasis)

Evidently, this portrait of Kautilya was especially gratifying for Du Bois, who seems to implicate himself directly in the idealization of Kautilya. Both the old and dull Du Bois and his young facsimile Matthew lavishly adore the radiantly lovely princess.

Kautilya is hardly a real woman to Matthew or to the reader. As "the high and beautiful lady whom he worshiped more and more," she is a feminized emblem for the superiority of colored people and thus an exalted symbolization of Du Bois's racial ideal (*Dark Princess*, 22).

However, this feminized emblem of racial loyalty fails to remain fully a political object but becomes instead an erotic object. With this transformation the novel imperils the possibility of sustaining practical propaganda. The danger becomes more pronounced when the eroticism inscribed in the settings, interior decor, and clothing amplifies Kautilya's sensuality. By the last part of the novel, what was eroticized propaganda is wholly narcissistic romance. The novel's association of Kautilya with both Titania of Shakespeare's *A Midsummer Night's Dream*, to whom Du Bois fondly dedicates *Dark Princess*, and with "her Mauve Majesty" of the "Envoy," to whom he appeals to endorse the novel's authority, makes Kautilya seem more a reflection of Du Bois's own erotic fixation than a political referent.

So compelling is the portrait of Kautilya that many of Du Bois's associates were prompted to speculate about the identity of the woman who may have served as the basis for her portrait. Herbert Aptheker refers to Du Bois's *Dusk of Dawn* and *Autobiography*, in which he writes about his enchantment at meeting a beautiful woman at Fisk (Introduction, 7). Mary White Ovington (a principal supporter of Du Bois and cofounder of the NAACP) suspects that Kautilya's inspiration was an Indian princess who attended the First Universal Races Congress in London in 1911 (Aptheker, 7). What is important to see is that Du Bois's creative writings—published and unpublished—reveal that he had long been enchanted with the idea of such a woman. She was the muse for Du Bois's racial strivings whom he envisioned as early as 1893 in his journal.

### Du Bois's Fantasmatic Pattern and Cognitive Model

On his twenty-fifth birthday, on February 23, 1893, as he reports in his journal, Du Bois consecrated his commitment to racial striving in a solitary ceremony with wine, candles, oil, and song. Alone in his room, he dedicated his library to his dead mother (Lewis, *W. E. B. Du Bois*, 134) and made a "sacrifice to the Zeitgeist" (Williamson, *Crucible*, 408). In that entry, which he entitles "Quarter-Centennial Celebration of My Life," Du Bois defines his racial commitment: "to make a name in science, to make a name in literature and thus to raise my race." "I rejoice as a strong man to win a race," he continues, "and

I am strong—is it egotism—is it assurance—or is it the silent call of the world spirit that makes me feel that I am royal and that beneath my sceptre a world of kings shall bow."[44] Such pronouncements and his wondering whether he was "a genius or a fool" (Papers, reel 88, frame 468) clearly cast him in a grandiose, indeed regal discourse.

This discourse identifies one of the great divides that Du Bois would struggle to traverse—the attempt to celebrate black folk in aristocratic terms. The fusion of the folk and the elite seems to be a defense for his own likely repressed feelings of class and caste inferiority. This journal entry also calls attention to another dilemma that would dominate Du Bois's critical vision, for in his writings and his life he would attempt to connect empiricism and romanticism. He would manage the alliance by invoking the Hegelian dialectic of synthesized opposition and by implicitly drawing on the cognitive equation between propaganda and eroticism.

Two journal entries, those of his twenty-fifth and twenty-sixth birthdays, manifest the imaginary products of Du Bois's fantasmatic pattern that cohere like a romantic narrative. In the former Du Bois writes,

> I will in this second quarter century of my life, enter the dark forest of the unknown world for which I have so many years served my apprenticeship. . . . I will seek till I find—and die. . . . What is life but life, after all? Its end is the greatest and fullest self—and this end is the Good: the Beautiful is its attribute—its soul, and Truth its being. . . . The greatest and fullest life is by definition beautiful, beautiful—beautiful as a dark passionate woman, beautiful as a golden-hearted school girl, beautiful as a grey haired hero. (Papers, reel 88, frames 469–70)

Like the extract from "The Criteria of Negro Art," this entry symbolizes racial politics as a chivalric adventure in a magic realm. His repetitive use of the word "beautiful" to describe Kautilya in *Dark Princess* reiterates the hyperbolic use of the expression "beautiful" in the description of "the dark passionate woman" in this journal entry. What Du Bois means by the "greatest and fullest life" becomes clearer in another journal entry, written on his twenty-sixth birthday, February 23, 1894. Here he writes that he spent this day "in my regular routine of work and musing." After outlining this day's itinerary, he continues, "I have finally proved to my entire satisfaction that my race forms but slight impediment between me and kindred souls. . . . Therefore I have gained for my life work new hope and zeal—the Negro people shall yet stand among the honored of the world" (Papers, reel 88, frame 490). The "greatest and the fullest life" of Du Bois's imagination is thus not constrained by race but elevated to the position of esteem by means of work, hope, and zeal among likeminded people. Such a life is not only intellectually satisfying to Du Bois but sexually gratifying as well, due to its association with the figures of the beautiful, dark, and passionate woman; the sincere, generous, and enlightened young girl; and the wise, aged hero.

What is important to observe here is that this string of images and prescriptions for the "greatest and fullest life" and "the greatest and fullest self" forms a signifying chain that intimates Du Bois's fantasmatic processes. This patterning process supplies the language for representing his racial activism. According to cognitive theorist George Lakoff, imaginative thought employs "metaphor, metonymy, and mental image to construct abstract thought—cognitive models—that exceeds the boundary of external reality."[45] When conscious, this process is an instance of what psychoanalysts term secondary image formation, and it is conditioned by "the nature of the organism doing the thinking—including the nature of its body, its interactions in its environment, its social character, and so on" (Lakoff, *Women*, xvi). Beneath conscious imaginative thought is the unconscious fantasmatic pattern. The woman, schoolgirl, and aged hero in Du Bois's entry are metonymies of beauty, generosity, and heroism—virtues that were integral both to Du Bois's self-conception and to his vision of his racial mission. Not only do these figures define his character; they also activate by eroticizing the racial discourses in Du Bois's fiction, verse, and pageants.

These secondary images signal the latent primary fixations of Du Bois's fantasmatic. Primary and secondary process thinking and image formation not only explain the symbolization of ideas but provide gratification as well. Psychoanalyst Mardi Jon Horowitz illustrates the effects of these mental processes by referring to Freud's "The Psychical Mechanism of Forgetfulness." Here Freud describes the infant's primary association of the breast with relief from hunger. Secondary thought processes occur when the infant is hungry and the breast does not immediately appear. Freud theorizes that the infant " 'hallucinates' the absent breast" by remembering it and the associated satisfaction.[46] Hence, the infant's fantasy of the breast allays hunger and frustration with the illusion of satisfaction.

The pattern of image formation in the 1894 journal entry has much in common with the gratifying hallucination of the hungry infant and for this reason is very provocative. This Freudian hypothesis suggests that throughout Du Bois's life, the image of a dark, beautiful woman partly allays the conflict he encounters with racism as well as the obstacle of his passionless first wife. This image then forms an essential element of Du Bois's image schemata and the basis of an important fantasy for him. Similarly, Matthew's encounter with the beautiful princess in *Dark Princess* allows him to invigorate his activist quest with phallic authority and permits him (and Du Bois as well) to suspend the fact that the effectiveness of his role as a race leader is in question. This displacement thus enables the novel to exchange the objective of successful racial agitation for sexual gratification.

The journal entries, then, do not simply represent the musings of an ambitious man about the work of racial uplift. When placed in context with a large body of Du Bois's early unpublished writings, many of which display a preoccupation with beautiful girls, especially princesses, jewels, locked jewel cases, stolen jewels, and railroad intrigue,[47] these entries further document an erotic fantasmatic that Freud made familiar as a standard sexual iconography. This fantasmatic schema regulated Du Bois's figurative and rhetorical repertoires, represented his social ambitions, and reproduced his personal desire.

Undoubtedly, the erotic image of Kautilya serves Du Bois's ideal personification of work and pleasure. If she were an isolated case, the erotic intensity of her character would make her a curiosity. However, facsimiles of Kautilya are plentiful in Du Bois's writings. For example, a similar beautiful, dark, and passionate ideal female appears as Zora

Cresswell in Du Bois's first novel, *The Quest of the Silver Fleece* (1911); the black heroine Ethiopia in his pageant *The Star of Ethiopia* (produced in 1915 and 1916; see Figure 5.2); the woman on the cover of the November *Crisis;* the "stunning-looking" brunette with "the most wonderful misty eyes" in "The Case" . . . (1907) . . . ; the woman with "great eyes all full and running over with tears" in an unpublished sketch "A Woman" . . . (1893) . . . ; and the princess in "The Princess of the Hither Isles," mentioned earlier. The recurrence of this figure in Du Bois's writing forms a personal "dialectic of style and content, sameness and difference" that coheres like an identity theme in a work of poetry or music.[48]

Such repetitions, in psychoanalysis, often indicate the site of repression for an original, idealized love object. As Freud explains in "On Narcissism," "[W]hen the original object of wishful impulses has been lost as a result of repression, it is frequently represented by an endless series of substitute objects, none of which, however, brings full satisfaction."[49] Whatever the explanation, some such theory of erotic displacement appears to characterize the narrative desire propelling the plot of *Dark Princess* forward in incidents that intimate Kautilya's symbolic identity as the specter of the lost mother, as the next section shall demonstrate. . . . [However], this section conclude[s] by exposing, first, a serious flaw in the characterization of this female ideal that symbolizes Du Bois's conception of heroic labor and, second, a discordance in his erotic symbolization of laboring for racial uplift.

Although Du Bois consciously racializes as dark the overdetermined feminine ideal in his creative writings, this intention is invaded by an effect of the white standard of female beauty.[50] For instance, Du Bois repeatedly describes *Quest's* Zora as dark, even as he makes her a "dull-golden" mulatta with "a great mass of immovable infinitely curled hair" in "thick twisted braids" rather than a typical black woman with negroid features.[51] Whether he was projecting a feminized version of his own hybridity or simply infatuated with light-skinned women is difficult to determine. The contradiction is clear. By using as uplift symbols ideal dark women who are, in actuality, golden-hued, he undermines his argument on black exceptionalism. Kautilya's portrait exacerbates this problem.

FIGURE 5.2 *Handbill for* The Star of Ethiopia. *Courtesy of Special Collections and Archives, W. E. B. Du Bois Library, University of Massachusetts, Amherst. Reprinted by permission of David Graham Du Bois.*

In *Black No More* (1931), George Schuyler satirized Du Bois for this inconsistency. Here Schuyler writes that Du Bois "deified the black woman but abstained from employing aught save octoroons."[52] Du Bois's preference for light-skinned women of the race is certainly not unique to him, for color prejudice in the black community has been as persistent as it has been controversial. The pervasiveness of this issue suggests that even as black Americans celebrate the physical and spiritual attributes of blackness (or what could be called a nascent black Symbolic), such celebrations are already unconsciously determined—indeed, subverted—by the white Symbolic. Despite the contradiction, this problematic love object symbolizes the imagined gratification of Du Bois's labors for racial uplift.

Indeed, Du Bois's dependency on this beloved object has much in common with Frantz Fanon's discussion of the black man's desire for the white woman in *Black Skin, White Masks*. Here the white woman becomes the signifier of racial equality for the black man because, as Fanon writes, "[b]y loving me she proves that I am worthy of white love. I am loved like a white man. I am a white man."[53] But in Du Bois's case, he abandons the white object of desire because white patriarchy uses perverse versions of this scenario to justify lynching. Yet Du Bois preserves a similar equation for racial equality by veiling the erotic object in color.

As early as 1894 Du Bois symbolically links erotic love and uplift work. In his journal entry of February 23, commemorating his twenty-sixth birthday, he associates his renewed zeal for his life's work with a romantic interlude during which, in his words, "a dear girl met and loved me" (Papers, reel 88, frame 490). To this female fantasy he attaches another about dedicated labor; thus, ideal work and ideal love become equivalent to "work and musing."[54] These identity themes and corresponding image schema (what I called a cognitive equation earlier) appear throughout Du Bois's writings and epitomize the politicized eroticism—or an eroticized politics—that energizes his quest for knowledge and social reform. As we will see, the balance between eroticism and politics in the image schema becomes destabilized in *Dark Princess*. While the tension between Matthew's political commitment and sexual desire is the source of power in the novel, the schema fails to make the eroticism serve the racial politics. As a result, the alignment between the "beautiful, beautiful" dark woman as the inspiration for racial propaganda splits off from the racial plot and becomes a full-fledged love story in its own right.

This misalignment is illustrate[d] by . . . Matthew's involvement in the train conspiracy, which he believes to be an appropriate expression of his racial outrage. However, the text does not represent this incident as radical protest but as a chivalric fantasy, again reminiscent of the tropes of valor inscribed in "The Criteria of Negro Art":

> Then again came sudden boundless exaltation. He was riding the wind of a golden morning, the sense of live, rising, leaping horseflesh between his knees, the rush of tempests through his hair, and the pounding of blood—the pounding and pounding of iron and blood as the train roared through the night. He felt his great soul burst in its bonds and his body rise in the stirrups as the Hounds of God screamed to the black and silver hills. In both scarred hands he seized his sword and lifted it to the circle of its swing. (*Dark Princess*, 88)

Full of the innuendo of sexual tumescence, the passage represents the attack rather than its motive or object. The reference to the "leaping horseflesh between [Matthew's] knees" and the personification of "the pounding and pounding of iron" of the train roaring "through the night" are standard Victorian icons for sexual desire moving to climax. These figurative representations call attention to an archaic euphemism—dying—for sexual climax, intimated in the extract. Hence the novel casts Matthew in the traditional chivalric pose as the valiant hero in a standardized ideational framework of sexual desire and consummation. This momentary fantasy of love and valor gratifies Matthew; however, it is at best only remotely associated with racial propaganda.

The text attempts to recover its racial plot by having Matthew attack the Klan, which is implicated in the porter's lynching. Matthew does not portray the Klan's heinous nature in either graphic detail or political terms; rather, the novel again resorts to romantic ideology. The appearance of the woman whom Matthew regards as his queen interrupts the fantasy of the charging black knight in a contest with the Klan and installs instead a tangible love story. Rather than expressing his racial commitment in terms of his devotion to this beautiful woman, at the midpoint of the novel Matthew collapses his commitment to her political ideal into his increasing erotic devotion to the woman. From there, the racial propaganda serves the novel's eroticism like metaphysical foreplay. Even when Kautilya is out of sight, she looms not only in Matthew's unconscious but in the unconscious and preconscious of the text.

## Dreaming of Kautilya

Kautilya is the ubiquitous dream of the text. It projects her much like the smiling face of the mother for whom the infant longs. For example, an oriental rug that Matthew places in one of his empty rooms alludes to Kautilya like a transitional maternal object for an infant. He sits before the rug for hours and dreams unconsciously of her presence: "The rug was marvelous. It burned him with its brilliance. It sang to his eyes and hands. It was yellow and green—it was thick and soft; but all this didn't tell the subtle charm of its weaving and shadows of coloring" (*Dark Princess,* 128). A second fantasy occurs while camping out en route to visit his mother. Imagining that he was "a boy again, with the world before him," Matthew "saw the sun rise, pale gold and crimson, over the eastern trees. . . . Beyond the frost, it lay magnificent—wonderful—beautiful—beautiful as one unforgettable face" (*Dark Princess,* 131).

The descriptions of the rug and sunrise are not simply ancillary textual features but discourses of displaced desire for Kautilya and ultimately the lost mother that cohere into powerful fantasies. They temporarily satisfy Matthew's repressed longing for Kautilya. These allusive, figurative projections partly form the preconscious of *Dark Princess,* which is recoverable because Western culture has taught us to associate landscapes and the interior decor of residential settings with the erotic female body.[55] Freud was the first to call our attention to such libidinal displacements, now recognized as sublimation. Thus, to write affectionately about such a setting is "to invest [it] with the ability to receive, give, or withhold love" (257). Du Bois drew on this pattern of erotic association to symbolize Matthew's unconscious desire for the princess and to inscribe latent maternal fantasies in the text of the novel.

The rug is an emphatic symbol for Kautilya; it is gorgeous, luminous, and sensual. Much like the infant in Freud's "Infantile Sexuality," . . . Matthew searches "for some pleasure which has already been experienced and is now remembered" (181). The rug links Matthew to gratifying memories of Kautilya, who, as we shall see, is increasingly associated with the primary object she displaces—the mother. This sublimated and regressive form of eroticism inspires an extensive illusion. For as he grows increasingly more sexually frustrated and emotionally disheartened, the text expands the compensatory fantasy by adding other maternal objects. For instance, an old chair provides Matthew with comfort and security, though he remains unconscious of the maternal associations that grant it the power to console him.

In the context of Freudian dream-work,[56] Matthew's problematic response to the sunrise fantasy is particularly meaningful. As he recalls his boyhood, the memory of "one unforgettable face," projected onto the sunrise, prompts him to leap "to the ground and clench his hand. A wave of red shame smothered his heart" (*Dark Princess*, 131). The text draws on the presumption that the face is Kautilya's, while simultaneously contesting that presumption with the inappropriateness of Matthew's shameful response. Matthew ought not feel guilty about his desire for this beautiful woman; nevertheless, the text is adamant. The intrusion of shame in Matthew's daydream associates Kautilya with the mother of the oedipal plot.

## Embracing Prohibited Desire

The dilemma that Matthew attempts to resolve by projecting his desire onto Sara is the same struggle with desire he has repeatedly fought throughout the novel in a variety of ways but failed to master: how to embrace the prohibited object of desire by means of displacement, regardless of whether the object is racial equality or the body of a proscribed woman. In fact, *Dark Princess* constructs gratification by superimposing the racial object onto the sexual object. As a result, the censors of white hegemony and the incest taboo become mutually signifying. When the text is unable to overcome one or the other and obtain the object, it relies on passive and regressive forms of satisfaction by depicting Matthew in the act of constructing compensatory infantile fantasies of transitional maternal objects.

The text thus structures its desire in the dynamics of Matthew's pursuit of Kautilya and characterizes his devotion to her in both a preoedipalized plot of infantile fusion with the mother and an oedipalized racial contest for freedom, symbolized as female, between the black son and Western, white patriarchy. Hence, desire in *Dark Princess* as well as Matthew's subjectivity coheres around his aggressive drive to dedicate, indeed, attach himself to Kautilya and the text's representations of this desire by means of figurative maternal displacements.

One key incident that relies on pre-oedipal imagery follows Matthew's initial retreat from Sara. He returns to his apartment, where he sits for hours in his big, old, shabby armchair. It puts "its old worn arms so sympathetically about him" (*Dark Princess,* 192). Here Matthew surrenders to an infantile fantasy of maternal holding. However, as desire develops in the text, it supplants the pre-oedipal fantasies with oedipal ones. Matthew's compulsion to purchase "a Turkish rug for the bedroom—a silken thing of dark, soft, warm coloring"—signals the onset of another oedipal allusion. When he got the rug to his apartment, he "threw it before his old bed and let it vie with the dusky gold of its Chinese mate" (*Dark Princess,* 193). Much like the Freudian primal scene in which the son imagines the site of his own conception and experiences the desire to displace the father, the text here casts Matthew as the voyeur of a figurative sexual embrace that signals oedipal gratification while preserving the pre-oedipal longing for holding. The text will eventually consolidate its pre-oedipal and oedipal illusions in Kautilya, who becomes an idealized reflection but not embodiment of the lost mother. I refer to this consolidation with the term "(m)other." I will also explain the significance of this distinction at the end of this essay. For the time being, though, what is important to see is that Matthew has transformed his apartment into a play space for his pre-oedipal and oedipal fantasies. They foreshadow Kautilya's return.

When Kautilya reappears, the text undermines its tenuous hold on the reality principle by resorting to melodrama to describe this woman, who has deliberately subjected herself to suffering as reparation for her ignorance of the history of Matthew's people. The text now sheds the golden gossamer of color that illuminated Kautilya in the first half of the novel:

> A dark figure stood by the table. An old dung-colored cloak flowed down upon her, and a veil lay across her head. Her thin dark hands, now bare and almost clawlike, gripped each other. They were colored hands. . . . And she came like a soft mist, *unveiled* and *uncloaked* before him. Always she seemed to come thus suddenly into his life. . . . [S]he was different, yet every difference emphasized something eternally marvelous. Her hair was cut short. . . . [H]er hands, hard, wore no jewels, but were calloused, with broken nails. The small soft beauty of her face had become stronger and set in still lines. Only in the steadfast glory of her eyes showed unchanged the Princess. (*Dark Princess*, 208–9)

Kautilya's noble endeavor to learn the effects of labor exploitation has transformed her into the emphatically dark—black—woman (Du Bois used the word "colored," which during the 1920s meant Negro). With her clawlike, calloused hands and wrinkled face, Kautilya's appearance has much in common with that of an old, poor, black woman.

The passage's references to veiling and unveiling and cloaking and uncloaking call attention to Kautilya's bodily representation of gratified latent desire and suggest another referent for Du Bois's metaphorical veil of race. At this point in the story, Matthew no longer needs to rely on thinly veiled and overdetermined pre-oedipal and oedipal fantasies; Kautilya now clearly reflects the beloved (m)other. In grateful recognition, "[h]e lifted his hands to heaven, stretched them to touch the width of the world, and swept her into his tight embrace" (*Dark Princess*, 209). The novel labels her rescue of Matthew from political corruption a "Benediction": she exhorts, "I have sought you, man of God, in the depths of hell, to bring your dead faith back to the stars." While the text insists that for Matthew "[t]he world was one woman and one cause" (*Dark Princess*, 210), the reader readily discerns the woman, but the cause has become rather obscure.

The text depicts the sexual consummation of Matthew's desire as an act of artistic expression, a sacrament of shared intimacy and self-revelation. Sex for Matthew and Kautilya is transfigured as a spiritual act. Theirs is true love—"spiritual, constant and altruistic, not sensual, short-lived and egoistic."[57] The apartment, which had been a kind of womb for the vulnerable Matthew, now becomes a love nest, filled with erotic stimulants of perfumes, seductive music, and delicious foods. Moreover, this episode fuses pre-oedipal and oedipal gratification, as Matthew possesses the beloved (m)other. However, his possession of her at this point in the story is not permanent.

When Kautilya departs to resume her work for racial equality, Matthew suffers the loss of his (m)other fantasy. He tries to give meaning to his life by atoning for his activist failures and sexual indulgence. The form of reparation he chooses repeats the stages in the story when he retreats in exile and is sentenced to ten years of hard labor. He now joins a subway crew whose job is to dig subway tunnels, an activity packed with allusion to the pre-oedipal desire to return to the womb. This incident repeats not only the regression of Matthew's imprisonment but that of the ocean voyage as well. Without Kautilya, Matthew feels dead. He digs beyond the point of exhaustion and "sleep[s] like death" (Dark Princess, 271).

And again Kautilya rescues him from an ineffective struggle to invest his life with meaning. In an urgent summons she commands that he join her at his mother's farm. In a personal letter accompanying the summons, she tells him as well that the

> Great Central Committee of Yellow, Brown, and Black is finally to meet. You are a member. The High Command is to be chosen. Ten years of preparation are set. Ten more years of final planning, and then five years of intensive struggle. In 1952, the Dark World goes free—whether in Peace and fostering Friendship with all men, or in blood and Storm—it is for Them—the Pale Masters of today to say. (Dark Princess, 296–97)

After an extraordinary flight and train ride, full of allusions to death and rebirth, Matthew reaches his mother's farm to find that Kautilya has delivered his son, who, as the new Maharajah, has rescued her from the life of a royal consort. The child, whom Kautilya has named "Madhu" (or "Matthew" in her language), is heir to her throne (*Dark Princess*, 308). After a brief wedding ceremony, the narrative explodes into the messianic masque of black supremacy discussed earlier.

## *Erotic Fantasy or Racial Propaganda in* Dark Princess *and Du Bois's* Quest of the Silver Fleece

The pageantry at the end of *Dark Princess* is both a masque and a mask of optimism. However, this apocalyptic ending is not so wholly hopeful as Arnold Rampersad suggests. He regards this epic ending as an expression of Du Bois's "ecstatic optimism," "the richest dividend of his awakened political consciousness." "Applied to his writing," Rampersad continues, "this optimism was compounded by his nostalgia for a vanished innocence within both a mythic Africa and humanity as a whole, by his sense of the history of the world as the history of progress" (Rampersad, [1976],"W. E. B. Du Bois," 70). What Rampersad has perceived as Du Bois's "ecstatic optimism" had to have been the resolve of his extraordinary willpower and undoubtedly the pleasurable effect of the fantasies about the lost mother, for his optimism could not have existed apart from his growing despair about the intractable color line. *Dark Princess*'s pageantry implores the reader to keep the faith, not by pragmatically addressing the race problem, but by escaping it with divine approbation, messianic proclamation, and erotic fantasy.

The novel's tactic of masking realism with pageantry is remarkably reminiscent of the supernatural setting that closes Pauline Hopkins's serial novel *Of One Blood; Or, the Hidden Self* (1902–1903). Here the black hero, conspicuously modeled on Du Bois, is anointed king of a legendary, underground African city, where he and his queen reside, waiting for God to reveal His resolution to the race conflict; for "none save Omnipotence can solve the problem." These lines conclude the story:

To our human intelligence these truths depicted in the feeble work may seem terrible—even horrible. But who shall judge the handiwork of God, the Great Craftsman! Caste prejudice, race pride, boundless wealth, scintillating intellects refined by all the arts of the intellectual world, are but puppets in His hand, for His promises stand, and He will prove His words, "Of one blood have I made all races of men."[58]

*Dark Princess* relies on similar displacements of time, place, and agency. As in *Of One Blood,* the resolution of the race problem in *Dark Princess* lies in the providential future, indeed, twenty-five years after the novel's setting, in 1952. But unlike Hopkins, Du Bois holds tenuously to human rather than divine agency. Instead of awaiting for Omnipotence to solve the race problem, Du Bois places that responsibility on a royal infant who claims divinity through Kautilya's lineage, an infant who is both a tribute to Du Bois's own dead son Burghardt and a projection of his own egotistical desire, inscribed in the journal entry of his twenty-fifth birthday.

The endings to *Of One Blood* and *Dark Princess* are similar because they originate in their authors' messianic racial outlook, a perspective that allowed them both to hold onto optimism even though it was tainted with continued disappointment. For during the last two decades of the nineteenth century and the first two decades of the twentieth, Hopkins and Du Bois, along with their black contemporaries, witnessed a severe re-entrenchment of racism that Rayford W. Logan called the "Dark Ages of recent American history."[59] By the onset of the 1920s the racial climate remained essentially unchanged despite the heroic efforts of legions of "race" men and women, including the monumental accomplishment of Du Bois himself, who was in his fifties. Resolving the problem of the color line no doubt seemed to defy human effort. Under these circumstances, it is not surprising that *Dark Princess,* like *Of One Blood,* maintains racial optimism by projecting it onto an apocalyptic tradition. While *Dark Princess,* unlike the earlier work, does not wholly subscribe to the existence of God, it does appeal to the ennobling potential of love, ethical conduct, and the virtues of labor, as evident in the novel's credo: "God is Love and Work is His Prophet" (*Dark Princess,* 279).

Du Bois's conviction in the efficacy of education, work, and organized protest is decidedly unconvincing in *Dark Princess.* While

Du Bois endorses this conviction in the novel by having Matthew make similar pronouncements, he abandons his education and fails to become involved in meaningful work or effective racial protest. This failure suggests that Du Bois himself might have been questioning the efficacy of such effort.

By contrast, his first novel, *The Quest of the Silver Fleece*, which appeared in 1911, is a more convincing work of propaganda. This novel appeared when Du Bois was also more secure in his role as race leader and thus more hopeful about the rational appeal of propaganda to mitigate the effects of racism. *Quest*, then, is a work more of reason than of passion. It focuses on the material consequences of slavery in the lives of black and white people in the context of the political economy of the cotton industry at the turn of the twentieth century. As the title suggests, the novel is a romantic, indeed, heroic quest for social justice. Despite the epic overlay, though, *Quest* is primarily a novel of social realism, grounded in the economic circumstances of black rural laborers, whose fate the central characters Zora Cresswell and Bles Alwyn share. Rather than escaping into an apocalyptic finale, they face the practical realities of achieving an educated and self-sufficient black populace in the face of severe racist oppression.

In sharp contrast, *Dark Princess* is a flight into fancy, as the novel's "Envoy" clearly indicates. *Dark Princess* turns from social realism to romance, from community enthusiasm to individual desire, from broad political objectives to narcissistic gratification. The novel's credo—"God is Love and Work is His Prophet" (*Dark Princess*, 279)—is more candid than even Du Bois may have suspected, for the controlling force in this text is not reason, God, or activist labor but unquestionably erotic desire. While Du Bois explicitly states that *Dark Princess* is a romance with the "deeper aim" of explaining the "difficulties and realities of race prejudices upon many sorts of people—ambitious black American youth, educated Asiatics, selfish colored politicians, ambitious self-seekers of all races,"[60] the novel does not fulfill that aim. Rather, it fulfills an even more essential but personal need, demand, and desire that a comparison of *Quest* and *Dark Princess* makes evident.

When these novels are placed side by side, they reveal very different textual intentions determined by their conscious and unconscious discourses of desire. *Quest* looks outward to social reform. The gratification of Zora and Bles's desire involves black community development as well as personal sexual pleasure. The postscript of *Quest* emphasizes the social perspective and entreats us to "Lay not these words aside for a moment's phantasy, but lift up thine eyes upon the Horror in this land;—the maiming and mocking and murdering of my people, and the prisonment of their souls" (*Quest*, 434). This appeal is reminiscent of the social mission to which Du Bois dedicates his life in the journal entry written on his twenty-fifth birthday. What is important is that *Quest* depicts racial activism by relying on the same figurative elements that appear in this journal entry. By abridging it somewhat, I can emphasize Du Bois's commitment: "I will in this second quarter century of my life . . . seek . . . the greatest and fullest self—and this end is the Good: the Beautiful is its attribute—its soul, and Truth its being. . . . The greatest and fullest life is by definition beautiful, beautiful— beautiful as a dark passionate woman" (Papers, reel 88, frames 469–70). *Quest* plots a story about committed self-development by repeating the scenario of the journal entry. Such a life, to paraphrase the entry, is as good and as beautiful as a beautiful, dark passionate woman. The social and erotic discourses cohere in the extract and in *Quest*. Thus, when the novel ends by imploring us to work together for social change, it retains a social obligation by projecting its message outward to the audience. Our charge is to duplicate the commitment of Zora and Bles, one sanctified by marriage. Moreover, this novel plots realistic strategies for that undertaking, the manipulated ending notwithstanding.

By contrast, the social (conscious) and erotic (partly unconscious) discourses do not cohere in *Dark Princess*. In fact, the latter undermines the novel's social objectives. The conscious narrative claims that Matthew is a proponent of racial activism, yet he is completely ineffective in this regard. His ambitions to be a doctor, an activist, and a politician are all ultimately supplanted by his desire for Kautilya. For these reasons, eroticism in *Dark Princess* dominates the site occupied by the reformist agenda in *Quest*. Work is *Quest*'s aspiration. Love—indeed, sexual coupling—is the ambition of *Dark Princess*. To put it another way, Matthew and Kautilya (pro)create a son who is yet another displacement for racial justice. Thus, the largely realistic racial argument that controls *Quest* becomes a fantastic, regal romance in *Dark Princess*. The conscious plot of propaganda in *Quest* shatters in *Dark Princess*, leaving the fragmented discourse little recourse but to regress into messianic pageantry.

Du Bois undoubtedly believed that the genre of romance could facilitate the expression of the propaganda in both novels. But in *Dark Princess*, the ideal object of the romantic Quest is eroticism instead of racial justice. The erotic, as Audre Lorde has convincingly argued in "The Uses of the Erotic," can provide the energy to pursue political change. And Du Bois no doubt believed he was tapping into that energy source with the question that concludes the novel in the "Envoy": "Which is really Truth—Fact or Fancy? the Dream of the Spirit or the Pain of the Bone?" This question invokes the novel's dedication to Du Bois's queen of fancy—Titania XXVII—and endorses what he evidently believed was the fine line between reality and providential history. However, in order for eroticism to fuel political change it must remain sublimated (or subsumed) within social activism. If the eroticism does not remain submerged within the political objective, its drive for pleasure becomes overly personalized, and its preoccupation with individual gratification subverts the collective goal. This is precisely what happens in *Dark Princess*. As a result, the novel's closing question about truth seems more the product of Du Bois's identification with Matthew's desire than with his identification with the novel's promotion of racial propaganda. *Dark Princess* more emphatically symbolizes the desire for a fulfilling, conjugal relationship and a son—two goals that in 1928 still eluded Du Bois—than for meeting the demands of political leadership. Moreover, the infant son in *Dark Princess* defines Kautilya's role as mother and thereby appeases the threat of female agency. As father and husband, Matthew holds the reins of power until his messianic infant son is a man.

The closing question of *Dark Princess*'s "Envoy"—"Which is really Truth—Fact or Fancy? the Dream of the Spirit or the Pain of the Bone?"—seems to pertain to Du Bois's own psychological reality at the time of the novel's creation, while the truthfulness of *Quest* pertains to the historical circumstances of the real people whom the characters represent. Although we may quarrel with the bequest that sustains the optimistic ending in *Quest*, this miraculous event does not preclude a realistic program of social activism. Neither does it prophesy the eradication of racism. The fanciful ending of *Quest* seems merely to be a modest concession to optimism. By contrast, the entire story of *Dark Princess* arises from fancy—"the Dream of the Spirit." And the fantasy interrupts rather than resolves the social issues with the unrealistic demand of deferral. The novel is thus suspended between a call to action and futility, between compromised ambition and ideal aspiration, between collective politics and personal desire. The fantasy accentuates rather than conceals the fact that *Dark Princess* is weighed down in the morass of racial despair that only the hiatus of pageantry can lift.

While the novel's message lies in Du Bois's insightful observations about the effects of white supremacy on people of color, its plot seems less concerned with fashioning social reform than with painting an idealized portrait of a love object in Kautilya. This character carries the burden of the novel's mythic glorification of peoples of color, a veneration that Edward Said might have called counter-Orientalism.[61] Kautilya and the dark-skinned members of her organization seek "to discover among them the genius, gift, and ability in far larger number than among the privileged and ruling classes" (*Dark Princess*, 225). That peoples of color possess such nobility (although he specifically meant the elite among them) is what Du Bois regarded as "essential and true," in Arnold Rampersad's words. According to Du Bois, such people were destined to assert their superiority. He maintained this viewpoint not only in *Dark Princess* but in all of his writings by consistently exposing the fallacious basis of white supremacy. However, rather than dismantling the ideologies of white supremacy, Du Bois inverts them to proclaim the dark "other" as the superior and foreordained leader. He clearly articulates this viewpoint in the "Credo" of *Darkwater* (1920): "the beauty of [the Negro's] genius, the sweetness of [his] soul, and [his] strength . . . shall yet inherit this turbulent earth" (3). This prophetic premise literally constructs part of the pleasure in *Dark Princess* by imagining the promise fulfilled in the birth of the messianic son. But most of the pleasure in this text is decidedly and distinctly erotic, even though Du Bois evidently believed or wanted to believe it was political.

While Du Bois took great pleasure in *Dark Princess,* his first readers, . . . did not. Like Kautilya's messenger, they perceived the novel to be a conflict "[b]etween self-indulgent phantasy and the salvation" of dark peoples (*Dark Princess,* 299). . . . [One] can trace their displeasure to a number of contradictory positions that the novel attempts to hold. First, it inscribes class ambivalence by appealing to the solidarity of the peoples of color with bourgeois and aristocratic leadership. Second, the novel attempts to erect black superiority while also venerating elite European art and music. Third, Du Bois's glorification of blackness is compromised by his enraptured depiction of the golden-skinned princess as the novel's ideal love object. Although the novel tries to represent all those who were not white by means of the sensuous hue of the dark princess, the polarized U.S. black/white racial discourse does not accommodate this conflation. Instead, the golden-hued princess, like Zora's mulatta background in *Quest,* endorses racial hybridity rather than blackness. This color dilemma is exacerbated by the choice of romance to structure the social message of *Dark Princess,* for implicit in romance is the ideological imperative of the status quo rather than its reformation. As Fredric Jameson has explained, the romance structure only substitutes an "enchanted space" of privilege for the "transformational scene" of the conflict ("Magical Narratives," 149). In this context the magical account and the Orientalized veiling of the dark princess are ultimately inhospitable to the novel's propagandist intent.

To be successful, to paraphrase Freud, a work must largely fuse its intellectual content and its "emotional attitude" or "mental constellation."[62] If a work achieves power, "it can only be the artist's intention, insofar as he has succeeded in expressing it in his work and in conveying it to us, that grips us so powerfully" ("Moses," 258). That intention, however, is not "merely a matter of intellectual comprehension"; intention must arise from "the meaning and content of what is represented in his work" ("Moses," 258). While Du Bois may have intended for the novel to be a powerful work of racial propaganda and indeed may have regarded it as such, the novel actually constructs a different story for those who do not share Du Bois's cognitive framework. For his rapport with *Dark Princess* is a very personal one that the reader at best can only partly share.

The ending of *Dark Princess* presents us with a dilemma. While we may generally sympathize with Matthew's frustrations and anxiety, his intense happiness at the novel's close has no corresponding significance for us. The novel's finale engenders our wonder and amazement but fails to evoke our empathy, compassion, or identification. This closed fantasy offers us no site for entry. Therefore, it certainly cannot inspire reformist zeal. In fact, the messianic ending undermines the novel's propagandist intent because it erodes the sympathy that we may have had for Matthew up to that point. The messianic ending compensates him for his suffering, as a *New York Times* reviewer points out: "it all turns out better for Matthew Townes than if he had become a doctor" (*NYT* Review of *Dark Princess*, 16). The novel thus fails to keep white society's culpability for racism in the foreground and makes Matthew's reward an ironic consequence of racism. In addition, the romantic signifier and its propagandistic meaning split apart. For if Kautilya symbolizes the ascendancy of "dark peoples," the allegory falls apart when the novel grants Matthew this love object but fails to secure his racial equality. The novel tries to recover this symbolic rift by forecasting that in twenty-five years "the Dark World goes free—whether in Peace and fostering Friendship with all men, or in Blood and Storm" (*Dark Princess*, 297). Rather than concluding by securing freedom as its objective, the novel sanctions the consummation of Kautilya's and Matthew's union with their marriage and celebrates the birth of their son, who will deliver freedom to the dark peoples of the world. As if the prophesy of racial liberation, which this child signifies, were not sufficiently compromised through its identification as fantasy, the novel closes with an envoy that privileges fancy over fact instead of transforming fact with fancy.

By symbolizing racial uplift as the beautiful and dark woman, Du Bois provided himself with a therapeutic mechanism for alleviating anxiety when the effects of racial trauma became severe. Because political desire assumes the cognitive form of eroticism in Du Bois's schema, overly stimulated political desire would demand intensified eroticism. This therapeutic model ultimately breaks down in *Dark Princess* because the eroticism cannot master the racial trauma. The eroticized symptoms are not contiguous with the political remedy.

Thus, the trauma continues to press its demands, and despite the ultimate futility of the erotic response, the novel continues to deliver ever
more extravagant images of the veiled and unveiled princess, the
chivalric Matthew, and her jewels—particularly the pearl between
her breasts that anticipates the suckling infant. Finally, the messianic
finale abandons virtually all semblance of political association.

Because *Dark Princess* relies so heavily on Du Bois's personal erotic
fantasies, it is essentially a private and, therefore, narcissistic political
romance not so much about reform as the gratification of what
seems to have been many of Du Bois's own personal desires: the role
of race leader for himself, a fulfilling marriage with a soulmate, a son
to carry forth the legacy of his leadership, his renunciation of black
participation in U.S. political corruption, and his affirmation of
social justice. Political scientist Harold R. Isaacs shares this viewpoint. He contends that "Du Bois poured his racial fantasies, his view
of the world, his obsession with color, his public judgments and his
secret hopes, and some of his own innermost dreams into [the] novel
he called *Dark Princess.*"[63] Isaacs goes on to explain that "much—if
not all—of Du Bois appears in this book, his thoughts and fantasies
about the world, and his dreams about himself, and about love and
about fulfillment" (219).

The erotic display was disconcerting for the Harlem literati. Yet
such symbolization is neither unusual, naive, nor absurd, for erotic
energy has provided the power for social change as writers as diverse
as Sigmund Freud and Audre Lorde have persistently argued. The
empathic failure between Du Bois and his readers is not due to the
inability of private fantasies to authorize social change but to a defect
in their representation in *Dark Princess.* Du Bois fails to maintain the
connection between the power of the erotic and the goal of social
reform in the novel. As a result, its superfluous desire merely makes
us uncomfortable.

Effective propaganda not only presents its point of view but also
obliges us to share that viewpoint and become activists in its behalf.
*Dark Princess* fails to accomplish such empathy because it cannot draw
us into the character's obsessions; it does not "reconcile the collective
nature of literary reception" with its unique logic of wish-fulfillment.[64]
The successful writer "softens the character of his egoistic day-dreams

by altering and disguising it, and he bribes us by the purely formal—
that is, aesthetic—yield of pleasure which he offers us in the presentation of his phantasies" (Freud, "Creative Writers and Day-Dreaming,"
quoted in Jameson, "Imaginary and Symbolic," 341). These tactics
seduce us into unconsciously recognizing our fantasies in the character's actions and emotions.[65] When this is the response, we become
vicarious participants in the work's argument, and the work proves
successful. This is precisely what Du Bois fails to accomplish in *Dark
Princess*. Rather, the novel transforms the desire to perform racial
activism into the desire to embrace the "single pearl shining at the parting of two little breasts" (*Dark Princess*, 299).

Like the child in an unmediated dyad with his imaginary identifications with the mother, Matthew vacillates between two possibilities. He can be "overwhelmed by the other, crowded out, taken over
(the fantasy of the devouring mother/voracious child); [or suffer] the
wretched isolation and abandonment of all self-worth by the other's
absence or neglect (the fantasy of the bad or selfish mother/child)."[66]
The latter describes Matthew's lot before Kautilya's restoration. To
protect his fragmenting sense of self, he tries to deaden his senses
with the physical exhaustion of digging subway tunnels in the bowels
of the earth. This incident is full of preconscious and therefore
unambiguous allusion to the regressive fantasy of being engulfed by
the omnipotent mother. Kautilya rescues Matthew from mental
death by offering herself as the mother surrogate. He joins her; he
even marries her, but still the narrative refuses to end.

The pleasure of Matthew's embrace of Kautilya is insufficient to
consummate and terminate all desire in the text because the narration continues. What else could *Dark Princess* possibly desire? Even
after the wedding, the story continues by supplementing the wedding
with a lavish naming ceremony for their child. Whatever final gratification the text demands is invested in this incident. What desire does
this incident represent?

The naming ceremony reestablishes the formation of a nuclear
family—Kautilya, Matthew, and extravagantly named child. The
triangular unit disrupts Matthew's narcissistic regression into dyadic
love by reestablishing individuated, parental gender roles for himself
and Kautilya. Moreover, the child is the physical proof of Matthew's

phallic power and his sexual difference from the mother and her surrogate. Therefore, the naming ceremony inscribes, preserves, and celebrates Matthew's masculine identity, and, I suspect, masculine textuality by symbolizing the phallus—the child, indeed a son. This incident then inscribes a defense for masculine heterosexual gender anxiety, for in desiring the fulfillment of heterosexual love, the male subject must confront the lost mother in the other woman, merge with her, *and still* preserve masculine individuation (Chodorow, *Feminism*, 73–74; Tyson and Tyson, *Psychoanalytic Theories*, 290).[67]

When Matthew's phallic potency is evident in the infant son, the text should end. But it does not. Again, the text attempts to end after speaking the son's prophesied social role in place of his name: "Messenger and Messiah to the Darker Worlds!" (*Dark Princess*, 311). With these words, the novel fulfills its conscious discourse of propaganda and maintains phallic difference. Therefore, the text should be ready to end. Well, almost.

The narrative now exhibits anxiety about audience response to so fanciful a story and delays the termination by appending an ancillary text in the Envoy. Here, the narrative concedes reason to desire altogether by imploring "her Mauve Majesty" to sanction the "Truth" in the novel that we mere mortal readers will undoubtedly fail fully to grasp. By offering "her Mauve Majesty," rather than us, the tale of *Dark Princess*, the narrative returns to a closed dyadic signifying system like that between the omnipotent mother and the pre-oedipal child. At this point the novel finally expresses its heavily concealed, much displaced, unconscious desire to exclude the social world and re-embrace the dyadic union with the sovereign dark matriarch, who is yet another displacement for the lost and clearly omnipotent mother.

Whereas Emma Kelley's *Megda* inscribes a fantasy of the daughter's pre-oedipal plenitude, *Dark Princess* complicates the son's oedipal resolution with residual pre-oedipal fantasies. Kelley's Meg becomes like the lost mother, while Du Bois's Matthew desires this mother and solicits her recognition. The finales of both novels symbolize the lost mother. *Megda* internalizes this figure in Meg's plenitude. The narrator of *Dark Princess* seeks the lost mother's approval in her loving gaze.

## *Notes*

1. Keith E. Byerman, *Seizing the Word: History, Art, and Self in the Work of W. E. B. Du Bois* (Athens: University of Georgia Press, 1994), 101. Subsequent references will be cited parenthetically in the text.

2. Griffith and Dixon appropriated the chivalric imagery and discourses of Sir Walter Scott's *Ivanhoe* (1819) to structure their portraits of the "Old South."

3. For a history of the Ku Klux Klan, see, for example, David M. Chalmers, *Hooded Americanism: The History of the Ku Klux Klan* (Durham, N. C.: Duke University Press, 1987).

4. Herbert Aptheker, Introduction to *Dark Princess: A Romance* (1928; repr. Millwood, N.Y.: Kraus-Thomson Organization, 1974), 14. Subsequent references will be cited parenthetically in the text.

5. Roland Barthes, *S/Z: An Essay,* trans. Richard Miller, 1974 (repr. New York: Hill and Wang, 1974), 17.

6. L. Laplanche and J. B. Pontalis, *The Language of Psycho-Analysis,* trans. Donald Nicholson-Smith (New York: American Psychoanalytic Assoc. and Yale University Press, 1990), 317.

7. Burness E. Moore and Bernard D. Fine, *Psychoanalytic Terms and Concepts* (New Haven: Yale University Press, 1990), 75.

8. Arnold Rampersad, "Du Bois's Passage to India: *Dark Princess*" (unpublished manuscript), 1. Subsequent references will be cited parenthetically in the text.

9. In 1909, Freud was invited to lecture at Clark University in Worcester, Massachusetts. During this first trans-Atlantic trip, Freud met with William James, one of Du Bois's favorite Harvard professors. James knew German (as did Du Bois) and had already been reading Freud's lectures with "great interest." James accorded the "future of psychology" to Freud's work (Ernest Jones, *The Life and Works of Sigmund Freud,* Vol. 2 (New York: Basic, 1957), 57. Inasmuch as Du Bois maintained contact with James long after he left Harvard and James was clearly impressed with Freud's work, I suspect that the two were likely to have discussed Freud's hypotheses (Lewis, *W. E. B. Du Bois* [see note 13], 225, 294, 366, 371, 565).

10. Conversation of January 20, 1994, with David Levering Lewis, Du Bois's principal biographer; quote from Du Bois, "My Evolving Program for Negro Freedom," in ed. Rayford Logan, *What the Negro Wants* (Chapel Hill: University of North Carolina Press, 1944), pp. 37–70, quote 49. Subsequent references will be cited parenthetically in the text.

11. Allison Davis, *Love, Leadership, and Aggression* (San Diego: Harcourt, Brace, Jovanovich, 1983), 130. Subsequent references will be cited parenthetically in the text.

12. Du Bois, *The Autobiography of W. E. B. Du Bois: A Soliloquy on Viewing My Life from the Last Decade of Its First Century* (New York: International Publishers, Inc., 1968), 277. Subsequent references will be cited parenthetically in the text.

13. David Levering Lewis, *W. E. B. Du Bois: Biography of a Race, 1868–1919* (New York: Henry Holt, 1993), 498. Subsequent references will be cited parenthetically in the text.

14. Arnold Rampersad, *The Art and Imagination of W. E. B. Du Bois (Cambridge, Mass.: Harvard University Press, 1976),* 204. Subsequent references will be cited

parenthetically in the text. Aptheker provides an excellent summary of the reviews of *Dark Princess* in his introduction to the novel. See Aptheker, Introduction, 21–29.

15. Jane Reitell, Review of *Dark Princess*, in *The Annals of the American Academy of Political and Social Science* 140 (Nov. 1928): 347; T. S. Review of *Dark Princess*, by W. E. B. Du Bois, *New York Evening Post*, May 12, 1928, 9; M. P. L. Review of *Dark Princess: A Romance*, by W. E. B. Du Bois, *New Republic*, August 22, 1928, 27. "Graustarkian" refers to the well-known romantic novel *Graustark* (1901), by George Barr McCutcheon, about the military and courtly adventures of a group of valiant characters in the fictional kingdom of Graustark. Another reviewer labels *Dark Princess* a "skyscraper problem novel of the Negro intellectual and the world radical," filled with "overelaboration" and "an epic theme . . . befogged by false romanticism" (Alain Locke, "The Negro Intellectual," *New York Herald Tribune*, May 20, 1928: 12). Another states that this "is by no means a dull novel, for the author's passion alone is enough to give it vigor and interest . . . [T]he book judged as a novel has only the slightest merit. As a document, as a program, as an exhortation, it has interest and value, but one can readily imagine the mirth it will provoke among the Harlem literati" (Review of *Dark Princess: A Romance*, by W. E. B. Du Bois, *Springfield Republican*, May 28, 1928; quoted in *Book Review Digest, 1928* (New York: H. W. Wilson Company, 1929), 216. And another reviewer asserts that the novel is "well written, but there is enough material in it for several novels and the plot is flamboyant and unconvincing" (Review of *Dark Princess: A Romance*, by W. E. B. Du Bois, *New York Times*, May 13, 1928: 19). Still another refers to the novel's "fantastic plot" and "Du Bois's old white-hot indignation against racial oppression and also his fierce pride in the beauty and deep tragic joy and rich loveliness of the dark peoples" ("The Throb of Dark Drums in Du Bois's Novel," *Honolulu Star Bulletin*, June 16, 1928, 12). The reviewer for *The Crisis* applauds *Dark Princess* for raising "the dead weight of our solid depression by propaganda at once eloquent and sane" (Allison Davis, "Browsing Reader," *The Crisis* 35 [November 1928]: 339). The reviewers generally agree, though, in the words of one, that *Dark Princess* "is not wholly successful" (Locke, "Negro Intellectual," 12).

16. After decades of neglect, Herbert Aptheker had the novel reprinted in 1971 as a part of a mammoth project to republish all of Du Bois's writings for library holdings. Even then only a few scholars of African American culture became acquainted with this obscure work. Consequently, *Dark Princess* has been a marginal novel despite the fame of its author. In 1995 the University Press of Mississippi reissued the novel and thereby provided contemporary readers with an opportunity to observe the passion of Du Bois's commitment to racial progress, manifested in the eroticism of *Dark Princess*.

17. Wilson J. Moses, *Black Messiahs and Uncle Toms: Social and Literary Manipulations of a Religious Myth* (University Park: Pennsylvania State University Press, 1982), 154; Saunders Redding, *To Make a Poet Black* (Chapel Hill: Univ. of North Carolina Press, 1948), 81; Hugh Gloster, *Negro Voices in American Fiction* (1948; repr. New York: Russell and Russell, 1965), 153; Amrijit Singh, *The Novels of the Harlem Renaissance: Twelve Black Writers, 1923–33* (University Park: Pennsylvania State University Press, 1981), 126–27.

18. Du Bois, "The Browsing Reader," *The Crisis* 35 (June 1928): 202.

19. Here Du Bois exclaims that "'Dark Princess' [is] my favorite book." Herbert Aptheker, a friend and colleague of Du Bois, has corroborated Du Bois's affection for

this work, recalling that he quite often "spoke [of the novel] with a special fondness" (Aptheker, Introduction, 29).

I am indebted to my colleague Marshall Alcorn for pointing out that the novel's failure arises not from Du Bois's choice of fusing erotic fantasy with political activism but from his inability to involve his reader in this fantasy.

20.  By 1940 Du Bois had written the following books: *The Suppression of the African Slave Trade to the United States of America, 1638–1870* (1896); *The Philadelphia Negro: A Social Study* (1900); *The Souls of Black Folk* (1903); *John Brown* (1909); *The Quest of the Silver Fleece* (1911); *The Negro* (1915); *Darkwater: Voices from within the Veil* (1920); *The Gift of Black Folk* (1924); *Black Reconstruction in America* (1935); and *Black Folk, Then and Now: An Essay in the History and Sociology of the Negro Race* (1939).

In addition to these nine books, between 1897 and 1915 Du Bois edited fifteen volumes on the study of Negro life that evolved from the proceedings of Annual Conferences on the Negro Problem at Atlanta University, which were published by Atlanta University Press: *Social and Physical Condition of Negroes in Cities* (1897); *Some Efforts of American Negroes for Their Own Social Betterment* (1898); *The Negro in Business* (1899); *The College-Bred Negro* (1900); *The Negro Common School* (1901); *The Negro Artisan* (1902); *The Negro Church* (1903); *Some Notes on Negro Crime, Particularly in Georgia* (1904); *The Health and Physique of the Negro American* (1906); *Economic Cooperation among Negro Americans* (1907); *The Negro American Family* (1908); *Efforts for Social Betterment among Negro Americans* (1910); *The Common School and the Negro American* (1912); *The Negro American Artisan* (1913); and *Morals and Manners among Negro Americans* (1915).

After *Dusk of Dawn* appeared, Du Bois wrote eight more books, three of which were novels that were written in the eighth decade of his life. These works include *Encyclopedia of the Negro: Preparatory Volume with Reference Lists and Reports* (1945); *Color and Democracy: Colonies and Peace* (1945); *The World and Africa: An Inquiry into the Part which Africa Has Played in World History* (1947); *Battle for Peace: The Story of My 83rd Birthday* (1952); The Black Flame Trilogy (*The Ordeal of Mansart* [1957], *Mansart Builds a School* [1959], and *Worlds of Color* [1961]); and *An ABC of Color: Selections from over a Half Century of the Writings of W. E. B. Du Bois* (1963, the year of his death).

The term "Negro" is a European historical designation for African peoples. . . . [In this essay]. . . . I use several terms in addition to Negro—colored, black, Afro-American, and African American—to designate New World people of African descent of different historical periods and political persuasions.

21.  Paul Gilroy, *The Black Atlantic: Modernity and Double Consciousness* (Cambridge, Mass.: Harvard Univ. Press, 1993), 114. Subsequent references will be cited parenthetically in the text.

22.  The term "Oedipus complex" first appears in Freud's "Special Type of Object Choice Made by Men," published in 1910. The Oedipus complex became linked with the nuclear family and what Freud called "family romances" (1909) when Jung began to question Freud's theories on the sexual etiology of neuroses. By 1920 the term had become the identifying feature that distinguished Freud's adherents from his opponents. Subsequent references to Freud's works cite Sigmund Freud, *The Standard*

*Edition of the Complete Works of Sigmund Freud,* trans. James Strachey et al (London: Hogarth Press and the Institute of Psycho-Analysis, 1953–1973); hereafter *SE.*

23. Freud's gender presumptions are a product of the patriarchal demands of his age and his own awareness of oedipalized conflicts with his father, whose death evidently exacerbated Freud's guilt.

24. In 1940 Du Bois attempts to alleviate the anxiety about the circumstances of his birth by inserting into his autobiographical record reference to the 1867 marriage registry for his parents at the Great Barrington Town Hall (*Dusk of Dawn: An Essay toward an Autobiography of a Race Concept* [New York: Harcourt, Brace and World, 1940], 109; Lewis, *W. E. B. Du Bois,* 588).

25. Allison Davis (1902–1983) a psychologist and educator, received a B.A. from Williams College in 1924, an M.A. from Howard University in 1925, and a Ph.D. from the University of Chicago in 1942. Davis knew Du Bois personally and reviewed *Dark Princess* for *The Crisis.* Davis was professor of sociology and educational psychology at the University of Chicago, where he taught from 1942 to 1965. His most famous book (coauthored with John Dollard) is *Children of Bondage* (1940).

26. Mary Anne Doane, *Femmes Fatales: Feminism, Film Theory, Psychoanalysis* (New York: Routledge, 1995), 52. Subsequent references will be made parenthetically in the text. Priscilla Wald associates Du Bois's symbolic use of the veil, especially his reference to the story "Of the Coming of John" in *The Souls of Black Folk* as a "tale twice told," with Nathaniel Hawthorne's *Twice-Told Tales,* published in 1837. Wald also notes an earlier prototype of the veil in Query 14 of Thomas Jefferson's *Notes on the State of Virginia* (Priscilla Wald, *Constituting Americans: Cultural Anxiety and Narrative Form* [Durham, N. C.: Duke University Press, 1995], 182–83). References to veiled female faces also appear in Du Bois's unpublished sketches, written while he was studying in Berlin, and later in the *Dark Princess.*

27. Ann McClintock, *Imperial Leather: Race, Gender and Sexuality in the Colonial Contest* (New York: Routledge, 1995), 184.

28. At the time Du Bois wrote this novel, he had already devoted thirty years of his life to his marriage to Nina Gomer Du Bois. He characterizes this marriage as "not . . . absolutely ideal" (*Autobiography,* 280). According to him, he had been "literally frightened into marriage" to a woman whose "life-long training as a virgin, made it almost impossible her ever to regard sexual intercourse as not fundamentally indecent." Du Bois goes on to explain that" [i]t took careful restraint on my part not to make her unhappy at this most beautiful of human experiences. It was no easy task for a normal and lusty young man" (*Autobiography* 281). "To the world," Du Bois adds in another context, "I was nearly always the isolated outsider looking in and seldom part of that inner life [of human beings]. Partly at role was thrust upon me because of the color of my skin. But I was not a prig. I was a lusty man with all normal appetites. I loved 'Wine, Women and Song' " (*Autobiography,* 3).

29. Peter Brooks, *Reading for the Plot: Design and Intention in Narrative* (New York: Random House, 1984); Peter Brooks, "The Idea of a Psychoanalytic Literary Criticism," in *Psychoanalysis and Storytelling* (Cambridge, Mass.: Blackwell, 1994), 20–45; cited 24.

30. See Jacques Lacan, *Écrits: A Selection,* trans. Alan Sheridan (New York: W. W. Norton, 1977), 169.

31. M. H. Abrams, *Natural Supernaturalism: Tradition and Revolution in Romantic Literature* (New York: W. W. Norton, 1971), 309. Subsequent references will be made parenthetically in the text.

32. During his years at Harvard in the late 1880s, Du Bois was a committed student of philosophy. He planned to study under George Herbert Palmer, who was a "profound and devoted Hegelian" (Joel Williamson, *The Crucible of Race: Black-White Relations in the American South since Emancipation* [New York: Oxford University Press, 1984], 406; subsequent references will be made parenthetically in the text.); however, Palmer went on sabbatical. Consequently, Du Bois enrolled in the class of William James, who at that time was developing Hegelian counterdiscourse in "pragmatic philosophy" (Williamson, *Crucible,* 406). No doubt, James's pragmatism fueled the dialectical dynamic of Hegelian metaphysics for Du Bois. Under the instruction of George Santayana, Du Bois also studied Immanuel Kant's *Critique of Pure Reason* (*Autobiography,* 143). Two other professors, Nathaniel Southgate Shaler and Albert Bushnell Hart, reaffirmed Du Bois's belief (which appears throughout *The Souls of Black Folk*) that each race has distinctive traits for fostering human progress. Du Bois's study at the University of Berlin would further develop this concept. Although Du Bois did not study philosophy at the University of Berlin, he arrived at a time when "Berlin was in the midst of a Hegelian revival" (Williamson, *Crucible,* 407). Hegel provided Du Bois with a philosophical model that influenced his thinking. This model explains the truth of human history as the positive or negative progressive reconciliation of contradictory propositions.

33. Du Bois, *The Souls of Black Folk,* 1903; repr. in ed., Eric Sundquist, *The Oxford W. E. B. Du Bois Reader* (New York: Oxford University Press, 1996), 102. Subsequent references will be cited parenthetically in the text.

34. Fredric Jameson, "Magical Narratives," in *The Political Unconscious: Narrative as a Socially Symbolic Act* (Ithaca, N.Y.: Cornell University Press, 1981), 103–50; 132.

35. Davis's portrait of the man on the rack in this citation is particularly meaningful, given the frequency that Du Bois uses the word "writhe" in his unpublished fiction. Davis knew Du Bois personally and therefore had the opportunity to observe him. His portrait of Du Bois has much in common with the biographical sketch of him that appears in *The New Worlds of Negro Americans* by Harold R. Isaacs. Isaacs includes transcriptions from an interview that he conducted with Du Bois when he was ninety-two. What is remarkable about the excerpts from this interview is that just as Du Bois had earlier predicted that the problem of the twentieth-century was the color line, he predicts here that in the twenty-first century the next stage in the battle would be for human dignity.

36. At sixteen, in 1885, Du Bois went to Fisk University, where he earned his A.B. He then fulfilled his childhood ambition to enter Harvard College. In 1888 he enrolled at Harvard as a junior. In 1890 he graduated cum laude and was one of six commencement speakers. In 1892 he secured the Slater Fund Fellowship for two years of study at the University of Berlin. In 1896 he received a Ph.D. from Harvard. His dissertation, *The Suppression of the African Slave-Trade to the United States of America, 1638–1870,* was published as the first volume in the Harvard Historical Series. He referred to this early period of extraordinary success and achievement as

"the age of miracles." Unfortunately, despite his brilliance and labor, he was never to recover the eminence of these early years.

37. For example, see Du Bois's famous *Souls of Black Folk* and *Darkwater* as well as the more obscure 1915 sociological treatise *The Negro* and reviews of his extravagant pageant *The Star of Ethiopia,* also staged that year.

38. Du Bois, *Dark Princess: A Romance* (1928; rpt. Jackson: University Press of Mississippi, 1995), 311. Subsequent references will be cited parenthetically in the text.

39. Du Bois, "The Drama among Black Folk," *The Crisis* 12 (August 1916): 169, 171–72.

40. Kautilya is the name of a well-known adviser of a Hindu kingdom before the Arabian invasion. Kautilya is also, as Arnold Rampersad points out, the name of the male author of the *Artha-sastra,* a political treatise written between 326 and 291 B.C. ("Du Bois's Passage" 11). Rampersad further identifies Du Bois's familiarity with Indian culture by referring to the respective Sanskrit and Hindi words for "black" and "the black one"—"Krishna" and "Kali"—as terms of endearment that he uses in *Dark Princess* ("Du Bois's Passage," 20).

41. Psychoanalyst Gilbert J. Rose explains in *Trauma and Mastery in Life and Art* (New Haven, Conn.: Yale University Press, 1987) that "creative and clinical processes follow the fundamental psychic principle of attempting to master passively experienced trauma by active repetition" (44).

42. For a provocative essay that uses psychoanalytic theory to analyze *The Scarlet Letter,* see Joanne Feit Diehl, "Re-Reading the Letter: Hawthorne, the Fetish, and the (Family) Romance," in ed. Ross C. Martin, *The Scarlet Letter by Nathaniel Hawthorne* (Boston: St. Martin's, 1991), 235–51. This essay focuses on Hawthorne's "repressed authorial desires" to expose "a subtext that links [Hawthorne's] motives for writing to a search for the lost mother" (237, 236). Diehl hypothesizes Hawthorne's "deep authorial conflict toward Hester as lover/mother" ("Re-Reading" 236). This is a deep-rooted conflict of male psychical development that Freud chronicled as the oedipal stage and that Du Bois symbolizes in *Dark Princess* with Matthew's attachment to Kautilya.

43. For discussion of the oceanic feeling, see Freud, *Civilization and Its Discontents,* 1930, in *SE,* 21: 64–65, 72.

44. *The Papers of William E. B. Du Bois,* Microfilm, Manuscript Division, Library of Congress, Washington, D.C.: reel 88, frames 468, 472, 473. Du Bois included the text of this entry in his autobiography. See *Autobiography,* 170–71.

45. Robin Lakoff, *Women, Fire, and Dangerous Things: What Categories Reveal about the Mind* (Chicago: University of Chicago Press, 1987), xiv.

46. Mardi Jon Horowitz, *Image Formation and Psychotherapy* (New York: Janson Aronson, 1983), 108.

47. Du Bois often wrote about girls in his weekly expository writing assignments for English 12 at Harvard. See, for example, those dated October 31, 1890 (Papers, reel 88, frame 329), January 21, 1891 (reel 88, frame 357), February 24, 1891 (reel 88, frame 362), and undated (reel 88, frames 350–51). He also made beautiful women, often in conjunction with stolen jewels and railroad intrigue, the subject of many of his early stories, published and unpublished. For unpublished examples, see "Fables from within the Veil" (reel 88, frames 970–71), "Princess Wata" (reel 88,

frames 927–28), "The Necklace of Emeralds" (reel 88, frames 1117–1121), "The Diamond Earring" (reel 88, frames 1058–1062), and "The Jewel" (reel 88, frames 1235–1242). For published examples, see "The Shaven Lady" and "The Case" (*The Horizon* 2 (July 1907): 4–10). The woman in "The Case" seems to be a replica of one in the unpublished sketch "A Woman" (1893, reel 88, frame 375).

Du Bois was also fond of the cloak-and-dagger story and plots of railroad intrigue. "The Case" and "The Shaven Lady" also employ these narrative devices. For representative published stories about princesses and noble women who rescue or are rescued by noble men, see "The Woman," in *The Crisis* 2 (May 1911): 12, and "The Princess of the Hither Isles," in *The Crisis* 6 (October 1913): 285, 288–89.

Representative messianic scenarios include Du Bois's staged pageant *The Star of Ethiopia*, which he says attracted audiences of 14,000. For details about this work see Du Bois, "The Star of Ethiopia," in *The Crisis* 9 (December 1915): 90–94; a detailed review in the *Washington Bee* (October 23, 1915) included in the Papers at the Library of Congress (reel 87, frames 1535, 1536), and the program (reel 88, frames 1528, 1529). Also see Du Bois's "Three Wise Men"; "Second Coming"; "Flight into Egypt"; "Gospel According to Mary Brown"; and "Black Man Brings His Gifts" in *The Creative Writings of W. E. B. Du Bois: A Pageant, Poems, Short Stories, and Playlets*, compiled and edited by Herbert Aptheker (White Plains, N.Y.: Kraus-Thomson Organization, Ltd., 1974).

Several of the above unpublished sketches also feature princesses; see, for example, "Princess Watta" (frames 928–29) and "Fables from within the Veil" (frames 970–71) in reel 88 of his Papers. Others feature mystery stories about jewels and jewel cachets; see "The Necklace of Emeralds" (frames 1059–1063), and "The Jewels" (frames 1236–1243), all in reel 88. In addition, see these representative fragments of unpublished pageants: "The Jewel of Ethiopia" (undated, reel 87, frame 1421) and "A Pageant of Negro History" (1913, reel 88, frames 1443–1459). For similar plays, see "The Christ of the Andes/Christ on the Andes" (undated, reel 87, frames 428–645) and "The Darker Wisdom: Prophecies in the Tale and Play, Seeking to Pierce the Gloom of 1940 . . ." (reel 87, frames 646–916).

48. For a discussion of the personal dialectic, see Heinz Lichtenstein, *The Dilemma of Human Identity* (New York: Hason Aronson, 1977), 258–60. For a discussion of the identity theme, see Norman N. Holland, *Brain of Robert Frost: A Cognitive Approach to Literature* (New York: Routledge, 1988), 38.

49. Freud, "On Narcissism: An Introduction," 1914, *SE*, 14: 111–40.

50. I appreciate Nell Painter's prompting me to focus on this issue and thereby to address the degree to which African Americans unconsciously struggle with the cultural duality Du Bois describes in *Souls*. This "two-ness" or hybridity of the Lacanian white Symbolic and the desire for a black counterpart manifests itself in Du Bois's (and in some other black people's) appreciation of selected white cultural artifacts (like classical music, European art, and Western fashion, for example), to say nothing of white values, especially Eurocentric beauty standards.

51. W. E. B. Du Bois, *The Quest of the Silver Fleece* (1911; repr. Boston: Northeastern University Press, 1989), 17, 123.

52. George Schuyler, *Black No More* (1931; repr. Evanston: Northeastern University Press, 1989), 90.

53. Frantz Fanon, *Black Skin, White Masks* 1952; repr., trans. Charles Lam Markmann (New York: Grove Press, 1967), 63.

54. On his twenty-sixth birthday, Du Bois wrote in his journal, "This is my twenty-sixth birthday—a fresh cold sunshiny day spent most in my regular routine of work and musing" (Papers, reel 88, frame 489). For Du Bois, working seems very similar to musing, day dreaming.

55. Peter Gay, *The Bourgeois Experience: Victoria to Freud*, Vol. 2, *The Tender Passion* (New York: Oxford University Press, 1986), 257. Subsequent references will be made parenthetically in the text.

56. In *The Interpretation of Dreams* (1900, *SE*, 4–5) Freud explains dreams as expressions of unconscious desire that cannot be fulfilled in the state of consciousness. Because such desire cannot seek satisfaction through action, dreams project satisfaction by encoding gratification in cryptic strings of images. Freud identified the stages of dream-work that produce the imagery as (1) condensation, (2) displacement, (3) considerations of representability, and (4) secondary revision. The first stage produces the overdetermined image by converging several latent wishes onto one manifest item. The second stage disguises elements in latent dream-thoughts by replacing them through a chain of associations. Condensation also occurs during this stage; it compresses elements in the latent content of the dream in associative links based on likeness and proximity. In speech, metaphor and metonymy embody these processes. The third stage translates dream-thoughts into manifest images. The fourth stage, known as secondary revision, imposes order, logic, and language on the manifest content of the dream in order to make it into a cohesive narrative. Because the manifest dream is a mediated formation, it bears a direct relationship to the demands of desire and the intensity of repression. Thus, the more obscure the encodings of dream-work, "the more intense the force of repression" (Elizabeth Wright, *Psychoanalytic Criticism: Theory in Practice* (London: Methuen, 1984), 19). But without repression, there would be shame.

57. Steven Seidman, *Romantic Longings: Love in America, 1830–1980* (New York: Routledge, 1991), 47.

58. Pauline E. Hopkins, *Of One Blood: Or, The Hidden Self,* 1903, repr. in *The Magazine Novels of Pauline Hopkins* (New York: Oxford University Press, 1988), 621. Du Bois seems to be the model for the heroes of Hopkins's *Of One Blood*, as well as her first novel, *Contending Forces* (1900). Hopkins lived in Cambridge during the period in which Du Bois attended Harvard, and I suspect that she came into contact with him then. She covered the 1900 Pan-African Conference for the *Colored American Magazine* (September 1900): 223–31. For a discussion of *One Blood*, see Chapter 7 in my *Domestic Allegories* (Claudia Tate, *Domestic Allegories of Political Desire: The Black Heroine's text at the Turn of the Century* [New York: Oxford University Press, 1992]).

59. Rayford W. Logan, *The Betrayal of the Negro* (New York: Collier, 1965), 9. See Chapter 7 of my *Domestic Allegories* for a discussion of the terms of representing the growing racial despair in the writings of Pauline Hopkins.

60. This statement is an extract from the second of two descriptions that Du Bois prepared describing the novel. In a letter of December 15, 1927, to Harcourt, Brace and Company, Du Bois inscribes a "general statement about the novel for your [the publisher's] use," which he sent "some time ago." Wondering whether that

statement was adequate, he included another with the final manuscript. See Aptheker, Introduction, 18–20.

61. In *Orientalism,* Said defines Orientalism as "a style of thought based upon an ontological and epistemological distinction made between 'the Orient' and (most of the time) 'the Occident' in which the latter is implicitly and explicitly understood as superior" (2). We late twentieth-century readers no doubt recognize Orientalism as a discourse about the sovereignty of Western consciousness, a discourse about its "desires, repressions, investments, and projections" (Edward Said, *Orientalism* [New York: Pantheon, 1978],8). This cultural discourse was/is intrinsic to the ideology of white supremacy that undergirded U.S. slavery and post-Reconstruction black disenfranchisement and racial segregation, as well as Western imperialism.

62. This is a paraphrase of Freud's thesis expressed in "The Moses of Michelangelo," 1914, *SE,* 23; repr. In *The Collected Papers of Sigmund Freud,* trans. Joan Riviere et al (New York: Basic Books, 1959), 4: 257–88; 258.

63. Harold R. Isaacs, *The New World of Negro Americans* (New York: John Day, 1963), 216.

64. Fredric Jameson, "Imaginary and Symbolic in Lacan: Marxism, Psychoanalytic Criticism, and the Problem of the Subject," in ed. Shoshana Felman, *Literature and Psychoanalysis: The Question of Reading, Otherwise* (Baltimore: Johns Hopkins University Press, 1978), 338–95; 340.

65. For a description of this process see Freud, "Psychopathic Characters on Stage," 1942, (1905–1906), *SE* 7: 305–10.

66. Elizabeth Grosz, *Jacques Lacan: A Feminist Introduction* (New York: Routledge, 1990), 51.

67. Nancy J. Chodorow, *Feminism and Psychoanalytic Theory* (New Haven, Conn.: Yale University Press, 1989), 73–74; Phyllis Tyson and Robert L. Tyson, *Psychoanalytic Theories of Development: An Integration* (New Haven, Conn.: Yale University Press, 1990), 290.

# 6

# Du Bois's Erotics

■ *Michele Elam and Paul C. Taylor*

> That the moralist of the Harlem Renaissance and
> author of impeccably feminist essays in *The Crisis* and
> of "The Damnation of Women" in *Darkwater* was a
> priapic adulterer compels appropriate disclosure, even
> though it inescapably smacks of the report of the
> private eye.
>
> David Levering Lewis, *W. E. B. Du Bois:*
> *The Fight for Equality and the American Century, 1919–1963*

Our epigraph, from David Levering Lewis's award-winning biography of W. E. B. Du Bois,[1] offers a glimpse into one of the many challenges involved in understanding Du Bois in the context of gender politics. Just how is it that Du Bois the "moralist" somehow coexisted with Du Bois the "priapic adulterer"? How is it that the feminist advocate was also, paradoxically, a retrograde rake? Lewis expresses some unease that the revelation, "smacking" as it does, he fears, of a vulgar critical voyeurism, places not only Du Bois's but also his own reputation at risk. Lewis's ambivalence about "appropriate disclosure" seems to stem further from his sense of risking a sideshow, of inappropriately diverting attention from his great man's political activism to, he implies, the very separate and less savory subject of Du Bois's private vices. Nevertheless, in documenting at length Du Bois's priapism, Lewis seems to conclude that politico-cultural piety should not block the potential apostasy of deflationary reportage.

Similarly, in her exploration of *Dark Princess* and other texts, Claudia Tate joins Lewis in cautious rejection of the long- and closely-held image of Du Bois as a blues-begrudging Victorian.[2] No longer the mouthpiece for the prudish Old Guard's resistance to the encroachments of a more sensual younger generation—Langston Hughes, Richard Bruce Nugent, Zora Neale Hurston, Claude McKay—Du Bois becomes a figure whose erotic fantasies and desires are inextricable from his political and literary work. In this regard, in fact, Tate moves beyond Lewis, whose unease seems to register the influence of what she sees as one of the main obstacles to adequate scholarship on black writers: the "popular racial story [that] calcifies our roles in . . . prescriptive racial plots" and that subordinates "private longing to racial politics" (see Tate, "Race and Desire," in this volume). While we would argue that Lewis does not give in entirely to what Tate identifies as prescriptive racial protocols, he does, however, leave standing the traditional gap between Du Bois's erotics and his literary politics: there is still a sense in which Du Bois's acknowledgments of desire are characterized as anomalous, related only inexplicably to the Harlem Renaissance moralist. Tate recruits psychoanalytic tools to improve upon this bifurcated picture. We can better understand the allegedly anomalous impulses, she argues, by examining the way the "individual and subjective experience of personal desire" creates what she calls unconscious "residual surplus," an "enigmatic presence" in the texts, marking out for itself sites of fantasy and freedom uncontained by any social message (Tate, "Race and Desire"). Yet in using psychoanalytic notions of unconscious textual desire to close the gap between erotics and politics, Tate in a sense relocates the gap by mapping it onto the division between conscious and unconscious. And while aiming to establish a more or less coherent source (the psyche) for all of Du Bois's supposedly conflicting impulses, her model tends somewhat to efface the intellectual-historical context that might have shaped his efforts to deploy them.

We propose to take another step altogether in the direction toward reconciling The Great Man with the priapic goat, examining Du Bois's erotics—particularly in *Dark Princess*—not as a moral lapse or an unconscious or anomalous effusion, but as part of a consciously avowed *perfectionist* agenda. "Perfectionism" is a species of the nineteenth-century ethics of self-realization, manifested in Friedrich Nietzsche's talk of Dionysian self-overcoming, in Margaret Fuller's and Ralph Waldo Emerson's transcendentalist focus on self-evolving, and in the progressive-era pragmatic emphasis on what Charlotte Perkins Gilman and John Dewey often called, simply, "growth." We are positing perfectionism as a site of philosophical convergence and an exegetical device rather than as causal influence. These cross-disciplinary models represent strains of thought in particular vogue in the early twentieth century and in which, we argue, Du Bois clearly participated; and we draw on them as compelling but overlooked interpretive paradigms for what Tate terms his "conjugal symbolism."[3] In short, we use resources roughly contemporaneous with Du Bois to explain and critique the priapic impulse in his literary and political agenda on his own critical terms and as it would have had cogency in his own time.

Much excellent scholarship has already considered the many and often competing philosophical paradigms, aesthetic traditions, and political agendas that shape Du Bois's work. These have included Calvinism, Hegelianism, pragmatism, Fabianism, collectivism, Marxism, Pan-Africanism, socialism—and in light of Susan Gillman's *Blood Talk* (2003),[4] we might add "occultism." Our work extends these reflections. We argue that reading Du Bois as a kind of "Dionysian perfectionist" means rejecting the claim that his eroticism was ethically or psychologically extraneous to his literary and political projects. This in turn means committing ourselves to saying more about Du Bois than scholars are typically encouraged to say of pioneering but ethically flawed historical figures—people that, so the argument goes, could not completely transcend the conventional moralities of their places and times. Often scholars are encouraged to exempt such figures from criticism, at least to some degree, on the basis of historical circumstance and environment: the "transgressions" become expressions of the agent's milieu, aspects of the contemporaneous culture that he or she uncritically absorbed while laudably attending to other issues.

In this light, then, even those who politely glance away from what are perceived as Du Bois's sexual lapses, and those who focus on the limitations of his sexual representations, share this impulse to historicize for damage control. Farah Jasmine Griffin, for instance, addresses Du Bois's representation (or lack thereof) of women by stating that his "masculinist" language is simply the "language of his time."[5] She juxtaposes his work on behalf of black women against his "masculinism" in order to insulate Du Bois's politically progressive tendencies from his philandering—as well as from the "sexism" that Beverly Guy-Sheftall and others find in both his "idealized image of black women" and, as Joy James cogently argues in this volume, his failure to acknowledge black women intellectuals as peers.[6] In her efforts to recuperate Du Bois, Griffin praises Du Bois as an exception among black intellectuals at that time in his advocacy for women's issues, however qualified it may appear to a contemporary audience. Herman Beavers similarly, if more gently, concludes that although "Du Bois's intellectual prowess with respect to the discourses of race and class was ahead of its time in the 1920s, his attitude regarding gender, while tending toward progressivism, was highly reflective of the historical moment."[7]

The risk with this move to historically quarantine Du Bois is not simply that the past is made a vehicle for the absolution of sins by the self-ordained ("we excuse our brother because it was just 'the times' that made him do it") but also that Du Bois's complex and apparently politically contradictory relations with and writings about women become sins in the first place—or at least a besmirching—to be, if not condemned, then at least isolated, excused, and exorcized from future enlightened practice. If utilized at all, Du Bois's "limitations and mistakes" in relation to women are cast as things that we can "learn from," a negative example rather than an exemplary model in our feminist primers.[8] Griffin's solution is that we grant due credit to Du Bois for putting "women at the forefront of his vision" and acknowledge debt to him as an "intellectual activist," but that we must "move on" from his paradoxes.[9] This move allows her to exculpate Du Bois while using the same measuring stick to single out "contemporary black male intellectuals and activists" for a bit of a spanking: Du Bois's black male intellectual heirs, she argues, "ought to be criticized for not moving beyond these limitations in matters of gender, sexuality, and class. Unlike Du Bois, they have access to the history and analytical frames and paradigms made available by the work of politically engaged black feminist intellectuals . . . ."[10]

Such criticisms of Du Bois and the male critics who inherit his legacy are of course perfectly fair, but we would like to begin rather than end with Beaver's conclusion that Du Bois's vision in the novel is "animated by patriarchal conventions."[11] That is, we wish to go beyond merely praising or condemning Du Bois's women—neither, as Alys Weinbaum characterizes it, extolling "his portraits of woman-hood, particularly those of the figure he repeatedly refers to as the black All-Mother,"[12] nor simply concluding with Beavers that Du Bois simply "cannot find a way to value [women] equally, to allow them to be the agents of political change, no matter how catalytic their presence may be."[13] These two interpretations, about whether women are represented realistically or are romanticized, whether they accrue potent symbolic power or are merely midwives to black men's creative projects, dovetail with earlier critiques by Nellie McKay, Bettina Aptheker, and Joy James (see her essay in this volume) over Du Bois's failure to grant proper professional recognition to his flesh and blood intellectual sisters—especially Jessie Fauset, Pauline Hopkins, and Anna Julia Cooper.

But in the last decade, some scholars have shifted focus from condemnations of stereotype or professional lapses to consider instead what Weinbaum denotes as the "sexual logic of the text," women's "rhetorical function in articulating a series of inextricable relations between gender and race, sexism and racism, and feminism and antiracism."[14] Thus Hazel V. Carby, in "The Souls of Black Men" (reprinted in this volume) seeks to "interrogate the ideological and political effects of the gendered nature of Du Bois's theoretical paradigm,"[15] particularly as it functions, as one critic puts it, as a "palimpsest for charting the masculinist roots of twentieth-century black intellectual production."[16] In Carby's reading of Du Bois, black women are proxy for "the folk" (as in "The Meaning of Progress") or for a race's failings (as in "On the Wings of Atalanta") while the black male body—namely, Du Bois's body—becomes social arbiter, bio-intellectual representative, and cultural "cipher . . . for an entire people" (as in "The Passing of the First-Born" and "The Coming of John"). In these places, Carby cogently argues, men supplant women as the site of reproduction; the "figure of the race leader is born of and engendered by other males," as in Du Bois's homage to Alexander Crummell in *The Souls of Black Folk* (see Carby, "The Souls of Black Men" in this volume). Similarly, we must ask, does the perfectionist model of the capacious and ever-improving self—a model that has historically lent itself to what R. W. B. Lewis termed the American Adam and to egalitarian promises of democracy—presume certain problematic class sentiments, conditions, and aspirations (e.g. a love of "the finer things," a "leisure class," a racial vanguard)? Do Du Bois's writings depict and dramatize the social conditions of perfectionism in gendered terms—specifically, do women merely become midwives for masculine self-creation? How does perfectionism figure the relation between male and female self-realization for Du Bois? With what implications is heterosexual union not only recruited into, but the central trope of, so many of his evolving geo-political visions? It is worth noting that since the 1970s, black feminist historiographers have sought to narrate the development of debates over the representation of black female sexuality; but they have not so carefully mapped the trajectory of black male sexual representation. Indeed, to hear Amiri Baraka tell it, the Black Arts Movement's portrayal of the "talented tenth" as "neutered" or "effete"(read: queer) effectively writes off Du Bois as intellectually impotent, ideologically unfit to contribute to heterosexual black masculine projects. Hence Du Bois is an interesting case in which he has been alternatively portrayed as Victorian prude, licentious pig, or, as in the case of Baraka, generally sexually suspect. Perfectionism, we feel, then enables us to outline a Du Boisian erotics that both engages in and against the historical tradition of very pointedly representing him as beyond the acceptable sexual pale. As we suggested earlier, we wish to resist the temptations of moralist condemnation, or conversely, the tendency to politely glance away; both discourage inquiry.

Our alternative frame of reference is an effort to make recourse to history without a bid for either redemption or condemnation. We are most interested in trying to understand the *constitutive* relation between Du Bois's priapism and his ethico-political project, to form a critical re-visioning of Du Bois's work which might render the contradictions perhaps not so contradictory after all.

## Erotic Commitments

Our claim is that Du Bois's priapic license was a consistent manifestation of his thoroughgoing interest in the sensual, affective, and especially sexual aspects of experience, and that the persistence of this interest reveals itself in the ethical commitments that frequently shape and permeate his nonfiction and fiction. The expression of the erotic in his work is, in many ways, not so much a departure from but an elaboration of the principle of pleasure that has always been lurking, and at times been front and center, throughout his life's work. Sometimes these are passing references that, accumulated, point to his belief, already developed by the turn of the century, that the sensual was to be celebrated if in the context of "love," and that "true love" in turn is always also understood to be in service of political work. Private desire and ethical fulfillment occurred when physical passion and political commitment were joined in what amounted to unions divinely sanctioned. As Arnold Rampersad puts it in his cogent reading of the moral of Du Bois's early work: "Self-denial is the start of self-fulfillment. The power of work is celebrated, but one must work with others and for others . . . . The grandeur of love is the greatest of human emotions and sanctifies sexual passion."[17] It is no slip of speech when, in "Criteria of Negro Art," Du Bois declares that he stands "in utter shamelessness and say that whatever art I have for writing has been used always for . . . gaining the right of black folk to *love and enjoy*."[18] Art serves emancipatory politics not (or not just) by securing rights or demonstrating equality, but by facilitating *love* and enjoyment. Aesthetic pleasure here is not an aside but an end in itself. Even bodily joy is validated: in "The Damnation of Women," he is saddened that he hears "all about me the unanswered call of youthful love, none the less glorious because of its clean, honest, physical passion" (952). His curtly disapproving reference to out-of-wedlock childbirth, prostitution, and marriages of convenience takes aim not at the individuals involved but at punitive conventions, the social rules that constrain and convert sexual impulse. Du Bois echoes this last line of complaint in the touching essay entitled "My Character," written near the end of his life, where he devotes several paragraphs to his experiences with, as he puts it, the overlapping goods of friendship and sex—though he is careful to leave aside the problems, reported by Lewis and others, that he had with Jessie Fauset and other women with whom he had working relationships. Near the middle of the piece he laments his wife's "life-long training as a virgin," which made it difficult for him, as "a normal and lusty young man," not to "make her unhappy at this most beautiful of human experiences" (1121). Uncoupling sex from reproduction—gone is the "day in the world when it was considered that by marriage a woman . . . simply became a machine for making men" (1170)—Du Bois nevertheless views the consummation of sexual desire as pivotal to social advance when spiritually purified by the fires of political labor.

### Dionysian Perfection

The full realization of this political-erotic ideal really takes shape in his fiction, particularly in his first novel, *The Quest of the Silver Fleece* (1911), in stories like "The Comet" in *Darkwater: Voices from Within the Veil* (1920), and most powerfully in *Dark Princess*. But before offering readings of the literature, we would like to develop more specifically the set of ethical commitments that we are claiming underwrites his investment in the erotic.

In his important book, *W. E. B. Du Bois and American Political Thought*, Adolph Reed urges us to approach Du Bois's views and the texts through which we encounter them as "historical artifacts of specific discursive communities," so that we can uncover the "deeper normative meanings" embedded within black political debates. Reed then models this approach for us by attending carefully, and convincingly, to Du Bois's debt to what he calls collectivism. This view developed in part as a response to the unsettling novelties of industrial capitalism and insists on "expertise as a . . . decisive social force," on "the neutrality of the state," and on "the neutral, guiding role of technology."[19] These commitments establish a special role for intellectuals and experts, who, in some instantiations of collectivism, serve as a leading elite—the role, for example, that Lenin assigns to his professional revolutionaries, or that Du Bois attributes to the Talented Tenth. According to Reed, this perspective provided the core commitments for early twentieth-century progressivism, managerialism, and socialism, and also "heavily conditioned" all of Du Bois's "intellectual and practical activity" (26). In Reed's account, "the unifying principles of the collectivist outlook" require excavation because Du Bois left them submerged and implicit. The principles, he says, "seldom are discussed in Du Bois's work, because they were generally shared through the discursive arena within which he operated. . . . Because they were not controversial, and were in fact part of the least common denominator of conventional attitudes . . . there was little reason for those principles ever to be discussed elaborately. Therefore, they are accessible to us . . . mainly through a reading that is sensitive to his [Du Bois's] text's location in relation to their audiences and the shared understandings that cement that relation" (89).

Reed does mention certain other widely shared elements of Du Bois's discursive arena. But he fails to mention some that contribute to the basic ethical motivation for collectivism (as opposed to its political or social-theoretic motivations). Like the principles of collectivism, these ethical commitments would have been familiar enough to escape detailed elaboration in Du Bois's work. We can start toward these other background perspectives by noting, first, that the basic problem that galvanized many Marxists, Fabian socialists, and American progressives was the stultification of human experience and personality. Capitalism, Marx says, is alienating: it separates the workers from their species-being, their activities, and themselves.[20] In much the same spirit, Dewey complains that industrial society separates the aesthetic from the practical, the useful from the meaningful, thereby frustrating the unavoidable human craving for meaning and beauty.[21] Charlotte Perkins Gilman, for her part, indicts an androcentric U.S. culture for what she thinks of as stunting the growth and wasting the personalities of its female participants.[22] These complaints emanate from a commonsense ethics of perfection, or self-realization. We might trace this tradition of thought to Aristotle's virtue ethics, but it takes on the forms with which we are concerned in the modern West, as it makes its way from Spinoza and Rousseau to eighteenth-century figures like Kant and, somewhat differently,

Hamann and Herder. From there it winds through Fichte, Hegel, and the Romantics, eventually taking explicitly political form in the liberalism that John Stuart Mill developed to accommodate his eudaemonist utilitarianism, and in the different calls for political self-determination that we find in nationalism and in Marxism. We can define this tradition in terms drawn from a venerable philosophical reference book, the *Dictionary of Philosophy and Psychology*, published in 1901.[23] Here we learn that adopting a perfectionist ethic means establishing "the perfection of character, or the complete and harmonious development of personal capacities" as the moral ideal.

As views committed to the many-sidedness of personality and to the importance of cultivating and expressing the innermost self (whether that self was a human individual or a world-spirit), romanticism and idealism cultivated perfectionists. They were also powerful influences on the United States in which Du Bois grew up. Many commentators have noted that Du Bois was particularly receptive to the seductions of idealism, often citing the Hegelian leanings of such texts as "The Conservation of Races."[24]

It is interesting to note that Harvard's philosophy faculty at the time also featured George Herbert Palmer, who espoused and taught what he referred to as "self-realization ethics." As Lewis tells us, Palmer was on sabbatical when Du Bois took the course that would otherwise have showcased the ethics of self-realization; we mention Palmer only to conclude our brief gesture at the cultural currency that this sort of ethical sensibility enjoyed: a popular teacher in the most prestigious philosophy department in the country publicly embraced it. In any case, Palmer's sabbatical left Du Bois to take Philosophy 4 from William James, who points us to a second ethical element of Du Bois's discursive arena. When Du Bois matriculated, James was just beginning to work out his version of a second important background perspective, which we might refer to as ethical anti-formalism. There are many documents of this tradition, but we can start with James's insistence, in his essay "The Moral Philosopher and the Moral Life," that "the highest ethical life consists . . . in the breaking of rules which have grown too narrow for the actual case."[25] We see similar ideas, and evidence of the influential voices that these ideas were able to enlist in their support, in Emerson's famous rebukes of consistency and in

John Dewey's writings on ethics. Dewey argued that ethical deliberation is a matter not of applying rules but of being sensitive to the various factors that make a situation ethically problematic.[26] For the anti-formalist, morally correct action requires fashioning an acceptable and creative response to novel conditions. For the pragmatist, all intelligent action meets this description, which is to say that all action has ethical import: ethical life demands the willingness to legislate for oneself in the truest sense, without the overweening regard for duty that allows one to avoid taking responsibility for oneself. This sometimes-pragmatic anti-formalism served many progressives well in their struggle against the obstacles that the newly industrialized United States was putting in the path of individual self-creation.

And they conducted their struggle in a way that leads us to a third element of Du Bois's intellectual milieu: the characteristically Victorian ambivalence about sex. In the grip of middle-class Victorian notions about propriety, thrift, and moral discipline, many progressives strove to "uplift" and "civilize" putatively at-risk populations, often by pushing for temperance laws, an old policy goal that received new purpose from late nineteenth-century shifts in gender roles and economic expectations. For these reformers, including the young Du Bois in his sociological studies of African American communities, moral discipline was necessary, and it was particularly important in the face of what seemed rampant sexual temptation and brutality.

While this determination to constrain sexual appetites and practices is consistent with the stereotype of Victorian prudery, Michel Foucault and others have encouraged us to see this focus on repression as simply one aspect of an *obsession*: the obsessive effort to understand sex, to find a place for it in human nature and society.[27] It was, of course, much more than this as well, especially for the reformers. They were determined to respond to sexual degradation as both sign and product of woman's overall degradation under broader social systems, whether of androcentrism, industrial capitalism, or white supremacy. But this attempt to discipline and constrain human sexual impulses also kept these impulses in the public eye, as reformers, scientists, journalists, and others struggled to define these impulses, to clarify their role in social life, and to make conceptual space for them in the newly scientific studies of the human condition.

So we take note of three important trends in nineteenth-century intellectual culture. Behind the progressive version of the ethics of self-realization, we find the idea of a multifaceted human personality, susceptible to development in a variety of directions, in need of cultivation and congenial conditions for growth. In the grip of this idea, Dewey and Gilman learned from idealists, romantics, and transcendentalists to take the notion of growth as their central ethical category, thereby providing a fitting metaphor for the non-conformist, organic, and ideally idiosyncratic process of ethical reflection that Emerson and William James imagined. We also find that many of the same progressives harbored typically Victorian worries about promiscuity, prostitution, and other untoward expressions of sexual impulse; but behind these worries we find the same obsessive focus on sex that preoccupied Freud.[28]

Du Bois worked at the intersection of these trends, inheriting the insights and shortcomings of post-idealist perfectionism, proto-pragmatic anti-formalism, and Victorian "erotomania", and adapting all of this to his own purposes. If we want to see how these elements of the late nineteenth and early twentieth-century intellectual environment might come together all at once, we might consider the Dionysian perfectionism of Friedrich Nietzsche. Nietzsche was perhaps the most uncompromising advocate for the cultivation of the self, and for reclaiming aspects of the self that, he believed, had been underemphasized by reigning theories of the human intellect. In his writings, Nietzsche insists on the importance of inner drives, and even, mostly seriously (and most relevant, as we will see, to our discussion of *Dark Princess*) on the importance of diet and digestion for intellectual activity. Predictably, even apart from his many misogynistic assertions and sexist analogies, he reclaims sexual desire as among these inner drives. He complains that Christianity turned Eros into Vice, and in *Ecce Homo* he offers the following as "a proposition against vice" from what he calls his moral code: "Every kind of contempt for sex, every impurification of it by means of the concept 'impure,' is the crime *par excellence* against life—is the real sin against the holy spirit of life."[29] Of course, Nietzsche says many things, on this subject especially, and some of his remarks are incompatible with others. But the basic points remain constant: life-enhancement is the key to what he sometimes consents to call virtue, and to what in any case stands opposed to decadence; virtue in this sense means claiming—and moderating—the expression of one's inner drives, of the non- and extra-rational aspects of human personality; and sexual desire is among these essential drives.

Nietzsche models this for us: a truly Dionysian perfectionism. For him, self-realization involves recognizing and celebrating one's inner drives, including the sex drive. And this celebration is constrained less by rules—which can, as James said, grow too narrow for the actual case—than by the pursuit of a classical harmony or balance. Nietzsche's insistence on revealing the hollowness of decadent Western traditions—on philosophizing, he says, with a hammer—leads him to overcompensate, to underemphasize ideas of balance and to overemphasize the ecstasy and vitality of Dionysian excess. This is a problem (if it is a problem) of rhetoric, caused in part by Nietzsche's continuing reliance on the Dionysian idea even as its meaning shifts in his later works, and in part by his determination to prevent readers from simply learning a system or set of answers from him. But this apparent celebration of excess, like the ultimate failure of the protagonist of *Zarathustra*, serves as a useful reminder of the difficulty of Nietzsche's ethical project. The willingness to break overly narrow rules can lead to real excess, to ethical mistakes and failures. Hence our claim that Du Bois, courting the risk of excess and moral error, was also something of a Dionysian perfectionist.[30]

## Race and Perfectionism

Du Bois's commitment to perfectionism and anti-formalism occurs in many of the same texts as does the erotic. In "Criteria," for example, he explains that the "world we want to create for ourselves and for all America" is "a world where men know, where men create, where they *realize themselves* and where they enjoy life" (*Writings*, 994–95, emphasis added). Somewhat later in the same essay he links this perfectionist project to a racialized, antiformalist defense of the erotic, in a diatribe against inappropriate constraints on artistic production that turns positively Emersonian: "The young and slowly growing black public," he says, "still wants its prophets...unfree. We are bound by all sorts of customs that have come down as second-hand soul clothes of white patrons. We are ashamed of sex and we lower our eyes when people will talk of it" (*Writings*, 1001). And in an entry from Du Bois's journal, we see again the way in which the sexual appetite can be understood as of a piece with political and spiritual desire. "What is life but life, after all? Its end is the greatest and fullest self—and this end is the Good. . . ."[31] He expands on these ideas much later, in a 1938 commencement address at Fisk University:

> Life is more than meat, even though life without food dies. Living is not for earning, earning is for living. . . . Life is the fullest, most complete enjoyment of the possibilities of human existence. It is the development and broadening of the feelings and emotions. . . . It is *the free enjoyment of every normal appetite.* . . . [H]ence rise Love, Friendship, emulation, and ambition, and the ever widening realms of thought, in increasing circles of apprehended and interpreted Truth (1061, emphasis added).

He emphasizes that the "freedom to create within the limits of natural law; *the freedom to love without limit*; the freedom to dream of the utter marriage of beauty and art; all this men may have . . ." (*Writings*, 1061–1062, emphasis added). Reminding us of the ethical vision behind the various forms of collectivism, these moments in Du Bois's writings evoke a Dionysian perfectionism: He establishes the multidimensional cultivation of human personality as his ethical ideal and as the aim of his political work. He insists that this self-realization include the erotic dimensions of human personality and interaction. He urges the pursuit of this ideal even if it means violating customary societal proscriptions—or, better put, he recommends the revaluation of these social rules so that the ideal can be freely sought. And he does all this at the risk of ethical mistake, or of slipping into an unbalanced character. This risk makes itself apparent in his personal behavior; but it also shapes his written work, perhaps nowhere more completely than in *Dark Princess* (1928).

## Dark Princess *and Political Desire*

The "couple" becomes the central trope and vehicle for social change for Du Bois as early as *The Quest of the Silver Fleece*, a "psychological

romance"[32] in which two African American lovers, Blessed Alwyn
and the dark-skinned Zora, must undergo political and sexual temptation (her fall is sexual; his, political) before marrying and crossing
the threshold into the modern era. Revolutionary in its figuring of a
dark-skinned heroine who falls but rises again (precisely the kind of
plot he finds lacking in white contemporary theatre, he will say years
later in "Criteria of Negro Art"), *The Quest* anticipates—in plot,
form, and global vision—the political nuptials of *Dark Princess*. In
"The Comet," the new world order glimpsed by the couple is brought
on by a freak apocalypse—importantly, in this case, it is an interracial
couple. Thinking that a comet has destroyed every living person in
the world (it turns out, only in New York), the black Jim and
unnamed white woman dimly come to realize that, despite their
racial differences, and most especially her racial antipathies, they
must become the new Adam and Eve if the human race is to survive:

All nature slept until—until, and quick with the same startling
thought, they looked into each other's eyes—he, ashen, and she,
crimson, with unspoken thought. To both, the vision of a mighty
beauty—of vast, unspoken things, swelled in their souls. . . .
Silently, immovably, they saw each other face to face—eye to eye.
Their souls lay naked to the night. It was not lust; it was not
love—it was some vaster, mightier thing that needed neither
touch of body nor thrill of soul. It was a thought divine, splendid.
Slowly, noiselessly, they moved toward each other—the heavens
above, the seas around, the city grim and dead below . . . She
stretched her jeweled hands abroad. He lifted up one of his
mighty arms, and they cried each to the other, almost with one
voice: "The World is dead." "Long live the—[33]

The romantic apostrophe, and the ideal itself, are literally interrupted
by the emergence of the woman's father and suitor who, it seems,
have survived the comet and immediately return the couple to the
world of racial stratification by calling Jim a racial epithet. Indeed,
Jim is accused of harming the woman and for his troubles risks being
lynched. The long poem, "A Hymn to The Peoples," follows
"The Comet" with a plea to God to "help make Humanity divine"
(*Reader,* 623); indeed the story is less a jeremiad than a plea for a

utopian dream. As in so much of Du Bois's fiction, literature makes extant a political reality in and for the imagination, and thereby offers a vision for, if not yet of, the "real" world in which he lived. Unlike *Dark Princess,* where the lovers are architects of social change, in "The Comet," catastrophic change (namely the comet) must happen *to* them in order for the world to reshape itself. This shift also reflects Du Bois's literary vacillations between a naturalist determination and the realist's faith in the possibility of human agency.[34] Importantly, miscegenation is figured as last resort, as only imaginable *after* the world's end. But it is also imagined as a brave new postlapsarian world which can be reimagined and repeopled, and although the latter is described almost as a kind of moral duty, the frequent references to the woman's blushing suggests that she, at least, will not find the duty onerous.

What in *Quest* cannot be narrated beyond the broken dash of the pledge, "long live—", finally finds expression, and generations of ambivalent audiences, in Du Bois's last published novel, *Dark Princess.*[35] Claudia Tate reports that contemporaneous critics "seemed to have regarded *Dark Princess* as a dirty old man's fantasy that should never have been published."[36] In the spirit of our discussion of Dionysian perfectionism, we suggest that what appears to be a dirty old man's fantasy is really a development in ethical expression. That is, the wedding of passion and politics in *Dark Princess* is not orthogonal to its political positions; rather, it inflects and gives content to the novel's arguments about antiracist activism.

Beavers argues that Du Bois's effort to align "the erotic with political agency" means that he must "find a way to link body and action."[37] We suggest further that the interest in the body, according to the novel's logic, is not to be confused with gross appetites or materialism. In fact, this is precisely the confusion that leads Matthew Townes, the novel's protagonist, to propose to the personally immaculate but sexually indifferent Sara. Settling for hygiene and domestic competence, Matthew is wooed by little more than the "perfect order" of her "machine-made . . . but wax-neat" flat, abetted by the "thick and sweet" cream that comes with his tea and by several helpings of "seed-cakes" (Du Bois, *Dark Princess,* 137). Ignoring the fact that she shows no interest in listening to music (Ivanoff), reading literature (Balzac), or experiencing love ("I've been fighting the thing men call love all my life," she says [138]), that is, all the very things that would fill the "void" for him, Townes is temporarily sidetracked from the "dream, the woman . . . the vision of world work" (136).

The scene in Sara's flat is important because she adopts an essentially Hobbesian worldview, in which political machination serves the ends of power rather than social justice. That alone should have made her an inappropriate mate for someone who, though disillusioned by this point in the novel, still imagines the possibilities of an international "union with all the dark and oppressed" (135). But this scene shows us what makes Sara initially attractive to Matthew, and what will ultimately make her truly unsuitable for him. It is because of, not in spite of, his longing for "beauty, music, [and] books" (136) that he mistakes (and then trades) cleanliness for aesthetic taste, political ambition for social commitment, and, importantly, domestic comforts for conjugal intimacy. Matthew will stray from the path that he and Sara set out on *not* because he lusted or was lulled away from "world work" by the sensual pleasures of seedcakes and tea cream, but because there were not *more* such pleasures. Just after their wedding, Matthew moves to embrace Sara, only to have her rebuff him with "mind the veil." (Of course, she means to warn him against rumpling her bridal regalia, though in language that recalls Du Bois's famous metaphor). The scene marks her as an unfit mate for Matthew and does so by using sexual desire to symbolize political sensibility, and anticipates Matthew's growing recognition of her political frigidity. This marriage does not wed what Du Bois really aims to couple: the sensual with the political. It is not simply that Sara is uninterested in love and its physical expressions, but that she is insensible to an entire continuum of sensual pleasures that the novel puts at the center of a global political vision, a vision that includes the body in its fullest expressions. Thus it is not just "bad taste" that Sara demonstrates, but—like her substitution of an electric log for a real fireplace (142)—a preference for the representation over the "real," and it is this that Matthew finally resists.

[S]lowly and half-consciously . . . revolt stirred within him against this political game he was playing. It was not moral

revolt. It was esthetic disquiet . . . . His revolt was against things
unsuitable, ill adjusted and in bad taste; the illogical lack of fundamental harmony; the unnecessary dirt and waste—the ugli-
ness of it all—that revolted him (147).

This is not mere class elitism, though it certainly partakes of it. Rather,
Epicureanism becomes the living embodiment and enactment of his
idealized politics, the development and fulfillment of the body as
called for by perfectionism. As we saw earlier, Du Bois argues that life
consists in "the free enjoyment of every normal appetite." *Dark
Princess* urges the enjoyment of a range of bodily appetites, from the
preparation and consumption of delicious foods to a sensual appreciation of the strenuous body in love and labor.

Matthew realizes his sexuopolitical ideal in his affair with the
Princess Kautilya. The lovers enjoy several weeks of languorous, sensual pleasure, foreplay to their shared struggle for racial justice.
According to Claudia Tate, Matthew here "seeks penance for his passionate excesses by joining a labor team, digging a tunnel for the new
subway"(1995, xxii). But, we argue, neither Matthew nor Kautilya
seem penitent for anything, least of all for their passion. Their separation performs a mutual sacrifice, which itself is an effort to recreate
their Edenic voluptuary on a broader scale for others to enjoy.
Arguably, Matthew embodies "a redemptive consciousness but . . .
eschews the impulse to channel this into religiosity, opting instead to
locate redemption as a secular phenomenon."[38] More than this, we
suggest, redemption for these two is an embodied, erotic, cultural,
and (not antithetically) political phenomenon.

Their erotic communion is not sanctioned by Sara's "smarter set"
(152), who call it a "five-minute infatuation—primitive passion"
(218), but the lovers are far from contrite; they see their relationship as
a "Benediction" (238). Lest an audience find the extramarital affair
merely a newfangled modern arrangement, Matthew's own "wise old
mother" approves of the relationship, and blithely dismisses his
marriage vows to Sara by saying that "her son ain't married. . . . He
only thinks he is" (224). Matthew's epistles to Kautilya make clear that
he willingly goes into isolation not out of shame but out of a sense of
the divine sanctity of their act, which, he says, expresses "the great love

of a man for a woman—the perfect friendship and communion of two human beings," which can never be "mere evil" (263). Their union may be contingent on the "physical urge of sex between us" but it "rises from the ecstasy of our bodies to the communion of saints, the resurrection of the spirit, the exquisite crucifixion of God. It is the noblest thing in our world" (259–60).

Matthew, yoking sexual climax with Christ's crucifixion, thereby weds bodily and religious ecstasies as conjugal partners. This merging of "high" and "low" also appears in Matthew's desire to have a relationship that is somehow a combination of his marriage to Sara, "hallowed by law and love" (153), and his experience with a prostitute who, he fondly remembers, "had twisted her young live body about his" and "whispered, 'There, Big Boy!'" (153). In short, Matthew wants his virgin to be a whore and his crucifixions to be climaxes. In fact, Matthew's desire for more does not lead to debauchery but to his efforts to make himself a worthier vehicle in order to realize his and Kautilya's world vision of leisure and pleasure for all. The couple's passion takes them beyond the bounds of social convention, but it is clear that their moral trespassing is necessary to the progressive perfection of the social order. Bystanders in Chicago hiss "shameless!" and "Fool" (264) at the "scarlet" couple, branded by his adultery and her unmarried status, as they walk down the streets publicly kissing and holding hands; but these critics are nothing to the pair. The novel associates them with Sara's sterile political set and even with an unnamed "East Indian" (298) in Kautilya's entourage, who, near the end of the novel, confesses to Matthew that he was almost moved to murder by the knowledge that "in a . . . wild excess of frenzy . . . she [Kautilya] sacrificed to you her royal person" (298).

Such moralism is clearly refuted in the novel. Townes and Kautilya reject these condemnations, and the novel's end amounts to a cosmic blessing of their courage to face the wrath of those who inhabit what Kautilya calls the "Place of Death and the city of the Face of Fear" (210). Importantly for our argument, Kautilya and Matthew understand their separation and their subsequent Spartan existence as temporary and spiritual—self-sacrifice but not self-punishment. Matthew, in fact, pointedly refutes the idea that he be "painted as punished with common labor for following lust and desecrating the home"

(263) and suggests instead that it is the "lustful scramble for place and power and show" (262) that is offensive. Kautilya understands their parting as spiritual preparation for work and possible reunion, suggesting that he "strip" himself of "everything material. . . . sit naked and alone before . . . God" (263) not as repudiation of their affair but as preparation for their work to improve the world: "Gentle culture and the beauty and the courtesies of life—they are the real end of living" (286).

Interestingly, consummation here is not the climax but the prelude. Du Bois's Matthew is not Richardson's Lovelace; the novel is not about pursuit, seduction, and fall from social grace. Rather, as the protagonists understand it, their unsanctioned liaison was not the end but rather a reward suggesting only more reward. Sex, Kautilya says, "was our due. We earned it. But now we must earn a higher, finer thing" (260). The separation functions as a way to earn anew what their "honeymoon of our high marriage with God alone as priest" (260) confirmed for them: that they must work to bring others toward the beauties of leisure and sensory luxury that they have tasted.

Significantly, the domestic props of the affair are proxy for the romance, which is in turn but a manifestation of the couple's politics of high culture and high color. When Kautilya announces her imminent departure, he explains that he'll have to leave the apartment they've shared: "the Chinese rug," he tells her, "was the splendid coloring of your skin; the Matisse was the flame of your high spirit; the music was your voice" (263). Kautilya, in a sense, comes to embody the representation of life that he had admired in his earlier life, in a painting that Sara had removed from their wall: an image of a nude "daringly drawn with a frame of color and a woman's long and naked body. It talked to Matthew of endless strife, of fire and beauty and never-dying flesh" (143). The contiguity and seeming interchangeability of body and cultural artifact reflect not so much the sensualization of the novel's political project but rather the politicization of the worldly senses. Matthew's description of his trials without Kautilya, for example, celebrates work in terms that evoke the homosociality of sport, and suggest the ways in which sensuality is a perfectible vehicle for political service. As a laborer, he goes down girded for a fight with a hundred others in jersies and overalls and thick, heavy shoes. We are like hard-limbed Grecian athletes . . . One can see the same ripple and swelling of muscles. . . . I am bare, sweating, untrammeled. My muscles already begin to flow smooth and unconfined. I have no stomach, either in flesh or spirit. My body is all life and eagerness, without weight" (265).

Work here is not just about the masses united; it is about getting in political shape. Such representations of bodily exertion and the classical beauty of sweating, muscular men reflect the way the body is political analog in *Dark Princess*. And thus Kautilya's body, too, is always a political spectacle and, in the logic of the novel, a spectacular register of political progress. Matthew's gazing on her, therefore, is not merely acquisitive, for the "rich and flowing grace of the dress out of which rose so darkly splendid the jeweled flesh" (19) makes the lush body a metonym for cultural riches and political ascendancy. We see this again when at novel's end, she has become a living cornucopia: "a king's ransom lay between the naked beauty of her breasts, blood rubies weighed down her ears and about the slim, brown gold of her waist ran a girdle such as emperors fight for" (307). Not accidentally, her body emerges from the clothing, in a subordinate position in the sentence, almost merely an adornment to the dress or the jewels. Not surprisingly, since a certain notion of "civilized" culture, not the cultivation of the body, is the political end to which the novel aspires, things acquire a physical sensuality often even more voluptuous than Kautilya's body. In a sense these things are the goal of all their striving and thus more to be narratively savored than their sex.

Take, for instance, the extended description of the *afterglow* of their ardor, in a scene in which Matthew in effect creates a spa for culture lovers. After a long hot bath, Kautilya finds "new silken things in the dressing room . . . . Beside the flaming dance of the fire was a low, white Turkish taboret . . . . The hot coffee steamed on the salver, with toast and butter and cream. There was an orange in halves and a little yellow rosebud" (220). After eating, they curl up in chairs by the fire, silently read poetry, and listen to the faint strains of Dvořák. "And so the day passed half wordless with beauty and sound, full of color and content . . ." (220). What Matthew longs for are "American Roses and new books and bits of silk and gold" (258), the "gorgeous dressing gown" (258) that Kautilya buys for him, the delicious food she prepares for him. Thus Matthew was misled by the tempting appearance of cream with his tea when he proposed to Sara, just as at his wedding to her, he is misled by the delicate titillation of "a single, shining pearl at the parting of two little breasts" (143)—misled not because, the reader learns, he should not have been looking at his betrothed's breasts but because her cleavage leads to no more. It is not Sara's frigidity that proves so unsatisfactory to him but that her frigidity is keyed to cultural sterility in the novel. The jewels at Kautilya's bosom—jewels which earlier the Machiavellian political operative, Sammy, sees just in terms of material wealth—are by the novel's end the couple's cultural dowry, signifying the multicultural blessings of Jesus, Allah, Brahma, Vishnu, and a host of other deities (310).

## Ethical Erotica

Du Bois's forays into the erotic, in his life and his writing, as products of a considered ethical sensibility, constitute the basic structure of which would have been familiar to many of his contemporaries. As suggested by his writings, including *Dark Princess*, Du Bois treats life as growth, and sees growth as a matter of cultivating, in a classically balanced and harmonious manner, all the potentialities of human embodied existence. Under these terms, right conduct is a matter of revaluing or breaking the rules that new conditions have rendered obsolete—what William James thought of as the highest ethical life and what Dewey and Jane Addams called, simply, intelligence. And he sees politics as the place to pursue the conditions under which growth and self-realization can take place, thereby making possible, as Emma Goldman put it, "the birth of what is fine and true in man."[39]

We use Goldman to make this last point in order to stress Du Bois's continuity with broader currents of thought during his time. Paradoxically, reading him in light of this continuity should also reveal his continuities with contemporary thinking. Postmodernists of a certain sort prize the breaking of overly narrow rules, and recommend that an aesthetic model of self-fashioning take the place of all casuistic ethics. Feminists and queer theorists of a certain sort argue for the value of embodied experience, the reclamation of sex as an arena for self-actualization, and the multiple connections between sex, gender, and politics. And social historians have come to insist on the links between identity formation in consumer societies and the cultivation of the possibilities of personal and sensory experience.

But there are familiar downsides to all of these recent developments. The challenge to ethical rules seems perilously close to the abandonment of ethics, with its promise of distinguishing good from bad, right from wrong. The embrace of aesthetic self-fashioning can come only after one decides—on what grounds?—between competing models of the aesthetic, between, say, the difficult shocks of avant-garde esoterica to the affirming accessibility of traditional practices. The reclamation of sex carries with it the danger of validating the status quo with regard to sexual and gender inequities. And folding the self into late capitalism's quest for possessions and enjoyments tends to subordinate the public to the market, the citizen to the consumer—and the poorer consumer to the wealthier.

Du Bois might be better equipped to deal with these problems if he were not so consistently an interstitial figure. Spending half his life in the nineteenth century and half in the twentieth, he often had to adjust his commitments to changed intellectual and social conditions. He struggled to make his romantic Crummellian racialism compatible with the realities of twentieth-century physical anthropology; to adjust his various optimisms—Enlightenment, progressive-era, and socialist—to the persistence of industrial capitalism and, as he says in one place, of unreason; and to reconcile his Victorian elitism to the consolidation of mass society. And, most relevant just now, he had to reconcile different conceptions of aesthetic self-fashioning.

## Notes

1. David Levering Lewis, *W. E. B. Du Bois: The Fight for Equality and the American Century, 1919–1963* (New York: Henry Holt, 2000), 267.

2. Claudia Tate, "Race and Desire: *Dark Princess: A Romance*, by William Edward Burghardt Du Bois," in *Psychoanalysis and Black Novels* (New York: Oxford

University Press, 1998); reprinted in this volume. Hereafter all references will be to the reprinted version and will be made parenthetically in the text.

3. Claudia Tate, Introduction to *Dark Princess: A Romance*, by W. E. B. Du Bois (Jackson: University Press of Mississippi, 1995), xviii. Hereafter all citations will be made parenthetically in the text.

4. Susan Gillman, *Blood Talk: American Race Melodrama and the Culture of the Occult* (Chicago: University of Chicago Press, 2003).

5. See Farah Jasmine Griffin, "Black Feminists and Du Bois: Respectability, Protection, and Beyond," *Annals of the American Academy of Political and Social Science* 568, no. 1 (March 2000): 28–40.

6. Farah Jasmine Griffin, "Black Feminists and Du Bois," 29; and Joy James, "Profeminism and Gender Elites: Du Bois, Anna Julia Cooper and Ida B. Wells-Barnett," in this volume.

7. Herman Beavers, "Romancing the Body Politic: Du Bois's Propaganda of the Dark World," *Annals of the American Academy of Political and Social Science* 568, no. 1 (March 2000), 250–64, 262–63.

8. Farah Jasmine Griffin, "Black Feminists and Du Bois," 36.

9. Ibid., 36.

10. Ibid., 36.

11. Herman Beavers, "Romancing the Body Politic," 231, 259.

12. Alys Eve Weinbaum, "Reproducing Racial Globality: W. E. B. Du Bois and the Sexual Politics of Black Internationalism," *Social Text* 19, no. 2 (Summer 2001): 15–41

13. Herman Beavers, "Romancing the Body Politic," 259.

14. Weinbaum, "Reproducing Racial Globality," 18.

15. Hazel V. Carby, "The Souls of Black Men," in *Race Men: The W. E. B. Du Bois Lectures* (Cambridge, Mass.: Harvard University Press, 1998). Reprinted in this volume, 16. Hereafter all references will be to the reprinted version and will be made parenthetically in the text.

16. Sharon Holland, "The Revolution, 'In Theory'," *American Literary History* 12, no. 1–2 (Spring/Summer 2000): 327–36.

17. Arnold Rampersad, *The Art and Imagination of Du Bois* (Cambridge, Mass.: Harvard University Press, 1976), 132. Rampersad is commenting on the moral statement of *The Quest of the Silver Fleece* (1911) here, but Du Bois's position seems only more emphatic on this point by the time he publishes *Dark Princess* in 1928.

18. W. E. B. Du Bois, *Writings* (New York: Library of America, 1987), 1000, emphasis added. Hereafter all citations will be made parenthetically in the text.

19. Adolph Reed, *W. E. B. Du Bois and American Political Thought* (New York: Oxford University Press, 1997), 19. Hereafter all citations will be made parenthetically in the text.

20. David McLennan, ed., *Karl Marx: Selected Writings* (Oxford: Oxford University Press, 2000).

21. John Dewey, *Art As Experience* (1934; New York: Putnam, 1958).

22. Charlotte Perkins Gilman (1912), "Our Brains and What Ails Them," in Leonard Harris, Scott L. Pratt, and Anne S. Waters ed., *American Philosophies* (Malden, Mass.: Blackwell, 2002) 122–33.

23. James Mark Baldwin, *Dictionary of Philosophy and Psychology* (New York: The Macmillan Company, 1901–1905), vol. 2.

24. Paul Gilroy gestures at Du Bois's debt to Hegel in chapter four of *The Black Atlantic: Modernity and Double Consciousness* (Cambridge, Mass.: Harvard University Press, 1993). To give the gesture more content, see Shamoon Zamir, *Dark Voices: W. E. B. Du Bois and American Thought, 1888–1903* (Chicago: University of Chicago Press, 1995); Russell A. Berman, "Du Bois and Wagner: Race, Nation, and Culture between the United States and Germany," *German Quarterly* 70, no. 2 (Spring 1997): 123–35; Sieglinde Lemke, "Berlin and Boundaries: sollen versus geschehen," *boundary 2* 27, no. 3 (Fall 2000): 45–78; Winfried Siemerling, "W. E. B. Du Bois, Hegel, and the Staging of Alterity," *Callaloo* 24, no. 1 (Winter 2001): 325–33; Robert Gooding-Williams, "Philosophy of History and Social Critique in *The Souls of Black Folk*," *Social Science Information* 26, no. 1 (1987): 99–114; and Ronald R. Sundstrom, "The Prophetic and Pragmatic Philosophy of 'Race' in W. E. B. Du Bois's 'The Comet,'" *APA Newsletter on Philosophy and the Black Experience* 99, no. 1 (Fall 1999): 2–5.

25. William James, "The Moral Philosopher and the Moral Life," *William James: The Essential Writings*, ed. Bruce Wilshire (Albany: SUNY Press, 1984) 294–308, 304.

26. John Dewey, "Moral Judgment and Moral Knowledge," in Larry A. Hickman and Thomas M. Alexander, eds., *The Essential Dewey, volume 23: Ethics, Logic, Psychology* (Bloomington: Indiana University Press, 1998) 328–40.

27. Gail Bederman, *Manliness and Civilization* (Chicago: University of Chicago Press, 1996), 48–49.

28. Michael McGerr, *A Fierce Discontent: the Rise and Fall of the Progressive Movement in America, 1870–1920* (New York: Free Press, 2003).

29. Friedrich Nietzsche, *Beyond Good and Evil*, Walter Kaufmann, trans. (New York: Vintage, 1966), 168; Friedrich Nietzsche, *Ecce Homo*, Walter Kaufmann, trans. (New York: Vintage, 1989), 6.

30. At this point Reed would likely urge us to adduce some evidence that Du Bois read or interacted with Nietzsche, or Dewey, or Gilman. But our point, once more, is not that he was influenced by these figures to adopt this view, but that his own words, and deeds, betray a commitment to a view that is at least quite similar, and as familiar in Du Bois's milieu as the collectivism that so interests Reed.

31. Reported in Tate, "Race and Desire."

32. Arnold Rampersad, *Art and Imagination of W. E. B. Du Bois*, 130.

33. W. E. B. Du Bois, *The Oxford W. E. B. Du Bois Reader*, ed. Eric J. Sundquist (New York: Oxford University Press, 1996), 618, 620. Hereafter all citations will be made parenthetically in the text.

34. On genre in Du Bois, see Arnold Rampersad, *Art and Imagination*, 128–32.

35. W. E. B. Du Bois, *Dark Princess* (1928; University of Mississippi Press, 1955). Hereafter all citations will be made parenthetically in the text.

36. Tate, Introduction to *Dark Princess*, xxiv.

37. Herman Beavers, "Romancing the Body Politic," 258.

38. Ibid., 257. An extension of this theme: Matthew and his new love, the Princess Kautilya have a son, and the novel ends by explicitly identifying the son with the political hopes of the darker races, a biracial love-child and emblem of anti-imperialist, anti-white-supremacist, interracial political mobilization.

39. Emma Goldman, "Anarchism," reprinted in *American Philosophies*, eds. Scott Pratt, Leonard Harris, and Ann Waters (Malden, Mass.: Blackwell, 2002), 410.

# 7

# The Souls of Black Men

■ *Hazel V. Carby*

Du Bois is the brook of fire through which we all must
pass in order to gain access to the intellectual and
political weaponry needed to sustain the radical
democratic tradition in our time.

Cornel West

In a grand Victorian gesture of self-sacrifice, W. E. B.
Du Bois, then a young man in the formative years of his intellectual
development, determined to subordinate his individual desires and
ambitions to promote a political project that would benefit the world
in general by advancing the particular interests of African American
peoples. In his journal entry of February 23, 1893, his twenty-fifth
birthday, Du Bois wrote:

I am striving to make my life all that life may be—and I am
limiting that strife only in so far as that strife is incompatible with
others of my brothers and sisters making their lives similar. . . .
I am firmly convinced that my own best development is not one
and the same with the best development of the world and here
I am willing to sacrifice . . . . I therefore . . . work for the rise of
the Negro people, taking for granted that their best development
means the best development of the world.

Du Bois decided, however, that the commitment he undertook did not require him to set aside the interests of selfish desire and ambition: the entry concludes that the advancement of his "race" will be intimately tied to his own personal achievements as an intellectual, a man who wishes to "make a name in science, to make a name in art and thus to raise my race."[1]

Through a close analysis of Du Bois's *The Souls of Black Folk*, I will argue that although he declares that he intends to limit his striving "in so far as that strife is incompatible with others of my brothers and sisters making their lives similar," beneath the surface of this apparent sacrifice of individual desire to become an intellectual and a race leader is a conceptual framework that is gender-specific; not only does it apply exclusively to men, but it encompasses only those men who enact narrowly and rigidly determined codes of masculinity.

This gendered framework negates in fact the opportunity offered in words for black women to make "their lives similar"; the project suffers from Du Bois's complete failure to imagine black women as intellectuals and race leaders. The failure to incorporate black women into the sphere of intellectual equality, I will demonstrate, is not merely the result of the sexism of Du Bois's historical moment, as evident in the language of his chapter titles in *The Souls of Black Folk*, such as "Of the Training of Black Men," and "The Sons of Master and Man."[2] It is a conceptual and political failure of imagination that remains a characteristic of the work of contemporary African American male intellectuals. Du Bois described and challenged the hegemony of the national and racial formations in the United States at the dawn of a new century, but he did so in ways that both assumed and privileged a discourse of black masculinity. Cornel West describes and challenges the hegemony of the national and racial formations at the end of the same century, but many of these discourses are still in place.

In a recent essay, West asserts that Du Bois's "patriarchal sensibilities speak for themselves."[3] On the contrary, I will argue that they do not "speak for themselves" but have to be rigorously examined so that we may follow and grasp their epistemological implications and consequences. West's easy dismissal suggests that there is no need to undertake the serious intellectual work necessary to understand the processes that gender knowledge.

West sets up three fundamental pillars of Du Bois's intellectual project: his "Enlightenment world view"; his "Victorian strategies" (the way his world view is translated into practice); and his "American optimism."[4] Is there no need to understand how these foundations articulate with ideologies of gender? If "patriarchal sensibilities speak for themselves," then they are merely superficial, easily recognized, and quickly accounted for, enabling real intellectual work to continue elsewhere.[5] If they "speak for themselves," then nothing of intellectual value or worth could result from demonstrating or exposing exactly what constitutes "patriarchy" or "patriarchal sensibilities." It is through such devices that members of the contemporary black male intellectual establishment, sometimes referred to by the media as "the new black intellectuals," disregard the need for feminist analysis while maintaining a politically correct posture of making an obligatory, though finally empty, gesture toward it.[6]

Du Bois constructed particular personal, political, and social characteristics of a racialized masculinity to articulate his definition of black leadership. He was particularly concerned about the "moral uplift of a people" and felt that this was best accomplished "by planting in every community of Negroes black men with ideals of life and thrift and civilization, such as must in time filter through the masses and set examples of moral living."[7] After weighing the political and social needs of what he imagined to be the race, he judged the worth of black male intellectuals and would-be race leaders according to those needs. In addition to focusing on that discussion, my analysis of *The Souls of Black Folk* will demonstrate how, in a similar fashion, Du Bois measured, judged, and lived his own multifaceted identity— as a black intellectual, as a race leader, and as a man. It is important not only to recognize the varied and complex ways in which Du Bois developed a public persona that was crafted to embody the philosophy he espoused, but also to analyze the ideological effect of such embodiment on his philosophic judgments. My contention is that these judgments reveal highly gendered structures of intellectual and political thought and feeling; these structures are embedded in specific ways in *The Souls of Black Folk*, first published in 1903, reprinted twenty-four times by 1940, revived in the 1960s and 1970s, and now regarded as a founding text in the study of black culture.[8]

First, let me anticipate and address possible objections to the feminist politics of this project. I decided to analyze the intellectual and political thought and feeling of *The Souls of Black Folk* from the perspective of its gendered structure precisely because it is such an important intellectual work. I absolutely agree with Wesley Brown that "Politically, Du Bois's activism always seems to anticipate struggles that followed . . . his crucial role in the formation of the N.A.A.C.P., the Pan African Movement, and the efforts to ban nuclear weapons paved the way for our own participation in the Civil Rights Movement and the Vietnam War protests of the 1960s. This link between Du Bois and struggles for self determination continues until this day."[9] I do not focus on *The Souls of Black Folk* because I feel that it is a particularly egregious example of sexist thinking; it isn't. Nor is it my intention to claim that W. E. B. Du Bois was a sexist male individual. In the public arena, as an African American intellectual and as a politician, Du Bois advocated equality for women and consistently supported feminist causes later in his life.

There is, unfortunately, no simple correspondence between anyone's support for female equality and the ideological effect of the gendered structures of thought and feeling at work in any text one might write and publish.[10] If, as intellectuals and as activists, we are committed, like Du Bois, to struggles for liberation and democratic egalitarianism, then surely it is not contradictory also to struggle to be critically aware of the ways in which ideologies of gender have undermined our egalitarian visions in the past and continue to do so in the present. Gendered structures of thought and feeling permeate our lives and our intellectual work, including *The Souls of Black Folk* and other texts which have been regarded as *founding* texts written by the *founding fathers* of black American history and culture.

In the North American and European academies, Du Bois has come to embody the ideal or representative figure of the African American intellectual, "the brook of fire through which we all must pass in order to gain access to the intellectual and political weaponry needed to sustain the radical democratic tradition in our time."[11] If we agree that our critical practice ought to include probing the various ways in which we constitute our fields of knowledge, I contend that we need to expose and learn from the gendered, ideological assumptions which underlie the founding texts and determine that their authors become the *representative* figures of the American intellectual. These authors and their productions are shaped by gendered structures of thought and feeling, which in turn actively shape the major paradigms and modes of thought of all academic discourse.

The significance of *The Souls of Black Folk* as a text which offered new and alternative ways to formulate complex issues of race and nation was immediately recognized by black intellectuals when it was first published in 1903.[12] In *The Autobiography of an Ex-Colored Man* (1912), James Weldon Johnson paid homage to *The Souls of Black Folk* as offering the country something previously unknown "in depicting the life, the ambitions, the struggles, and the passions of those of their race who are striving to break the narrow limits of traditions."[13] In his autobiography *Along This Way*, first published in 1933, Johnson asserted that *The Souls of Black Folk* "had a greater effect upon and within the Negro race in America than any other single book published in this country since *Uncle Tom's Cabin.*"[14]

Johnson's enthusiasm was kindled by the ambitious attempt of *The Souls of Black Folk* to create a genealogy for what Benedict Anderson has called an *"imagined community"* among a specific assemblage of fellow readers.[15] Through its representations of individuals, Du Bois's book aims to bring into being a community. Imaginatively, he forges a people from his articulation of the material terms of their historical existence.[16] Because *The Souls of Black Folk* was so successful in the creation and imagining of a black community, it was an important text to academics and political activists outside of the academy who fought to establish African American Studies as a coherent and structured field of knowledge—a process which also needed to bring its own imagined community into being through the intellectual and political work of identifying intellectual ancestors; situating and classifying their texts; establishing literary canons and genres of writing; and establishing traditions of thought and intellectual practice.

As one of these rediscovered ancestors, Du Bois became many things to many people: in response to the needs of various agendas, he was situated as an important precursor of different traditions and strands of thought. For Houston Baker, for example, *The Souls of*

*Black Folk* established the general significance of Du Bois as "the black man of culture"; Darwin Turner has argued for the importance of situating Du Bois in relation to a theory of a "Black Aesthetic"; and Wilson J. Moses has stressed the importance of Du Bois's poetics of "Ethiopianism" in order to position him as an important figure in a tradition of "literary black nationalism."[17] As a literary critic, Arnold Rampersad believes that

> The greatness of *The Souls of Black Folk* as a document of black American culture lies in its creation of profound and enduring myths about the life of the people. . . . If all of a nation's literature may stem from one book, as Hemingway implied about *The Adventures of Huckleberry Finn,* then it can as accurately be said that all of Afro-American literature of a creative nature has proceeded from Du Bois' comprehensive statement on the nature of the people in *The Souls of Black Folk.*[18]

Similarly, Robert Stepto has defined the African American literary canon as those texts which expressed a "primary pregeneric myth of the quest for freedom and literacy," and positioned *The Souls of Black Folk* as "a seminal text in Afro-American letters."[19] "Seminal" is, perhaps, the most appropriate (if gendered) adjective to describe the present canonic status of *The Souls of Black Folk,* not just as a work of literature but also as a major contribution to the study of African American history, sociology, politics, and philosophy.[20]

Perhaps the most influential contemporary recovery of Du Bois as a major influence in African American intellectual thought and practice is the work of Cornel West.[21] In West's opinion "W. E. B. Du Bois is the towering black scholar of the twentieth century. The scope of his interests, the depth of his insights, and the sheer majesty of his prolific writings bespeak a level of genius unequaled among modern black intellectuals."[22] In addition to being considered the *greatest* American intellectual of African descent, Du Bois is also the *only* African American intellectual whom West includes in his *The American Evasion of Philosophy: A Genealogy of Pragmatism.*[23]

In this book West argues that pragmatism is a viable and necessary alternative to epistemology-centered philosophy. Pragmatism, he proposes, is "a conception of philosophy as a form of cultural criticism in which the meaning of America is put forward by intellectuals in response to distinct social and cultural crises." As a form of cultural criticism, "American pragmatism is less a philosophical tradition putting forward solutions to perennial problems in the Western philosophical conversation initiated by Plato and more a continuous cultural commentary or set of interpretations that attempt to explain America to itself at a particular historical moment." West situates his own intellectual work within this tradition, and sees himself as a direct descendant of the form of cultural criticism which he has thus defined.[24] And, because Du Bois is the only other black intellectual in this schema, he is West's only representative African American ancestor.

For West, the ideal black intellectual acts as a "critical organic catalyst," a practitioner of "prophetic criticism,"[25] and someone who can become, as West regards himself, "a re-transcending prophet."[26] While all of West's books both criticize and praise the work and ideas of a wide range of intellectuals, only Du Bois is consistently present in all of his texts and the focus of most of the analysis. West self-consciously situates himself as a contemporary embodiment of Du Bois, but he neglects to interrogate the ideological and political *effects* of the gendered nature of Du Bois's theoretical paradigms.

It is a necessary critical task, then, to examine the gendered intellectual practices which structure the way *The Souls of Black Folk* imagines a community and organizes its "framework of consciousness," its "soul."[27] Du Bois creates this community through a complex evocation of the concepts of race, nation, and masculinity.[28] My discussion of the gendering of Du Bois's genealogy of race, of nation, and of manhood will evolve from an analysis of the general narrative structure of the essays and a consideration of the order in which they occur.

If African American writing in North America has its source in the eighteenth- and nineteenth-century texts now identified collectively and variously as slave narratives, personal histories, and spiritual or secular autobiographical texts that give voice to and authenticate black existence, then the narrative structure and genealogy of race, nation, and manhood to be found in *The Souls of Black Folk* imagines its community by reversing the direction of the archetypal journey of these original narratives. The conventional movement of the earlier narratives is away from the conditions of physical and/or mental bondage or despair associated historically with the political, economic, and social formation of the southern states, and toward the attainment of physical and spiritual freedom in the North.[29] But what is understood to be a literary convention has specific political effects: as these narratives moved away from the context in which the majority of African American peoples lived and moved toward a predominantly white society, the direction of the journey determined the imaginative and symbolic landscape in which the conscious desires and ambitions of black humanity could be created and asserted.

Before 1865 it was difficult, if not impossible, for black writers even to imagine the option of returning to the South once black humanity and freedom had been gained in the North. Even after emancipation the American literary imagination was shackled in this respect. For as Mark Twain acknowledged in his 1885 *Adventures of Huckleberry Finn*, once Huck and Jim missed the Ohio river and sailed deeper and deeper into the South, it was necessary for Jim to "belong" to someone; he could no longer belong to himself and survive. As Huck replied when asked if Jim was an escaped slave, "Goodness sakes, would a runaway nigger run *south*?"[30]

In 1903, W. E. B. Du Bois confronted the political dilemmas of previous American narrative forms while also revising many of the conventional concerns expressed in African American literature. The trajectory of *The Souls of Black Folk* is toward the Black Belt of the South, but the text does enact two cultural imperatives from earlier African American literature: freedom and knowledge.[31] The desire for freedom in *The Souls of Black Folk* is a dual quest, both spiritual and physical, while the desire for knowledge emerges in a number of different ways: it is at various times practical, political, philosophical, and spiritual. The text consistently shifts between a predominantly white and a predominantly black world, but its overall narrative impulse gradually moves the focus from white terrain to an autonomous black one.

Out of a total of fourteen chapters that comprise *The Souls of Black Folk*, nine had been previously published as essays in journals, four of them in *The Atlantic Monthly*. When Du Bois organized them into a book, he did not put them in chronological order according to previous dates of publication or in the order in which he had written them, but arranged them according to an interesting set of themes.[32] Two-thirds of the book, the first nine chapters, imagine a black community in relation to its negotiations with the white world of the text. Chapter one, "Of Our Spiritual Strivings," provocatively poses the question that white America dare not ask of black Americans: "How does it feel to be a problem?" It then sets up the existential lament, "Why did God make me an outcast and a stranger in mine own house?" to which the following eight chapters provide the response. Readers are guided through the history and stark present realities of relations of dominance and subordination at the "dawn" of the twentieth century. The story that Du Bois outlines is a story of disappointment, "a vain search for freedom" (48).

The history of this disappointment structures the progress of Du Bois's genealogy, a narrative which is organized through various struggles to claim national citizenship for black people: struggles to emancipate the slaves, struggles to gain the right to vote, struggles for access to education, and the ever-present struggle against economic inequality. Du Bois reconstructs this history in order to envision an alternative future for the nation.[33] In addition to responding to the questions raised in the first chapter, each of the following eight chapters sets up a call: are all these struggles meaningless for black men? The final third of the book, the last five chapters, answer the call with a clear and resounding "no."

The structure of *The Souls of Black Folk* might be described as what Benedict Anderson calls "an idea of steady, solid simultaneity through time."[34] The political meanings to be derived from this form of organization are embodied in a number of individual figures. Du Bois uses anonymous metaphorical figures like the "blighted, ruined form" of the southern man and the brooding black mother; he draws upon the figures of contemporary intellectuals like Booker T. Washington, Alexander Crummell, and himself; and he attempts to create a narrative of the African American folk. I will discuss the gendered characteristics of the first two types of figuration at some length later, but first I wish to consider the way in which Du Bois genders his narrative of the folk.

The folk are first introduced in the fourth chapter, "Of the Meaning of Progress," in a narrative based upon Du Bois's memories of being a teacher in the rural district of Wilson County, Tennessee. Du Bois taught there for two consecutive summers, while he was a student at Fisk University, and he stayed with the Dowell family. One member of that family, a young woman, Josie Dowell, is transformed by Du Bois into a particularly interesting and memorable character whose life and death become a measure for the historical progress of the folk as a whole. Josie is the center of her family and essential to its survival. She harbors a "longing to know" and is the first student to enroll in Du Bois's school. Josie, in other words, becomes a symbol for the desires and the struggles of the African American folk, struggles which are epitomized by attempts to obtain an education. When Du Bois returns to visit the family ten years later—a passage of narrative time during which the liberal reader would expect to see evidence of progress and the fruition of Josie's desires—we learn abruptly that "Josie was dead" (103). Josie's life and death become a metaphor for what progress has meant for the folk; her body is the ground upon which the contradictions between African American desires and ambition and the ambition and desires of white society are fought.[35]

The individual story of Josie is immediately followed by the collective narrative of Atlanta, a city Du Bois describes as a site of contradictions, lying "South of the North, yet North of the South" (109). Atlanta is portrayed as embodying the desires and ambitions of the white world of the South, desires and ambitions that are founded on material greed. If Atlanta represents a possible future for the nation, it will be a future that grows from the outcome of the struggle for the "soul" of the black folk, Du Bois asserts. If that is so, it would seem to be a future built upon the literal and metaphoric deaths of all Josies.

In the fifth chapter, "Of the Wings of Atalanta," Du Bois personifies and genders the city as female and elevates it to the position of a central character in his narrative. He uses the myth of Atalanta and Hippomenes, in which Atalanta, who could outrun and outshoot any man with whom she came into competition, was betrayed by her own greed. Constantly chased by suitors, Atalanta declared that she would only marry the man who could beat her in a foot race, knowing that no one ran faster than she. Hippomenes decides that only guile can help him win, and during the course of his race with Atalanta rolls golden apples in her path, knowing that she will not be able to resist retrieving them. Atalanta falls to temptation and when she swerves to pick up the final apple loses the race to Hippomenes.

Du Bois's particular interpretation of this myth is sexually charged. He reflects that "Atalanta is not the first or last maiden whom greed of gold has led to defile the temple of love," and a greed for gold becomes entwined with a narrative of sexual lust, a mark that stains the city. "If Atlanta be not named for Atalanta, she ought to have been," he concludes (110–11).[36] In particular, Du Bois fears for "the black young Atalanta" who, instead of running a noble race to a glorious future, might stoop for the golden apples strewn by the American Mammon (114).

At this point in the text we can see the gendered consequences of the order of the chapters. Atlanta, as a city embodying the gold-lust of Atalanta, is the center of the section that depicts a predominantly white world. The heart of first section of *The Souls of Black Folk*, then, is organized as a primarily female symbolic space dominated by the figures of Josie and the city of Atlanta. But even though the heart of the text at this point is female, this does not mean that concern with what is female is central to Du Bois's conceptual frame of reference. On the contrary, the metaphoric and symbolic characteristics of Josie and Atlanta determine that neither is a symbol of hope for the future of the African American folk, indeed neither have a viable political, social, or intellectual future in Du Bois's text. Although as a student at Fisk he was surrounded by black female intellectuals who were his peers, he was not yet able to imagine a community in which positive intellectual and social transformation could be evoked through female metaphors or tropes.[37]

Chapters seven and eight, in the middle of the book, begin to mark the transition from a predominantly white to a predominantly black world, a journey of descent into the black belt of the southern states and through an economic history of black immiseration under a system of forced labor. This descent is not only into a black world but into a world of disappointed, embittered men who are also hopelessly in debt. The narrative exposes the reality of an apartheid system in housing, in economic relations, in political activity, and in the legal system. The white South is shown in utter spiritual as well as political turmoil, without a soul. The account of this turbulent white world is merely a coda, however, for a journey into the wholesome, spiritual, and soulful existence of black people in chapter ten, "Of the Faith of Our Fathers," which begins the final third of the book.

Within the opening pages of *The Souls of Black Folk,* Du Bois establishes his ability to speak as a race leader and grants himself the authority to evoke a convincing portrayal of the black folk by integrating his own commanding narrative voice, as a black intellectual, with the life of the folk, and his own body with his philosophy. From Genesis Du Bois takes the words of Adam and, transforming the pronouns, uses them to mark his own body as an essential part of that wider community his text imagines. "And, finally, need I add," he declares in the last sentence of his introduction, "that I who speak here am bone of the bone and flesh of the flesh of them that live within the veil" (xii). It was Du Bois's ambition to fashion a book that could create and make tangible the "soul" of a race in space and time, and he utilizes his own body to enable that soul to be imagined. Such embodiment is also an important trope to Cornel West:

> The Victorian three-piece suit—with a clock and a chain in the vest—worn by W. E. B. Du Bois not only represented the age that shaped and molded him; it also dignified his sense of intellectual vocation, a sense of rendering service by means of a critical intelligence and moral action. The shabby clothing worn by most black intellectuals these days may be seen as symbolizing their utter marginality behind the walls of academe and their sense of impotence in the wider world of American culture and politics.[38]

West's claim is that moral and ethical values of intellectual practice are inscribed in the clothed body, and these clothes secure the status of the intellect within. The clothes can then be read, unproblematically, as clear signs of intellectual worth.

A comparison of the widely circulated photographs of Du Bois and Cornel West demonstrates how the male body can be sculpted to model an intellectual mentor.[39] But to define this appearance as the *only* acceptable confirmation of intellectual vocation, critical intelligence, and moral action is also to secure these qualities as irrevocably and conservatively masculine. Just as Du Bois constantly replaces and represses images of sexual desire (in his chapter on Atlanta) with evocations of a New England work ethic, so West equates the body and mind as disciplined and contained within a dark, severely cut three-piece suit, buttoned shirt, and tightly drawn tie.

As the readers are gradually drawn into the center of the spiritual and cultural life of Du Bois's black folk, that life becomes increasingly African in its soul and masculine in its body. With the entry into the black world, the multiple narrative personae (historian, sociologist, and philosopher) are gradually stripped away. While *The Souls of Black Folk* are to be revealed through religion and music, the heart and soul of the author are revealed through the grief of a father after the death of his son.

Chapter eleven, "Of the Passing of the First Born," is one of the most direct and passionate revelations of a male soul in American literature.[40] Children are commonly figured as embodiments of the hopes and fears of the previous generation, and this is how Du Bois represents his son. As he does so, in his role of narrator Du Bois becomes a cipher, simply the transmitter of the frustrated dreams and fears of an entire people, the black folk.

> Within the veil was he born . . . and there within shall he live,— a Negro and a Negro's son. Holding in that little head—ah, bitterly!—the unbowed pride of a hunted race clinging . . . to a hope not hopeless but unhopeful, and seeing with those bright wondering eyes that peer into my soul a land whose freedom is to us a mockery and whose liberty is a lie. . . . I . . . saw the strength of my own arm stretched onward through the ages through the newer strength of his; saw the dream of my black fathers stagger a step onward in the wild phantasm of the world; heard in his baby voice the voice of the prophet that was to rise within the veil. (227–28)

Here Du Bois attempts to fuse his own body with a racialized way of knowing the world, "a Negro and a Negro's son . . . saw the dream of my black father." But he also situates himself as an intellectual and spiritual mediator between the world and his people and interpreter of the meanings of their dreams and fears for their collective future.

For Du Bois the contradictions and ambiguities of his genealogy of race and nation exist metaphorically within the boundaries of his own soul, in which a deep pessimism wars with an emergent sense of optimism about the future of black men within the national community. This struggle of and for the soul of a people, which is enacted within the soul of the narrator, culminates in a recognition that the loss of his son reveals the consequences of the sacrifice that Du Bois was willing, in the abstract, to make in 1893: "now there wails, on that dark shore within the veil, the . . . deep voice, *Thou Shalt Forego!* And all have I foregone at that command, and with small complaint, all save that fair young form that lies so closely wed with death in the nest I had builded" (232). The death of his son places the fate of the race, figuratively, back within the hands of Du Bois, a leader with no heir.

Du Bois's reflections on the life of Alexander Crummell, in the following chapter, lie in startling juxtaposition to the meanings he derives from the death of his son. The issue of who shall inherit the mantle of intellectual leadership is again the central question. Although Crummell lived long enough to become a man who gained the "voice of the prophet," this voice could not bring into being its own prophecies, for Crummell has no acolytes. Therefore Crummell's name remains unknown, despite his devoting his entire life to intellectual leadership. Here, again, Du Bois locates himself as the only remaining conduit for disseminating Crummell's work and principles among the race, and the only possible agent for translating those principles of leadership into action.

The story of "The Coming of John" elaborates these paradigms and continues to evoke tension and anxiety about a lack of a viable future for the race, as white and black male desires and hopes violently conflict and result in their mutual destruction. But in this essay Du Bois also consciously confronts and contradicts claims that white male aggression is met only by black male passivity—Black John actually kills his white childhood companion, also named John, for attempting to rape his sister. In this struggle over the control of female sexuality and sexual reproduction, John gains self-respect in his own black manhood. Although his bravery leads to his death, his manner of dying can be a model of manhood for future generations. Here again, the future of Du Bois's imagined black community is to be determined by the nature of the struggle among men over the bodies of women.

As an intellectual, Du Bois was obviously concerned about the continuity of intellectual generations, what I would call the reproduction of Race Men. This anxiety permeates and structures the essays on his son, on Alexander Crummell, and on the two Johns. The map of intellectual mentors he draws for us is a map of male production and reproduction that traces in its form, but displaces through its content, biological and sexual reproduction. It is reproduction without women, and is a final closure to Du Bois's claim to be "flesh of the flesh and bone of the bone," for in the usurpation of the birth of woman from Adam's rib, the figure of the intellectual and race leader is born of and engendered by other males.

This anxiety continues to be evoked in the work of contemporary black male intellectuals. In an eloquent and moving passage, Henry Louis Gates, Jr. gives an account of his generation at Yale: "Some of the black students I knew at Yale dropped out, or pursued militancy to a point of no return, or went mad." But the premature deaths of two who did not drop out, who could have become intellectuals and race leaders, leads him to mourn an even greater loss:

> It is also true that some of the black students I knew at Yale have gone on to serve in Congress, as big-city mayors, as presidents and vice-presidents of major conglomerates. This is what members of the crossover generation are supposed to do: cross over. This is what the civil activists and social engineers who recruited us had in mind. It's how the trope of the "Talented Tenth" was to be retrieved and refashioned for modern times. And yet there's a sense in which DeChabert and Robinson [who did not cross over] represented more to me than any of the "success stories"; and their failures of fulfillment (the oldest college story of all) grieved and rankled me as my own. I didn't go to their funerals: the truth is, I wasn't ready for them to be dead, either of them. We were supposed to storm the citadel

together, to summer at Martha's Vineyard together, to grow old together. They would be on hand to explain to me the difference between selling out and buying in. Our kids were supposed to marry each other; to graduate from schools where we would give the commencement addresses. Ours was to be the generation with cultural accountability, and cultural security: the generation that would tell white folks that we would not be deterred—that, whether they knew it or not, we too were of the elite.[41]

Gates's generational map, like that of Du Bois, is permeated by a particular anxiety of masculinity, an anxiety which is embedded in the landscape of a crisis in the social order. The particularity of the loss of men who are called by name, and grieved in part for the failure of intellectual reproduction, contrasts dramatically with the generality of the social crisis of poverty which he documents as reproduced through the figures of anonymous single mothers.[42]

Having considered the consequences of the narrative structure of *The Souls of Black Folk*, I want to consider its conceptual structure, drawn from Du Bois's creative interrelation of the complex meanings of race and nation. The individual essays that comprise *The Souls of Black Folk* are composed and tied to each other to form a series of tightly bound ideological contradictions, contradictions which are themselves inherent in the particularities of the racial ordering of the United States as a modern nation-state. The text exposes and exploits the tension that exists between the internal egalitarian impulse inherent in the concept of nation and the relations of domination and subordination that are embodied in a racially encoded social hierarchy.[43] Du Bois recognized that the question of the relation between nationalism and racism was a matter of understanding their historical articulation, and he therefore attempted to rewrite the historical as well as the sociological genealogy of black people, situating them as equal citizens within the national community.[44]

Du Bois did not contest the claim that black people should be viewed as a race. On the contrary, his intellectual strategy was to utilize the concept of race and transform it into a means of political unification. In *The Souls of Black Folk* he imagines black people as a race in ways that are conceptually analogous to imagining them as a nation. Processes of racialization are usually understood to be fragmentary in their historical effect on national political communities, and, indeed, *The Souls of Black Folk* was produced at a time when the nation was internally organized into a system of rigid racial segregation maintained and policed by the politics of terror. Adopting a strategy of direct confrontation with the historical conditions under which he wrote, Du Bois asserted that processes of racialization could create *unified* communities existing in harmony with the national community. He stated:

> Work, culture, liberty,—all these we need, not singly but together, not successively but together, each growing and aiding each, and all striving toward that vaster ideal that swims before the Negro people, the ideal of human brotherhood, gained through the unifying ideal of Race; the ideal of fostering and developing the traits and talents of the Negro, not in opposition to or contempt for other races, but rather in large conformity to the great ideals of the American Republic. (52)

Conceptual tension arises from the differing inflections of the concept of race in this passage. While Du Bois attempted to avoid the use of the term in the sense of the limited genetic concept which had historically condemned the descendants of African peoples in the United States to exclusion from the framework of national citizenship, he retained the metaphorical and familial language of racial kinship. At this point in his intellectual life, Du Bois used the concept of race to signify cultural difference (a designation now more frequently associated with the concept of ethnicity). He paid little attention to analyzing or criticizing actual material *processes* of racial categorization, and concentrated instead upon documenting the historical *effects* of racialization by focusing upon the historically constituted and conventional racialized meanings inscribed in the social and political constitution of blackness.[45]

In the opening chapter, "Of Our Spiritual Strivings," Du Bois challenges the dominant ideological definitions of the historical, sociological, and political position of black people within the boundaries of the national community. His initial philosophical premise is that black people and black cultural forms do not exist in opposition to the ideals of an American republic but, on the contrary, embody them. Consequently, instead of participating in the contestation over categories of racial differentiation, he locates the symbolic power of nationalism, of Americanness, squarely within the black cultural field.

> We the darker ones come even now not altogether empty-handed: there are today no truer exponents of the pure human spirit of the Declaration of Independence than the American Negroes; there is no true American music but the wild sweet melodies of the Negro slave; the American fairy tales and folk-lore are Indian and African; and, all in all, we black men seem the sole oasis of simple faith and reverence in a dusty desert of dollars and smartness. (52)

The reference to the "pure human spirit of the Declaration of Independence" evokes "the pervasive *republicanism* of the newly-independent [national] communities" of the eighteenth century.[46] Claiming this particular genealogy for black peoples has very particular political and ideological effects. It is a demand for inclusion in the "imagined community" of the nation-state produced by the cultural revolutions of the modern world. This demand contrasts dramatically, for example, with the way in which Marcus Garvey would, in the coming years, structure the U.N.I.A. (United Negro Improvement Association), an organization ideologically and politically incompatible with the idea of a modern nation-state: a racialized fraternity, it was conceived in the terms of a premodern dynastic order.[47]

*The Souls of Black Folk* is organized and framed by the symbolic unification of race and nation, and in its closing pages Du Bois repeats his strategy of placing black bodies at the center of the national discourse. Black people, he asserts, are integral to the very formation and maintenance of the nation-state to which they have donated their particular gifts: "a gift of story and song—soft, stirring melody in an ill-harmonized and unmelodious land; the gift of sweat and brawn to beat back the wilderness, conquer the soil and lay the foundations of this vast economic empire two hundred years earlier than your weak hands could have done it; the third, a gift of the Spirit.... Actively we have woven ourselves with the very warp and woof of this nation" (275).

In language simultaneously evocative of the history of the frontier and of the industrial cotton mills, Du Bois rejects the marginalization of black people in American national life, whom he sees as integral to the founding and formation of the republic. In *The Souls of Black Folk* it is the descendants of African peoples who are proclaimed the legitimate inheritors of the principles of the Declaration of Independence, and Du Bois inscribes the symbolic power of nationalism directly onto black bodies. It is the bodies of the previously enslaved which inherit, and therefore become the primary site for, the preservation of national ideals. It is black bodies which offer the only vision of spiritual sustenance in a desert of rampant materialism, and it is the conditions of *their* social, political, and economic existence, Du Bois asserts, which are the only reliable measures of the health of the national body politic. In the body of America dwells a black soul.

What is at stake for Du Bois is to convince his readership that what appear to be ideologically and historically oppositional categories, namely race and nation, are not, in fact, incompatible. Yet crucial to Du Bois's structure of thought is the way he uses gender to mediate the relation between his concept of race and his concept of nation. This enables him to negotiate his way between the contradictions of a nationalist discourse of equality, on the one hand, and a fragmentary and hierarchical discourse of race, on the other.[48] The process of gendering at work in *The Souls of Black Folk* distinguishes not only between concepts of masculine and feminine subject positions but makes distinctions within his definition of masculinity itself.

The multiplicity and complexity of Du Bois's intellectual project, which integrates the discourses of history, philosophy, and social science, is bound with the thread of an apparently unified gendered subject position. In "Of Our Spiritual Strivings," the title of the first chapter, the opening pages establish the "I" of an autobiographical narrator, an "I" that quickly links itself to the "Our," the black community, through the experience of being regarded as a problem. The basis for this shared experience, however—a racist social order—is the same ground which establishes the narrator as an exceptional male individual. Du Bois's intellectual and political intention to integrate *his* voice with the voice of the wider black community displaces a number of ideological contradictions, not the least of which is his class position. In order to retain his credentials for leadership, Du Bois had to situate himself as both an exceptional and a representative individual: to be different from and maintain a distance between his experience and that of the masses of black people, while simultaneously integrating his existential being with that of his imagined community of the people. The terms and conditions of his exceptionalism, Du Bois argues, have their source in his formation as a *gendered* intellectual.

The "striving" that was required in order to exist in a racist society was of a different order for Du Bois than for most black men, he states. As a schoolboy, he was able to beat his white classmates at examination time, and this success, he concludes, enabled him to overcome his contempt of them. Attributing to his success in school the source of his emotional maturity emphasizes Du Bois's intellectual ability and superiority. In this, however, his becoming a man differed from the way most other black boys grew to manhood. As Du Bois describes this distinction: "With other black boys the strife was not so fiercely sunny: their youth shrank into tasteless sychophancy, or into silent hatred of the pale world about them and mocking distrust of everything white; or wasted itself in a bitter cry, Why did God make me an outcast and a stranger in mine own house?" (44–45).[49] Du Bois's intellectual and sexual formation are twin aspects of the constitution of black masculinity, and their interdependence is manifest in the gendered language of his text.

For Du Bois the "problem" of being black was an issue of both commonality and exceptionalism; it was not just about learning that he was black but also about learning how to *become* a black man. The story of his first memorable racist incident is also the re-creation of a highly charged moment of gender formation. He describes how all his classmates decided to exchange visiting cards. A white girl arrogantly refused to accept the card Du Bois offered her and at that moment, he writes, he knew that he was "different" from his white peers and became aware of the "veil" that separated their two worlds.

This realization disrupts the smooth passage of the formative years of his male adolescence, but the practice of challenging and overcoming such obstacles enables the transition from boy to man.[50]

The conceptual structure of Du Bois's genealogy of race and nation has, at its center, the dilemma of the formation of black manhood. Gender mediates Du Bois's presentation of the relation between race, nation, and a fully participatory citizenship for black people. Integral to the "problem" of simultaneously being black and being American is coming into manhood, and it is the latter that is the most vulnerable to attack. For racism shrank the youth of most black boys into a "tasteless sychophancy" which not only disrupts adolescence but dooms these young men to a life of mimicry, to a mere parody of masculinity, a parody which results in their being denied a full role in the patriarchal social and political order.

Du Bois's characterization of a parody of masculinity echoes today in Cornel West's descriptions of the "nihilism" of black America, and in his analysis of the formation of black male sexuality. West makes a clear distinction between "black male sexuality" and "black female sexuality"; he argues, for instance, that "black men have different self-images and strategies of acquiring power in the patriarchal structures of white America and black communities. For most young black men, power is acquired by stylizing their bodies over space and time in such a way that their bodies reflect their uniqueness and provoke fear in others." West is convinced that it is these "limited stylistic options" which lead to their patriarchal subordination. This stylizing of bodies is "an instance of machismo," West insists, which "solicits primarily sexual encounters with women and violent encounters with other black men or aggressive police. . . . This search for power . . . usually results in a direct confrontation with the order-imposing authorities of the status quo, that is, the police or the criminal justice system."[51] West's argument about the style of young black men stands in direct contrast to his image of the successful black intellectual in a three-piece suit and is directly analogous to Du Bois's arguments about the deformation of the process of young black men becoming gendered beings at the turn of the century. What Du Bois regards as a black male style that is a parody of a national discourse of masculinity is equivalent to Cornel West's "machismo" style of young black men, which "solicits primarily sexual encounters with women and violent encounters with other black men" and brings them into direct confrontation with the authority of the nation-state.

It is significant that Du Bois claims that his first encounter with racism was the moment when his courtly, nineteenth-century advances were rejected by a young white woman. Du Bois clearly believed that women (and, I will argue, certain men whom he regarded as having compromised their masculinity) could become the mediators through which the nation-state oppressed black men. For most black men, he argues, the burden of racism was not only poverty and ignorance but a burden carried through black mothers and imposed upon their sons. "The red stain of bastardy, which two centuries of systematic legal defilement of Negro women had stamped upon his race," Du Bois concludes, fell upon the shoulders of black men, as they had to carry "the hereditary weight of a mass of corruption from white adulterers" (50). This "hereditary weight" is the burden imposed on black men by history because they could not control the sexual reproduction of black women. Under this weight of betrayal by black women, most black men stumbled, fell, and failed to come into the full flowering of black manhood.

Most black men, in Du Bois's genealogy, suffer from a deformation in their process of becoming gendered beings; the result is their patriarchal subordination in the national community. Du Bois's language in *The Souls of Black Folk* is passionately gendered in its symbolic power as he describes such subordination. In addition to the weight that the black man had to bear because of the defilement of Negro women, Du Bois describes how the "shadow of the vast despair" that darkens "the very soul of the toiling, sweating black man" was made even more unbearable by white sociologists who "gleefully count his bastards and his prostitutes." For Du Bois the figure of the black woman, whether prostitute or mother, has a surplus symbolic value upon which he liberally draws in his illustrations of the denigration of the black man. The illicit sexuality that Du Bois inscribes upon the bodies of black women contributes to rendering the male impotent, so that the black man "stands helpless, dismayed and well-nigh speechless; before that personal disrespect and mockery, the ridicule and systematic humiliation, the distortion of fact and wanton license of fancy" (50).

Although paralysis of mind and body is the fate of most black men, *The Souls of Black Folk* stands as evidence that Du Bois is an exception:[52] he retains an ability to speak in a voice that has overcome the vast despair that defeats lesser men; he has lifted the burden of illegitimacy and female sexual complicity from his shoulders, and he has conquered the impotence caused by such a burden.[53] It is the process of becoming an intellectual that Du Bois offers as an alternative route to manhood, as a way to avoid gendered and racialized subordination, deformation, and degradation. Indeed, becoming an intellectual is, perhaps, the only sure route to becoming a certain type of man, a man whose "style" is not in direct confrontation with the nation-state. Du Bois insists that it is his *intellectual* achievements that enable him to make a successful transition from adolescence into a socially acceptable style of manhood, and that it is the power of his intellect which gives him the ability to analyze the burden, the vast shadow, which stunts and deforms the growth of other black men. The practice of intellectual analysis, as narratively encoded within *The Souls of Black Folk,* conquers political impotence and leads to an attainment of masculine self-respect. It is this theory of conquest by intellect that I would now like to consider.

In *The Souls of Black Folk* Du Bois not only challenges his readers to reconsider the ways in which the national community has been historically constituted, but he also creates an alternative cultural identity for the nation-state. Despite the apparent idealism of this project, Du Bois was certainly aware that even if he succeeded, neither the cultural recognition of the historic role of black people in the formation of the nation-state nor their inclusion in the nationalist symbolic order would automatically result in the granting of universal suffrage and political citizenship: acts which would signify their inclusion within the imagined boundaries of the nation-state. Thus it was essential for Du Bois to provide a framework for the future political praxis of black leadership.

Through a series of reflections, Du Bois developed what he regarded as the necessary conditions for producing black political and intellectual leadership. In the sixth chapter, "Of the Training of Black Men," Du Bois appraises black education and argues for the importance of producing a college-educated elite, a "Talented Tenth" which would teach and provide leadership for the race. This "Talented Tenth," however, was not to remain an isolated intellectual elite but would evolve in alliance with its constituency, an alliance he describes as a "loving, reverent comradeship between the black lowly and the black men emancipated by training and culture" (138). Black intellectuals are to become the means for inducting the "lowly" into the national community; as teachers, their role becomes that of missionaries for the nation-state.[54]

In the ninth chapter, "Of the Sons of Master and Man," Du Bois elaborates upon these ideas and insists that leaders who had assimilated "the culture and common sense of modern civilization" play an important role in imagining the "race" as part of the national entity, a role, I have argued, that Du Bois himself was effecting by bringing black people into the boundaries of the national imagination through *The Souls of Black Folk*. However, representing the race as part of the national entity bespoke the obligation to turn the representation into reality: in order to effect change those leaders needed access to political power. The ballot was recognized to be an important *mechanism* for the production of actual and symbolic national subjects but it was through the *practice* of exercising their right to vote that black men could imagine their own relation as subjects to a political community. In 1903, Du Bois regarded the ballot as perhaps the most important means for a black political and intellectual elite to acquire political power and signify black political citizenship.

The philosophy and practice of black intellectual leadership was to be bound by the same limits and commitments that Du Bois imposed upon himself in 1893. Although there are specific passages in *The Souls of Black Folk* where Du Bois discusses the present and future condition of black leadership in the abstract, and occasionally in relation to specific individuals such as Booker T. Washington and Alexander Crummell, the narrative is stitched together by an authorial persona who enacts the ideal qualities of intellectual and political leadership and black masculinity. Du Bois himself is textually present in three important ways: first, he acts as an embodiment of his own ideal of an intellectual and graduate of the humanistic education he advocates; second, he appears as a contestant for black leadership whose voice gains authority through the process of critiquing other male leaders; and, finally, he quite deliberately uses his own body as the site for an exposition of the qualities of black manhood.

In Du Bois's genealogy of race and nation, black people are both integral to the nation-state and essential to its future. An important political element of his blueprint for black intellectuals is the development and elaboration of a critique of rampant materialism. In a period which gives rise to the global expansion of capitalism and secures the rapid "incorporation" of the United States, black men are "the sole oasis of simple faith and reverence in a dusty desert of dollars and smartness" (52).[55] In chapter five, "Of the Wings of Atalanta," Du Bois elaborates this world view and places himself at its axis.

The chapter opens with his critique of materialism and fear that within the black world as well as the white, "the habit is forming of interpreting the world in dollars" (113). The city of Atlanta, epitome of industrialization and material greed, is what gave birth to the new South, Du Bois asserts. He describes how "the city crowned her hundred hills with factories" (110) and warns that "Atlanta must not lead the South to dream of material prosperity as the touchstone of all success" (112). But in this "desert" bloomed Atlanta University, a world that was not obsessed with the dream of material prosperity and had a vision of life with "nothing mean or selfish" in it.

> Not at Oxford or at Leipsic, not at Yale or Columbia, is there an air of higher resolve or more unfettered striving; the determination to realize for men, both black and white, the broadest possibilities of life, to seek the better and the best, to spread with their own hands the Gospel of Sacrifice,—all this is the burden of their talk and dream. Here, amid a wide desert of cast and proscription, amid the heart-hurting slights and jars and vagaries of a deep race-dislike, lies this green oasis. (115–16)

Using the language of sacrifice and commitment which in 1893 he had confined to his personal diary, Du Bois creates an image of the University of Atlanta as a body politic which could be the source of alternative humanistic values and ideals and, at the heart of it, putting the "air of higher resolve" and "unfettered striving" into practice, Du Bois places himself.

The language and narrative structure of *The Souls of Black Folk* define the university as being at once the foundation of a civilization under threat and, through its production of professional intellectuals, the promise of a new social order for the nation. As Eric Hobsbawm put it, "the progress of schools and universities measures that of nationalism just as schools and universities become its most conscious champions."[56] By explicitly situating himself as speaking from the University of Atlanta, Du Bois establishes himself as a professional intellectual in a position of authority from which he could, as an intellectual and as a critic of culture, intervene in and shape debate about the boundaries of culture and civilization, broadening its parameters to imaginatively include black men and black folk culture.

But the professional intellectual needs not only a site from which to speak but a "true self-consciousness" to determine what is spoken. The concept of double-consciousness is generally regarded as one of Du Bois's major contributions to philosophic thought. Explicated in the first chapter of *The Souls of Black Folk*, double-consciousness is the product of a world that has allowed the black man no "true self-consciousness but only lets him see himself through the revelation of the other world" (45). While double-consciousness is, indeed, a product of the articulation between race and nation, I would argue that we need to revise our understanding of how this double-consciousness works in order to understand how gender is an ever-present, though unacknowledged, factor in this theory. For Du Bois, the gaining of the "true self-consciousness" of a racialized and national subject position is dependent upon first gaining a gendered self-consciousness.

In order to explicate this assertion I want to return to the second chapter, "Of the Dawn of Freedom," and its two contrasting figures which typify the gendered nature of the history of Reconstruction. Each figure is imagined to bear the history of its race in the South. The first one is white: "a grey-haired gentleman" who, although "his fathers had quit themselves like men," is unable to father future generations or leave a legacy of patriarchal power because his sons "lay in nameless graves." This figure is an unmanned and "blighted, ruined form, with hate in his eyes." The second figure is black: a mother with an "awful face" who "quailed at that white master's command," loved his sons and his wife, and "laid herself low to his lust." Her legacy is a "tawny manchild" born out of an act of submission—an act of racial betrayal which compromises the black man's masculinity because it does not recognize his control over her sexual being.

Two acts of compromise, one political and one sexual, lead to the perpetual subordination of black manhood. The act of sexual compromise by Du Bois's anonymous figure of the black mother, which contributes to the black man's failure to become a man, is deliberately situated in the narrative of Reconstruction so as to parallel the Act of Compromise of 1877 between the northern and southern states, an act which put an end to the work of the Freedmen's Bureau, led to the withdrawal of northern troops from the South, and resulted in further oppression of black men. Each act of compromise renders the nation impotent, unable and unwilling to fully emancipate the black man. "For this much all men know" wrote Du Bois, "despite compromise, war and struggle, the Negro is not free" (77). The integrity and the autonomy of race, of nation, and of masculinity are destroyed by such acts of compromise in which the sexual and political subordination of black manhood are figuratively intertwined.

The gendered nature of the language in chapter three, "Of Mr. Booker T. Washington and Others," continues to allude to the sexual compromise evoked by Du Bois's figure of the black mother. The "most notable thing in Mr. Washington's career," Du Bois states with undisguised irony, is his "Atlanta Compromise" (80). Washington's body becomes a spectacle set against the landscape described as a "dusty desert of dollars and smartness." Initially, Du Bois characterizes Washington as a sycophant and as destructive as the materialistic idols in front of which he prostrates himself. In a bitter tone he writes of him: "And so thoroughly did [Washington] learn the speech and thought of triumphant commercialism, and the ideals of commercial prosperity, that the picture of a lone black boy pouring over a French grammar amid the weeds and dirt of a neglected home soon seemed to him the acme of absurdities" (81). Sycophancy and selling out to commercialism are cited as evidence of a stunted or deformed manhood, a masculine style incompatible with the incorporation of the race into the modern nation-state. Because Du Bois makes his narrative of the transition from male adolescence and immaturity to full manhood and maturity so entirely dependent upon becoming an intellectual, Washington's standing as an intellectual and as a race leader is challenged at the same time as his masculinity is undermined.

Du Bois deliberately constructs his figure of Washington as analogous to that of his anonymous black mother: both betray the sons of the race, both undermine the possibility of black patriarchal power, and both of their acts of submission are condemned with equal vehemence. When Washington mimics the speech and ideals of commercialism, he becomes the metaphorical equivalent of the black mother (or the black female prostitute) who succumbs to the lust of white men. Washington also stands accused of succumbing to the lust of his historical moment: his "oneness with his age" is ironically described as "the mark of a successful man" (81), but his "counsels of submission," Du Bois concludes, "overlooked certain elements of true manhood" (82). Not only is the reader left in little doubt that Washington is not a man by Du Bois's measure of black masculinity, but his compromise with the dominant philosophy of his age is to be understood as a form of prostitution.

The chapter on Booker T. Washington immediately precedes the two chapters that I describe as the female symbolic space of the white section of the book. The discussion of Washington is, therefore, separated and excluded from the black masculine world with which the text concludes, and juxtaposed with a feminized symbolic territory of illegitimate and negative sexuality. The city of Atlanta—whether evoked through Washington's "Atlanta Compromise" speech or as the symbolic landscape of commercial degradation in *The Souls of Black Folk*— is a female entity, historically compromised and starkly contrasted to the modern nation evoked as "this common Fatherland" (91).

Du Bois's gendered language grows increasingly complex and sexually explicit when he considers the future of the Union. "We have no right," he says, "to sit silently by while the inevitable seeds are sown for a harvest of disaster to our children, black and white" (92). Washington is situated at the crux of two illegitimate symbolic sexual unions: he prostituted himself because he sold his soul and betrayed the best interests of black men; and he promoted the national reconciliation of the (female) South and "her co-partner in guilt," the North (94).

Du Bois contrasts Washington's inadequate manliness and consequent lack of the attributes of leadership with a history of black male revolt and self-assertion led by such revolutionary figures as the maroons, Toussaint L'Ouverture, Nat Turner, and other rebels against Washington's acts of compromise. The heirs of these revolutionaries, Du Bois argues, are leaders like David Walker, Frederick Douglass, and William Wells Brown—a list that excludes Washington but is the genealogy of the progenitors of Du Bois. These revolutionary figures appear in Du Bois's narrative both as "true" black men and genuine leaders of black men.

Washington, in contrast, figures as the equivalent of the bastard child: "Booker T. Washington arose as essentially the leader not of one race but of two—a compromiser between the South, the North and the Negro" (86). He is twice a compromiser, a man who prostrates himself to whites and black alike and is himself a product of a national compromise. Washington's compromise, declares Du Bois, surrendered the civil and political rights of black men in the same way that the compromise between the North and the South betrayed these rights. Washington's policy of submission withdrew "many of the high demands of Negroes as men and as American citizens" (87). His policies were "bound to sap the manhood of any race" (88). They directly undermine the genealogy of race and nation Du Bois constructs in *The Souls of Black Folk*, just as the historical compromise between the northern and southern states undermines his political and philosophical ideals. In short, *The Souls of Black Folk* effectively dethrones Booker T. Washington from his position as a preeminent leader, questions his political and intellectual integrity, and condemns him as a collaborator.

The complex cultural politics of gender at work in *The Souls of Black Folk* are an important means of producing political displacement. The narrative demise of Booker T. Washington, of course, significantly advances Du Bois's own claim to speak with the authority of a representative black intellectual, leader, and man. But, we should ask, at what cost has this figure of the representative black intellectual been produced? And to what extent do we still live with the politics of gender implicated in its production?

## *Notes*

1. See Julius Lester, ed., *The Seventh Son: The Thought and Writings of W. E. B. Du Bois* (New York: Vintage, 1971), 24. Cornel West characterizes the sacrificial nature of Du Bois's intellectual project as a "Victorian strategy." See Henry Louis Gates, Jr. and Cornel West, *The Future of the Race* (New York: Knopf, 1996), 64.

2. W. E. B. Du Bois, *The Souls of Black Folk* (1903; repr. New York: New American Library, 1982). Page numbers to this edition will hereafter be cited in parenthesis in the body of the text.

3. Gates and West, *Future of the Race*, 65.

4. Gates and West, *Future of the Race*, 58–79.

5. The use of the phrase "real intellectual work" points to what I believe is the relegation of feminist analysis to the realm of domestic intellectual labor. Male intellectuals do the real work of intellectual labor, whereas feminist or gender analysis applies only to the separate sphere of women.

6. West severely criticizes Du Bois's model of the "Talented Tenth" for being elitist; see Gates and West, *The Future of the Race*, 65–67. West is equally uninterested in and dismissive of feminist work. See, for example, p. 185, note 20, on Ida B. Wells, which ignores all scholarship on Wells by women. One can only assume that West does not read it.

7. W. E. B. Du Bois, "The Development of a People" (1904), repr. in David W. Blight and Robert Gooding-Williams, eds., *The Souls of Black Folk* (Boston: Bedford Books, 1997), 238–54.

8. I am, of course, rather freely but I hope not disrespectfully, both adopting and revising the term "structures of feeling" from Raymond Williams. While Williams applied this term to the "culture of a period," I want to retain this sense of history, but also to evoke the cultural meanings of a particular text as I apply it to my readings of the essays collected in *The Souls of Black Folk*. Though I deviate slightly from Williams in my use of his insights, I am following the spirit and method of the conceptual framework, which he describes as follows: "The analysis of culture is the attempt to discover the nature of the organization which is the complex of these relationships. Analysis of particular works or institutions is, in this context, analysis of their essential kind of organization, the relationships which works or institutions embody as parts of the organization as a whole. A keyword, in such analysis, is pattern: it is with the discovery of patterns of a characteristic kind that any useful cultural analysis begins, and it is with the relationships between these patterns, which sometimes reveal unexpected identities and correspondences in hitherto separately considered activities, sometimes again reveal discontinuities of an unexpected kind, that general cultural analysis is concerned." Raymond Williams, *The Long Revolution* (1961; repr. London: Pelican Books, 1965), 63–66.

9. Wesley Brown in Louis Massiah, dir., *W. E. B. Du Bois: A Biography in Four Voices* (San Francisco: California Newsreel, 1995), part 1.

10. It is, however, the case that in his private life, as a father and as a husband, Du Bois was a consummate patriarch, but that is not the subject of my concern in this chapter. For further consideration of the contradictions that existed between Du Bois's public politics and his private life, contradictions that are not uncommon in the lives of men who publicly support feminist causes, see David Levering Lewis, *W. E. B. Du Bois: Biography of a Race, 1868–1919* (New York: Henry Holt, 1993).

11. Gates and West, *Future of the Race*, 55.

12. See also William Andrews, *Critical Essays on W. E. B. Du Bois* (Boston: G. K. Hall, 1985), for a selection of early reviews of the book.

13. James Weldon Johnson, *The Autobiography of An Ex-Colored Man* (1912; repr. New York: Hill and Wang, 1960), 168–69. Johnson also evokes Du Bois's metaphor of the veil in his Preface: "In these pages it is as though a veil had been drawn aside: the reader is given a view of the inner life of the Negro in America, is initiated into the freemasonry, as it were, of the race" (xii). Johnson, like Du Bois, privileges discourses of masculinity and assumes that these will reveal the inner life of the race as a whole. See Robert B. Stepto, *From Behind the Veil: A Study of Afro-American Narrative* (Urbana: University of Illinois Press, 1979), 111–27, for a detailed explication of Johnson's use of *The Souls of Black Folk*. See also Valerie Smith, *Self-Discovery and Authority in Afro-American Narrative* (Cambridge: Harvard University Press, 1987), 56–58.

14. James Weldon Johnson, *Along This Way: The Autobiography of James Weldon Johnson* (1933; repr. New York: Viking Penguin, 1990), 203.

15. The phrase "imagined community" is, of course, taken from Benedict Anderson, *Imagined Communities: Reflections on the Origins and Spread of Nationalism* (London: Verso, 1983), 62. For a description of genealogies and their relation to "homogenous empty time," see 68–69.

16. In the context of discussing religious pilgrimages, Benedict Anderson argues that "a vast horde of illiterate vernacular-speakers provided the dense, physical reality of the ceremonial passage; while a small segment of literal bilingual adepts drawn from each vernacular community performed the unifying rites, interpreting to their respective followings the meaning of their collective motion" (Anderson, *Imagined Communities*, 56). I see *The Souls of Black Folk* as performing a similar interpretive function of bringing a people into existence, and regard the intellectual act of producing the text as analogous to "performing the unifying rites."

17. See Andrews, *Critical Essays*, for reprints of these essays: Houston A. Baker, Jr. (1972), "The Black Man of Culture: W. E. B. Du Bois and *The Souls of Black Folk*," 129–38; Darwin T. Turner (1974), "W. E. B. Du Bois and the Theory of a Black Aesthetic," 73–91; and Wilson J. Moses (1975), "The Poetics of Ethiopianism: W. E. B. Du Bois and Literary Black Nationalism," 92–105.

18. Arnold Rampersad, *The Art and Imagination of W. E. B. Du Bois* (Cambridge, Mass.: Harvard University Press, 1976), 88–89.

19. Stepto, *From Behind the Veil*, 99.

20. Indeed, I find the text very useful when I address the inherently interdisciplinary nature of work in African American Studies and American Studies, and as an example of the critical potential of African American cultural studies. However, it is also important to note that other works by Du Bois have not acquired such status and are not always in print. To state the obvious, there is a very real material relation between the process of the academic canonization of a text and the politics of the publishing industry.

21. W. E. B. Du Bois has been a consistent presence in the work of Cornel West as the figure of an ideal or representative African American intellectual. See, for example, *Prophesy Deliverance! An Afro-American Revolutionary Christianity* (Philadelphia: Westminster Press, 1982); *Prophetic Fragments* (Grand Rapids, Mich.: Africa World

Press, 1988); *The American Evasion of Philosophy: A Genealogy of Pragmatism* (Madison: University of Wisconsin Press, 1989); *Race Matters* (Boston: Beacon Press, 1993); and *Keeping the Faith: Philosophy and Race in America* (New York: Routledge, 1993).

22. Gates and West, *Future of the Race*, 55.

23. West, *American Evasion of Philosophy*, 138.

24. West, *American Evasion of Philosophy*, 5. Later, West describes his position as follows: "I began this work as an exercise in critical self-inventory, as a historical, social and existential situating of my own work as an intellectual, activist and human being. I wanted to make clear to myself my own contradictions and tensions, faults and foibles as one shaped by, in part, the tradition of American pragmatism" (7).

25. West, *Keeping the Faith*, 27, 82–83, 23.

26. West, *Race Matters*, 46.

27. See Anderson, *Imagined Communities*, 65. "Liberalism and the Enlightenment clearly had a powerful impact, above all in providing an arsenal of ideological criticisms of imperial and *ancien régimes*. What I am proposing is that neither economic interest, Liberalism, nor Enlightenment could, or did, create *in themselves* the *kind* or shape, of imagined community to be defended from these regime's depredations; to put it another way, none provided the framework of a new consciousness—the scarcely-seen periphery of its admiration or disgust. In accomplishing *this* specific task, pilgrim creole functionaries and provincial creole printmen played the decisive role."

28. The theoretical framework for my thinking about the narrative shape of genealogies is influenced by the work of Etienne Balibar and Immanuel Wallerstein, *Race, Nation, Class: Ambiguous Identities* (London: Verso, 1991).

29. See, for example, the analysis of Stepto, *From Behind the Veil*, 3–31 and 67–72.

30. Mark Twain, *Adventures of Huckleberry Finn* (1885; repr. New York: Library of America, 1982), 704–16, 784.

31. Stepto, *From Behind the Veil*, 66.

32. For details of previous publication see Blight and Gooding-Williams, *Souls*, viii.

33. Cornel West shares this intellectual and political motivation with Du Bois: "I have written this text convinced that a thorough re-examination of American pragmatism, stripping it of its myths, caricatures, and stereotypes and viewing it as a component of a new and novel form of indigenous thought and action, may be a first step toward fundamental change and transformation in America and the world" (*The American Evasion of Philosophy*, 8).

34. " . . . we have seen that the very conception of the newspaper implies the refraction of even 'world-events' into a specific imagined world of vernacular readers; and also how important to that imagined community is an idea of steady, solid simultaneity through time" (Anderson, *Imagined Communities*, 63).

35. "How shall man measure Progress there where the dark-faced Josie lies? How many heartfuls of sorrow shall balance a bushel of wheat? How hard a thing in life to be lowly, and yet how human and real!" (Du Bois, *The Souls of Black Folk*, 108).

36. It is interesting that Du Bois himself recognizes the temptations of sensuality. "Golden apples are beautiful—I remember the lawless days of boyhood, when orchards in crimson and gold tempted me over fence and field" (112). One can only

wonder if writing the essay caused him to reflect upon his sexual relationship with Josie's mother. See note 37.

37. Du Bois clearly had somewhat ambivalent and complex attitudes toward female sexuality. In his autobiography he claims that when he taught in Tennessee he was "literally raped by the unhappy wife who was my landlady." David Levering Lewis states that this "unhappy wife" was Josie's mother. The claim of rape seeks to establish Du Bois's (male) innocence in the face of a predatory (female) sexuality. Du Bois appears to have considered female sexuality in binary terms as a conceptual dilemma. Whenever "I tried to solve the contradiction of virginity and motherhood I was inevitably faced with the other contradiction of prostitution and adultery." It is interesting to reflect upon what Du Bois calls here, "a contradiction," in light of the binary gendered structures of thought and feeling in *Souls*. See W. E. B. Du Bois, *The Autobiography of W. E. B. Du Bois* (New York: International Publishers, 1968), 280; and David Levering Lewis, *W. E. B. Du Bois: Biography of a Race, 1868–1919* (New York: Henry Holt, 1993), 68–72. (As Claudia Tate has reminded me, Du Bois does later use a female figure for social transformation as the character of Zora in *The Quest of the Silver Fleece.*)

38. West, *Race Matters*, 40. As West's clothing duplicates Du Bois's, one assumes that he may be adopting the values that Du Bois imagined went along with the way he dressed. Indeed, the photograph on the cover of *Race Matters* would seem to confirm this analogy. However, one must take issue with West's cavalier dismissal of how other black intellectuals dress, and with the intellectual and political implications he draws from it.

39. The photographs can be found in Hazel V. Carby, *Race Men* (Cambridge, Mass.: Harvard University Press, 1998), 22–23.

40. David Levering Lewis considers that the "elegiac prose of 'The Passing of the First-Born' verges on bathos today." I have called it "passionate" but we both seem to agree that the focus of the tragedy is Du Bois himself. However, because I see such continuity between this essay and the other essays in *The Souls of Black Folk*, I would disagree with Levering Lewis's opinion that the essay is merely an "apostrophe" in the book. See Levering Lewis, *W. E. B. Du Bois*, 227.

41. Gates and West, *Future of the Race*, 48–49.

42. Gates and West, *Future of the Race*, 27–29.

43. As Etienne Balibar has described the particular conditions of racism in the modern world: "societies in which racism develops are at the same time supposed to be 'egalitarian' societies, in other words, societies which (officially) disregard status differences between individuals, this sociological thesis . . . cannot be abstracted from the national environment itself . . . it is not the modern state which is 'egalitarian' but the modern (nationalist) nation-state, this equality having as its internal and external limits the national community and, as its essential content, the acts which signify it directly (particularly universal suffrage and political 'citizenship'). It is, first and foremost, an equality in respect of nationality." See Balibar and Wallerstein, *Race, Nation, Class*, 49–50. Benedict Anderson has also pointed out the force of these contradictions: the nation "is imagined as a community, because, regardless of the actual inequality and exploitation that may prevail in each, the nation is always conceived as a deep, horizontal comradeship" (Anderson, *Imagined Communities*, 16).

44. Balibar and Wallerstein, *Race, Nation, Class*, 50. As Balibar describes this process, "the connection between nationalism and racism is neither a matter of

perversion (for there is no 'pure' essence of nationalism) nor a question of formal similarity, but a question of historical articulation."

45. See also Du Bois's essay, "The Conservation of the Races," and the discussion of it by Blight and Gooding-Williams in their Introductory essay to *The Souls of Black Folk*, 9.

46. Anderson, *Imagined Communities*, 53: "The success of the Thirteen Colonies' revolt at the end of the 1770s, and the onset of the French Revolution at the end of the 1780s, did not fail to exert a powerful influence. Nothing confirms this 'cultural revolution' more than the pervasive *republicanism* of the newly-independent communities. Nowhere was any serious attempt made to recreate the dynastic principle in the Americas, except in Brazil."

47. I refer to the trappings and hierarchy of Empire that were reproduced in U.N.I.A. parades and costumes and in the titles given to U.N.I.A. officials.

48. It would be an interesting and fruitful project to trace the use of gender as a term of mediation between the concept of race and the evocation of the premodern dynastic order in the work of Marcus Garvey and in the U.N.I.A.

49. Gates's experience as described in his essay "The Parable of the Talents" bears an uncanny similarity to Du Bois's account of his educational success and the failures of the other boys. At the end of the section which includes the passage of loss and mourning quoted above, Gates concludes: "But I was fortunate; I loved the place [Yale]. I loved the library and the seminars, I loved talking with the professors; I loved 'peeping the hole card' in people's assumptions and turning their logic back upon themselves. I had more chip than shoulder, and through it all I demanded of every person with whom I chanced to interact that they earn the right to learn my name. . . . Only sometimes do I feel guilty that I was among the lucky ones, and only sometimes do I ask myself why." For both Gates and Du Bois, their success in negotiating their way as intellectuals lies in the complexity of their formation as particular types of men. (Gates and West, *Future of the Race*, 51–52).

50. David Levering Lewis directs our attention to how very many different autobiographical versions of the moment of Du Bois's discovery of the significance of race there are in his writings. However, he also seems to agree that Du Bois's awareness of race is consistently gendered. "Whatever the personal dynamics of racial self-discovery were, by his thirteenth birthday Willie came to have an informed idea of what being a black male meant even in the relatively tolerant New England." See Levering Lewis, *W. E. B. Du Bois*, 33–34.

51. West, *Race Matters*, 88–89.

52. It is worth noting that Cornel West too treats himself as an exception among other black men in his analysis of the politics of contemporary black male sexuality, and that he consciously styles his body to be a conspicuous sign of that distinction. Of course, using the body to display masculine distinction as "race leader" is not limited to Du Bois and Cornel West. Marcus Garvey, for example, comes immediately to mind. All three have used their bodies to articulate masculine exceptionalism in particularly interesting ways.

53. David Levering Lewis speculates how possibly "evasive, ambivalent and wretched Du Bois's feelings for his mother might have been as she became an 'albatross' to him" (Levering Lewis, *W. E. B. Du Bois*, 52).

54. I am concentrating upon the function of intellectuals here and following a Gramscian definition of intellectual practices, as follows: "Can one find a unitary

criterion to characterise equally all the diverse and disparate activities of intellectuals and to distinguish these at the same time and in an essential way from the activities of other social groupings? The most widespread error of method seems to me that of having looked for this criterion of distinction in the intrinsic nature of intellectual activities, rather than in the ensemble of the system of relations in which these activities (and therefore the intellectual groups who personify them) have their place within the general complex of social relations . . . . All men are intellectuals . . . but not all men have in society the function of intellectuals. When one distinguishes between intellectuals and non-intellectuals, one is referring in reality only to the immediate social function of the professional category of the intellectuals." Antonio Gramsci, *Selections from the Prison Notebooks* (London: Lawrence and Wishart, 1971), 8, 9.

55. The use of "incorporation" refers to the thesis Alan Trachtenberg developed in his book, *The Incorporation of America: Culture and Society in the Gilded Age* (New York: Hill and Wang, 1982).

56. Eric Hobsbawm, as quoted in Anderson, *Imagined Communities*, 69.

# 8

# "W. E. B. Du Bois": Biography of a Discourse

■ *Roderick A. Ferguson*

Can we be sure that we are speaking of a person when we think we are speaking of a person? Isn't it possible that we could be silently evoking an assemblage of norms, concepts, and ideals when all the while we presume we are only discussing a "real" historical figure? In this essay, I am not actually concerned with a historical person but with the discourse that goes by that person's name. This is a discourse whose power is concealed by the apparent transparency of its referent's fame and notoriety, a discourse that convinces us not to scrutinize its deployment. The person that I am not concerned with is W. E. B. Du Bois, but the discourse that intrigues me has assumed Du Bois's identity.

Among its many emblems, African American intellectual formation wears that of "talking Du Bois." Much more than a living, breathing historical figure, Du Bois has been the general metaphor for African American intellectual history and disposition, as well as the symbol of antiracist thought and struggles. In the space of a century, we have been led to direct the question of who we are—as intellectuals, as African Americans, as racial subjects within modernity—to Du Bois. Now is the time that we focus our attention on Du Bois as a discursive operation, asking ourselves what are the reasons for its incitement, the conditions and modes of its deployment, and its effects on intellectual life and practice.

Part of the inspiration for this very speculative inquiry comes from Hazel Carby's "The Souls of Black Men." In that text Carby looks at how black men have historically stood as representatives of African American intellect and culture; tracing this genealogy of the heterosexual black male intellectual as representative figure to *The Souls of Black Folk*, Carby writes

> Within the opening pages of *The Souls of Black Folk*, Du Bois establishes his ability to speak as a race leader and grants himself the authority to evoke a convincing portrayal of the black folk by integrating his own commanding narrative voice, as a black intellectual, with the life of the folk, and his own body with his philosophy. From Genesis, Du Bois takes the words of Adam and, transforming the pronouns, uses them to mark his own body as an essential part of that wider community his text imagines. "And finally, need I add," he declares in the last sentence of his introduction, "that I who speak here am bone of the bone and flesh of the flesh of them that live within the veil." It was Du Bois's ambition to fashion a book that could create and make tangible the "soul" of a race in space and time, and he utilizes his own body to enable that soul to be imagined.[1]

Carby's essay suggests that there are actually two Du Bois's, one historical and the other discursive. The term "historical Du Bois" does not suggest that this historical figure is outside of discourse. It is merely an analytic that might help us differentiate Du Bois the person from Du Bois the discourse, knowing that in practice the two were often inseparable. While historical analysis would grasp Du Bois primarily as a historical being, a genealogical analysis would address Du Bois as a central discursive component within the mechanisms of power. Genealogy assumes that discourses have different temporalities than living persons. History thinks in terms of timelines: things begin and things end. For a discourse, however, there might be a beginning, but who knows when the end will be. Put plainly, discourses are not obliged to history's temporal constraints. William Edward Burghardt Du Bois was born in 1868 and died in 1963. But Du Bois the discourse had a "life" during and after its historical referent.

Incited constantly, that discourse has produced effects and inspired practices in the contemporary moment. Continuing to discuss the impact of Du Bois on African American intellectual formation, Carby offers the example of Du Bois's influence on Cornel West's *Race Matters*. In this quote from *Race Matters*, West states:

> The Victorian three-piece suit—with a clock and a chain in the vest—worn by W. E. B. Du Bois not only represented the age that shaped and molded him; it also dignified his sense of his intellectual vocation, a sense of rendering service by means of a critical intelligence and moral action. The shabby clothing worn by most black intellectuals these days may be seen as symbolizing their utter marginality behind the walls of academe and their sense of impotence in the wider world of American culture and politics.[2]

West implies that Du Bois's style was not simply an aesthetic matter but a pedagogical and political concern. Du Bois's suits communicate dignity, communal responsibility, masculinity, moral authority, and political agency. The suit thus becomes a measure of the state of contemporary African American intellectual practice, implying its distance from the ideals suggested by Du Bois's style, a distance that links intellectual and political integrity to corporeality. In this instance, Du Bois becomes a discursive mode of evaluating African American intellectual practice, a mode that links intellectual and political agency with the corporealization of the intellectual.

As a discursive mode that links intellect to politics and corporeality, Du Bois affects black subjects who do not conform to the moral properties associated with black heteropatriarchal masculinity, subjects who do not cohere with the gender and sexual properties ascribed to Du Bois. Discussing the material effects of symbolizing African American intellectual practice through black male bodies, specifically how such symbolic maneuvers have led to a particular organization of knowledge and subjects within African American Studies, Carby argues,

In the late 1990s the work of black women intellectuals is still considered peripheral by the black male establishment. It is true that, superficially, the situation appears to have improved. The words "women and gender" are frequently added after the word "race" and the appropriate commas, and increasingly the word "sexuality" completes the litany. On occasion a particular black woman's name will be mentioned, like that of Toni Morrison. But the *intellectual work* of black women and gay men is not thought to be of enough significance to be engaged with, argued with, agreed or disagreed with. (Carby, *Race Men,* 20–21)

Linking intellectual and political agency to corporealization through the discourse known as Du Bois betrays two things: First, the corporealization of African American intellectual agency posits black heterosexual masculinity as its ideal. Second, that corporealization works to devalue black queer and black female subjects and their intellectual production. The discourse known as "Du Bois," in this context, acts as a mode of epistemological and social exclusions. Hence, "Du Bois the discourse" operates, in part, as a standard of evaluation that links critical agency to corporealization. That corporealization seeks to resolve itself in heteropatriarchal masculinity and acts as a system of epistemic and social exclusions that resonate at the level of gender and sexuality.

Carby's remarks about the late 1990s as a period characterized by the marginalization of work by black women and black gay male intellectuals suggest what Raymond Williams has termed a "structure of feeling." By way of definition, he writes,

We are talking about characteristic elements of impulse, restraint, and tone; specifically affective elements of consciousness and relationships: not feeling against thought, but thought as felt and feeling as thought. We are then defining those elements as a structure: as a set, with specific internal relations, at once interlocking and in tension. Yet we are also defining a social experience which is still in process, often indeed not yet recognized as social but taken to be private, idiosyncratic, and even isolating.[3]

One way of reading Carby's statements about the 1990s as a period marked by the simultaneous regulation of black feminist and black queer work is to say that she is suggesting that the affective residues of heteropatriarchal regulations within African American Studies form a structure of feeling that claims black feminist and black queer subjects. As that structure of feeling points to the social parameters of patriarchal and homophobic suppression, heteropatriarchy ceases to be a "private" and "idiosyncratic" matter and becomes a vital element in African American intellectual formations.

As one mode of authorizing those regimes, the discourse of Du Bois has possibly come to underwrite African American intellectual practice and African American Studies as a field. A certain way of imagining Du Bois, thus, may have unleashed a discourse that has stolen his identity and has likely built the institution we know as African American Studies, determining which projects belong in that jurisdiction and which endeavors don't, outlining which subjects are fit to embody African American critical thought and which ones are inappropriate for that enterprise. Indeed, Carby's observations about the 1990s suggest a structure of feeling among black feminist and black queer intellectuals, one constituted out of repression but one interested in breaking away from the very regimes of normativity that account for its predicament. My critique is also motivated by this structure, and in its spirit, I am less concerned with providing exhaustive documentation of the discourse that I am calling "Du Bois," and more interested in acknowledging a structure that operates outside the terrain of the evidentiary. Indeed, we needn't assume that a project of this type requires evidence of the gendered and sexual regulations that comprise much of African American Studies and its discursive deployment of Du Bois. To do so would be to misunderstand power's own interest in concealment and its penchant to polemicize that which contests its own regimes of truth. Inasmuch as structures of feeling denote formations that do not even appear to be social, those structures do not necessarily signify as evidence. Indeed, we might say that the marginalization of work by black women and black queer intellectuals is coextensive with efforts to withhold the facts of that marginalization from the realm of evidence. If we appeal to evidence, we risk dismissing these structures and all that they have to tell us. Rather than accumulate evidence in hopes that this accumulation will constitute truth, I shall discuss this structure of feeling that seems to intuit regimes of gender and sexual normativity, sensing them acutely in the invocation of Du Bois and all that it represents. And in doing so, I am well aware that sometimes a "feeling" is all the "evidence" you need.

## The Itineraries of Power within Radical Agency: The Incitement to Du Bois

That the discourse of Du Bois unites intellectual and political agency to the body seems to be borne out historically. In Martin Summers' wonderful *Manliness and its Discontents: The Black Middle Class and the Transformation of Masculinity, 1900–1930*, he discusses student protests at Fisk University during the 1920s—protests inspired, in part, by an address given by W. E. B. Du Bois. In his speech, Du Bois raised the importance of manhood for black racial formation, and the ways in which the administration at Fisk was placing black manhood in jeopardy:

> [Self-expression] and manhood are choked at Fisk in the very day when we need expression to develop manhood in the colored race . . . We are facing a serious and difficult situation. We need every bit of brains and ability that we have for leadership. There is no hope that the American Negro is going to develop as a docile animal. He is going to be a man, and he needs therefore his best manhood. This manhood is being discouraged at Fisk today and ambition instead of being fostered is being deliberately frowned upon.[4]

For Du Bois the speaker, manhood was a way of coming into the self, a means of articulating identity. It was also a racial project: the masculinist articulation of the self helped to enunciate and develop the race. This racial project was an intellectual one, requiring "brains," "ability," and "leadership," and as far as Du Bois the person was concerned, the administrative arrangement of Fisk was interfering with this racial project.

As Summers notes, we must contextualize Du Bois's speech within the tense social environment at Fisk during that time and the student rebellions against "the imposition of late–Victorian standards of morality" (243) at black colleges and universities. Fisk students were subject to curfews, to increased surveillance of male–female fraternizing, to prohibitions on dancing to jazz and blues (243). The student protests at Fisk University in the 1920s illustrate the ways that Du Bois functioned not simply as a person, but as a discourse that incited heterosexual masculinity. For instance, at a rally that lasted for seven hours and called for the resignation of then president Fayette A. McKenzie, students chanted, "Hey Boys! Who Boys? *Du Bois*. Down with McKenzie" (266, emphasis added). One Fisk undergrad informed Du Bois, "At the football games . . . they gave rousing cheers for Du Bois and yelled 'down with the Fisk parasites and job holders! Give us *men* on your faculty'" (266). In another protest, a group of male students violated curfew and chanted throughout the campus, "Du Bois! Du Bois!" and "Before I'd be a Slave" (267). The student protests illustrate the ways in which the incitement to Du Bois functions in many instances as an incitement to heteropatriarchal masculinity. In the context of the protest, "Du Bois as discourse" stood for the ideal of black masculinity as distinguished from feminized university administration and faculty, feminized presumably because of their allegiance to accomodationism inside and outside the university. Against the purportedly feminized disposition of the university administration, the students evoked Du Bois as a means to create and pose an insurrectionary masculinity situated against the university establishment and positioned in favor of their own sexual autonomy.

The student protests illustrate how the discourse of Du Bois assembles subjects for the health of gendered and sexualized regimes of power, in this case regimes of power that were oppositional. Such regimes do not establish themselves through the suppression of racialized gender and sexuality, but through the articulation of racialized gender and sexuality as modes of agency. This formulation of power intersects with Foucault's work on power by illustrating how the enunciation of agency, rather than the abolition of it, is power's trademark. Discussing the birth of a new form of power after the decline of power symbolized through the sovereign body, Foucault states,

> As always with relations of power, one is faced with complex phenomena which don't obey the Hegelian form of the dialec-tic. Mastery and awareness of one's own body can be acquired only through the effect of an investment of power in the body: gymnastics, exercises, muscle-building, nudism, glorification of the body beautiful. All of this belongs to the pathway leading to the desire of one's own body, by way of the insistent, persistent, meticulous work of power on the bodies of children or soldiers, the healthy bodies.[5]

The student protests, and their demands for the unfettered interaction between men and women, and the freedom to dance to jazz and blues music, represent the students' call for a mastery and awareness of the black male body. Indeed, students at Fisk were evoking Du Bois as a way to designate their own bodies as sites of social and sexual desires. The particular notion of power that Foucault tried to evolve was not a description of the degradation of the subject but of the amplification of the body and its powers. In the context of the Fisk protests, the stu-dents were charging the administration with degrading the body and its desires; in the name of Du Bois, the protests tried to achieve the body's fulfillment. As the discourse of Du Bois demonstrates how the amplification of the body helps constitute racial projects and forma-tions, the idea of Du Bois as a mode of corporealization veers from Foucault's interest in the body as a site of power. The protests at Fisk illuminate the ways that the black body can function as a critical *and* rational (i.e. heteronormative) domain of sexual and intellectual agency, that is as the insurrectionary project of a rational black self. But to the extent that the Fisk protests called for a sexual mobility and reclamation of the body that left heteropatriarchy undisturbed, their critical interventions folded into, rather than departed from the itineraries of power.

For Foucault, power's agentive properties not only applied to the body but to what he called governmentality as well. Foucault theo-rized governmentality as a way to link different venues that expressed power's agentive properties. We might say, provisionally, that Du Bois is the name of a discourse that operates continuously at the levels of episteme, corporeality, and institutionality. Discussing the continuities that are presumed by governmentality, Foucault states,

> ... there are three fundamental types of government, each of which relates to a particular science or discipline: the art of self-government, connected with morality; the art of properly governing a family, which belongs to economy; and finally the science of ruling the state, which concerns politics ... What matters, notwithstanding this typology, is that the art of government is always characterized by the essential continuity of one type with the other, and of a second type with a third (91).

Governmentality implies power's encampment in social institutions as well as power's constitution of the subject and the subject's agency. Hence, Foucault implies that governmentality is an art of the self intended to connect the fashioning of the self to the management of family, economy, and state. Governmentality is thus a means for subjects to articulate forms of agency in relation to the various aspects of society. As such, participation in the public sphere and supervision of the private become the destination of "the art of self-government."

To the extent that the discourse of Du Bois functions as a way of connecting intellectual and political agency to corporeality and the creation of the self, it coheres with Foucault's understanding of governmentality. Foucault uses the category "upward continuity" to describe the connection between self-making and the administration of the social world. He states, "in the art of government the task is to establish a continuity, in both an upwards and a downwards direction ... Upwards continuity means that a person who wishes to govern the state well must first learn how to govern himself, his goods and his patrimony, after which he will be successful in governing the state" (91). In other words, upwards continuity suggests that the creation of agency for the self moves outward toward possessions and family and then upwards toward the state. The Fisk Protests presumed a continuous relation between the regulation of the body and the Fisk administration so that the emancipation of black male bodies would move outward to a radical transformation of the university itself.

## The Two Governmentalities of Dark Princess

Interestingly enough, we can find in Du Bois's novel *Dark Princess* an engagement with racialized forms of governmentality. We can also discern traces of the discourse called "Du Bois." Indeed, the novel presents a radical black heterosexual masculinity as the critique of the gender and sexual itineraries of liberalism. In doing so, that version of masculinity recommends itself as the appropriate critic of liberal forms of governmentality. We might read Du Bois's novel *Dark Princess* as a narrative about forms of governmentality, but one that eschews black assimilation into liberal institutions. Instead, the novel promotes a form of radical governmentality that is antiracist and internationalist. The novel is significant for our purposes, as it connects the creation of a critical self to the governance of the race. In doing so, *Dark Princess* provides an illustration of how the elaboration of critical agency becomes power's intention rather than its objection. We must analyze the discourse that organizes the novel. We need to understand the ways in which that discourse presumes a regime of gender and sexual normativity in opposition to liberal pronouncements about state, citizenship, and marriage.

While the discourse of the novel assumes the necessity of governmentality, we require a mode of analysis that can hold all forms of governmentality under inspection in an effort to possibly move beyond them. As we will see, both forms of governmentality link agency to heterosexual normativity. These regimes of governmentality are both responsible for gender and sexual suppressions during Du Bois's day and our own. These governmentalities and their resultant regulations have become part of the genealogy of African American intellectual formations. We need a hermeneutic that can reckon with that genealogy in the name of a distant but possible intellectual practice not commanded by regimes of governance.

We may place *Dark Princess*, and the radical governmentality espoused by the novel, broadly within the interwar period, which historian Bill V. Mullen describes as a period characterized by Indian nationalist movements: "the emergence of Black radicalism within the United States and the role of black and Asian radicals in revising Soviet policy on both 'Negro' and Asian liberation during the formation of the third International after 1919 and the crucial 1922 and 1928 Comintern in Moscow."[6] *Dark Princess* was published in 1928, and as Claudia Tate argues in her introduction to the reprint of this novel, it allowed Du Bois to "[promote] racial propaganda by countering the ideology of white supremacy with black exceptionalism."[7] Black exceptionalism functions both as a vehicle for acceptance within a racial state organized around liberal ideals and as the means to a more radical future. The novel is in part about the very bright and educated Matthew Townes and whether or not he can help awaken the black masses to a radical revolt against the white domination by the United States and European nations.[8] In doing so, Matthew must also inspire blacks to an awareness of how white supremacy in the states is part of a worldwide racial domination of European races over people and nations of color. That question becomes the central concern of the novel as Matthew is brought into the confidences of a revolutionary and elite coalition of leaders from North Africa, Asia, and the Middle East—a gathering convened by a beautiful Indian princess named Kautilya. At a dinner party to discuss the possibility and means of an international struggle against the global reach of the color line, Matthew asserts that blacks should be a part of such an agenda. One of the guests, a Japanese man, responds by raising the question of the Negro race's capacity for revolutionary action and for founding an antiracist, international, and coalitional society:

It would be unfair to our guest not to explain with some clarity and precision that the whole question of the Negro race both in Africa and America is for us not simply a question of suffering and compassion. Need we say that for these peoples we have every human sympathy? But for us here and for the larger company we represent, there is a deeper question—that of the ability, qualifications, and real possibilities of the black race in Africa or elsewhere. (21)

Matthew understands clearly the anti-black racism at work in the Japanese man's remarks. As the narrator tell us, "Suddenly there loomed plain and clear the shadow of a color line within a color line, a prejudice within a prejudice, and he and his again the sacrifice" (22). It is also clear that the "ability, qualifications, and real possibilities of the black race in Africa or elsewhere" are defined in terms of the ability of the race to conform to nationalist standards of modernity. Suggesting such a possibility, Princess Kautilya states,

> . . . Moscow has reports—careful reports of the world's masses. And the report on the Negroes of America was astonishing. At the time, I doubted its truth: their education, their work, their property, their organizations; and the odds, the terrible, crushing odds against which, inch by inch and heartbreak by heartbreak, they have forged their unfaltering way upward. If the report is true, they are a *nation* today, a modern *nation* worthy to stand beside any *nation* here (22, emphasis added).

It is crucial to understand the extent to which the internationalism that the assemblage is calling for is predicated on modern definitions of a nation. As Kautilya implies, the criteria for modern nation status is denoted through labor, education, property ownership, and organizational development. Another criterion is the demonstration of progressive development in the face of adversity. The assemblage also assumes the distinctiveness and discontinuity of societies, nations, and cultures. Indeed, the members of the group are the empirical evidence of distinct and discontinuous national histories and ideals. Historically, we might situate the nationalist foundations of internationalism within the Communist Party's articulation of the nation within a nation thesis. Black intellectuals like Claude McKay and Harry Haywood helped to shape the contours of this thesis. Haywood stated in his autobiography, "As the theory was put into practice, we learned that national cultures could be expressed with a proletarian (socialist) content and that there was no antagonistic contradictions, under socialism, between national cultures and proletarian internationalism . . . Thus the Bolsheviks upheld the principle of 'proletarian in content, national in form.'"[9] As Haywood implies, the Party sanctioned the production of discontinuous national formations, understanding the accumulation of those formations as internationalism. In their article, "Beyond 'Culture': Space, Identity, and the Politics of Difference," Akhil Gupta and James Ferguson discuss how narratives of cultural, social, and national discontinuity have shaped modern thought. They write,

> Representations of space in the social sciences are remarkably dependent on images of break, rupture, and distinction. The distinctiveness of societies, nations, and cultures is predicated on a seemingly unproblematic division of space, on the fact that they occupy "naturally" discontinuous spaces. The premise of discontinuity forms the starting point from which to theorize culture, conflict, and contradiction between cultures and societies.[10]

We might say that the radical assemblage has internalized social scientific understandings of nations and cultures and fashioned their standard of internationalism upon those understandings. Indeed, the premise of discontinuity is the starting point from which the group theorizes internationalism and enacts its politics. While the novel may represent Du Bois's internationalist turn, that move in no way suggests the abdication of nationalist ideologies. In fact, this brand of internationalism seems to require them.

As Gupta and Ferguson argue, the narrative of discontinuity presents culture in isomorphic relation to national entities. In this sense, culture is made to bear witness to national difference. They say, for instance,

> It is so taken for granted that each country embodies its own distinctive culture and society that the terms "society" and "culture" are routinely simply appended to the names of nation-states, as when a tourist visits India to understand "Indian culture" and "Indian society" or Thailand to experience "Thai culture" or the United States to get a whiff of "American culture."[11]

Hence, culture becomes a way of demonstrating modern subject and nation status as well. At the heart of *Dark Princess* is the question of how to make a case for blacks as modern radical subjects who can frame their racial condition within an international framework, and thus participate in an international struggle against white supremacy. *Dark Princess* answers this question by offering up African American culture as the evidence of modern development. Matthew responds to the group's doubts about black national and revolutionary agency with a spiritual:

> . . . Matthew let go restraint and sang as his people sang in Virginia, twenty years ago. His great voice, gathered in one long deep breath, rolled the Call of God:
>
> Go down, Moses!
> Way Down into the Egypt land,
> Tell Old Pharaoh
> To let my people go!" (26)

With the sorrow songs, Matthew democratizes culture, demonstrating that "ability and talent and art is not entirely or even mainly among the reigning aristocrats of Asia and Europe, but buried among millions of men down in the great sodden masses of all men and even in Black Africa?" In doing so, he presents African American culture and indeed African Americans as at the vanguard of democratic possibilities. Understanding that Matthew offers African American culture as confirmation of the modern status of African Americans, Princess Kautilya asks, "You assume then . . . that the mass of the workers of the world can rule as well as be ruled?" Matthew replies,

> Yes—or rather can work as well as be worked, can live as well as be kept alive. America is teaching the world one thing and only one thing of real value, and that is, that ability and capacity for culture is not the hereditary monopoly of a few, but the widespread possibility for the majority of mankind if they only have a decent chance in life. (26)

This capacity for culture suggests a specific type of upwards continuity—one in which the creation of culture implies that self-governance and creation could extend upwards into the international overthrow of white supremacy and the founding of a new antiracist world order. As participation in an international coalition against white supremacy presumes self-constituted nations, Matthew's song thus presents African American culture as the evidence and outcome of a national consciousness that can win participation in radically internationalist politics.

The geopolitical narrative of discontinuity organizes interracial heterosexual desire in the novel as well. When Matthew observes how the color line separates him from the assemblage, he also realizes that the color line might separate him from the young princess. After the Japanese gentlemen's remarks, Matthew

> . . . left the piquant salad and laid down his fork slowly. Up to this moment he had been quite happy. Despite the feeling of being out of it now and then, he had assumed that this was his world, his people, from the high and beautiful lady whom he worshipped more and more, even to the Egyptians, Indians, and Arab who seemed slightly, but very slightly, aloof or misunderstanding. (21–22)

Blacks' status as modern subjects is not all that is jeopardized by the racialization of blacks as outside modern agency and subjectivity. Matthew's status as potential sexual partner of Princess Kautilya is also jeopardized. In doing so, the novel demonstrates the ways in which notions of social and cultural discontinuity distinguish social spaces geopolitically as well as sexually. Matthew's admittance to the international coalition is thrown into question along with a potential romantic relationship with the Princess. Indeed, the dinner symbolizes the political and sexual hope of two national cultures represented in Matthew and Kautilya coming together. The novel thus makes the achievement of modern subject status a political and (hetero) sexual endeavor.

In keeping with that political endeavor, Matthew pursues a plan to rally black masses in the south, but through a series of misadventures he winds up in jail with his hopes of revolutionary incitement and a romance with Princess Kautilya dashed. The failure of the revolutionary plan convinces Matthew to reject the possibilities of a radical governmentality, and so he begins his capitulation to liberalism, a capitulation symbolized most powerfully through legalized marriage. Matthew is freed from jail thanks to the ingenuity of a social climbing African American secretary named Sara Andrews. Despite his freedom, Matthew is enthralled by his desire to participate in revolutionary struggle. To withstand the appeals of a radical governmentality, he throws himself into the embrace of a liberal one, an embrace symbolized by his marriage proposal to Sara. To himself, he thinks, "Why not marry Sara? Marriage was normal. Marriage stopped secret longings and wild open revolt. It solved the woman problem once and for all. Once married, he would be safe, settled, quiet; with all the furies at rest, calm, satisfied . . . " (138). Here marriage is presented not only as that which will direct Matthew's attention away from Kautilya but as that which will neutralize insurrectionary desires. Sara understands the marriage to work in favor of her desires for respectability and power as well, telling Matthew "I've been fighting the thing men call love all my life, and I don't see much in it. I don't think you are the loving kind—and that suits me. But I do think enlightened self-interest calls us to be partners. And if you really mean this, I am willing" (138). For Sara, marriage to Matthew is a chance to advance her plans of power by putting Matthew up as Chicago's new black political leader. Marriage, according to the novel, is a technique of liberal governmentality that gives legitimacy to black middle-class efforts to assimilate into liberal democracy, and acquire power according to its rules of engagement. Marriage to Sara ensures his launch into a liberal governmentality denoted through bourgeois advancement, participation within electoral politics, and assimilation into Chicago civil society. By marrying Sara, Matthew would supplant radical governmentality by placing liberal governmentality in its stead.

While Matthew's relationship with Kautilya becomes the context for revolutionary struggle, his marriage to Sara becomes the condition for traditional political pursuits. The narrator informs us of Sara's plans:

> First she was going to elect Matthew to the legislature, and then in the glory of his triumph there was going to be a wedding that would make black Chicago sit up and even white Chicago take notice. Thirdly, she was going to reveal to a gaping world that

she already owned that nearly new, modern, and beautifully equipped apartment on the South Parkway which had just been sold at auction. (139)

Matthew soon discovers that his marriage to Sara is filled with emptiness. He is elected to the legislature but unfulfilled. The grand apartment is the place-to-be for Chicago socialites, black and white, but it is "an immaculate place that must not be disturbed for mere living purposes . . . " (152). The marriage arches toward an upward continuity designed to capture the attention, recognition, and approval of liberal civil society. As Sara's interest in hailing black Chicago and white Chicago illustrates, liberal governmentality is a racial project intended for assimilation. But the novel suggests that in addition to being compromised by racism, liberal civil society and its accoutrements offer no hope of ethical improvement, political fulfillment, or sensual pleasure. Through the loveless marriage to Sara and the social arrangements that come with it, the novel communicates the impotence of liberal forms of participation and agency.

Eventually, Matthew leaves Sara for Kautilya and is thus put back on the road to revolutionary intentions. After a lengthy separation, Matthew and Kautilya are reunited toward the end of the novel, when Kautilya presents Matthew with their infant son, Madhu. In contrast to the coldness that characterized Matthew's relationship with Sara, he pours affection onto Kautilya: "He kissed the tendrils of her hair and saw silver threads lurking there; he kissed her forehead and her eyes and lingered on her lips" (307). In this scene, the novel suggests that the radical governmentality symbolized by Matthew's union with Kautilya and the birth of their child promises gender and sexual fulfillment, as well as a political vision for a more radical and just tomorrow—but one that resolves itself in heterosexual normativity. Upon this reunion, Matthew's mother says, "An now, son, we'se gwine to make dis little man an hones' chile—Preacher!" (309). After Matthew and Kautilya are married, Matthew's mother [stiffens], [closes] her eyes, and [chants] to her God: "Jesus, take dis child. Make him a man! Make him a man, Lord Jesus—a leader of his people and a lover of his God!" (309). In similar fashion, an impromptu court has gathered in the woods, extolling the infant as "Messenger and Messiah to all the Darker Worlds!" (311).

By presenting the hope of revolutionary struggle in the form of the child, the novel accomplishes two things—it establishes radical governmentality as an agenda designed to create not just an abstract political subject, but a program intended to foster subjects and social formations gendered and sexualized in a certain direction. As Alys Weinbaum argues in her analysis of *Dark Princess*, "[Du Bois through *Dark Princess*] directly connects romance to struggle against imperialism and colonialism and thus situates it as an artistic form that lends itself to expression of triumph over oppression."[12] Hence, as Weinbaum suggests, the task of producing a radical movement against Western imperialism and for an anti-imperialist world depends upon the constitution of heterosexual reproduction and also, as this essay argues, on the constitution of heterosexual subjects. The discourse of Du Bois as it works within the novel attempts to argue that radical political agency is continuous with intellectual agency as well as gender and sexual identity.

If we read *Dark Princess* as a narrative of governmentality, we must do so with two points in mind: the type of governmentality that the novel arches toward is not identical to the one that Foucault theorizes. Foucault based his theory of governmentality on civil society within a liberal regime. In the novel, this version of civil society is symbolized by Chicago high society and electoral politics. It represents civil society as it is given. The mode of governmentality that the novel favors belongs to a society that does not exist, one that is projected into a radical tomorrow. Madhu represents the possibility of that society organized around interracial and international cooperation, a messianic possibility far off in the future. While the novel invests its hope and imagination within that radical tomorrow, we need a counter-discourse that is suspicious of that version of tomorrow, one that organizes critical agency around heterosexual gender and sexual normativity. We need to theorize processes of governmentality for revolutionary projects—that is, if we wish to apprehend the genealogy of African American intellectual formations and fully appreciate the governmentalizing discourse known as Du Bois.

We must study Du Bois as a discourse to deepen our appreciation of power and its manifestations in radical subject and social formations. One of those manifestations is the regulation and exclusion of subjects who violate the gendered and sexual presumptions of black critical agency. In fact, we might read Carby's passage about the regulation and management of black women and black queer men within African American Studies as a statement that homophobia and patriarchy are two salient effects of the governmentalizing agenda called "Du Bois." As an intellectual figure, Du Bois has been used to promote governmentality. Again, Du Bois ceases to be simply an historical figure that lived and died and becomes the pseudonym for systems of normativity that have been internalized and enacted. To put it bluntly, learning and internalizing Du Bois may never have simply represented the acquisition of knowledge. More pointedly, regimes of normativity might have been acquired in the name of that erudition. In sum, the incitement to Du Bois has authorized more than curiosity. African American intellectual formations have been produced within certain regimes of power that have yet to be reckoned with. Those regimes have legislated the gender and sexual economies of African American intellectual formations. Those economies have determined for African American Studies which gender and sexual practices, knowledges, and corporealities should be deemed worthy of production and distribution. Confronting this history means that we need biographies not so much of African American intellectuals but of those economies that account for our then and now.

## Notes

1. Hazel V. Carby, "The Souls of Black Men," in *Race Men* (Cambridge: Harvard University Press, 1998), 20–21. Reprinted in this volume. Hereafter all references will be to the reprinted version and will be made parenthetically in the text.

2. Cornel West, *Race Matters* (Boston: Beacon Press, 1993), 40. Quoted in Carby, "Souls of Black Men," reprinted in this volume.

3. Raymond Williams, *Marxism and Literature* (Oxford and New York: Oxford University Press, 1977), 132.

4. Martin Summers, *Manliness and Its Discontents: The Black Middle Class and the Transformation of Masculinity, 1900–1930* (Chapel Hill and London: The University of North Carolina Press, 2004), 265. Hereafter all citations will be made parenthetically in the text.

5. Michel Foucault, *Power/Knowledge: Selected Interviews and Other Writings, 1972–1977,* edited by Colin Gordon (New York: Pantheon Books, 1980), 56.

6. Bill V. Mullen, "Du Bois, *Dark Princess*, and the Afro-Asian International," *positions* vol. 11, no. 1 (Spring 2003): 218.

7. W. E. B. Du Bois, *Dark Princess: A Romance*, with an Introduction by Claudia Tate (Jackson, Mississippi: Banner Books, 1995), xx. Hereafter all citations will be made parenthetically in the text.

8. Masses of blacks never show up in novel but act as a powerful absent presence that organizes much of the rhetoric and plotline of the novel.

9. Harry Haywood, *Black Bolshevik: Autobiography of an Afro-Communist* (Chicago: Liberator, 1978), 158. Quoted in Mullen 229.

10. Akhil Gupta and James Ferguson, "Beyond 'Culture': Space, Identity, and the Politics of Difference," in *Culture, Power, Place: Explorations in Critical Anthropology*, edited by Akhil Gupta and James Ferguson (Durham, N.C.: Duke University Press, 1997), 33–34.

11. Ibid., 34.

12. Alys Eve Weinbaum, "The Sexual Politics of Black Internationalism: W. E. B. Du Bois and the Reproduction of Racial Globality," in *Wayward Reproductions: Genealogies of Race and Nation in Transatlantic Modern Thought* (Durham N.C.: Duke University Press, 2004), 202.

# 9

# Father of the Bride: Du Bois and the Making of Black Heterosexuality

■ *Mason Stokes*

When Countee Cullen, unofficial poet laureate of the Harlem Renaissance, married W. E. B. Du Bois's daughter, Yolande, in 1928, the result was both a spectacular and a failed moment of black heterosexuality. Cullen's subsequent decision to travel to Paris not with his new bride, but with his, well, pick your euphemism, "special friend," "longtime companion," "fellow traveler" Harold Jackman revealed the extent of the marriage's failure, a failure that was made official when the couple divorced in 1930. While newspapers in Harlem reported the existence of an alleged "other woman" as cause of the breakup, Yolande revealed to her father the true nature of the "problem": Cullen's homosexuality. Because the Du Bois/Cullen union was widely staged and reported as a specifically racial triumph, this episode offers a unique window on the racial logics of heterosexuality in the twenties. In short, I'm interested less in the "question" of Cullen's homosexuality than I am in the assumption and construction of his "heterosexuality" as the public face of the "New Negro." The fact that W. E. B. Du Bois played an active role in that assumption and construction raises the stakes of this black wedding, making it, finally, the story not just of two people, but of a new black nation.

To call the wedding of Cullen and Yolande the "Harlem social event of the decade," as most critics eventually get around to doing, is probably an understatement.[1] In fact, when one considers the competition—namely the annual Hamilton Lodge drag ball at Eighth Avenue and 155th Street, which had been held just over a month before the wedding—it's worth thinking of the Cullen/Du Bois wedding in the same category: as a wonderfully over-the-top drag performance, the drag ball to beat all.[2] This is heterosexual drag par excellence, which, as Judith Butler has famously pointed out, makes sense, given the extent to which heterosexuality depends for its very existence on performance as a mode of being.[3] Without invoking the context of Harlem drag culture, Nathan Huggins gets at a similar idea when he calls the Cullen/Du Bois wedding "a parody or travesty of ceremony, no less striking in its mimicry than the pomp-filled parades of Marcus Garvey."[4]

A third context for the Cullen/Du Bois wedding lurks in the near background: African American Pageantry. In 1915, Du Bois wrote that "the Pageant is the thing. This is what the people want and long for. This is the gown and paraphernalia in which the message of education and reasonable race pride can deck itself."[5] Du Bois's first experience with black Pageantry came when he authored *The Star of Ethiopia*, which was first staged in New York City in 1913. *Star* begins with the cry of the Herald:

> Hear ye, hear ye! Men of all the Americas, and listen to the tale of the Eldest and Strongest of the Races of men whose faces be Black . . . . Upon this night a world shall pass before your souls, bathed in color, wound with song and set to the dancing of a thousand feet. And this shall be the message of this pageantry: Of the Black man's Gift of Iron to the world; of Ethiopia and her Glory . . . . Men of the world keep silence and in reverence see this holy thing."[6]

As this passage makes clear, and as Katharine Capshaw Smith argues, "the political, the didactic, the reformative all coalesced for Du Bois in the pageant format, and he found, as did other pageant writers, an eager and responsive audience for his vision."[7]

Ten years later, and just before the wedding of his daughter and Countee Cullen, Du Bois wrote that "a new Negro theatre is demanded and it is slowly coming."[8] This new theatre must be, Du Bois continued, "about us . . . , by us . . . , for us . . . , [and] near us."[9] In this context, it's not too much of a stretch to see his daughter's wedding—with all of its pomp and performative circumstance—as yet another kind of pageant, a drama that creates, through its very performance, the new world it augurs. Du Bois seems to have realized as much himself when, in an essay on the wedding for *The Crisis*, he referred to the ceremony as "a great pageant."[10] The wedding of Countee and Yolande was a kind of New Negro art, and as such it was designed with an appropriately large audience in mind: not only those who were lucky enough to gain entrance, but those across the ages and the pages who would experience it as story, as Pageant. Du Bois, after all, had famously written in "The Criteria for Negro Art," "I do not care a damn for any art that is not used for propaganda."[11] In the context of its performativity—its pageantry—his daughter's wedding surely qualifies as just the kind of propagandistic art he had in mind. As art, Yolande's wedding was meant to prophesy and inaugurate the new black future.

According to accounts in the *Amsterdam News*, three thousand people were packed into the Salem Methodist Episcopal Church in Harlem on April 9, 1928, and "an equally large number were kept outside" by policemen.[12] The *News* continues, "baskets of mixed flowers and cages of canary birds were hung on the balcony railing. At the altar were tall green palms, ferns, calla and Easter lilies, roses and tulips. From the ceiling, and directly over the altar, was a white dove suspended from a cord."[13] According to some accounts, two thousand doves were to be released after the wedding vows were exchanged, but given the logistical, not to mention hygienic, nightmare of releasing two thousand doves in a church, this part of the story is most likely apocryphal.[14] We do know, however, that Langston Hughes and Arna Bontemps numbered among the ushers, and that Harold Jackman, Cullen's devastatingly handsome companion on his upcoming trip to Paris, served as the best man.

Despite his usual love of extravagant display (*The Star of Ethiopia* was not a subtle enterprise), Du Bois put up a gallant fight against extravagance in the days and months preceding the wedding, largely for financial reasons. Quite simply, he lost this battle, and letters from Du Bois to Yolande offer a record of his efforts. As he wrote in January, "as to the size and cost of the wedding, we must be careful not to be so ostentatious and showy as to be vulgar .... I am especially alarmed about the number of bridesmaids. It seems to me that fifteen is beyond all possibility .... Can't you some way cut this down to four or five?" (January 13, 1928).[15] Six days later Du Bois again wrote to Yolande, "I am still alarmed about those bridesmaids" (January 19, 1928). Not surprisingly, the size of the reception was also a concern: "We [and by "we" Du Bois meant Countee and himself] have decided that two hundred ought to be the outside limit for persons invited to the reception. Even this is an awful mob, and the thought of feeding them makes me feel weak" (January 13, 1928).

Of course, this largely financial hesitation should not be viewed as a lack of enthusiasm on Du Bois's part for the upcoming wedding, or for what it symbolized. His enthusiasm was so great, in fact, that he devoted significant column inches in the June issue of *The Crisis* to the wedding, including a full-page bridal photo of Mrs. Yolande Du Bois Cullen and half-page shots of the bridal party. In the rather odd essay that anchors this pictorial tribute, called "So the Girl Marries" (one piece of the oddness is that Yolande is called "The Girl" throughout), Du Bois goes on at some length about marriage in general, and about this one in particular. He talks about his own role in what he calls "Mate-selection": "We talked the young men over— their fathers and grandfathers; their education; their ability to earn particular sorts of living; their dispositions .... Once or twice I went on long letter hunts for facts; usually facts were all too clear and only deductions necessary. What was the result? I really don't know."[16] But if "facts were all too clear and only deductions necessary," it's hard to understand how Countee slipped through, for Du Bois does recognize a certain "difference," if you will, about Countee. In this same essay Du Bois describes Cullen—unnamed here unless you consider "The Boy" a name—as "a rather unusual boy with a promise of fine manhood."[17] And earlier, Du Bois had written in a moment of fatherly exasperation, "Boys! queer animals."[18] Indeed.

Du Bois ratchets his prose up a bit when he talks about the symbolism of the wedding. And given the importance of this to the argument I want to make here, I quote at some length:

> The symbolism of that procession was tremendous. It was not the mere marriage of a maiden. It was not simply the wedding of a fine young poet. It was the symbolic march of young and black America. America, because there was Harvard, Columbia, Smith, Brown, Howard, Chicago, Syracuse, Penn and Cornell. There were three Masters of Arts and fourteen Bachelors. There were poets and teachers, actors, artists and students. But it was not simply conventional America—it had a dark and shimmering beauty all its own; a calm and high restraint and sense of new power; it was a new race; a new thought; a new thing rejoicing in a ceremony as old as the world.[19]

Clearly, Du Bois sees this wedding in terms that go well beyond this specific bride and groom, beyond these specific families. A man and woman come together in order to give birth not to something so mundane as children, but to a new black America, a new race. More specifically, this passage again calls to mind Du Bois's *The Star of Ethiopia*, which, according to Lewis, featured "a thousand creamy-complexioned young women and tawny, well-built men, and flocks of schoolchildren marching through history."[20] It is, then, not simply the "symbolic march of young and black America," but the symbolic march of black heterosexuality, complete with the schoolchildren destined to be its product.

The metaphorics of Du Bois's description of the ceremony shouldn't be too surprising once we remind ourselves of that which seems too obvious to mention, but which never actually *gets* mentioned: that the language of a "Harlem Renaissance"—a new birth in Harlem—is itself already the language of heterosexuality, the language of birthing. Heterosexuality, then, has become an organizing trope—a central metaphor—for America's black future.

Du Bois is aware that all of this is perhaps a bit over the top, a bit much. As he puts it:

> Why should there have been so much pomp and ceremony—flowers and carriages and silk hats; wedding cake and wedding

music? After all marriage in its essence is and should be very
simple: a clasp of friendly hands; a walking away together of Two
who say: "Let us try to be One and face and fight a lonely world
together!" What more? Is that not enough? Quite; and were
I merely white I should have sought to make it end with this.

But it seems to me that I owe something extra to an Idea, a
Tradition. We who are black and panting up hurried hills of
hate and hindrance—we have got to establish new footholds on
the slipping by-paths through which we come.[21]

In other words, Du Bois recognizes that there is a specifically racial
aspect to this moment of performative heterosexuality—that, given
the burdens and trials of history, a black wedding can be anything but
simple. However, if his goal is to normalize blackness through a public performance of heterosexuality, it's important to realize that
"heterosexuality" isn't the completely stable force he had imagined.
As Judith Butler writes,

hegemonic heterosexuality is itself a constant and repeated
effort to imitate its own idealizations. That it must repeat this
imitation, that it sets up pathologizing practices and normalizing sciences in order to produce and consecrate its own claim
on originality and propriety, suggests that heterosexual performativity is beset by an anxiety that it can never fully overcome,
that its effort to become its own idealizations can never be
finally or fully achieved, and that it is consistently haunted by
that domain of sexual possibility that must be excluded for
heterosexualized gender to produce itself.[22]

What Du Bois may not have realized is that a wedding in 1928 may
not be one of those "new footholds" he was looking for, but may, in
fact, be just another "slipping by-path." The "domain of sexual possibility that must be excluded" haunts the story of Countee and
Yolande from beginning to end.

Du Bois had talked at greater length of the difficulties of African
American marriage in a column he wrote for *The Crisis* six
years before his daughter's wedding. In that column he begins by

positioning marriage as a problem "among colored people, especially the advancing groups."[23] The problem is related to what seems to be not only an overly idealized series of expectations linked to marriage, but to a fundamental incompatibility that lies at the heart of the married state. As he puts it, "Here is a man and a woman. The natural and righteous cry of their bodies calls for marriage to propagate, preserve and improve mankind. But there are difficulties" (247). These difficulties begin, it seems, with the man, whom Du Bois describes as "an educated Negro American of 1922," who is invariably "a spoiled child. He has been catered to and petted by a mother" (247). Then there are the qualities that this spoiled, catered to, and petted American Negro must see in his intended: "thinking of his own mother, he conceives his wife also as a trained, efficient Upper Servant, who can cook, serve, wash, clean, market and nurse; she must also be able to dance, play the piano, talk on politics and literature, entertain with daintiness, play tennis and drive an automobile" (248). Of course, this well-trained tennis-playing Upper Servant also has her own list: her mate must have "money and good looks. He must be a college graduate, a professional man, or at least a business man; hardly a mechanic, and certainly never a menial servant. He must have, ready for delivery on the wedding day: a well-furnished home in a good neighborhood, a servant or a day's worker, a car and a reputation that brings his picture to the pages of leading colored weeklies" (248). To put it simply, marriage in the twenties seems a difficult business indeed.

Du Bois's picture of the Negro Man as "spoiled," "catered to and petted by a mother" is, in the particular case of Countee, striking for the extent to which it reflects the then-emerging misogynist notion of what makes the homosexual man: the domineering and possessive mother, the distant, absent father. Planting a seed that would bloom in full force in the 1950s, Freud had written as early as 1910 that all of his male homosexual patients

> had had a very intense erotic attachment to a female person, as a rule their mother, during the first period of childhood, which is afterwards forgotten; this attachment was evoked or encouraged by too much tenderness on the part of the mother herself, and further reinforced by the small part played by the father during their childhood. Sadger emphasizes the fact that the

mothers of his homosexual patients were frequently masculine women, women with energetic traits of character, who were able to push the father out of his proper place. I have occasionally seen the same thing, but I was more strongly impressed by cases in which the father was absent from the beginning or left the scene at an early date, so that the boy found himself left entirely under feminine influence. Indeed, it almost seems as though the presence of a strong father would ensure that the son made the correct decision in his choice of object, namely someone of the opposite sex.[24]

Du Bois's "educated Negro American of 1922," overly mothered, essentially fatherless, would seem utterly incapable of making this "correct decision." Du Bois's vision of the difficulty of marriage "among colored people" may actually understate the case.

This is particularly true if this demonization of motherhood is placed in a specifically racial context. Du Bois's representations of black motherhood are always anxious and ambivalent. His writings on Africa as "the land of the mother" are caught between two conflicting but related possibilities: first, the black mother as the rock on which the race is founded and, second, the black mother as a rather disturbing and controlling force.[25] In "The Damnation of Women" Du Bois proudly claims that "the great black race . . . gave the world . . . the mother-idea" (954). At the same time, however, he portrays Africa as being under the thrall of an immensely powerful black sorceress: "In subtle and mysterious ways, despite her curious history, her slavery, polygamy, and toil, the spell of the African mother pervades her land" (954). This spell seeps into the heart of all black families, whether African or diasporic. As Du Bois reminds us, quoting a commentator on African families, "'The hand that rocks the cradle rules the world'" (955).

Shifting his attention from Africa to Great Barrington, Du Bois discovers the spellbinding centrality of black women in his own family as well:

As I remember through memories of others, backward among my own family, it is the mother I ever recall . . . , the brown velvet of her skin, the sorrowful black-brown of her eyes, and the tiny brown-capped waves of her midnight hair as it lay new parted on her forehead. All the way back in these dim distances it is mothers and mothers of mothers who seem to count, while fathers are shadowy memories. (955–56)

Du Bois's anxious repetition—"mothers and mothers of mothers"— reproduces syntactically the over-mothering of his hypothetical and potential candidate for marriage, that sissified New Negro, no longer fit for the requirements of heterosexuality.

Which brings us back, of course, to Cullen: while Du Bois's portrait of the overly petted New Negro contains an unconscious awareness of homosexual possibility, it's ironic that his idealized listing of "the perfect husband" remains utterly unaware of such a possibility. For, in the long list of what makes the perfect husband—the money, the job, the house, the servant, the fame, the general lack of dirt under the nails—the most important thing seems oddly missing: this man's heterosexuality. Surely this would be more important than, say, the college degree or the good looks. But of course this omission is readily understood. Du Bois doesn't think to mention it because its lack doesn't occur to him as a possibility. He seems unaware that such a requirement would need articulation, since he also seems unaware that there are good-looking, famous, college-educated poets who would lack this fundamental quality. What we see, then, when we combine the comments about the domineering mother with the absence of heterosexuality in the list of demands, is Du Bois firmly situated in a moment of real and important transition: between a naturalized and always assumed heterosexuality and the possibility of something else entirely; between the invisibility of the homosexual and the first glimmerings of homosexual possibility.

The best way to understand this new visibility of homosexual possibility is, ironically, to think first about the new visibility of heterosexuality. As scholars are now demonstrating, heterosexuality has a history; there's a new scholarly emphasis on the ways in which culture "makes" heterosexuality, apart from what might be called the biological and reproductive imperatives of male/female sexual relations. While this male/female sexual commerce has obviously been around for some time, the making of modern heterosexuality is a relatively recent phenomenon. Jonathan Ned Katz traces what he calls "the invention of heterosexuality" in medical literature of the late nineteenth century, charting the ways in which heterosexuality made its gradual and deeply ironic journey from *perversion*—its first incarnation—to its current status as an immensely powerful normalizing force. According to Katz, "heterosexuality" first appeared in the American medical lexicon in 1892 in an article by Dr. James G. Kiernan.[26] For Kiernan, "heterosexuality" signified the perverse, since it referred, in part, to male/female sexual behavior divorced from reproductive imperatives. Since reproduction normalized eroticism, sexual pleasure occurring outside of a reproductive context was seen by Kiernan and others as unhealthy, as pathological. For Kiernan, then, a heterosexual is someone whose sexuality is, in a very real sense, out of control. At the time of Kiernan's article, Richard Von Krafft-Ebing was also using the word "heterosexual" in his landmark study *Psychopathia Sexualis.* Krafft-Ebing shares Kiernan's sense that "heterosexual" signifies a non-reproductive, pleasure-centered pathology, but, contrary to Kiernan, Krafft-Ebing begins to position heterosexuality as a normalized, healthy, different-sex erotic standard. Because Krafft-Ebing discusses heterosexuality alongside case studies of men troubled by homosexual desire, heterosexuality begins to assume its shape as a cure for deviance, as a thing to strive for. This process of normalizing heterosexuality was continued by Freud in his "Three Essays on the Theory of Sexuality" (1905), where "heterosexuality" comes to mean the healthy, natural endpoint of one's sexual maturation. As Katz writes, Freud "helped to constitute our belief in the existence of a unitary, monolithic thing with a life and determining power of its own: 'heterosexuality'" (66). Katz continues, "Freud's explicit uses of the word *heterosexual* helped to constitute a different-sex eroticism as modern society's influential, dominant norm" (66).

We get a sense of the same movement if we shift from the relatively obscure arcana of medical jargon to the more populist etymologies of *Webster's.* "Heterosexuality" first appeared in Merriam Webster's *New International Dictionary* in 1923, where it was defined as a medical term meaning "morbid sexual passion for one of the opposite sex"—"morbid" here clearly signifying the pathological, the diseased (Katz, 92).

By 1934, however, a short eleven years later, *Webster's Second Edition* gives it the definition we associate with it today: a "manifestation of sexual passion for one of the opposite sex; normal sexuality" (Katz, 92). In the space of a decade, as Katz demonstrates, "heterosexuality" had morphed from perversion to norm. And back again, if the Countee Cullen wedding is any guide.

It's become a piece of received wisdom that Countee Cullen went on his honeymoon not with Yolande, but with his best man and best euphemism, Harold Jackman. This is, in fact, a story that appears in several critics' accounts of these events, and it gets so frequently passed along without dissent, no doubt, because it offers such an appealing encapsulation of this Yolande/Countee fiasco. Unfortunately, it's not quite true. Countee and Yolande did in fact go on their honeymoon together, sans Jackman. They went first to Atlantic City, then to Philadelphia, and finally to Great Barrington, Massachusetts, the Du Bois family seat. The Jackman/honeymoon story concerns events of a few months later: Cullen's departure for Paris, where he was going to spend the period of his recently awarded Guggenheim. This trip he did make without Yolande, accompanied solely by his father and Harold Jackman. He explained the rather complicated reasoning for these travel arrangements to Du Bois in a letter, the short version being that he had to leave earlier than expected, and, as Yolande wasn't quite ready, she could come at a later date.

But the troubles had begun on the honeymoon, where, as Lewis reports, things "had not gone smoothly."[27] Although these troubles remain unspecified, a somewhat more detailed account begins to emerge from the letters that journeyed back and forth across the Atlantic between Du Bois, Cullen, and Yolande in the fall of 1928. Not all of these letters have survived, but we get our first hint that things are amiss in a letter from Du Bois to Yolande, dated September 7, 1928. Du Bois is responding, presumably, to a letter from Yolande indicating her unhappiness in Paris. Du Bois writes, "First of all, remember that life is and must be compromised. We cannot have everything we want, and the sooner the young person realizes this the happier and more well balanced he becomes. The panacea is work. As long as you have interesting work, on which your heart is set, nothing else matters." Du Bois then recommends that Yolande "get to work immediately and work hard. First, at drawing. You should study anatomy, the human body and the human face, the laws of perspectus and all that." This, however, is really Yolande's secondary task; her first, according to Du Bois, is that of "helping a great poet to become greater." As Du Bois puts it, rather cruelly,

> You should make it easy for Countee to write and keep him regularly at it. You should not distract him or make him spend too much time catering to your entertainment. For once in your life and in your own thought, get out of the center of the picture. Stop thinking of yourself or being sorry for yourself or regarding the world as revolving about you and concentrate on the main job of having Countee Cullen do a year's work to which the world will listen.

The rest of this letter is a quick dig at Yolande's financial extravagance. "Think of the assembled beauty about you in Paris," Du Bois writes, "which you can enjoy for practically nothing."

The record gets more detailed in Du Bois's letters to Countee, which are consistently more loving and affectionate than the ones he had written to Yolande. Although we don't always have the letters to which he's responding, we're able to fill in the gaps a bit from his responses. For instance, the first real sign of trouble comes in a letter he wrote a mere four days after the one urging Yolande to get to work. It begins, "Dear Countee: I am more grieved and overcome than I can say. I had never dreamed of this. I knew Yolande was spoiled and often silly but if I had not thought she respected and loved you I would not thought [sic] of marriage. I knew your honeymoon was trying but I thought it due to weariness and excitement." Setting a theme that is to dominate the rest of his letters to Countee on the subject, Du Bois continues:

> I still think the main trouble is physical and psychological . . . a girl has been trained to continence and then suddenly, loved, the universe trembles. Yolande does not know what she wants or loves or hopes for. If perhaps you could just bear with her and try again perhaps, all would yet be well . . . . remember that

this inexperienced girl—despite her years—does not really know what she is doing.

His closing is particularly dismissive of Yolande's "problems": "At any rate keep her till Xmas if any way possible and then—God show us all the way."

His letter of seven days later adopts a more pragmatic tone, admitting that his previous was "incoherent and unsatisfactory." If it is indeed "impossible now for the marriage to continue," he suggests that he will send Mrs. Du Bois over to stay with Yolande until summer, which "will keep down unkind gossip and enable the break to come after a decent interval." "Meantime," he writes, "I hope and pray that this terrible thing will not slow *your work*. Your career has been very dear to me from the beginning and I had dreamed fine things from this marriage."

Du Bois then shows himself to be firmly embedded in the Victorian logics of sexual desire, logics which imputed all such desire to men, and none to women. As he puts it, "the sex mating of a man and a girl is often disappointing . . . . I do not believe that in any case or with any husband Yolande's initiation into marriage would have failed to have been unpleasant and disconcerting. Men—young men, usually assume that their brides will immediately have the same sexual desire for them as they have. This I believe is seldom so." In closing Du Bois writes, "Try again if you can—if you cannot, I shall understand. In any case you have my love and trust and I shall always be your affectionate father."

A letter of a few weeks later, however, finds Du Bois in a much better mood, presumably the result of letters from Countee and Yolande indicating that they were trying to reconcile. Describing himself and his wife as "overjoyed," Du Bois then goes into his most detailed mini-sermon on matters sexual, saying that this "whole trouble comes because we are not frank on sex and do not teach the young" (October 11, 1928). In the rest of this letter Du Bois seemingly tries to make up for this lack of frank sex talk. "A girl," he writes, "usually has not had her sexual desire localized and is extremely sensitive in her organs. That then which gives her husband pleasure may be exquisite torture physically and mental humiliation for her." Switching back to the specific case at hand, he advises Countee, "Don't approach her too often and put her in terror lest every kiss and caress end in sexual commerce." More specifically, he advises, "never over do it—for the sake of your brain work and your wife's more slowly developed desire, let your intimacies be at intervals—once in 3 or 4 days or once a week or even two weeks." This renewed optimism, however, was not to last long. His shortest letter of the batch, written on November 29, 1929, says simply, "Dear Countee, Won't you write me right off and tell me the status of the court case? Also the name and address of the lawyer."

Du Bois's letters to Yolande and Countee offer a revealing window into an early moment of heterosexual instability and revision. At the same time, they help us to move beyond the oft-repeated but unsatisfactory claims concerning Du Bois's feminist progressivism. At some level, Du Bois understood the no-win situation imposed upon women in the early part of the twentieth century. As he wrote in "The Damnation of Women," "only at the sacrifice of intelligence and the chance to do their best work can the majority of modern women bear children. This is the damnation of women."[28] This awareness of the intellectual sacrifices seemingly required by reproductive imperatives seeped into his parenting; as he wrote to the headmaster of Yolande's boarding school, he wanted Yolande "trained for efficient work and not simply for breeding."[29] In short, Du Bois is trying to find his way between the real and the ideal, between his theoretical feminism and his deeply pragmatic investment in a black future. Not surprisingly, however, when compromise is required, it's black women—including his own daughter—who become the sacrificial offerings to the gods of black pragmatism. As Joy James writes, "Du Bois's sexual politics suggest that he navigated between increasingly nonclassist and democratic ideologies and a moribund gender progressivism into a quagmire of contradictory progressive and paternalistic racial-sexual politics."[30]

Nowhere is this field of contradictions on clearer display than in Du Bois's letters to Yolande and Countee, which serve to re-encode traditional heterosexual power dynamics. Although Yolande should "get to work," it's not really her own work that she should get to; rather, it's Countee's. She must give up her selfish ways (one can only imagine what these are: the desire for happiness, satisfaction, love?) and resign herself to the fact that "life is and must be compromised."

Du Bois had been training Yolande for the compromises of married life—one might say for the compromises of heterosexuality—from a very early age. When Yolande was fourteen, and away from home at school for the first time, Du Bois wrote her a letter that took a less-than-sympathetic approach to soothing the pangs of homesickness: "Take the cold bath bravely," he writes. "Enter into the spirit of your big bedroom. Enjoy what is and not pine for what is not. Read some good, heavy, serious books just for discipline: Take yourself in hand and master yourself. Make yourself do unpleasant things, so as to gain the upper hand of your soul."[31] Such advice extended to realms more bodily than the soul. For example, when Yolande was twenty-two her father wrote her, "Your bowels must move daily at a regular hour. Let nothing interfere—meals, classes, engagements, study or prayers. Every day at that hour be at your toilet."[32]

On the other hand, Countee must also resign himself to the notion of compromise, though his task is decidedly different from Yolande's. He must, apparently, learn to rein in his sexual desire for Yolande; he must compromise his yearning. He must not "approach her too often," must "never over do it." He must somehow find it in him to settle for "intimacies" at "intervals"—once every week or two tops. (We can only imagine that Countee did not find this particular enjoinment to be a burden.) In short, and ironically, he must somehow become *less* heterosexual until Yolande has learned to become *more* heterosexual. In fact, there's a way in which the perversion that Du Bois is saving Cullen from isn't homosexuality but heterosexuality, which, as I mentioned earlier, carried, in the twenties, the connotation of a "morbid sexual passion for one of the opposite sex." The irony is almost too rich: under Du Bois's tutelage, the homosexual is being cured of heterosexuality.

Further, Du Bois's advice about reining in the excesses of modern-day heterosexuality is particularly odd, coming from someone whom Lewis has called a "priapic adulterer."[33] As Lewis puts it:

By the mid-twenties, the emotional core below the Du Boisian layers of public virtue and personal vigor implicated him in an evolving state of affective being in which he seemed ever more driven to exploit the enormous fascination he exercised over many women, a fascination intensified in the eyes of some by Du Bois's advanced ideas about women's rights.[34]

This "evolving state of affective being" becomes more explicit when Lewis quotes a 1926 letter from Du Bois to the writer Georgia Douglas Johnson: "Dear Georgia, I'm thinking of you. I'd like to have you here. Write me. I['m] coming to see you at midnight. Please come down half-dressed with pretty stockings. I shall kiss you."[35] (It turns out that Du Bois was capable of simple, unornamented prose after all—when the situation was urgent enough.) The record of Du Bois's "affective being" gets perhaps too explicit when Lewis quotes a "distinguished scholar-diplomat" on Du Bois's, well, charms: "He was very well hung . . . , and I always had an impression that when sex was concerned, he was well endowed and was interested [in women] and his wife certainly was never around."[36]

From Du Bois's perspective, then, Yolande clearly had some work to do if she were to find herself in the world of heterosexuality. But how was she to learn? Perhaps the answer lies in Du Bois's rather odd earlier advice that she study drawing, concentrating first on "anatomy, the human body." One can't help but think that in offering this advice Du Bois had found the thin line that would allow him to encourage his daughter's sexual appetite while maintaining the necessary fictions of decorum and gentility. Once again, art comes to the rescue of Eros.

Du Bois wasn't the only one to blame Yolande for whatever sexual failures existed in her marriage to Countee. Blanche Ferguson, author of the only book-length biography of Cullen, also sees Yolande as the problem. In a scene conjured up in Ferguson's rather unrestrained biographical imagination, Countee "lolls" in his steamer chair on the deck of an ocean liner taking him to Paris, where he will spend the period of his Guggenheim fellowship. Yolande is, of course, not with him. Ferguson enters Countee's thoughts, which are understandably troubled:

He had cause for concern. They were spending less time together now than they had during their courtship. Countee was not unaware of some of the talk that had been going on. He knew that some of Salem's members had thought the DuBois girl was haughty. And the relationship between his father and Yolande was less warm than he had hoped it would be . . . . Then too, each of the young people was an only child, and Yolande in particular (from Countee's point of view) found it hard to adjust to the compromises necessary in a marriage. It seemed a little unreasonable of her to take the job. On the other hand, his income as a Guggenheim fellow was hardly sufficient for him to insist on her not working.[37]

In this little duet of blame and recrimination, Ferguson and Countee collude in some interesting ways. Though he can't afford for Yolande not to work, he resents that her work has kept her behind. And it's not Countee and Yolande whose relationship is "less warm than he had hoped it would be"; rather, it's the relationship between Yolande and Countee's father that's the problem, an interesting substitution, to say the least. And, of course, people are talking—though not about Countee, and not about Jackman, who is surely lolling on the steamer chair next to Countee at this very moment, but who never makes an appearance in Ferguson's staging of this little scene. No, the whispering in the pews is not about Countee, not about Jackman, but instead about Yolande, that "haughty" Du Bois girl. Like Du Bois, though for different reasons, Ferguson's version of this drama casts Yolande as the wrench thrown in the works of heterosexuality.

Having heard Ferguson's version of what people were whispering in the pews, it's worth taking a moment to hear what they were saying outside the pews, in the streets of Harlem. Given the spectacle of the wedding, surely tongues were wagging when Countee sailed for Paris without his bride. As Lewis puts it, "Harlemites, along with a significant portion of the Talented Tenth elsewhere, were roiled by gossip and innuendo. There were strong suspicions that Countee Cullen was gay. Indeed, many of the groom's friends had no doubt that he was . . . . A female friend at Hampton, still struggling to accept the arrangement, wrote the groom a month after the marriage, 'My! How strange.'"[38]

The press, however, reported a slightly different story. The *Amsterdam News* of March 6, 1929, offered the headline, "Poet and Wife Live Apart in Paris, But Still Seem Friends." The accompanying article reported that "the two are said to regard themselves as incompatible and to further complicate matters is a report to the effect that Cullen is in love with a girl on this side of the Atlantic ocean."[39]

Almost a year later the *News* blares the headline, "Daughter of *Crisis* Editor Gets Divorce From Poet Son of Rev. F. A. Cullen." The article reports that the agreement was reached "under the most amicable relations between herself and her husband."[40] It also admits, however, that "New York was shocked in March, 1929, when the first hint of a rift in the domestic bliss of the young couple came from the French capital in the form of reports that they were maintaining separate establishments." This line about "amicable relations" isn't entirely surprising, since "amicable" was about as much as the pair could muster up in the relations game. One is tempted, however, to hear the voice of Claude Raines in the *News*' claim to have been "shocked, shocked" over the first hints that the marriage was crumbling. As a letter from Jackman to Cullen in January of 1929 states, "So the inevitable has come about! Well, well, well, I didn't think it would be so soon really. Of course the Negroes in America have had it out for a long time." Veering charmingly off course, Jackman then writes that "Everybody is raving about my cigarette case . . . . It is the cats."[41]

There were others who were in the know from the beginning, and that beginning came rather shockingly early. In a letter to Alain Locke dated August 26, 1923—almost five full years before the wedding—Cullen mentions Yolande as someone who might be "the solution of my problem."[42] Cullen elaborates on this instrumentalist appropriation of Yolande in another letter to Locke, this one written in September of 1923. Cullen writes, "You will recall that in my last letter I spoke of a presentiment of happiness with a certain young lady. All that has come to nought [*sic*]—as yet. And then there are complications—her age and experience above my own, and then *that fear which is always at my heels*."[43]

So, was Yolande the only person *not* to know about Cullen? Lest we wallow too long in the rather tawdry world of gossip on the street, now seems a good time—in fact an overdue good time—to hear from Yolande herself. I've been holding back Yolande's voice for a reason, for I wanted first to put in place the *story* of these events without complicating that story by, well, the truth. Which is to say I'm actually more interested in the ways in which the failure of the marriage gets narrativized—by Du Bois, by the parishioners, by the press—than I am in what *literally* happened there. Yolande did in fact weigh in on these matters, and she did so in a clearer, more revealing, and more informed manner than either her father or her husband had managed to. Since Yolande seems to have been the least of her father's consideration, I think it's important that *we* hear Yolande's version of events nearly in their entirety, and so I quote at some length from her letter to Du Bois of May 23, 1929. It begins "Dearest Father," and after some preliminary small talk, it gets down to the issue at hand:

> About Countee and myself—the reason I haven't said much is because I hated to . . . . Shortly after our attempt at reconciliation Countee told me something about himself that just finished things. Other people told me too but I thought & hoped they were lying. If he had not told me *himself* that it was true I wouldn't have believed it but since he did I knew then that eventually I'd have to leave him. I never loved him but I had a enormous amount of respect for him. Having lost that—and having an added feeling of horror at the abnormality of it I couldn't "make it." I knew something was wrong—physically, but being very ignorant & inexperienced I couldn't be sure what. When he confessed that he's always known that he was abnormal sexually—as far as *other men were concerned* then many things became clear. At first I felt terribly angry—I felt he'd no right to marry any woman knowing that. Now I feel only sorry for him—all I want is not to have to be anywhere near him. I've heard of such things of course but the idea of it being true of anyone close to me gives me a feeling of horror & disgust. I've heard gossip but I've never *known* it before about anyone. I haven't told mama. She doesn't like Countee much & it's no use to worry her. Besides, I promised him I would not tell it or use it as a grounds for divorce so you can tear this up. You seemed to be "smelling a rot" so I thought I'd better tell you frankly. Of course, if any of this had reached me *before*—I'd never have married him. If he was born that way I can't help it. I'm sorry—but I cannot understand it. I think I prefer my own more natural inclinations. Anyway, that's that.

While just about everything in this letter is interesting—and deeply sad—I'm particularly struck by the fact that homosexuality—or some notion of gay identity—is never actually spoken here. In fact, the letter engages in a rather excruciating series of seemingly endless deferrals. The letter begins with a "something," an "it," that Countee told her. Other people also told her this "thing," this "it" that must be true, but it's well into the letter before we—and Du Bois—get any specific sense of what this thing is. And even then our sense isn't that specific. As Yolande finally writes, "When he confessed that he's always known that he was abnormal sexually—as far as *other men were concerned* then many things became clear."

Now, much of this language sounds familiar to us here at the beginning of the twenty-first century because it's a language—a series of tropes—that now dominates our thinking about sexual identity. The language of the "confession" is the language of "coming out," of revealing some central truth that's always been there but has previously been unspoken. Yolande's response—"then many things became clear"—echoes the process of reinterpretation that such coming-out episodes trigger.

What's equally important, however, are the *differences* between Countee's moment and our own, between his "confession" and more recent incidents of "coming out." Nowhere in Yolande's reportage does she assign—or does Cullen assign himself—an *identity* based on this newly revealed knowledge. He doesn't produce the truth of his homosexuality, which is to say, the truth that he is something called a homosexual; rather, he positions himself in a continuing—though pathological—relationship to heterosexuality. He had written, in that letter to Locke, of "my problem." In other words, rather than saying, "I am a homosexual"—the identity-based language of our current moment—he says instead, "I am a bad heterosexual," I am "abnormal sexually." By insisting on the language of abnormality rather than identity—of pathology rather than newly liberated homosexuality— Cullen and Yolande continue to tell a heterosexual story, though one with a twist.

I make this claim not to discount the "truth" that Countee suppos- edly tells, but to let that truth be a truth about *heterosexuality* as much as it wants to be a truth about *homosexuality*. In other words, I don't want to be too quick to disentangle Countee from the story of heterosexuality. I don't want, in some burst of gay pride, to swoop in and sweep him away to some place apart from heterosexuality. Why? Because that road leads to a story we've come to know almost as well as the fairy-tale story of heterosexuality. It's an important, though increasingly familiar, story about gay and lesbian pride, gay and lesbian resistance, gay and lesbian history. And while that's certainly a story worth telling, it's not the story I'm interested in telling here.

So, as a way of keeping the spotlight on heterosexuality, I want to return to Du Bois, that most heterosexual of heterosexuals. If Yolande can claim to have been shocked by Cullen's claim, it's worth asking how shocked her father would have been. Near the end of 1927, just months before the wedding, Augustus Granville Dill, business manager of *The Crisis* (and close friend of Du Bois), was arrested for homosexual activity in a subway washroom. Du Bois fired him in a letter dated December 29, 1927, a letter that was obviously a difficult one for Du Bois to write. In it he calls Dill his "friend and loyal helper for near twenty years," and he says that he had "never contemplated continuing my life work without you by my side." This last phrase is particularly interesting in this context, since it invokes the classic language of heterosexual partnership. In this formulation, Du Bois casts Dill as his wife, someone who will support the more serious labor of the man, but whose own work—and life—is clearly secondary. It's as if in writing to this newly discovered homosexual, Du Bois unconsciously finds a language that produces, for him, the truth of Dill's abandonment of masculinity.

The letter gives two reasons for Dill's firing: the diminishing economic health of *The Crisis* and the diminishing physical health of Dill. The first is rather straightforward; as Du Bois writes, "THE CRISIS cannot longer afford your salary." The second reason—Dill's physical condition—requires a bit more comment. As Du Bois writes,

> You are not well. You can be restored to health and vigor if you will take yourself in hand . . . . You need peace and quiet; out door air and sunshine; good and continuous physical exercise; and deep, dreamless sleep. A few years of this will make you a new man—strong, well, vigorous, ready for the battle of the world. Then with a loving sympathetic wife you can be happy and successful.

It's hard not to hear in Du Bois's recipe for making Dill a "new man" the same ingredients that were making "the new Negro": "strong, well, vigorous, ready for the battle of the world." And his advice about the necessity of "a loving sympathetic wife" is utterly in keeping with his picture of the New Negro's future. It's also in keeping with medical advice at the time on the issue of homosexuality: according to medical authorities, Dill's behavior in the washroom would have been thought of as just that: behavior. And behavior, so the story went, is always a thing that can be fixed. So, like Countee's sense of himself as abnormal—as a bad heterosexual—Du Bois views Dill through the continuing lens of heterosexuality as the only site of identity. Dill's heterosexuality is flawed, but it can be restored with the addition of a "loving sympathetic wife." One wonders if he had the same thing in mind when, only three months later, he would give his daughter to Countee Cullen in marriage.

Although Du Bois claims that "the little incident" of Dill's arrest "has nothing at all to do with" Dill's firing, it's hard not to feel, in the paragraph I just quoted, that the two events are in fact related. In fact, looking back on this event some thirty years later, Du Bois *does* connect the firing to his new knowledge of Dill. As he writes in his *Autobiography*:

> In the midst of my career there burst on me a new and undreamed of aspect of sex. A young man, long my disciple and student, then my co-helper and successor to part of my work, was suddenly arrested for molesting men in public places. I had before that time no conception of homosexuality. I had never understood the tragedy of Oscar Wilde. I dismissed my co-worker forthwith, and spent heavy days regretting my act.[44]

So, just a few months before Yolande was to marry Countee, Du Bois came face to face with the fact of homosexuality. It's possible that he simply never connected the dots, that he never made the leap from the rather sad but dutiful Dill to the promising and ambitious Countee, poet of the black future. And yet, this possibility seems increasingly hard to swallow. Surely Du Bois knew about Countee. Like others in Harlem, he must have heard the rumors and, in the aftermath of the Dill arrest and subsequent firing, allowed his new awareness of homosexuality to spill over onto his awareness of Countee. If this is true, though, why would he possibly consent to Yolande marrying him? The answer to this one is easy, since Du Bois provides it himself. As he told Dill, "with a loving sympathetic wife you can be happy and successful."

But Du Bois's own happiness—his own self-interest—is surely at stake as well. One has to ask, who's actually being married here: Countee and Yolande, or Countee and Yolande's father? After all, the most important relationship in the Du Bois-Cullen union was not between Yolande and Countee, or even between Countee and Harold Jackman. The central relationship seems to have been between Countee and Du Bois, the father of the bride. The story of this wedding is, quite simply, the story of men coming together over the body of a woman, a story in which a silent female facilitates male bonding. This is the age-old "traffic in women," a homosocial story of heterosexual exchange. Du Bois's eager participation in this exchange supports Hazel Carby's theory of the "reproduction of Race Men."[45] As Carby writes, "the map of intellectual mentors [Du Bois] draws for us is a map of male production and reproduction that traces in its form, but displaces through its content, biological and sexual reproduction. It is reproduction without women."[46]

The strange ménage à trois of Du Bois, Yolande, and Cullen seems a perfect instance of this "reproduction without women." That Yolande's role is both central and utterly subordinate becomes clear once we understand what Du Bois was really after. As Lewis has observed, Du Bois saw Countee Cullen as a surrogate son, a kind of prophet who, through his poetry and through his marriage to Yolande, might embody the future of the race, carrying both the Du Bois bloodline and the Talented Tenth into the next generation.[47] Given this desire— and desire seems precisely the right word—Du Bois took the failure of the marriage particularly hard, referring to it many years later as a "needless tragedy." Du Bois had lost a son.

In fact, Countee Cullen was not the first son Du Bois had lost. Yolande had been preceded by Burghardt Gomer Du Bois, born in October of 1897. Burghardt died just shy of his second birthday, an event that Du Bois takes up in *The Souls of Black Folk* under the title "Of the Passing of the First-Born." In the understandably overheated tones of this essay, Du Bois reveals the hopes he had for the boy: "I . . . saw the strength of my own arm stretched onward through the ages through the newer strength of his; saw the dream of my black fathers stagger a step onward in the wild phantasm of the world; heard in his baby voice the voice of the Prophet that was to rise within the Veil."[48]

In a piece written for *The Crisis* in 1922, Du Bois had called marriage "the center of real resurrection and remaking of the world"; he saw his daughter's marriage as the almost literal resurrection of his dead son in the person of Countee Cullen.[49] Then the tragedy of Burghardt's death was reprised, thirty years later. In each instance we see a procreative failure, a promise betrayed—the rebirth of a nation, aborted.

As for Yolande, whatever chance she may have had for happiness had long since passed her by. Countee was not her first romantic interest; he was simply the first to receive her father's approval. At the age of twenty-two Yolande had met Jimmie Lunceford, who would go on to a successful career as a jazz band conductor. Lewis calls Lunceford Yolande's "enduring passion, the man about whom she would spend much of her life dreaming, wondering how different things could have been if they had married."[50] She could only wonder, however, because her father shut this relationship down. Not thrilled with the prospect of a jazz musician for a son-in-law, Du Bois told Yolande, "I am not taking Jimmie very seriously."[51] Du Bois continued, "Nothing is more disheartening and idiotic than to see two human beings without cultivated tastes, without trained abilities and without power to earn a living locking themselves together and trying to live on love."[52]

As for Yolande's life after Countee, she remarried in 1931, a little over a year after her divorce from Cullen was finalized. This time she married the anti-Cullen, a football player named Arnette Franklin Williams. This marriage soon disintegrated amid Williams' alcoholism and physical abuse, and they divorced a little less than five years after they were married. Yolande's life after this second divorce provided a constant stream of worry and embarrassment for her parents. Her mother "really felt quite alarmed" about Yolande's subsequent affairs, which included "a male lover ten years her junior and much else that was deplorable."[53] It's hard not to hear, hanging over Yolande's various attempts at happiness, her father's most persistent advice: "make yourself do unpleasant things."[54]

If Du Bois saw the marriage of his daughter as a renaissance in and of itself—as a new birth of blackness—it's fair to say that the fruits of that birth were going to differ radically from what he had imagined. As Alain Locke wrote in 1925, those who "have traditionally presided over the Negro problem have a changeling in their laps. The Sociologist, the Philanthropist, the Race-leader are not unaware of the New Negro, but they are at a loss to account for him. He simply cannot be swathed in their formulae."[55] Although there is surely some irony in the fact of Countee Cullen becoming the public face of the "New Negro," Locke reminds us that irony tells only half of the story. Yes, it's ironic that a decidedly queer Countee Cullen became the poster boy for New Negroism. But it's also, I would argue, entirely appropriate. For as Locke writes elsewhere in his essay, "Harlem . . . isn't typical— but it is significant, it is prophetic."[56]

The New Negro has remained Harlem's most enduring prophesy, a radically hybrid category, a decidedly queer species of identity. In its location at the borders—between old and new, whiteness and blackness, art and politics, masculinity and femininity, heterosexuality and homosexuality—the New Negro defied the attempts of Du Bois and others to circumscribe its shape and behavior. Countee Cullen foreshadowed, in his own queer way, New Negroes to come: in the realm of the fictional, Larsen's Clare Kendry, Ellison's Invisible Man, Morrison's Sula; in the realm of the real, James Baldwin, Audre Lorde, Essex Hemphill—characters and people hovering on the margins of identity, trying to find a shape for their shape, a place to be in. Cullen— that most circumspect and correct of poets and men—turns out to have prefigured a new world coming, to have offered "significant prophesy," to borrow again from Locke. And nowhere is this significant prophesy more apparent than in that queer moment when he and Yolande Du Bois stepped up to the altar of the Salem Methodist Episcopal Church to say, for all of Harlem to hear, "I do."

## Notes

1. David Levering Lewis, *W. E. B. Du Bois: The Fight for Equality and the American Century, 1919–1963* (New York: Henry Holt & Co., 2000), 221.

2. The Hamilton Lodge drag ball is best described by quoting a surveillance report from the Committee of Fourteen, an anti-prostitution organization: "About 12:30 a.m. we visited this place and found approximately 5,000 people, colored and

white, men attired in women's clothes, and vice versa. The affair, we were informed, was a 'Fag/(fairy)Masquerade Ball.' This is an annual affair where the white and colored fairies assemble together with their friends, this being attended also by a certain respectable element who go here to see the sights." George Chauncey, *Gay New York: Gender, Urban Culture, and the Making of the Gay Male World, 1890–1940* (New York: Basic Books, 1994), 130.

3. Judith Butler, *Bodies That Matter: On the Discursive Limits of "Sex"* (New York: Routledge, 1993), 125.

4. Nathan Irvin Huggins, *Harlem Renaissance* (New York: Oxford University Press, 1971), 306.

5. W. E. B. Du Bois, "The Star of Ethiopia," *The Crisis* 11 (Dec. 1915): 91.

6. W. E. B. Du Bois, "The Drama Among Black Folk," *The Crisis* 12 (Aug. 1916): 169.

7. Katherine Capshaw Smith, "Constructing a Shared History: Black Pageantry for Children during the Harlem Renaissance," *Children's Literature* 27 (1999): 42.

8. W. E. B. Du Bois, "Krigwa Players Little Negro Theatre," *The Crisis* 32 (July 1926): 134.

9. Ibid., 134.

10. W. E. B. Du Bois, "So the Girl Marries," in *W. E. B. Du Bois: Writings*, ed. Nathan Huggins (New York: Library of American, 1986), 1008.

11. W. E. B. Du Bois, "The Criteria for Negro Art," in *W. E. B. Du Bois: Writings*, 1000.

12. Thelma E. Berlack, "Wedding Guests sans Invitations Arrive Very Early," *Amsterdam News* 11 (Apr. 1928): 1.

13. Ibid., 1.

14. Lewis, *Fight*, 222.

15. All letters from Du Bois, Yolande, and Countee Cullen are taken from the W. E. B. Du Bois Papers, available at University of Massachusetts, Amherst, and in the microfilm version of this collection. Dates will be noted in the text.

16. Du Bois, "So the Girl Marries," 1006.

17. Ibid., 1007. While "the girl" and "the boy" appear parallel in Du Bois's usage, they are actually quite different. It's one thing to refer to one of an un-named string of suitors as "the boy": it's quite another to borrow the same generic title for one's daughter. The affectional dynamic revealed by this seeming semantic parallelism reveals a larger attitude toward Yolande that I will take up later.

18. Ibid., 1005.

19. Ibid., 1008.

20. David Levering Lewis, *W. E. B. Du Bois: Biography of a Race, 1868–1919* (New York: Henry Holt & Co., 1997), 460.

21. Du Bois, "So the Girl Marries," 1008–1009.

22. Butler, *Bodies*, 125.

23. W. E. B. Du Bois, "Marriage," *The Crisis* 24 (Oct. 1922): 247. Hereafter all citations will be made parenthetically in the text.

24. Sigmund Freud, "Leonardo da Vinci and a Memory of His Childhood," in *The Standard Edition of the Complete Psychological Works of Sigmund Freud*, ed. and trans. James Strachey (London: Hogarth Press, 1957), 11:99. Magnus Hirschfeld notes this Freudian wisdom only to refute it: "The attachment of homosexual men to their mothers is so typical that the Freudian school sees a cause of homosexuality in

this 'mother complex.' I consider this conclusion to be false." Magnus Hirschfeld, *The Homosexuality of Men and Women*, trans. Michael A. Lombardi-Nash (1913; repr., New York: Prometheus Books, 2000), 143. Nevertheless, this mother-blaming would gradually seep into the cultural commonsense, most notoriously through Philip Wylie's 1942 bestseller *Generation of Vipers*, in which Wylie would coin the term "momism" to "describe the destructive tendency among the overwhelming majority of American mothers to stifle, dominate, and manipulate their children—particularly sons—into submission and crippling weakness." Jennifer Terry, "Momism and the Making of Treasonous Homosexuals," in *"Bad" Mothers: The Politics of Blame in Twentieth-Century America*, ed. Molly Ladd-Taylor and Lauri Umansky (New York: New York University Press, 1998), 175.

25. W. E. B. Du Bois, "The Damnation of Women," in *W. E. B. Du Bois: Writings*, 954. Hereafter all citations will be made parenthetically in the text.

26. Jonathan Ned Katz, *The Invention of Heterosexuality* (New York: Penguin, 1995), 19. Hereafter all citations will be made parenthetically in the text.

27. Lewis, *Fight*, 223.

28. Du Bois, "Damnation," 953.

29. Lewis, *Biography*, 452.

30. Joy James, "Profeminism and Gender Elites: W. E. B. Du Bois, Anna Julia Cooper, and Ida B. Wells-Barnett," in *Transcending the Talented Tenth: Black Leaders and American Intellectuals* (New York: Routledge, 1997). Reprinted in this volume.

31. Lewis, *Biography*, 453.

32. Lewis, *Fight*, 106.

33. Ibid., 267.

34. Ibid., 185–86.

35. Ibid., 183.

36. Ibid., 186.

37. Blanche E. Ferguson, *Countee Cullen and the Negro Renaissance* (New York: Dodd, Mean, 1966), 103.

38. Lewis, *Fight*, 224.

39. "Poet and Wife Live Apart in Paris, But Still Seem Friends," *Amsterdam News* 6 (March 1929): 1.

40. "Daughter of Crisis Editor Gets Divorce from Poet Son of Rev. F.A. Cullen," *Amsterdam News* 2 (April 1930): 1.

41. Harold Jackman, letter to Countee Cullen, 3 January 1929, Amistad Research Center, New Orleans.

42. Alden Reimonenq, "Countee Cullen's Uranian 'Soul Windows,'" *Journal of Homosexuality* 26 (1993): 149.

43. Ibid., 150.

44. W. E. B. Du Bois, *The Autobiography of W. E. B. Du Bois: A Soliloquy on Viewing My Life from the Last Decade of its First Century* (New York: International Publishers, 1968), 283.

45. Hazel Carby, "The Souls of Black Men," in *Race Men* (Cambridge and London: Harvard University Press, 1998). Reprinted in this volume.

46. Ibid.

47. Lewis, *Fight*, 223.

48. W. E. B. Du Bois, "Of the Passing of the First-Born," in *W. E. B. Du Bois: Writings*, 507–8.

49. Du Bois, "Marriage," 248.

50. Lewis, *Fight*, 107.

51. Ibid., 108.

52. Ibid., 108.

53. Ibid., 458.

54. Ibid., 453.

55. Alain Locke, "The New Negro," in *The New Negro: Voices of the Harlem Renaissance*, ed. Alain Locke (1925; repr. New York: Simon and Schuster, 1992), 3.

56. Ibid., 7.

# 10

## Uplift and Criminality

Fred Moten

This is an essay about stolen life, where uplift and criminality converge in the ani*mater*iality of W. E. B. Du Bois's fugitive voice. Considering stolen life requires that we move, in the words of Du Bois and in their transformative amplification by Nahum Chandler, in the sphere—the open set—of "the Negro Question." The plain of the ordinary, of common ground or of a common underground, of the common underground or outskirts of the city, before the distinction between urban and rural and the formation of modernity and its opposite that distinction engenders, is where such movement, such structuring incommensurability, resides. What is given in Du Bois's composed and scholarly production of the question of the Negro is the possibility of an improvisational discovery: of a politics of the black ordinary and of everything that is both enabled and endangered by such a politics, which is to say by the anthropological and/or sociological attitude that the discovery of the concept of the object of the black ordinary demands. Focus on the danger is part of what I'll focus on here in the interest of saving the saving power. This means working by way of the paralinguistic and its chances, of mechanically reproduced aesthesis and its foreshortening effects on the distance the ethnographer seems to require. The political opening Du Bois's work marks and helps to conjure is the function of a double step: the first element of this choreography is the step away or outside, the movement of analytic detachment with regard to black sociality that is characterized, as Chandler has established, by a fundamental ontological question: *Who are they?*[1] The second step, which is only properly understood as that which lies *before* the first, as that which is productive of a second and, as it were, improvisational (fore)sight, is a voluntary, identificatory address of and entrance into the politico-theatrical scene of black sociality. It is characterized by an answer to the first of the questions it anticipates: *They are me.* In Du Bois's case, he associates this address and entrance with his matriculation at Fisk University at the beginning of the 1880s. Such entrance has all the indeterminate force of an always already cut and augmented act of will whose effect stays with Du Bois, drives him every day and in a way that is always manifest as what might be called the constitutive and disruptive supplement to everything in Du Bois that would operate under the sign of regulation.

It seems necessary and just to speak of this paradoxically foundational ornament as surface, as materiality, as ordinary, but one must reserve the right, so to speak, to ask that it also be considered under the rubrics of the archi-trace, the maternal, the one who is fully and problematically before the law. The discernment of this scar that is deep in the heart and at the start of Du Bois's work demands gentle, militant reading, a reading that is governed by a particular poetics and by commitment to the rich content of a lyricism of the surplus, of the dangerous, salvific, (im)pure sonority of unaccounted for things or of the unaccounted in things, of the ruptural accompaniment, of murmur and mummery, of the folding or invaginative residue moving at the excessive interchange (the moving bridge-like object) of a set, which is to say a history, of loss(es). It demands a reading that is possessed and, above all, dispossessive, one that moves in a cut romance with the criminal burn of the very idea. The extraordinary is in the ordinary like freedom is in unfreedom as the trace of the resistance that constitutes constraint. John Coltrane spoke of a set of harmonic devices that he knew would take him out of the ordinary path. This transport out of the ordinary path within the ordinary; this extraordinary path within the ordinary; this wandering in search of the extraordinary in the ordinary (where what Du Bois calls the "evident rhythm of human action" and the "evident incalculability in human action" interarticulate) is the distressed rationality that drives the romantic poetic reading Du Bois requires, and whose discovery is made possible by reading Du Bois and by reading in Du Bois what he calls, in a great 1905 essay called "Sociology Hesitant" (made available again by Chandler's and Ronald A. T. Judy's work), the "sudden rise at a given tune."[2]

So let's begin again by indexing the discourse on a set of given tunes—a strain or string of the black radical tradition that moves in (mis)translation, (mis)transliteration, (mis)transcription and in the phrasing that emerges from the difficulty of these. Here is a passage from C. L. R. James's *The Black Jacobins* that recovers and elucidates a "Haitian Fight Song" irrupting from the gap between enlightenment and romanticism, enlightenment and darkness, among other constructs and continents:

> But one does not need education or encouragement to cherish a dream of freedom. At their midnight celebrations of Voodoo, their African cult, they danced and sang, usually this favourite song:
>
> Eh ! Eh ! Bomba! Heu! Heu!
> Canga, bafio té!
> Canga, mouné de lé!
> Canga, do ki la!
> Canga, li!
>
> "We swear to destroy the whites and all that they possess; let us die rather than fail to keep this vow."

> The colonists knew this song and tried to stamp it out, and the Voodoo cult with which it was linked. In vain. For over two hundred years the slaves sang it at their meetings, as the Jews in Babylon sang of Zion, and the Bantu to-day sing in secret the national anthem of Africa.[3]

And here is Amiri Baraka in *Blues People:*

> It is impossible to find out exactly how long the slaves were in America before the African work song actually did begin to

have extra-African references. First, of course, there were mere additions of the foreign words—French, Spanish, or English, for the most part, after the British colonists gained power in the United States. Krehbel lists a Creole song transcribed by Lafcadio Hearn, which contains both the French (or Patois) and African words (the italicized words are African):

*Ouendé, ouendé, macaya!*
Mo pas barrasse, *macaya!*
*Ouendé, ouendé, macaya!*
Mo bois bon divin, *macaya!*
*Ouendé, ouendé, macaya!*
Mo mange bon poulet, *macaya!*
*Ouendé, ouendé, macaya!*
Mo pas barrasse, *macaya!*
*Ouendé, ouendé, macaya!*
*Macaya!*

Hearns's translation was:

*Go on! Go on! eat enormously!*
I ain't one bit ashamed—*eat outrageously!*
*Go on! Go on! eat prodigiously!*
I drink good wine!—*eat ferociously!*
*Go on! go on! eat unceasingly!*
I eat good chicken—*gorging myself!*
*Go on! go on! etc.*[4]

In his explication of this "extra-African" song and its translation, Baraka writes,

> It is interesting to note, and perhaps more than coincidence, that the portions of the song emphasizing excess are in African, which most of the white men could not understand, and the portions of the song elaborating some kind of genteel, if fanciful, existence are in the tongue of the masters. . . . What is called now a "Southern accent" or "Negro speech" was once simply the accent of a foreigner trying to speak a new and unfamiliar language,

although it was characteristic of the white masters to attribute the slave's "inability" to speak perfect English to the same kind of "childishness" that was used to explain the African's belief in the supernatural. The owners, when they bothered to listen, were impressed that even the songs of their native American slaves were "incomprehensible" or "unintelligible."[5]

In placing such importance on the resistant force of African inflected new world song—and on the forging of a politics and aesthetics of excess and ornament from conditions of constraint by way of the simultaneous and ongoing loss and transfer of Africa—Baraka, and James before him, follows in the footsteps of Du Bois whose long life came to an end in 1963, the year *Blues People* was published. This was also the year after James added his famous postscript to *The Black Jacobins* on the line that stretches from Toussaint to Castro. Together they echo, in particular, the following oft-noted passage from the final chapter of *The Souls of Black Folk:*

> The songs are indeed siftings of centuries; the music is far more ancient than the words, and in it we can trace here and there signs of development. My grandfather's grandmother was seized by an evil Dutch trader two centuries ago; and coming to the valleys of the Hudson and Housatonic, black, little, and lithe, she shivered and shrank in the harsh north winds, looking longingly at the hills, and often crooned a heathen melody to the child between her knees, thus:

> Do bana coba, gene me, gene me!
> Do bana coba, gene me, gene me!
> Ben d'nuli, ben d'le..

"This was primitive African music," Du Bois asserts—"the voice of exile."[6] In the first volume of his massive biography of Du Bois, David Levering Lewis provides some context and background for Du Bois's musical excursion:

> As with much else to do with early Burghardt history, Du Bois has left several confusing and contradictory accounts of the

"little black Bantu" ancestor who sang a sad West African tune, still heard at the fireside of his childhood . . . Willie never learned the meaning of her song, the exact origin and translation of which have continued to defy linguists . . . [B]ut it was the influence of the song, rather than the singer, that finally mattered to Willie. It was his one truly palpable tie to that African homeland he would spend an academic and political lifetime trying to interpret and shape. "Africa is, of course, my fatherland," he would write sixteen years after spending a few months during 1923 in Monrovia, Liberia. "What is it between us that constitutes a tie which I can feel better than I can explain?" [The] song had been the earliest prompting of a very New England and supremely intellectual great-grandson to try to discern a few notes of a remote, vestigial and mysterious heritage.[7]

In a footnote Lewis takes advantage of the independent research into the song's provenance and meaning conducted by Mrs. Denise Williams, a collateral descendant of Du Bois, quoting Sulayman S. Nyang, who writes that

If the song is a creolized version of a Wolof song, it should go like this: "Duga na chi pah, gene ma, gene ma/Duga na chipah, gene ma, gene ma/bena njuli, njuli." Translation: "I have fallen into a pit, get me out. Get me out!/I have fallen into a pit, get me out. Get me out!/One circumcised boy, one circumcised boy, one circumcised boy, one circumcised boy."[8]

Lewis adds that this is "A strange song, it would seem, for a female ancestor to sing. I have not been able to solve this mystery."[9]

The discourse on such songs is rich with such addenda (marked by confusion in the face of an impudence to which we shall return). James' appeal to song is anticipatory, prophetic, reaching back to a not fully approachable Africa in the name of a postcolonial African future we still await. Meanwhile, Baraka, highlighting the fruitful impossibility of a direct appeal to African origin that James constantly discloses and retrospectively admits, lingers in an unintelligibility that works at the site of a rebellious excess whose condition of possibility is, paradoxically, an African origin and which manifests itself most fully in the unbridgeable distance that separates it from that origin. That sound which both never arrives at and goes past home is directed towards a future politics that exists as a function of such non-arrival. Finally, Lewis marks the chain of references to that origin that links Du Bois's texts over half a century and links himself to that chain. It's a chain of impossible interpretation correspondent to a broken matrilinearity that Du Bois and Lewis after him reveal and repress (whether by an assertion that the song can be detached from, or matter more than, its maternal singer, or by folding that remote maternal claim on Du Bois into the long trajectory of the claim he makes on the "fatherland"). The song of the mother is given in a resistant, forceful materiality that emerges most clearly after the fact of a deprivation, the ongoing—which is to say substitutive—loss of the mother and of meaning, sense, depth. Such songs—which is to say the performative, overdubbed circulation of these songs, embedded in a kind of literary recording that Hortense Spillers characterizes as "put[ting] down tracks for some future investigation" and understands as the instructive, repressive, reiterative engagement of a radical black male tradition with the fantastic and *material* black female archi-trace that lies before it—are why it seems necessary to speak of black radicalism as a new thing, as something James might specifically think of as a new world thing (or that James Brown might think of as a new breed thing), even as we recognize the absolute necessity of thinking it as the old-new thing, the "sexual cut," the ruptural and regenerative ungendering or regendering that Lewis finds so mysterious. In the end, this is just a way of repeating with a difference Cedric Robinson's formulation—whose depth and beauty is inevitably cut even by what hopes to be a genuine augmentation—regarding the impossibility of understanding black radicalism within the particular context of its genesis.[10]

The period in Du Bois's career between 1896 and 1903, when he was researching and writing both *The Philadelphia Negro* and some of the essays that would be collected in *The Souls of Black Folk,* is a crucial moment in the history of black radicalism in part because it shows the massive tension between what Kevin Gaines, in his important book *Uplifting the Race,* describes as

> two general connotations of uplift. On the one hand, a broader vision of uplift signifying collective social aspiration,

advancement and struggle [which] had been the legacy of the emancipation era. On the other hand, black elites made uplift the basis for a racialized elite identity claiming Negro improvement through class stratification as race progress, which entailed an attenuated conception of bourgeois qualifications for rights and citizenship.[11]

One of the objectives of Gaines's research is the historicization of the concept of race that arises as a result of the "tension between elite racial and popular social images of uplift within black leadership and culture" (xv). He is interested in exposing and challenging "[t]he limitations of black elites' defensive appropriation of dominant racial theories for the purpose of erecting a supposedly positive black identity" (xv). These limitations resulted, he argues, finally more from "[white] power, black vulnerability, and the centrality of race in the nation's political and cultural institutions" than from the "complicity of black elites" (xv). I want to follow Gaines in his attempts to explicate the tension between these modes of uplift while veering off from his enabling path in order to show how that tension operates at a deep and fundamental level in the work of Du Bois at the turn of the last century. This is to say that there is at work in Du Bois, even when his discourse is most colored by the elitism Gaines astutely critiques, another voice that Nathaniel Mackey, after Robert Duncan, might call a meta-voice, whose features carry some important information regarding the history of blackness as politico-aesthetic assertion. One might even say that this meta-voice marks, in its most essential office, not the tension between two modes of uplift but that between a certain lingering with the ordinary and what Chandler might call the construction of a horizon.

This tension is bound to Du Bois's contribution to the discourse of black urban pathology. Gaines explicates that contribution, arguing that Du Bois thinks of urban fallenness in contradistinction to a kind of organic ruralism that has, as its most important feature, a connection to soil and earth that fosters the maintenance of the patriarchal family model or, at least, militates against the most thorough post–Civil War degradation of female sexuality—the descent into prostitution that is figured by Du Bois as an almost inevitable corollary of women working outside the home. But if you look at the chapters in *Souls* detailing black peasant life in the south, you see something that operates in a less agonistic manner with regard to the Du Boisian critique of urbanization, something that prefigures Gaines's own assertions regarding the structuring force of white power and black vulnerability. First, urbanization is seen as the effect of a kind of enclosure. In this case enclosure doesn't refer to (though it ought not be understood to operate in some simple contrast to) the peasant's forced removal from expropriated common land. Rather, this enclosure is *of* the peasant, a literal entrapment and attachment to the land by way of the disciplinary—indeed, carceral—managerial techniques imposed on debt-ridden tenant farmers by landholders and enforced by the state. Urbanization is, in this regard, a kind of fugitivity, an incapacitated mobilization that works not in contradistinction to idyllic southern life but in chorographic articulation with southern oppression, which itself responds to the irregular rhythms of ordinary movements already in place, under the feet, as it were, of whoever enacts, every day, the revaluation of their own irreducibly political being. If Du Bois understands the flight to town as available only to "the better classes of Negroes," such understanding ought itself be understood as an attempt to misunderstand the low-class, country conspiracy that constitutes our smuggled, runaway modernity.[12]

As Gaines knows, the reconstruction of the pastoral *in Souls*—the black reconstruction of the pastoral that it begins to narrate—contains no simple scenes of the gallant or even organic South. This is to say not only that Du Bois is unsparing in his attention to the details of southern oppression but also, as Gaines argues, that even in what might be read as a certain rural nostalgia in *Souls* there is room for "innovative social analysis" (176). The question is how such analysis comes to occupy Du Bois's text and this question is inseparable from other modes of disruptive inhabitation. Put differently, the other factor that strains (against) the pastoral in Du Bois—that he sees the black belt as a kind of breeding ground for the very pathology that Gaines understands Du Bois to locate more originarily in the urban north—is so closely related, along a maternal and material line, as to be practically inseparable from the condition of possibility of innovative social analysis. That this is so is inextricably bound to the fact that the extension of regimes of forced and stolen labor beyond "emancipation" is also fertile ground for a certain mode of critique of their life-situation by Southern blacks. That this is so could be said, in turn, both to emerge from and body forth the social life Du Bois pathologizes—a social life that is not reducible to the structures of oppression to which it responds and which respond to it. Du Bois addresses the brutal plight of the black tenant farmer whose indefinitely deferred emancipation is putatively justified by the "opinion among the merchants and employers of the Black Belt that only by the slavery of debt can the Negro be kept at work." We should join Gaines in his attunement to Du Bois's barely veiled confirmation of that opinion, which he describes as an "honest and widespread" response to the supposed listlessness, laziness, and ignorance of black workers. But Du Bois's normative elitism comes most sharply into relief when he seeks to explain and extenuate the social life of black laborers by referring to

> the obvious fact that a slave ancestry and a system of unrequited toil has not improved the efficiency or temper of the mass of black laborers. Nor is this peculiar to Sambo; it has in history been just as true of John and Hans, of Jacques and Pat, of all ground-down peasantries. Such is the situation of the mass of the Negroes in the Black Belt to-day; and they are thinking about it. Crime, and a cheap and dangerous socialism, are the inevitable results of this pondering. I see now that ragged black man sitting on a log, aimlessly whittling a stick. He muttered to me with the murmur of many ages when he said: White man sit down whole year; Nigger work day and night and make crop; Nigger hardly gits bread and meat; white man sittin' down gits all. *It's wrong.*[13]

Some of what is problematic in this passage is so glaring that Gaines doesn't have to attend to it—the offhand invocation of "Sambo" that carries with it so much of the contempt that it is meant to combat; the facile confirmation of the idea that peonage might have been a legitimate response to the shiftlessness of the newly emancipated. What Gaines does note, however, is the way Du Bois so easily conflates crime and socialism, thereby marking, at this moment in his career, a particular commitment to bourgeois norms. Gaines goes on to express surprise at Du Bois's interpolation of "the ragged black man's" analysis, thinking it, along lines Lewis establishes, a mysterious song for Du Bois to sing.

If Du Bois's song is strange, marking the irreducible, material presence of a stranger in Du Bois, one who leaves the mark or gift of a certain estrangement for Du Bois that will await his claim, it is so because the thinking, the moral reasoning, of the ignorant worker disrupts and constitutes its own regulation. The class stratification that is signaled by land ownership and the internal differentiation that attends self-possessive discursive composure enact a kind of re-doubled distancing. This is how Du Bois domesticates flight in the dramatization of a question about what the "better classes" of Negroes do to improve their situation and the answer that either they buy land or they migrate to town. It is, at the same time, how Du Bois comes to ventriloquize the pathologization of fugitivity, as Gaines shows in his reading of Du Bois's analysis of the transfer of certain plantation irregularities from rural South to urban North. In the end, I want primarily to investigate "the murmur of many ages" that works as a vexed, multiplied coding of the voice, recorded in Du Bois's literary phonography but recorded also in the phonographic recording of his voice, disrupting a condescension at once regulative, elitist, and detached even as it troubles the very affective attachment that the writing fitfully implies. This murmur sets and keeps the time of that originary encounter of Du Boisian (onto-sociological) questioning and answering with which I began. Later we'll hear (of) a kind of whistle, a pathogen in Du Bois's speech, that I have come to think of as this murmur of many ages, a transported maternal trace intensified by technological feedback like a scar in and on the body of the voice. This whistle is a disruptive augmentation of the voice that I wish to place under the rubric of the criminal. This criminal essence of the black voice is mediated, technological, accidental, contingent, historically sedimented, performed, constructed, and no less essential for being all of these. I say this in critique of labeling or constructionist theories of criminality, blackness and what might be called, by way of a movement that can be traced back to Althusser, their articulated but incommensurable and unbridgeable combination.[14] Those criminologists, who are known as labeling theorists, argue along lines established in Marx's critical ontology of the commodity. Just as the commodity's (exchange) value is understood by Marx to have been conferred from outside, so is deviance or criminality understood by labeling theorists as a function of nomination—"a consequence of the application by others of rules and sanctions"—and not as a quality of the act or the person that is called deviant or criminal. But the hope for and history of resistance demands that we consider the question concerning the specific interiority of the deviant (act or person or act-as-person). Again, this is not to challenge claims of the constructedness of the category but to initiate an investigation into the essence of the constructed in this case and in general. In the end, black social life as innovative social analysis bears an outlaw sound.

What Gaines refers to as Du Bois's "telling juxtaposition" (177) of crime and cheap/dangerous socialism moves as if in some appositional derivation from a more properly Marxian attachment to the revolutionary capacity of the proletariat that is, itself, dependent upon a discourse of uplift implied in the dismissal of the *lumpen*. *Souls* and *The Philadelphia Negro* are bound by the valorization of hierarchical stratification and black leadership that Gaines so cogently diagnoses as fundamental to the ideology of normative uplift. This is to say that for Du Bois the cheapness and danger of the socialism that emerges in some articulated combination with crime in the south is all bound up with the fact that it is a socialism that will have emerged from the peasantry and/or urban *(lumpen)* proletariat without the guidance or the leadership of the better classes.

It's important here to note that this new enclosure that determines the character of the system of so-called free labor—an enclosure not of the common lands but of the peasant on private land—reifies the conflation of slave and prisoner that defines both these categories. It therefore lies at the heart of the experience of blackness in a transition from slavery to freedom that is so fundamentally (de)formed and rendered so fundamentally delusional by convict-leasing (not to mention the no less intense non-extremities that attend what Saidiya Hartman teaches us more accurately to regard as the transition from subjection to subjection).[15] That system extends the criminalization of black social life that emerged as a central accomplishment of the power that black social life—as black resistance—brought into being. This is to say that the social death of slavery and imprisonment can only be understood as operating in some articulated combination with necessarily political, necessarily aesthetic, necessarily erotic black social life. Each is the other's condition of possibility; and this is to understand the criminality of black life in its relation not to laws codified and enforced by power but to power itself as the self-(re)generating mystical foundation of its own authority.[16] In this sense criminality is a drive originarily inscribed in constructed blackness or black radicalism, but this criminality cannot be understood within the context of its genesis. It is constructed, exists as a function of construction, and yet it is before construction.

This makes it possible and necessary to understand Du Bois's adherence to the ideology of normative uplift as always disrupted by his deviance from it and from the morality of bourgeois production that attends it as means, end, and cause. A deviance is inscribed on the very discourse that puts that morality forward and this deviance must be attended. Movement between the critique of the interplay in elite black constructions of black social life between class stratification and bourgeois respectability and the racist imposition of the minstrel stereotype—renders difficult such attention to this other writing, this other phonography that works like a kind of dissonant echo, some kind of accompaniment, held a fraction after the initiative sound of its "original," and moves as if such harmonic thickness implied some perspectival time in the recording—the aspect or internal temporal constituency of the overdub. It's the overdub of or accompaniment to Du Bois's normative ideals—their doubleness, the repetition (with a difference) that is internal to them—in which I am interested and which I want to try to enter and unpack in order to extend (along with and against the normativity that in/voluntary, fugitive Du Boisians like Gaines and I share) the ongoing discovery of a particular concept of the criminal that animates black radicalism. It's recorded in Du Bois's writing and is evident in the recording of his speech as the form of a quite specific content towards which we are pointed (as the deviance from progress, rationalism, objectivity, scientific observation), and which we'll hear even in Du Bois's most severe adherence to these ideals.

Meanwhile, if, as Gaines points out, Du Bois helps to initiate the problematic discourse of black urban pathology that had its fullest flowering in the infamous report on the causes of urban unrest produced by the allegedly deceased Daniel Patrick Moynihan and others about thirty-five years ago and which still shapes much of the discourse on black urban life, then it is also worth noting that Du Bois's thoughts on the origin of black criminality had a more immediate scholarly impact, prefiguring the notoriously racist but inescapably valuable work of the historian of slavery Ulrich B. Phillips and his discourse on slave crime.[17] This convergence—unlikely given their mutual dismissal of each other's work—shows, in a way that Gaines's work predicts, how the assimilationist cultural politics of normative uplift can never be fully separated from the white supremacism it is supposed to combat. Here's Phillips at the opening of "Slave Crime," the penultimate chapter of his *American Negro Slavery*:

> The Negroes were in a strange land, coercively subjected to laws and customs far different from those of their ancestral country; and by being enslaved and set off into a separate lowly caste they were largely deprived of that incentive to conformity which under normal conditions the hope of individual advancement so strongly gives. It was quite to be expected that their conduct in general would be widely different from that of the whites who were citizens and proprietors. The natural amenability of the blacks, however, had been a decisive factor in their initial enslavement, and the reckoning which their captors and rulers made of this was on the whole well founded. Their lawbreaking had few distinctive characteristics, and gave no special concern to the public except as regards rape and revolt.[18]

Phillips's belief in black biological inferiority and cultural backwardness—a belief that constitutes a major aspect of his retrospective defense of slavery; a belief that Du Bois will have characterized as both honest and dishonest; a belief to which Du Bois will have adhered in his understanding of the effects of slavery and from which he will have detached himself in his retrospective attack on slavery—does not restrict him from offering the kind of environmentalist account of the origins of black crime that Du Bois puts forward a couple of decades earlier in Chapter XIII of *The Philadelphia Negro*, "The Negro Criminal." Moreover, black criminality, according to Phillips, has no "distinctive characteristics," and presents "no special concern" except for rape and revolt. The presumption here seems to be that special characteristics would arise as a function of some essential difference and that such a difference only manifests itself as a kind of propensity to rape and to rebel that magically lives in harmony with "natural amenability." Finally, note that these two distinctive characteristics give concern to a public that is understood, by definition and in a way so commonplace as to be almost unnoticeable, as excluding slaves and/or blacks. The slave is not a part of the public and yet this does not mean that the question of the slave's publicity or public—which is to say *political*—life is not a problem. As Phillips says a few pages later, "In general the slaveholding South learned of crimes by individual negroes with considerable equanimity. It was the news or suspicion of concerted action by them which alone caused widespread alarm and uneasiness."[19] Phillips slightly contradicts himself here, since now it seems that the special concerns regarding slave criminality are really a function of rebellion alone and not rape and, more specifically, are bound up with slave sociality and social organization, with the specter of an uncontrollable public life of slaves which was tantamount to revolt. Indeed, Phillips is valuable in part because of the rather lengthy catalogue of slave revolts— in the north, the south, as well as the Caribbean—that he produces. In some ways, Phillips picks up on the work of Thomas Wentworth Higginson and anticipates that of Herbert Aptheker, giving the lie to the old commonplace of slave historiography that happy and/or shiftless slaves never lifted a hand in the struggle for their liberation. Instead, the chapter on crime in Phillips is largely taken up with slave revolt and gives us some occasion for thinking the relation between rebellion and crime in such a way as to make possible a new understanding of the relation between criminality and blackness, taking care to think criminality as, first and foremost, black sociality, social life, social organization.[20]

If we jump back to Du Bois's formulations on the Negro criminal, we can hear what Phillips echoes.

Crime is a phenomenon of organized social life, and is the open rebellion of an individual against his social environment. Naturally then, if men are suddenly transported from one environment to another, the result is lack of harmony with the new conditions; lack of harmony with the new physical surroundings leading to disease and death or modification of physique; lack of harmony with social surroundings leading to crime. Thus very early in the history of the colony [of Pennsylvania] characteristic complaints of the disorder of the Negro slaves is heard.[21]

Du Bois goes on to enumerate complaints regarding the "tumultuous" gathering of blacks, folks swearing, cussing and engaging in a supposed general kind of disorderliness. The environmentalist explanation that Du Bois offers constitutes a kind of justification of the colony's "anti-tumult" ordinances precisely by taking at face value the complaints against black gatherings. (Note in particular one such ordinance, passed in 1700 and recorded in Appendix B of *The Philadelphia Negro*, where blacks assembled in groups of more than four were subject to whipping if unable to certify that they were on their master's business.[22]) Moreover, as Gaines suggests, Du Bois is interested in promoting black assimilation to bourgeois norms of social organization precisely in the interest of racial uplift.

Black criminality as discord and disorder—or as the gathering of an ensemble that works outside of normative harmony; the atonality of another totality—is figured as a sign that black people need to develop social skills, as it were, to engage in already established normative modes of publicity that include not only high-minded social and political organization devoted to racial uplift but wholesome forms of popular amusement that would form a vital supplement to respectable private domesticity.[23] This overlooks the fact, of course, that the supposed definitional impossibility of a black public, on the one hand, and the fear of this impossible or unreadable black publicity, on the other, is at the heart not only of notions of black criminality but founds or constructs blackness—black social life—as criminality. To be black, to engage in the ensemblic—necessarily social—performance of blackness, is to be criminal. This is essential to the construction of blackness and is to be indexed by neither environment nor genetics. It is of interest—and will be taken up later—that crime is figured by Du Bois both as discord (between men and their conditions) and as a phenomenon of social organization. This ensemblic organization is something we'll come to think about under the rubrics of frenzy and fugitivity, where crime-as-revolt might be thought of as what Miles Davis came to understand as an ineluctably "social music" whose perceived disharmony and arrhythmia operates as an enactment of surreptitiousness and fugitivity, a harmonic and rhythmic reorganization, if not disorganization, reconstruction, if not destruction. It is, therefore, not amiss to think the musicality of black criminality-as-black rebellion and, moreover, it is of importance to consider what's at stake in the feat of black (musical) gathering. The first and most serious black crime is black sociality, something Robinson might understand as the preservation of an ontological totality and something I hope to understand as the continual and foundational cutting and expansion of this totality's masculinist circumference.[24]

This means that the question of a certain criminalized sexuality is not to be put on the back burner. A fundamental issue, for Du Bois, is precisely illicit and uncontrollable black sexuality. The locus of this sexuality is, however, not the predatory male but the insatiable female. This is a stereotype that Du Bois believes in and disbelieves at the same time, one that he must strive to address and overcome. Anna Julia Cooper's unprotected black female is at the heart of Du Bois's problem, as Gaines astutely points out. And the problem for Du Bois is not so much her supposed sexual insatiability but the fact of her being sexual at all. The black woman's transgression of domestic respectability—in working outside of the home, in seeking public and communal forms of sociality, amusement and pleasure— is problematic for Du Bois in a way that recalls the ambivalences of normative uplift in Frederick Douglass where music and the discourse on music and rebellion in the second chapter of the *Narrative* emerges from a black woman's assertion of sexual autonomy and the resistance to sexual violation recorded in the first chapter. In that first chapter, the one who is constructed as property causes the very idea of the proper to tremble between the poles of appropriation and expropriation. Douglass—in the midst of his moral denunciation of the master's cruelty—imagines some possible rehabilitative justification for his Aunt Hester's brutal and violative "punishment" by the master since, after all, she has attempted to determine the disposition of a sexuality she embraces and enacts. In so doing he prefigures the justifications of peonage or policing—in response to the black worker's attempt to determine the disposition of her labor—that are explicit and implicit in *The Philadelphia Negro* and *Souls*. Aunt Hester's "resistant aurality," less than and in excess of the brilliant account/ing that Harryette Mullen offers by way of a term that sounds like that term, is a political phonography moving over the edge of speech, is part of that chain of song with which I began, a history of recording that Du Bois calls "the murmur of ages;" but his normative view of black women's publicity and sexuality—their engagement in forms of reappropriative challenge to the extraction of surplus from their bodies—leaves him unable fully to valorize a criminality by which he is, at the same time, possessed. It is a criminality attached, finally, to a black maternity that is at once constitutive and substitutive and that is construed, as Spillers first points out, as necessarily illegitimate and impossible. Du Bois intimately knows and obsessively indexes and represses this maternity. It is an inheritance that touches and unmans him, something handed to him that cannot be handled.[25]

The murmur is a sound, a grumble or rumble, given on the outskirts of normal, as opposed to the center of (speech) pathological, articulation. It's tied to acting and performance where mummery coincides with murmuring, where the dumb show would seem to indicate an otherness if not absence of articulacy, as in *A Midsummer Night's Dream*, where murmuring and mummery, in the figure of Bottom, verge on animality (and I should just point out here, that we're moving now in a constellation in which animality, sociality, criminality, blackness and femininity circulate around a sound against or above speech, one that has, as Akira Lippit points out, the effect of making possible the construction, deconstruction and reconstruction of the human, a project in which black radicalism is intimately engaged).[26] For Du Bois the murmur is laden with history, is the dubbed and overdubbed recording of a history of complaint, where the phonic materiality of maternal song operates, again, over the edge of speech, over the edge of meaning. If we take Nathaniel Mackey's work more fully into account we see that complaint is better understood if seen and heard in its articulation with rebellion and escape at the place where expropriation and (re)appropriation combine idiomatically and accentually to disrupt the very idea of the proper—of property and proper speech. The murmur is an interminable doubling in and of what is supposed to be most properly one's own, namely one's speech. It's a phonography or deviant recording already inscribed upon or embedded in proper speech such that speech will have never been proper. Speech breaking from propriety, on the run from ownership. This is what Mackey thinks about, by way of Baraka on Federico García Lorca and saxophonist John Tchicai, under the rubric of fugitivity. Mackey begins by quoting Baraka's citation, in the epigraph to his poem "Lines to García Lorca," of lines from an African American spiritual: "Climbin' up the mountain, chillun/Didn't come here for to stay/If I'm ever gonna see you agin/It'll be on the judgment day." He continues:

> Gypsies, though they do not appear explicitly in this poem, come in elsewhere in Baraka's early work to embody a mobile, mercurial noninvestment in the status quo. One of the things going on in "Lines to García Lorca" is the implicit connection between that mercuriality, that nomadism, and the lines "Didn't come here for to stay," behind which lies a well-known, resonant history of African American fugitivity and its well-known, resonant relation to enslavement and persecution. Thus the resonant apposition of the poem's opening lines, "Send soldiers again to kill you, García./Send them to quell my escape." At the end of the poem Lorca's voice, "away off," invested with fugitive spirit, laughs
>
> > But away off, quite close to daylight,
> > I hear his voice, and he is laughing, laughing
> > Like a Spanish guitar.
>
> The way in which fugitivity asserts itself on an aesthetic level, at the level of poetics, is important as well. The way in which Baraka's poems of this period move intimates a fugitive spirit as does much of the music that he was into. He writes of a solo

by . . . Tchicai on an Archie Shepp album, "It slides away from the proposed." That gets into, again, the cultivation of another voice, a voice that is other than that proposed by one's intentions, tangential to one's intentions, angular, oblique—the obliquity of an unbound reference. That sliding away wants out.[27]

Mackey illustrates his analysis of fugitivity and the meta-voice with a fragment of multi-instrumentalist Rahsaan Roland Kirk's recording of his composition "The Business Ain't Nothing But the Blues," taking care to note how the voice and the instrument—in this case the flute—mutually cut and augment one another in a way that illuminates their already given internal difference and multiplicity.[28] Fugitivity, then, is a desire for and a spirit of escape and transgression of the proper and the proposed. It's a desire for the outside, for a playing or being outside, an outlaw edge proper to the now always already improper voice or instrument. This is to say that it moves outside the intentions of the one who speaks and writes, moving outside their own adherence to the law and to propriety. This fugitivity is at the heart of the murmur of many ages that Du Bois records. His recording of it is bound at once to his desire for it and for the outside that it desires and to his proper fear of that fugitivity to the extent that it marks and carries that thinking or pondering that he associates with the combination of crime and, more generally, a certain lawlessness of imagination, with cheap, dangerous socialism, and with the improper as such.

There are a couple of things left to consider: how are we to understand the transition that occurs in Du Bois, the one that moves from the rejection to the embrace of socialism in every bit of what had been understood to be its cheapness, danger and criminality? This question is all bound up with others: how are we to understand the constellation of (unsupervised, non-patriarchal) maternity, sexuality, promiscuity in its relation to the nexus of socialism and criminality? What's the relation between the phonics of fugitivity, the phonics of maternity and socialism? This question is crucial precisely because it requires us to call into question the very idea of transition even as we explain it's workings in the trajectory of Du Bois's thought. This is about the place of fugitivity in a maternal song that is inseparable from transgressions of proper bourgeois kinship. It's also about the trace of such song in Du Bois's speech and writing as not only his recording of the rural folk but also his bearing of the maternal mark that bourgeois respectability demands be relinquished. In other words, we must be concerned with his operation within and ongoing reproduction (of the opening of discovery) of the political line formed by the tumultuous convergence of phonic materiality and maternity, criminality and socialism, (what has often been dismissed as a kind of *lumpen*) peonage and (what has often been hoped for under the rubric of) proletariat.

At the end of his discussion of Du Bois, Gaines associates what might be called the revolutionary in Du Bois—the deviant, fugitive excess of normative uplift discourse and ideology—with Du Bois's affective critique of his own faith in the gathering and ordering of objective social facts as a necessary precursor to reform. This moment of reflection is prompted by the lynching of Sam Hose shortly after Du Bois moved from Philadelphia to Atlanta and Gaines reads it as the beginning of Du Bois's never fully successful attempt to detach himself from the discourse of urban pathology he helps to found and which continues to dominate discourse on the so-called black underclass to this day. Du Bois's recounting of this moment of self-analysis was recorded in 1961.[29] The truth of this recording lies precisely in a certain infidelity it bears that could be indexed to age, technology and/or the oscillation between objective distancing and objectional identification. This interplay of truth and infidelity— which Adorno argues is art's *Bewegungsgesetz*, its law of motion—is pierced by the criminality that lies before it, one that, in the end, ought to give a certain pause right in between fidelity and its various modifiers and prefixes, since it is perhaps more precise to say that the high fidelity of the recording accurately offers us a sound-image of Du Bois's scholarly and political intentions and commitments not only pierced but constituted by the low's high pitch.[30] I'm interested in the form as well as the content of a vocal performance that is almost everywhere cut and augmented by what might be perceived as a pathological disruption wherein every sibilant sound is subject to the rude extension of a whistle. It's as if Du Bois, prefiguring Kirk, is playing flute in accompaniment to speech that is already also his own improper, unowned disruption of the opposition between speaking and singing. Such broken form has something to tell us about that content and it's condition of possibility, though perhaps I make too much of an involuntary impediment—or the surplus effect of the overcoming of this impediment—that you will not be able not to hear. I think, however, that this disruptive augmentation of Du Bois's *Sprechgesang* is emblematic of some things that certainly require attention. Is the whistle an effect of microphone distortion, of technological mediation and reproduction? Can it be attributed to, and dismissed as, an effect of old age as if the nonagenarian Du Bois is afflicted by the kind of micro-tonal, micro-fugal disorder that is sometimes said to characterize "late work," from Beethoven's to Holiday's, like some combination of natural disaster and supernatural depth? In a sense this doesn't matter since what I'm after, again, is some recognition of the accidental, contingent and extra-intentional nature of the voice's essential quality, some acknowledgement of the transgressive scar on the body of the instrument that is, nevertheless, inseparable from a pronounced politico-aesthetic agency of the ages (and the aged). Such scarring is important precisely because, in the end, it can't be detached from the vocal instrument it remakes, like the mutative force of the combination of muting and amplification that characterizes a fundamental aspect of Miles' exilic approach to the trumpet and to speech. It's as if he can't help but make this dirty sound, the black noise of overdubbing and overcoming, the disruptive addition to the instrument or the instrumental, the irruptive, resistant aurality of a runaway tongue in all its phonoerotic, pathographic materiality. Du Bois's whistle bespeaks (and exspeaks) the graphic wear and tear of long days on speaking, a kind of distress, the inscription of that against which a certain voice is raised, the ordinary over(tonal)writing of everyday trouble, an irreducible immanence taking the way back into the strife between transcendental claims for and on the moral law within and the vicious invocation of the transcendental as justification for an appeal to such law that is, at once, violation and enforcement—as if starry heavens are made possible by the dust we can't shake from our feet, the dust of daywork and journeywork, of lynching as the disciplinary outrage of whiteness, which is to say, of dispersed, degraded, defeated and, nevertheless, dominant, modernized sovereignty. This is to say that the troubled voice is not only where the trace of the spectacle is laid down on top of the ordinary track, but also where the abstractions of a discourse of (violated) rights and citizenship are animated by material that is before the law and outside the house and its restricted economy. Audio cuts and augments the autobiography with another writing, the ordinary and inaugural inscription of and onto Du Bois. It's not just that Du Bois is, but that he also depends upon, a writing that overwrites his own attempts to erase it, a dilemma that is both before and after, inside and out of, Du Bois's exemplary position in the life and line of the thinking of black radicalism, the question of the question of the Negro. Du Bois's speech is shadowed by walking panthers and working women; haunted by citified Farmville promiscuity and Lowndes County outlaw audiobiography. The whistle is also a clue regarding the necessary phonographic aspects of the enterprise of reading and one needs to listen to (the racial-sexual force of [the sound of] phantasmatic and material) criminality in Du Bois, *especially in his denunciations of it*. The criminality to which we listen is of another order or is something at the high or low and hitherto undetectable end of criminality's politico-aesthetic spectrum. More than the denunciation of Du Bois's moralism and more than the renewed—because de-moralized—correction of stereotype is the audition of the criminality that inhabits Du Bois's speech and writing.

In beginning with the question of an open set, one might have moved this way: What is open to exploration in and by way of the phrases "criminal ontology" and "ontological criminality"?[31] What is opened in the distinction between crime and criminality? What is given in the range of movement that ensues from this (before or beyond Marxian) declension: being, wealth, city? Is criminality a thing realized in crimes? What commerce is there between *metoikos* (the stranger, the foreign resident, whom Robinson, in *Black Marxism*, calls "the eternal internal alien"), *zoon politikon* and the criminal? What's the relation between what might appear to be the priority of ontology over history and the priority within ontology of criminality over law? These are members of the open set of The Negro Question, where color and democracy are situated relative to a gender line, where the historical and ontological relation between blackness and radicalism is set to work. Perhaps their effectivity can be maximized if in posing them one understands radicalism to be a kind of out rooted-ness, an irreducibly interior and transversal transformationality, and blackness to be an archive of performances, at once disrupted and expansive, moving by way and in excess of its points (Africa, the Antilles, Arkansas, Amsterdam [Avenue], the city, the City) and events (confinement, transport, exchange, confinement, employment, emancipation, confinement, the city, the City) of origin. The question of the City is an open set as well, operating before urbanization and its dialectic of modernity and regress, that constantly brushes up against the en-gendering of the ordinary, of the everyday and its economies. The question of the city is inseparable from that concerning what it is to be, at once, of and outside of the house, of an impossible domestic-ity, of the broken generation/s of the *metoikos*. It demands that the questioner consider the one outside the house, be concerned with what the outside does to the one, explore territories that have been thought to be outside the house of being, outside language. It requires an attempt to attune oneself to the outside language of the outside woman, the common law outlaw, the shacked-up outside/r and, above all it seeks to investigate and to inhabit that mode of interiority, that politico-aesthetic assertion, that inaugural, errant criminality that is the law of the outside, that the outside and everyday-laboring growl and hum of everyday people enforces and allows.

When Robinson speaks of "the eternal internal alien," impossible domesticity is indexed. Deeper still, it is the impossible domestic who is indexed, the one who does the labor of the house that is constitutive of the economy and yet remains irreducibly outside of the economy and the house, not just as stranger, but as outside the law, outside of the law's protection even if open to the law's assault. This is what I mean by criminality—the status of the outlaw in all of its constitutive force in relation to the law, the house, the commune, the family; the status of the outlaw in all of the deconstructive force and danger to the law and the house of its ordinary imagination. This criminality is essential and historical. The outlaw, the impossible domestic, is before the law but not subject to it because not under its protection. She is, rather, the law's object or, more precisely, the thing or gathering or vessel of and before the law, up ahead and destructive of it. She can be prosecuted but she cannot and chooses not to prosecute. Citizenship is denied to the thing who denies citizenship. She enacts an ordinary apposition to, a denial-in-abolition of, citizenship. The impossible domestic apposes the citizen-subject. What a problem and what a chance she is for Du Bois (or for Marx, each in their own challenging adherence to certain Aristotelian and Kantian fundaments of political theory). She? A voice or meta-(metrical-madrigal-) voice disruptive of speech; the outside sound of the outside woman and her chorus, the lawless freedom of the imagination (improvising, not not looking in the very reconstitution of foresight as something Robin Kelley might call a "freedom dream," the surreal political "nonsense" of a utopian vision, the freedom we know outside of the opposition of sense and intellection by way of and *as* the transcendental and immanent aesthetic [clue] of the sound we make when we sing about it, such song's flavor, the movement that produces it and that it induces[32]) that is constitutive of the political animal. The infusion of maternal song in Du Bois, the murmur of ages, indexes her. So that this is about what the impossible domestic carries in her (pan-)toting, her handing and passing on of her little all, of everything, in her singing, her stealing and stealing away from being stolen, from being carried off, in her carrying and carrying off and carrying on, her production and re-accumulation of the wealth she is and carries where wealth is understood, in a new revision of the old Marxian way. Marx says wealth will not have been the aim of production. Rather,

> when the limited bourgeois form is stripped away, what is wealth other than the universality of individual needs, capacities, pleasures, productive forces, etc., created through universal exchange? The full development of human mastery over the forces of nature, those of so-called nature as well as of humanity's own nature? The absolute working-out of his creative potentialities, with no presupposition other than the previous historic development, which makes this totality of development, i.e. the development of all human powers as such the end in itself, not as measured on a *predetermined* yardstick? Where he does not reproduce himself in one specificity, but produces

his totality? Strives not to remain something he has become, but is in the absolute movement of becoming?[33]

But our revision will have so cut mastery as to free up the forces of nature. This is about stealing and/in singing, out of which emerges another, voluntary, organization; another garden, another life outside, another city, another day/work and play, improvising through house and field. So this is also akin to Deleuze's and Guattari's rhizomatic irruption into the arbor and hinges on the relationship between the volunteer (the plant or shoot or tendril that grows in spite of, and also in the absence of, cultivation) and the meta-voice.[34] It demands concern with what the volunteer does to voluntarity, on the one hand, and, on the other hand, an aesthetics of criminality that is inseparable from, or is articulated through and as, art's *law* of movement. The occasion of the volunteer is, as it were, a movement between the force of (the out)law and the (out)law of movement.

What kind of organization comes from this? She is outside the house she structures and makes possible by entering, and she is outside her own impossible home within this "national" homelessness by leaving. She is embedded in and works a kind of leave-taking—at once palimpsestic and montagic—in the radical absence or absenting of home/origin. She leaves without origin, is not understandable within the context of her geneses and natal occasions, generally and ordinarily cuts and augments understanding with work-songs. This exteriority preserves the house that it dismantles so radically as not only to trouble or make impossible a certain tension between inside and outside but also fundamentally to disfigure, refigure, reconfigure ownership. This is a problematic, more specifically, of tools, of the ownership of tools. The master's tools can never dismantle the master's house, according to Audre Lorde, who would know. Only the master's tools can dismantle the master's house, according to Henry Louis Gates Jr., who would know.[35] This impossible domestic, this female slave (a conflation Aristotle sees as barbaric), is the master's tool who will have never belonged to the master; the master's object who can make or break him. The one who will have never been the master's tool because she is the master's object anticipates the one who is assuredly the tool of mastery precisely by being subject to it.

The point, however, is that what's happening here is beyond or before the problematic of dismantling or, perhaps more precisely, is of a dismantling that can only be spoken of within the context of something like an originary rebuilding. We have to move, rather, in what Chandler might call an originary displacement of building and dismantling, a displacement that emerges, paradoxically, from leaving (without) origin. We live in an impossible originarity, the impossible domesticity, of reconstruction. We enact a deconstruction that only moves in its relation to reconstruction. You could call this improvisation, too. Impossible domesticity begins with irruptive reconstruction. It's marked and instantiated by a fugitive sound that is not just on the run from ownership but blowing a run that enacts a fundamental dispossession of ownership as such so that owning is, itself, disowned. This is black Marxism, black communism, where the originary reconstruction is understood as the preservation of the ontological totality, the reconstructive conservation, if you will, of wealth, of the wealth of who and what we are and will be. This is the condition of possibility of accumulation, primitive or otherwise; but it is also its disruption, deferral, originary displacement or anoriginal differing. Anoriginal stealing, anoriginal dispossession at the level of a disruption of regulative and lawful self-possession, the citizen-subject's necessary mode, his rational grammar and tone, the transformation, by way of protection, of voice into speech, a distinction that the impossible domestic operates before, as it were. There's much more to be said about teleological principle and certain outlaw actualities of black reconstruction through an analysis of some migratory outwork that Du Bois turns away from in *The Philadelphia Negro* before a long, tentative and discomfiting embrace that his *Black Reconstruction* signals; for now it must be sufficient to take note, *in the interest of the city,* of the imagination of the impossible domestic, of the lawless freedom and/of the law of motion, her (every)day work, the work of the ordinary, the ordinary outwork, the madness, the flight, the *criminality,* in the presence of (the) work.

What more can be said about this criminality, this being against the law, to which the whistle brings us? Where else do we have to go in order to develop our understanding of it? The essence of blackness—as political, economic, sexual, aesthetic formation—is expropriative (or, both more and less precisely, ecstatic). Frenzied (in the way that Du Bois elucidates in his description of a certain highly eroticized black religiosity in *Souls*). Tumultuous. Plaintive. Trialed. Trailed. What happens when the law becomes the discourse to which we turn in order to get at the essence of what that very law is meant both to control and to slander? What does it mean to speak of the essence of a historical, constructed thing? This is not meant to romanticize crime; it is to say, however, that what we valorize as revolutionary or radical has to do with the criminal in a sense that is both very specific and extraordinarily broad, where the criminal can be understood as the resistant, cut augmentation of the proper. This means thinking criminality not as a violation of the criminal law (however il/legitimate one thinks such law to be) but rather as a capacity or propensity to transgress the law as such, to challenge its mystical authority with a kind of improvisational rupture.

The anti-tumult law—which Du Bois ineffectively sought to apply to his own text (as the univocal voice of reason which, of course, bears itself as a kind of schizoid difference or transversal) and which is broken by the plexed multiplicity of his speech and writing—is a privileged place from which to begin an investigation of this criminality and its revolutionary or radical qualities. The whistle is, finally, a kind of clue at once immanent and transcendental and the return of it or its like seems inevitable when and where righteous transgression and brutal repression meet. Deeper still, in cases such as this, what returns is a rich anticipation. But one shouldn't attach too much significance to such impediments of speech without having a conceptual apparatus that understands that surplus sound effect as something way more than an impediment. After the formation of such an apparatus what will remain, as always, is this: How will this event/music—and the content it breaks and bears—continue visibly to mark the occasion of the volunteer?

## Notes

1. Nahum D. Chandler, "Delimitations: The Positions of W. E. B. Du Bois in the History of Thought," unpublished.

2. W. E. B. Du Bois, "Sociology Hesitant," *boundary 2* 27, no. 3 (Fall, 2000): 37–44. All preceding quotations, 14. In that volume see also Ronald A. T. Judy, "Introduction: On W. E. B. Du Bois and Hyperbolic Thinking" (1–35) and Nahum

Dmitri Chandler, "Originary Displacement" (249–86). While the essay should be read as Du Bois's call for sociology to escape its hesitancy in thinking black life, it is necessary to recognize that hesitation will have been, in fact, the method of such movement. This abiding, (loco)motive immanence in the pause, in the delay, in the interval, in the break, is understood by Du Bois as confounding the "two sorts of human uniformity," chance and law. He therefore advocates inhabiting a polyrhythmic caesura that will have been the precise point of an interruptive conjunction of, say, the death rate and the women's club. But you'd have to get so into the deaths that both make up and disturb the rate, the measurement, of death, as well as so faithfully attend the activity of women that both make up and disrupt the club, as to actually enact a recalibration of fugitivity as the traversal of the bridge between things and the whole they (de)form.

　3. C. L. R. James, *The Black Jacobins: Toussaint L'Ouverture and the San Domingo Revolution,* Second Edition, Revised (New York: Vintage Books, 1989), 18.

　4. Amiri Baraka (LeRoi Jones), *Blues People: Negro Music in White America* (New York: Morrow, 1963), 20–21.

　5. Baraka, *Blues People,* 21–22.

　6. Du Bois, *The Souls of Black Folk,* in *Writings,* ed. Nathan Huggins (New York: The Library of America, 1986), 538–39.

　7. David Levering Lewis, *W. E. B. Du Bois: Biography of a Race, 1868–1919* (New York: Henry Holt, 1993), 14–15. Brent Hayes Edwards discusses the series of recordings of this song that Du Bois offers throughout his long autobiographical career in relation to Guadeloupean Suzanne Lacascade's 1924 novel *Claire-Solange, âme africaine.* Lacascade's (writing of) music, Edwards forcefully argues, bears the cultural difference, mix and transport that mark the necessary articulation of blackness and internationalism. Through the character whose name is also given to the novel, Lacascade indexes yet another song that lingers in the gap between transcription and translation: a song the figure of Claire-Solange describes as both "savage revolt" and the echo or trace of "the blow of the lash on the naked back of negro slaves"; a song of (dis)possession, contortion and suspension (of traffic, of the bridge in Zanzibar where Claire-Solange first encounters its performance); a song of repetitive, even recidivist, insistence. In its resistance to, if not flight from, meaning and its regulations—whose manifestation in the novel's apparatus occurs at and as the convergence of fiction and fieldwork as Edwards illuminates—Lacascade joins Du Bois and others before and after him in a certain phonographic insurgency; in my attendance to this insurgency, where blackness and internationalism must now be seen as interarticulate with vaga/bondage, I'm attempting to follow the example of Edwards. For the real thing see *The Practice of Diaspora: Literature, Translation, and the Rise of Black Internationalism* (Cambridge, Mass.: Harvard University Press, 2003). Take note, especially, of Edwards's discussion of Claude McKay's *Banjo* (187–233) as well as his discussion of *Claire-Solange, âme africaine* (51–58).

　8. Lewis, *W. E. B. Du Bois,* 585, n. 7.

　9. Lewis, *W. E. B. Du Bois,* 585, n. 7.

　10. See Hortense Spillers, "All the Things You Could Be by Now If Sigmund Freud's Wife Was Your Mother': Psychoanalysis and Race," in *Black and White and in Color: Essays in American Literature and Culture* (Chicago: University of Chicago Press, 2003), 382; and Cedric Robinson, *Black Marxism: The Making of the Black Radical Tradition* (Chapel Hill: The University of North Carolina Press, 2000), 73.

11. Kevin K. Gaines, *Uplifting the Race: Black Leadership, Politics and Culture in the Twentieth Century* (Chapel Hill: The University of North Carolina Press, 1996), xv. Hereafter cited parenthetically in the text.

12. Du Bois, *The Souls of Black Folk,* 467.

13. Du Bois, *The Souls of Black Folk,* 466–67. All quotations in the preceding paragraph, 466.

14. I am thinking of the following passage from an exegesis of a few sentences of Marx's *Grundrisse* in Althusser & Etienne Balibar, *Reading Capital,* trans. Ben Brewster (London: Verso, 1979), 48. "It is precisely this *Gliederung,* this articulated-thought-totality [or "articulated combination"/*"combinaison articulée"*] which has to be produced in knowledge as an object of knowledge in order to treat a knowledge of the real *Gliederung,* of the real articulated-totality which constitutes the existence of bourgeois society. The order in which the thought *Gliederung* is produced is a specific order, precisely the order of the theoretical *analysis* Marx performed in *Capital,* the order of the liaison and 'synthesis' of the concepts necessary for the production of a thought-whole, a thought-concrete, the theory of *Capital.*" Perhaps the articulated combination of blackness and criminality makes possible a thought of another totality, a futurity given every day. Edwards offers his own (thinking on) articulation, his own conceptualization of *decalage,* translation and the enactment of diaspora, in a way that anticipates the line I am trying to trace or, better yet, follow. He moves by way of Stuart Hall's engagement with Althusser. See *Reading Capital,* 108, where the notion of "structure in dominance" is derived from an analysis of "articulated combination." See also Edwards, *The Practice of Diaspora,* 11–15. And for another, deeper engagement with Althusser that thinks the relation between the protocols of reading and the necessity of a conceptualization of the object in/of black studies, see Part III of Spillers, "The Crisis of the Negro Intellectual: A Post-Date," *Black and White and in Color,* 444–58.

15. Saidiya V. Hartman, *Scenes of Subjection: Terror, Slavery and Self-Making in Nineteenth-Century America* (Oxford: Oxford University Press, 1997).

16. See Jacques Derrida, "Force of Law: The 'Mystical Foundation of Authority,'" Drucilla Cornell, Michael Rosenfeld, and David Gray Carlson, ed. *Deconstruction and the Possibility of Justice* (New York: Routledge, 1992), 3–68.

17. See Daniel P. Moynihan, *The Negro Family: The Case for National Action* (Washington, D.C.: U.S. Department of Labor, 1965). Spillers' exposure of the historical and theoretical conditions of possibility of Moynihan's argument is definitive. See her "Mama's Baby, Papa's Maybe: An American Grammar Book," *Black and White and in Color,* 203–29.

18. Ulrich B. Phillips, *American Negro Slavery* (Baton Rouge: Louisiana State University Press, 1966), 454.

19. Phillips, *American Negro Slavery,* 463.

20. I am indebted, here, to the valuable work of Steven Hahn. In his *A Nation Under Our Feet: Black Political Struggles in the Rural South from Slavery to the Great Migration* (Cambridge, Mass.: Harvard University Press, 2003), Hahn exhaustively records the very kind of black political activity that Phillips represses, noting that "Southern slaveholders and their representatives (and, we might add, their historiographical apologists) . . . could scarcely acknowledge, let alone dignify, the disruptive or communal behaviours of their slaves as worthy of the name political" (15). Hahn's work does much to rectify this problem even as it might also be said to reify it, not

only in its insistence on a distinction between resistance and politics that deeper consideration of the very idea of organization requires us to challenge, but also in its adherence to a notion of political subjectivity that forecloses further investigation into the possibilities of the slaves having produced new modes of agency that will have strained against the very modes of disciplinary citizenship they might be said to have called into being. In this respect, however problematic Phillips's discourse on slave crime may be, it bears the trace of political modes to which Hahn's brilliant corrective is not fully attuned even though it prepares us for a more faithful listening.

21. Du Bois, *The Philadelphia Negro: A Social Study, Revised Edition* (Philadelphia: University of Pennsylvania Press, 1996), 235.

22. *The Philadelphia Negro,* 411.

23. Such domesticity has its own music, as Du Bois's tutor Max Weber shows in his discourse on the piano in *The Rational and Social Foundations of Music,* trans. and ed. Don Martindale, Johannes Riedel, and Gertrude Neuwirth (Carbondale, IL: Southern Illinois University Press, 1958). The "instrumental rationality" of the piano's harmonic construction is inseparable from its iconic position in the bourgeois drawing room and its symbolic relation to proper (feminine) accomplishment and proper (feminized) domesticity.

24. Robinson, *Black Marxism,* 171.

25. See Frederick Douglass, *Narrative of the Life of Frederick Douglass, An American Slave,* in Henry Louis Gates Jr. ed., *The Classic Slave Narratives* (New York: Mentor Books, 1987), 259. For a striking analysis of the constitutive trace of "resistant orality" (a verbal, that is inseparable from a sexual, impudence) in black women's writing see Harryette Mullen, "Runaway Tongue: Resistant Orality in *Uncle Tom's Cabin, Our Nig, Incidents in the Life of a Slave Girl,* and *Beloved*" in Shirley Samuels ed., *The Culture of Sentiment: Race, Gender, and Sentimentality in Nineteenth-Century America* (New York: Oxford University Press, 1992), 244–64. On the question of sexuality, labor, and the challenge to bourgeois domesticity and Du Bois's problematic attitudes towards working-class black women's autonomy, see Tera Hunter, "The 'Brotherly Love' for Which This City is Proverbial Should Extend to All: The Everyday Lives of Working-Class Women in Philadelphia and Atlanta in the 1890s," Michael B. Katz & Thomas J. Sugrue, eds., *W. E. B. Du Bois, Race, and the City: The Philadelphia Negro and its Legacy* (Philadelphia: University of Pennsylvania Press, 1998), 127–51. Also see Hunter's extraordinary *To 'Joy My Freedom* (Cambridge, Mass.: Harvard University Press, 1997). For more on Hester's resistant aurality, see my *In the Break: The Aesthetics of the Black Radical Tradition* (Minneapolis: University of Minnesota Press, 2003). My formulations attempt, weakly, to enact what would have been infinitely more adequately given under Spillers's hand. On page 15 of *In the Break* you'll see that here, now, I am late in imagining the incalculable difference between *handled* and *handed* to which Spillers gestures ("The African-American male has been touched, therefore, by the mother, *handed by* her in ways that he cannot escape . . ."). What's at stake is some more efficacious approach to inheritance-in-dispossession, the hand-me-down im/possibility embedded in passing on and in what inheres outside and against grasping. See Spillers, "Mama's Baby, Papa's Maybe," 228. For a bracing challenge to the anthropological overinvestment in the phonic mode see Gina Dent, *Anchored to the Real: Black Literature in the Wake of Anthropology* (Durham: Duke University Press), forthcoming.

26. See Akira Lippit, *Electric Animal: Toward a Rhetoric of Wildlife* (Minneapolis: University of Minnesota Press, 2000).

27. Nathaniel Mackey, "Cante Moro" in *Sound States: Innovative Poetics and Acoustical Technologies* ed. Adalaide Morris (Chapel Hill: The University of North Carolina Press, 1997), 199–200.

28. Roland Kirk, *I Talk With the Spirits* (New York: Verve Records, 1964).

29. W. E. B. Du Bois and Moses Asch. *W. E. B. Du Bois: a Recorded Autobiography* (New York: Folkways Records, 1961).

30. I'm thinking of two passages in Adorno's late work. In the first, Adorno writes, "Brecht said once that the [Lenin] book on empirio-criticism obviated any further need to criticize the philosophy of immanence. It was a shortsighted remark. Materialist theory is subject to philosophical desiderata if it is not to succumb to the same provincialism that disfigures art in Eastern countries. The object of theory is not something immediate, of which theory might carry home a replica. Knowledge has not, like the state police, a rogues' gallery of its objects. Rather, it conceives them as it conveys them; else it would be content to describe the façade. As Brecht did admit, after all, the criterion of sense perception—overstretched and problematic even in its proper place—is not applicable to radically indirect society. What immigrated into the object as the law of its motion [*Bewegungsgesetz*], inevitably concealed by the ideological form of the phenomenon, eludes that criterion." See Theodor W. Adorno, *Negative Dialectics*, trans. E. B. Ashton (New York: Continuum, 1972), 206. In the second passage, Adorno argues, "The semblance character of artworks, the illusion of their being-in-itself, refers back to the fact that in the totality of their subjective mediatedness they take part in the universal delusional context of reification, and, that, in Marxist terms, they need to reflect a relation of living labor as if it were a thing. The inner consistency through which artworks participate in truth always involves their untruth; in its most unguarded manifestations art has always revolted against this, and today this revolt has become art's own law of movement [*Bewegungsgesetz*]. Traditional aesthetics possessed the insight that the primacy of the whole over the parts has constitutive need of the diverse and that this primacy misfires when it is simply imposed from above." See Theodor W. Adorno, *Aesthetic Theory*, trans. Robert Hullot-Kentor (Minneapolis: University of Minnesota Press, 1997), 168–69.

31. It might appear that I risk privileging the ontological over the historical. I hope that the passages from Adorno I quoted above justify the direction I have taken. Those passages contain what Herman Rapaport might call transcendental clues regarding the relation between blackness and radicalism, the politics and aesthetics, the history and ontology of criminality, which has everything to do with the *Bewegungsgesetz*, the (im)migrant law irrupting into and thereby constituting the object from outside. The methodological point, for me, is this: that the re-emergence of the aesthetic and the ontological allow a more rigorous engagement with the political and the historical. These fields are no more to be divided, their terms no more to be fixed or hypostasized, than law and criminality or the *polis* and its *metoikoi*. Of course, the self-described criminal's self-description is mediated by the state; at the same time, the state is constituted by the very criminal/ity that it constructs and defines. This paradoxically contingent priority is what Cedric Robinson is already after when he says that black radicalism cannot be understood within the context of

its genesis; and this is not negated but invaginated and augmented by the assertion that the priority of such radicalism, its broken and scarred ontological totality, is inseparable from a definable historical constitution. As E. P. Thompson says in the preface to his masterpiece: "The working class was present at its own making."

It is important, then, not only to exhume the ontological in contexts or in relations to things that are thought only to defy it, but also to begin to consider a certain ontological notion of the city and of wealth that is tied to his formulations on the modes of primitive accumulation that have traditionally been linked to economies of the outskirts or the underground, to broken homes or black markets. This notion of the City/wealth that is operative in Marx is crucially tied to his analysis of enclosure. The two types of enclosure that I cite are mirror images of one another and are important to my attempts to consider the relationship between blackness, radicalism and the City. That they are mirror images of one another and need to be understood in their difference from one another is not at all to suggest that they are not continuous (though my quick treatment of them may give that impression). I just want to maintain the tension between them so that I can explore it elsewhere (i.e., consider enclosure within the context of a more general ontological history of the City.) In the end, it seems to me that the most concrete levels of historical analysis either require or, more modestly, are improved by raising those ontological questions that animate Du Bois's long historical and sociological engagement with the black ordinary.

32. See Robin D. G. Kelley, *Freedom Dreams: The Black Radical Imagination* (New York: Beacon Press, 2002), 157–94.

33. Karl Marx, *Grundrisse: Foundations of the Critique of Political Economy*, trans. Martin Nicolaus (New York: Vintage, 1973), 487–88.

34. See Gilles Deleuze and Felix Guattari, *A Thousand Plateaus*, trans. Brian Massumi (Minneapolis: University of Minnesota Press, 1987), 11–12.

35. See Audre Lorde, "The Master's Tools Will Never Dismantle the Master's House," in *Sister Outsider: Essays and Speeches* (Freedom, CA: The Crossing Press, 1984), 110–13; and Henry Louis Gates Jr., "The Master's Pieces: On Canon Formation and the Afro-American Tradition," in Dominick LaCapra ed., *The Bounds of Race* (Ithaca: Cornell University Press, 1991), 34.

# 11

# Second-Sight: Du Bois and the Black Masculine Gaze

■ *Shawn Michelle Smith*

In the well-known scene in which W. E. B. Du Bois describes his first recognition of the color line and his dawning double consciousness, he figures "race" through a gaze:

It is in the early days of rollicking boyhood that the revelation first bursts upon one, all in a day, as it were. I remember well when the shadow swept across me. I was a little thing, away up in the hills of New England. . . . In a wee wooden schoolhouse, something put it into the boys' and girls' heads to buy gorgeous visiting-cards—ten cents a package—and exchange. The exchange was merry, till one girl, a tall newcomer, refused my card,—refused it peremptorily, with a glance. Then it dawned upon me with a certain suddenness that I was different from the others.

What the young Du Bois recognizes in the dismissive glance of the white girl is that he is unlike the other children, or rather he is "like, mayhap, in heart and life and longing," but *seen* as different. It is the white girl's look that racializes Du Bois's self-perception, opening his eyes to the force of the color line.[1]

As Hazel Carby has noted, "It is significant that Du Bois claims that his first encounter with racism was the moment when his courtly, nineteenth-century advances were rejected by a young white woman."[2] Du Bois's social world is divided by the force of the color line, split along racial lines, but also, it would seem, in the very recognition of the color line, divided by gender. The color line is brought home to Du Bois, made intimate and self-transforming through the vehicle of a white girl's gaze. The assumed cultural privilege of a masculine gaze is trumped by race in this scene, as whiteness bestows the prerogative of looking (and refusing to look) on the white girl. Indeed, the trauma of racialization, for Du Bois, is marked by a disavowal of his masculine claim to the gaze.[3] Du Bois thus poses the process of racial recognition as a visual dynamic that is not only racialized, but also gendered, that figures "race" through a gendered gaze.

Du Bois paints the scene of the white girl's rejecting glance to exemplify double consciousness as the imperative of "looking at one's self through the eyes of others."[4] The visual scene of racial rejection is one in which Du Bois is asked to see himself differently, to see what is cast aside in the white girl's glance. The look that initiates double consciousness projects a specter of blackness that splits consciousness into "two-ness."[5] But Du Bois quickly reminds readers that the bifurcated gaze of double consciousness does not only look inward at the newly figured double self, but also outward, at the white world, at those who would look and deny him the gaze. Therefore, while double consciousness may require Du Bois to look at himself through a white gaze, it also enables him to see "race" differently, with what he calls "second-sight." In this sense, then, a white girl's look produces a new vision for a masculine black subject. If a racialized and gendered gaze crystallizes double consciousness, splitting self-recognition into "two-ness," double consciousness also produces second-sight, a gaze that is also racialized and gendered, albeit differently from the look that prefigures it. Thus, even as he poses the revelation of racism (double consciousness) as the effect of objectification produced for a black male subject through a white feminine gaze, Du Bois also claims, through second-sight, the prerogative of a reconfigured black masculine gaze.

Du Bois poses the denial and reconstitution of a black masculine gaze in a historical moment in which that gaze, especially upon a white female body, was violently prohibited by the cultural logics of lynching. Indeed, as Vron Ware has argued, in the post-Reconstruction South, "If a black man so much as looked a white woman in the eye he risked being accused of lechery or insolence, and in some cases this was as good as committing an actual assault."[6] According to the gendered and racialized logics of lynching, the black man's gaze upon a white woman signaled his desire to possess her sexually; the black man's gaze was perceived as a gesture of sexual appropriation that threatened white patriarchal privilege.

The rhetoric of lynching, which aimed to justify the torture and mutilation of African American men by calling it retribution for the crime of rape, figured black male sexuality as "savage." In the scenarios construed by the white lynch mob, a reconfigured white patriarchy was called upon to protect white women, always posed as the sexually pure, passive victims of black male sexual aggression. While dominant and culturally effective, this racialized sexual mythology did not go unchallenged at the turn of the century. In her antilynching work, Ida B. Wells questioned the purity and passivity of the white female victim, and also the absence of African American women from the lynch mob's outcry over the crime of rape. According to Wells, the rape scenarios so often rehearsed by a white mob worked to obscure consensual relationships between white women and African American men, as well as white men's rape of African American women, institutionalized during slavery, and continuing in the post-emancipation and post-Reconstruction periods.

White anxiety over interracial reproduction, over the blurring of physical racial markers called on to differentiate the races, at least partly informed the lynch mob's outrage over an African American man's imagined access to a white woman's body. In many ways, that anxiety figured a return of a white patriarchy's repressed legacy of interracial rape and reproduction, a legacy often attributed, in white supremacist discourses, to African American women, represented not as victims, but as themselves the aggressors in sexual "encounters" with white men. In the intertwined legacies of white rape and lynching that worked to consolidate a white patriarchy, black male and female sexuality were construed as uncivilized in order to mask the violence of white male sexuality.

As Ida B. Wells observed in the 1890s, lynching ultimately served as a form of economic terrorism, as racialized class warfare translated into the terms of sexual purity and transgression.[7] The cry of rape of a white woman that legitimized lynching in the eyes of many, was seen by Wells to be a cover that enabled whites to lash out and resist the African American progress they perceived to be a threat to their own economic and cultural capital. The African American man who posed a financial threat to white business was transformed, by the lynch mob's cry of rape, into a man who threatened the sexual purity of white women. Thus, as one pillar of white patriarchy, the control of capital, was challenged, it was displaced in a psychosexual domain into a threat to another cornerstone of white patriarchy, namely, white women and their reproductive power.

Within this highly charged cultural context, Du Bois's reinscription of a black masculine gaze through second-sight is a bold act of defiance. In this essay I would like to consider further the function of that gaze by examining a remarkable collection of photographs that Du Bois compiled as part of his Georgia Negro studies for the American Negro Exhibit at the 1900 Paris Exposition.[8] I propose to read the Georgia Negro photographs as a lens through which to focus thoughts about Du Bois's reconfiguration of black masculinity at the turn of the century. By and large, the images represent an African American elite, Du Bois's Talented Tenth. Hundreds of photographs of well-to-do African American men and women contest the discourses of lynching that sought to deem the African American man a sexual savage, and thereby obliterate his economic power and class standing. In the context of such discourses, Du Bois poses a vision of an elite African American patriarchy, of an African American middle and upper class making claims to both economic advancement and cultural privilege through the performance of gendered respectability and sexual control. Du Bois founds an African American middle class on gender differentiation and sexual discipline. His evidence of racial equality is figured through gender hierarchy as a sign of class stratification, and that gender hierarchy is made manifest in Du Bois's photographs of an African American patriarchy, images that both project and confirm the vision of a reconfigured black masculine gaze.

## *The Georgia Negro Exhibit: Dismantling the "Negro Type"*

In the spring of 1900, Du Bois sent his Georgia Negro Exhibit to the Paris Exposition, to be installed in the American Negro Exhibit, under the direction of Thomas J. Calloway. The Georgia Negro studies, made in collaboration with Atlanta University students and graduates, include a series of charts and graphs documenting the social and economic history and progress of African Americans in Georgia, a copy of the complete legal code of Georgia pertaining to African Americans, and a series of 363 photographs of African Americans in Georgia. Du Bois organized the photographs into albums, entitled *Types of American Negroes, Georgia, U.S.A.* (Vols. I-III), and *Negro Life in Georgia, U.S.A.* About two-thirds of the photographs are portraits, generally paired on a page, with two images representing one individual, and many of these images are surprisingly objectifying, approximating the closely cropped frontal and hard-profile headshots of mugshots. Other photographs are more typical middle-class portraits, showing individuals in three-quarter poses, surrounded by studio props; many of these latter portraits were made by Thomas E. Askew, a prominent African American photographer in Atlanta. The remaining photographs in the Georgia Negro albums include group portraits of families, bands, and sport teams, as well as documentary photographs of stores and businesses, churches, wealthy and impoverished neighborhoods, and agricultural fields.

The closely cropped mugshots that introduce Du Bois's albums of "Negro Types" replicate the formal codes of nineteenth- and turn-of-the-century scientific photography; they signify on the visual texts constructed by biological racialists and eugenicists as "evidence" of innate African American inferiority.[9] The initial portraits in Du Bois's *Types of American Negroes, Georgia, U.S.A.*, Vols. I and II, reproduce the formal characteristics of "objective" scientific photography: Individuals are photographed against a plain background, in the standardized, paired poses of closely cropped headshots and hard profiles, the very poses early physical anthropologists, biological

racialists, and eugenicists fashioned in order to define racial "types."
Early race scientists utilized photographs to codify what they argued
were the physical signs of innate, inherent racial characteristics, the
physical markings of inferiority or superiority.

FIGURE 11.1  *W. E. B. Du Bois,* Types of American Negroes, Georgia, U.S.A.
*(1900), volume 1, no. 11. Reproduced from the Daniel Murray Collection,
Library of Congress, Washington, D.C.*

FIGURE 11.2 *W. E. B. Du Bois,* Types of American Negroes, Georgia, U.S.A. *(1900), volume 1, no. 12. Reproduced from the Daniel Murray Collection, Library of Congress, Washington, D.C.*

I suggest, then, that the initial photographs in Du Bois's albums of "Negro Types" offer views of African Americans as projected "through the eyes of [white] others." With these images, Du Bois demonstrates that the racialized gaze of second-sight perceives white projections and understands them to be constructions. Ultimately, Du Bois appropriates a scientific, white masculine gaze to dismantle its racist vision, to disrupt its image of the "Negro type," and finally, to scrutinize African American bodies on his own terms.

While the first images in Du Bois's 1900 Paris Exposition albums formally recall the photographs that biological racialists and eugenicists used to codify and distinguish bodies in racial terms, Du Bois's albums as a whole dismantle the physical coherence of the imagined racial type. For the "Negro type," as represented in Du Bois's photograph albums, is plural—*Types of American Negroes, Georgia, U.S.A.* Indeed, the albums represent a diverse array of individuals who are not bound by physical appearance, by the "hair and bone and color" that Du Bois rejects as singular signs of racial belonging in his essay of 1897, "The Conservation of Races."[10] In Du Bois's albums, blond and pale "Negro types" are placed beside brunette and brown "Negro types," a juxtaposition that challenges the color line as a marker of racial difference and the body itself as sign of racial meaning. The divergence of physical characteristics along Du Bois's "color line" also reminds viewers that the interracial mixing whites proclaim to fear and resist has already taken place, and largely at their own hands.[11] Looking back on this period later in his life, Du Bois would declare: "I was of course aware that all members of the Negro race were not black and that the pictures of my race which were current were not authentic nor fair portraits."[12] In his 1900 Paris Exposition albums, Du Bois loosens the narrow circumscription of the racial type as codified by biological racialists and eugenicists; he unfixes the "Negro type."

In the scientific paradigms of biological racialists and eugenicists, the purported degeneracy of biracial individuals served as evidence of the essential differences between the races, as evidence that the races were unequal and should remain separate. The figure of the biracial individual or "mulatto," then, became an important site through which to challenge eugenicist claims about essential racial

FIGURE 11.3 *W. E. B. Du Bois,* Types of American Negroes, Georgia, U.S.A. *(1900), volume 2, no. 144. Reproduced from the Daniel Murray Collection, Library of Congress, Washington, D.C.*

differences and "Negro" inferiority. If one could demonstrate that there was nothing degenerate about the so-called mulatto, one might also suggest that the different races were not so terribly distinct. This is precisely what Du Bois endeavored to prove in his sociological studies at the turn of the century, and to suggest with his Georgia Negro photographs. In *The Health and Physique of the Negro American* (1906), a text in which he recycles many of his 1900 Georgia Negro photographs, Du Bois concludes: "A word may be added as to race mixture in general and as regards white and black stocks in the future. There is, of course, in general no argument against the intermingling of the world's races. 'All the great peoples of the world are the result of a mixture of races.'"[13]

Du Bois's portraits of white-looking African Americans in the Georgia Negro albums contest a white supremacist racial taxonomy of identifiable (because visible) otherness. The images of young African American men, women, and children who could pass for white in *Types of American Negroes, Georgia, U.S.A.*, highlight the paradoxes of racial classification in Jim Crow America. By the turn of the century, several states had laws that deemed one-thirty-second African or African American ancestry the key that distinguished "black" from "white," a distinction so narrow as to make explicit the invisibility of "blackness" and "whiteness" as racial categories.[14] As Mary Ann Doane has argued, the individual of mixed ancestry, "whose looks and ontology do not coincide, poses a threat to . . . the very idea of racial categorization."[15] The physical appearance of the person of mixed ancestry "always signifies a potential confusion of racial categories and the epistemological impotency of vision."[16] Individuals of mixed racial ancestry challenge visual codes of racial distinction, showing a racial taxonomy founded in visual paradigms of recognition to be a fiction, albeit a powerful one. Thus, at the very moment in which segregation and science required whites and blacks to be distinguished, "white" and "black," as legally defined, could not necessarily be differentiated visibly. Du Bois uses photographic "evidence" to demonstrate the inefficacy of visual paradigms in delimiting racial identities that are, in turn, falsely rooted in biology.[17]

White hysteria over the "threat" of racial passing at the turn of the century both spurred an increased fervor in racial surveillance, and marked the extent of forced interracial mixing across generations during and after slavery. Du Bois's photographs of a young, blond, very pale African American child in the Georgia Negro albums challenge white supremacists' investment in separating the races by signaling an undeniable history of physical union between them.

FIGURE 11.4 *Photograph by Thomas E. Askew. From W. E. B. Du Bois,* Types of American Negroes, Georgia, U.S.A. *(1900), volume 1, no. 59. Reproduced from the Daniel Murray Collection, Library of Congress, Washington, D.C.*

As Robert J. C. Young has argued, "The ideology of race . . . from the 1840s onwards necessarily worked according to a doubled logic, according to which it both enforced and policed the differences between the whites and the non-whites, but at the same time focused fetishistically upon the product of the contacts between them."[18] In Du Bois's visual archive, photographs of white-looking African Americans create a space "for an exploration and expression of what was increasingly socially proscribed"[19] at the turn of the century, namely social and sexual contact between the races, and also for an examination of a white patriarchy's brutal practices of consolidation through the racialized and gendered crime of rape.

Within this cultural context of repressed desire and racialized sexual violence, Du Bois's photographs of white-looking African American women take on especially resonant meaning. White supremacists posed the light-skinned woman of color as both the object and instigator of interracial mixing, as both the sign and cause of racial degeneration. Discourses imagining the lusts of women of color were long-evoked in efforts to legitimize institutionalized rape in slavery, and to perpetuate rape and concubinage after slavery. The pale African American woman was the enticing object of long-standing white supremacist discourses that sought to justify the rape of women of color by blaming it on the seductive wiles of the beautiful "quadroon" or "octoroon."

In *Types of American Negroes, Georgia, U.S.A.*, Du Bois reclaims the image of the pale African American woman so highly fetishized in racial hierarchies, re-presenting her as a woman of grace, elegance, and refinement. He poses the white-looking African American woman as the object of a black masculine gaze, and then secures her within the structure of an African American patriarchy as future wife and mother. His photographs celebrate her innocence and purity, to then contain and circumscribe her sexuality by laying out the future roles she is to assume within a patriarchal African American family. The thin, pale woman with brown wavy hair who meets the viewer's gaze directly in Du Bois's albums is the epitome of elegance and innocence.

Her high-necked, white, ruffled dress with its delicate pattern and lacy trim is an emblem of feminine grace and purity, and the whiteness

**FIGURE 11.5** *W. E. B. Du Bois*, Types of American Negroes, Georgia, U.S.A. *(1900), volume 1, no. 63. Reproduced from the Daniel Murray Collection, Library of Congress, Washington, D.C.*

of her dress underscores the whiteness of her complexion. She stands straight to accept the gaze that is bestowed on her, and she meets and returns that gaze. Her direct look and softly hinted smile would seem to signal recognition, sympathy, and admiration for the viewer, a position inhabited, after the photographer, and before later viewers, by Du Bois himself.

In this highly controlled "interaction" between Du Bois as viewer and this young woman, frozen in time and mute, Du Bois may reformulate his decisive experience of racialized rejection through the glance of a young white girl. Du Bois refigures that earlier scene through the sympathetic gaze of this photographed subject whose position is imaginatively doubled, for she is represented as a white-looking African American woman in an album of "Negro Types." Here, then, Du Bois can transpose and reimagine his traumatic experience of fragmentation vis-à-vis a white feminine gaze, through the inviting gaze of a woman both white enough to revisit that experience in fantasy, and also African American, a potential maternal anchor for a black patriarchy. Her doubled position enables Du Bois to reinscribe the gendered scene of racialization, reclaiming the privilege of a (racialized) masculine gaze upon a white-looking woman. Her symbolic duality also allows Du Bois to "safely" enact the forbidden scene of the black man's gaze upon a white woman prohibited by the discourses and practices of lynching. Indeed, the African American man's gaze upon the white-looking African American woman challenges a white patriarchy's claims over both white and African American women. This woman's sympathetic gaze would seem to affirm both the (black, male) viewer's positive self-image and his claim to look; her gaze would seem to be one of recognition and acceptance. But in order to function as suturing salve in this racialized scene of masculine reconstitution, she must be fixed—in the photograph, in Du Bois's gaze, in her own gaze upon him, and finally, as we shall see, within the bounds of an African American patriarchy.

## Envisioning an African American Patriarchy

In the family portraits included in the Georgia Negro albums, Du Bois figures patriarchal authority as the sign of class consolidation.

A series of group portraits of families posed in front of homes announces a prosperous middle class founded along patriarchal lines. In these images, wives-as-mothers and children are posed as the possessions of African American men, the products of an African American patriarchy. Black masculinity is supported and defined by the solidity of large homes and a web of gendered family relations. An African American patriarchy is literally envisioned in these photographs, its gender dynamics focused through the lens of a reconfigured black masculine gaze.[20]

In one photograph, in a rather distant view (as if taken from across the street), a man and his family are arranged carefully in the garden approaching the house. The image is constructed to emphasize the expanse of property; indeed, the family is dwarfed by the size of the house and the breadth of the garden. Individual faces are just barely discernible, and they do not seem to be the point of this photograph. And yet the people are particularly placed in this image; the photograph clearly has been orchestrated to emphasize their positions, if not their individuality. A man, in suit and hat, poses at the bottom of the steps that lead up to the garden.

In order to "enter" this space, one must move past him, up the wooden stairs, to a garden walkway that leads past immaculately groomed children, to the steps of the house where three women, one sitting, two standing, introduce the viewer to the house proper. The women are posed on the steps of the house, they are associated with the interior space that beckons from the large, shaded entry made by the frame of the patio. The man has one foot rooted in the street; he is, symbolically, the liaison between public and private realms. He is separated from his family by the sharp rise of the wooden stairs and the brick wall which divides his garden, house, and family from the street. This vertical rise behind him visually separates the image into two planes: the framed and enclosed portion of the photograph, including the family, the garden, and the house, provides a kind of backdrop to the man in the foreground. The image appears to be primarily about his identity as a middle-class man, a father and husband; the "backdrop" situates him and lends him his individual importance— the family and house provide the scale by which the viewer is meant to measure his worth as a middle-class man and a "metonymic racial representative."[21]

**Figure 11.6** *W. E. B. Du Bois,* Negro Life in Georgia, U.S.A. *(1900), no. 354. Reproduced from the Daniel Murray Collection, Library of Congress, Washington, D.C.*

In another family portrait of a lawyer's home in Atlanta (an image I have identified as a photograph by Thomas E. Askew), the camera has been placed much closer to its subjects; it is perched in the very garden itself.[22] This image, included in *Negro Life in Georgia, U.S.A.* in 1900, and again in *The Negro American Family* in 1908, is dominated by the house, which looms up large, spilling over the edges of the photographic frame. The family, in turn, is circumscribed by the steps that lead up to the patio, by a simple, carved wooden railing that encloses the porch, and by the decorative corners of Victorian beams that recall the scalloped edges of picture frames. The three women who stand, and the single woman who sits, child in her lap, are rigidly posed in this image. They adopt the far-off looks of nobility and striving, gazing out in different directions.

Their stiffness belies their performance for the camera; it is only the small children seated on the steps who appear actively engaged in the process. Two of these children look back at the camera with some uncertainty, but the child in the middle strains and stretches her neck

FIGURE 11.7 *The home of an African American lawyer, Atlanta, Georgia. Photograph by Thomas E. Askew. From W. E. B. Du Bois,* Negro Life in Georgia, U.S.A. *(1900), no. 352. Reproduced from the Daniel Murray Collection, Library of Congress, Washington, D.C.*

to look up and over at something else, perhaps a neighbor made curious by the camera and commotion. The single adult male represented in this photograph is positioned just slightly behind the women and children he appears to preside over. He stands with hand on hip, and another propped against the back of the large chair in which sit his wife (presumably) and child. His posture is both relaxed and commanding, and he is distinguished from the rest of the group by the relative ease of his pose (the others stand stiffly with hands at sides). And yet his position is also carefully crafted to reveal the wedding band on his left finger, to signal his status as husband and father. The angle of his gaze, and the foregrounding of his face against shadow, highlight and sharply define his cheekbones, chin and nose, creating an individual portrait within the group photograph. Women and children sit beneath him, some literally at his feet. It is almost as if they are seated around a hearth, as if an intimate, interior family scene has been turned momentarily inside out, and then literally taken outside, for the gaze of the viewer.

With his photographs of well-to-do African American patriarchs, Du Bois challenges the image of the African American man posed in the white supremacist rhetoric surrounding and enabling lynching. Du Bois's men are emblems of masculine respectability and familial responsibility. However, Du Bois's representational strategies concerning African American women within an African American patriarchy remain complicated and problematic, particularly when read through his sociological texts of the turn of the century. While he celebrates the "purity" of African American women, protected by upstanding African American men, he does so only after condemning their potential sexual "looseness," which he argues must be harnessed and disciplined to sexual restraint and gendered submission. Du Bois first condemns the African American woman's sexuality to then "reform" her, not as a victim of white (or black) male aggression, but as a victim of her own sexual promiscuity. In Du Bois's vision, the African American patriarch, by virtue of his sexual discipline, will "save" the sexually unbridled African American woman from herself. Du Bois's gendered challenge to the tenets of white supremacism thus leaves in place one of the mainstays of its founding sexual mythologies.

For Du Bois, racialized sexual deviance must be rooted out by controlling and containing African American women's sexual desires within the patriarchal African American family. Du Bois thus makes a case for "disciplining" African Americans and the African American bodies he sexualizes in a highly gendered manner. Indirectly countering white representations of the African American man as sexually rampant in the discourses of lynching, Du Bois forwards an image of patriarchal restraint, shifting the locus of sexual aggression onto African American women. Further, Du Bois is careful to consign sexual "aberrations" to the lower classes, dividing and distinguishing them from his elite, Talented Tenth, the mold and model of gendered sexual respectability to which he would make others conform. As white Americans constructed images of African American sexual deviance to reinforce their claims to cultural privilege, Du Bois also distinguished his vision of an African American elite from a sexually suspect African American underclass.

Du Bois adheres to antebellum models of gender protocol as the signs of moral strength and the measures of "civilized" middle-class "evolution" in *The Philadelphia Negro* (1899), as well as *The Negro American Family* (1908), a text that is illustrated with some of the images from the Georgia Negro albums, as noted above. In the earlier sociological study, he divides the population of Philadelphia's Seventh Ward into four "grades": (1) "The 'Middle Classes' and those above," which includes "families of undoubted respectability" that adhere to patriarchal models of domesticity and housewifery; (2) "The Working People—Fair to Comfortable," consisting of "respectable" "laborers"; (3) "The Poor," but "honest"; and (4) "Vicious and Criminal Classes," including "the lowest class of criminals, prostitutes and loafers; the 'submerged tenth.'"[23] Du Bois's scale of social respectability is measured by the African American patriarch's ability to keep his wife at home, devoted to the work of motherhood and middle-class housewifery in *The Philadelphia Negro*, and such gender roles become markers of "civilization" in *The Negro American Family*. Condemning illegitimacy in particular, Du Bois proclaims: "Without doubt the point where the Negro American is furthest behind modern civilization is in his sexual mores."[24] For Du Bois, the African American woman registers her family's moral status, marking its place in the scale of civilization: In her most elevated role she is a housewife supported by her husband; from there she sinks to the role of co-worker who must help to support the family financially; and finally, in her most degraded role as prostitute, her (sexual) work situates her outside the bounds of patriarchal familial respectability altogether.

In Du Bois's juxtaposition of a "talented" tenth to a "submerged" tenth, he distinguishes members of the middle and upper classes, individuals of "undoubted respectability," from sexual deviants, such as prostitutes. Du Bois appears to adopt a strategy parallel to the racist ones he would critique, dismissing a portion of the population as inherently inferior, as debased beyond the reach of uplift. In the words of Mia Bay, Du Bois is "very much given to moralizing about lower-class manners and behavior," and "inclined to blame at least some area's problems on the failings of its 'bottom class' denizens."[25] Du Bois constructs a class hierarchy within a diverse racial group, deflecting the biological arguments of race scientists onto a portion of the African American population he is content to "submerge" under the expectations he rejects for himself and others of an elite class. Du Bois's vision of a gendered Talented Tenth would appear to rely upon his construction of a sexualized "submerged tenth."[26]

Du Bois's "lowest class" is the site of sexual "irregularity" from which he distances an African American elite. In *The Negro American Family* he celebrates "the great and most patent fact [of] differentiation: the emergence from the mass, of successive classes with higher and higher sexual morals."[27] As Kevin Gaines has argued, Du Bois depicts a black urban working class as sexually promiscuous, and criminally inclined, in order to shore up the cultural distinction of a Northern black bourgeoisie. In doing so, he falls in line with racial "uplift" rhetoric, through which, Gaines suggests, the black middle classes represented themselves as an intellectual, moral and cultural elite by evoking standards of Victorian sexual morality rooted in a patriarchal gender paradigm. In the final footnote to a chapter devoted to the "conjugal condition" in *The Philadelphia Negro*, Du Bois condemns what he deems the lax sexual morals of the African American working classes: "Sexual looseness is to-day the prevailing sin of the mass of the Negro population."[28] He ameliorates that statement with caveats pointing to the historical dissolution of and disregard for African American marriage bonds and family connections during slavery, and by noting that white men continue to disrespect and dishonor African American womanhood. And yet, throughout this chapter he is exceptionally nervous about the numbers of men and women living together outside of wedlock in Philadelphia's Seventh Ward. Du Bois is concerned particularly about "the unchastity of a large number of women"—"unmarried mothers"—and suggests that "lax moral habits" signal grave "moral disorder."[29]

"Unmarried women," and even women per se— that "large excess of young women"[30] —need to be woven into the fold of an economically strong patriarchy in Du Bois's vision of social reform.[31] Addressing the (sexual) "fall" of "the poorly trained colored girl" in *The Philadelphia Negro*, Du Bois states, "Nothing but strict home life can avail in such cases."[32] For Du Bois, a middle-class, gendered family structure is the sign and salvation of good (gender) character: "The mass of the Negro people must be taught sacredly to guard the home, to make it the centre of social life and moral guardianship. This it is largely among the best class of Negroes, but it might be made even more conspicuously so than it is."[33] Indeed, the patriarchal family, for Du Bois, is the very sign of civilization itself. Arguing that "sexual irregularity" "belongs to the undifferentiated mass: some of them decent people, but behind civilization by training and instinct," he proclaims: "Above these and out of these, are continually rising, however, classes who must not be confounded with them. Of the raising of the sex mores of the Negro by these classes the fact is clear and unequivocal: they have raised them and are raising them. There is more female purity, more male continence, and a healthier home life today than ever before among Negroes in America."[34]

Du Bois holds up his patriarchy of "undoubted respectability" as a disciplining and civilizing force to curb the sexual excess of the working classes. He seeks to bind African American women especially to the patriarchal structures of middle-class family norms that reproduce direct lines of inheritance. In contrast to the image of the sexually aggressive black man construed in lynching discourses, Du Bois intimates that uncontrolled sexuality is not a characteristic of African American men, but a failing of African American women. Indeed, in *The Philadelphia Negro*, Du Bois suggests that it is only the sober African American man, the middle-class patriarch, who, as father and husband, can rein in the wiles of African American women.

The racialized and gendered vision of African American "uplift" that Du Bois articulates in his early twentieth-century sociological texts is subtly inscribed in his 1900 Georgia Negro photographs. As we have seen, some of the images represent African American homes and families, focusing on the exterior signs of a middle-class patriarchy; other images represent the interior spaces of domesticity most often associated with middle-class women. Many of these latter photographs show parlor rooms devoid of the individuals who enjoy the material wealth on display, but one image depicts a man and a young woman seated at a piano within an elegant, retouched room. The young woman, with long wavy hair flowing down her back, places ivory fingers upon ivory keys; she is slightly hunched forward, staring intently at the music before her eyes. A man with a wonderful mustache sits just behind her, his eyes also focused on her practice.

Placed on top of the piano that looms in front of the girl are two photographs in ornate frames, two vases, and a small statuette of a

FIGURE 11.8 *W. E. B. Du Bois*, Negro Life in Georgia, U.S.A. *(1900), no. 363. Reproduced from the Daniel Murray Collection, Library of Congress, Washington, D.C.*

toga-clad figure that resembles popular representations of Liberty, Justice, or Virtue. The photographs that peer down at the young woman from either side of the piano are hard to make out, but one appears to be an image of an infant, and the other a photograph of a young girl, with shoulder-length hair cascading down the sides of her face. Perhaps these are photographs of the young woman herself, images that mark various stages in her growth and maturity. The two images frame the girl at the piano, and they also frame the small statuette, which stands in the middle, directly over the young woman, as symbol of an ideal, an abstract notion of virtue or justice embodied in an ivory white figure with long flowing hair. The small statuette functions, perhaps, as the mark toward which this young African American woman is meant to strive, as a cornerstone in the history of her development toward womanhood.

The young woman's long flowing hair, her white fingers on ivory keys, the piano itself, and the gaze of the man seated just behind her, all work to delineate the complicated nexus of racialized gender relations that defines Du Bois's vision of an elite African American patriarchy. The young, light-skinned woman of color represents the fetish of white supremacist desire, and perhaps the evidence of white sexual aggression, but here she is woven into the protective restraint of an African American patriarchy as the object of a black masculine gaze. The piano represents wealth and cultural refinement, and the young woman's practice suggests that she is being trained for a life of leisure, a life of "undoubted respectability" as a housewife. As the young woman pursues her artistic training, her progress is measured by the man who watches from just behind her, the man whose gaze, perhaps, figures Du Bois's own. For as Du Bois challenges the white feminine gaze so formative in disrupting his gendered self-vision, and reconstitutes a black masculine gaze, he does so by fixing that gaze upon African American women. Pretending to discipline the sexualized black female phantom of white supremacist discourses, Du Bois founds an African American patriarchy by making African American women the objects of his surveillance. He reasserts the gender privilege of a racialized masculine gaze by directing his attention toward African American women. And often, as we have seen, the African American women upon whom Du Bois's photographs focus are pale enough to enable an imaginative slippage whereby they may stand in for white women, those objects most violently forbidden to a black masculine gaze. In this way the photographs may assert a double challenge to the prerogatives of a white patriarchy, suggesting black masculine claims over white and African American women. The limitations of such representative strategies for African American women are, of course, salient. While the paleness of the women caught in Du Bois's gaze may enable him to revisit and conquer the scene of his racialization in a "safe" realm of fantasy, his seeming preference for pale women also threatens to subsume African American women under the sign of white womanhood. And as we have seen, regardless of their complexions, Du Bois's African American women are honored foremost as reformed subjects of patriarchal discipline, as sexually errant beings reined in by patriarchal control. Once again, as the eyes of the young woman at the piano are trained on the music she will master as the sign of an elite femininity, her progress is monitored by an African American man who watches her from behind; her actions are circumscribed by a black masculine gaze. Crystallizing the gender dynamics that inform Du Bois's Georgia Negro photographs, the image suggests that an African American patriarchy establishes itself by keeping African American women firmly fixed within the sights of its reconfigured black masculine gaze.

## Notes

This essay is a distillation of an extended argument I make in *Photography on the Color Line: W. E. B. Du Bois, Race, and Visual Culture* (Durham: Duke University Press, 2004). I am grateful for permission to rework portions of my argument here. I would also like to thank Susan Gillman, Alys Weinbaum, and Ralph Rodriguez for their help in fine-tuning this essay, and Joe Masco for his substantive engagement with this work over many years.

1. W. E. B. Du Bois, *The Souls of Black Folk,* intro. John Edgar Wideman, The Library of America Edition (New York: Vintage Books, 1990), 7–8.

2. Hazel V. Carby, *Race Men* (Cambridge, Mass.: Harvard University Press, 1998), 32–33. Reprinted in this volume.

3. In Du Bois's scene of gendered racial trauma, part of the shock for the young Du Bois is in recognizing, through the rejection of the white girl (racially empowered in relation to him, despite her gendered position), the disavowal of his gender privilege as a *black* man in a white patriarchal world. In her analysis of gender in the work

of Frantz Fanon, Gwen Bergner similarly suggests that Fanon experiences his racial objectification under a white supremacist gaze as particularly destructive because such objectification places him "in the 'feminine' position." Gwen Bergner, "Who Is That Masked Woman? or, The Role of Gender in Fanon's *Black Skin, White Masks*," *PMLA* 110, no. 1 (January 1995): 75–88, 80. Du Bois's vision of gendered racialization would also seem to accord with the racialized gender dynamics assessed by Jean Walton in her examination of the racial fantasies of white women. Discussing the fantasies of the white female patient who is the focal point of Joan Riviere's influential essay "Womanliness as a Masquerade" (1929), Walton asserts: "As a white woman, her appearing to have the phallus is culturally permitted when it is a question of her relation to a black man." In critiquing Riviere, and those white feminists influenced by her work, for failing to recognize the racial specter of the black man in Riviere's patient's fantasy, Walton remains committed to discerning the (racialized) gender identifications of the white woman. In my discussion of Du Bois, conversely, I am interested in how the specter of the white woman informs the (gendered) racial identification of the African American man. Jean Walton, chapter one, "Masquerade and Reparation: (White) Womanliness in Riviere and Klein," in *Fair Sex, Savage Dreams: Race, Psychoanalysis, Sexual Difference* (Durham: Duke University Press, 2001), 17–40, 22.

4. W. E. B. Du Bois, *The Souls of Black Folk*, 8. David Marriott and Maurice O. Wallace also offer important examinations of black masculinity and visual culture. David Marriott, *On Black Men* (New York: Columbia University Press, 2000). Maurice O. Wallace, *Constructing the Black Masculine: Identity and Ideality in African American Men's Literature and Culture, 1775–1995* (Durham: Duke University Press, 2002).

5. Claudia Tate similarly suggests that this event is traumatic for Du Bois because it "disrupts his admirable self-image." *Psychoanalysis and Black Novels: Desire and the Protocols of Race* (New York: Oxford University Press, 1998), 185.

6. Vron Ware, *Beyond the Pale: White Women, Racism, and History* (London: Verso, 1992), 182. See also bell hooks, "The Oppositional Gaze: Black Female Spectators," in *Black Looks: Race and Representation* (Boston: South End Press, 1992), 115–31, and Jane M. Gaines, "White Privilege and Looking Relations: Race and Gender in Feminist Film Theory," *Screen* 29, no. 4 (Autumn 1988): 12–27.

7 Wells came to this conclusion after three of her friends were lynched for the "crime" of operating a successful grocery store that undermined the business of a white-owned shop in the same neighborhood. Ida B. Wells's antilynching work is documented in *Crusade for Justice, A Red Record*, and *Southern Horrors*. Ida B. Wells, *Crusade for Justice: The Autobiography of Ida B. Wells*, ed. Alfreda M. Duster (Chicago: University of Chicago Press, 1970), *A Red Record* (1895) and *Southern Horrors: Lynch Law in All Its Phases* (1892), in *Selected Works of Ida B. Wells-Barnett*, intro. Trudier Harris (New York: Oxford University Press, 1991), 138–252, 14–45. Vron Ware, Hazel Carby, and Paula Giddings follow Ida B. Wells in assessing lynching as a form of economic terrorism. Vron Ware, *Beyond the Pale*, 167–224, 179; Paula Giddings, *When and Where I Enter: The Impact of Black Women on Race and Sex in America* (New York: Morrow, 1984), 26; Hazel V. Carby, *Reconstructing Womanhood: The Emergence of the Afro-American Woman Novelist* (New York: Oxford University Press, 1987), 115, and "'On the Threshold of Woman's Era': Lynching, Empire, and Sexuality in Black Feminist Theory," in *"Race," Writing, and Difference*, ed. Henry

Louis Gates, Jr. (Chicago: University of Chicago Press, 1986), 301–16. For additional analyses of Ida B. Wells's radical work, see Gail Bederman, "'Civilization,' the Decline of Middle-Class Manliness, and Ida B. Wells's Antilynching Campaign (1892–1894)," *Radical History Review* 52 (1992): 5–30, and Sandra Gunning, *Race, Rape, and Lynching: The Red Record of American Literature, 1890–1912* (New York: Oxford University Press, 1996).

8. While Du Bois did not make these photographs himself, it is his gaze that is forwarded in their organization and presentation, for he is the attributed "author" of the photograph albums he compiled, and it was Du Bois who was awarded a gold medal for this work by Paris Exposition judges.

9. See Shawn Michelle Smith, *Photography on the Color Line: W. E. B. Du Bois, Race, and Visual Culture* (Durham: Duke University Press, 2004). I first began to articulate this argument in chapter six, "Photographing the 'American Negro': Nation, Race, and Photography at the Paris Exposition of 1900," in *American Archives: Gender, Race, and Class in Visual Culture* (Princeton: Princeton University Press, 1999), 157–86.

10. W. E. B. Du Bois, "The Conservation of Races," *A W. E. B. Du Bois Reader,* ed. Andrew G. Paschal, intro. Arna Bontemps (New York: Macmillan, 1971), 19–31.

11. Susan Gubar has argued that "the secret the biracial infant holds" is "the lie commingled bloodlines put to the historical accounts of a segregated culture." Susan Gubar, "What Will the Mixed Child Deliver? Conceiving Color Without Race," in *Racechanges: White Skin, Black Face in American Culture* (New York: Oxford University Press, 1997), 203–39, 207.

12. W. E. B. Du Bois, *Dusk of Dawn: An Essay Toward an Autobiography of a Race Concept,* in *W. E. B. Du Bois: Writings,* ed. Nathan Huggins, Library of American College Edition (New York: Literary Classics of the United States, 1986), 549–802, 627. According to Arnold Rampersad, in discussing his own racial identity and ancestry, Du Bois "would not accept the white racist convention that denied the truth of his mixed genealogy." Arnold Rampersad, *The Art and Imagination of W. E. B. Du Bois* (New York: Schocken, 1990), 17.

13. Ibid., 37. Du Bois is quoting Jas Bryce, "The relations of the advanced and backward races of mankind" (Oxford, 1892).

14. According to Susan Gillman, as late as 1970 in Louisiana, "the legal fraction defining blackness was still one thirty-second 'Negro blood.'" Susan Gillman, *Dark Twins: Imposture and Identity in Mark Twain's America* (Chicago and London: The University of Chicago Press, 1898), 81–86. As Barbara J. Fields has argued, "The very diversity and arbitrariness of the physical rules governing racial classification prove that the physical emblems which symbolize race are not the foundation upon which race arises as a category of social thought." Barbara J. Fields, "Ideology and Race in American History," in *Region, Race, and Reconstruction,* ed. J. Morgan Kousser and James M. McPherson (New York: Oxford University Press, 1982), 143–77, 151.

15. Mary Ann Doane, "Dark Continents: Epistemologies of Racial and Sexual Difference in Psychoanalysis and the Cinema," in *Femmes Fatales: Feminism, Film Theory, Psychoanalysis* (New York: Routledge, 1991), 209–48, 235.

16. Ibid., 234.

17. In her work on passing, Samira Kawash describes "the color line" as "a social system of classification and identification that insisted on absolute difference between white and black, even as it warily acknowledged the existence of certain

bodies that seemed to violate the very possibility of distinction." Samira Kawash, *Dislocating the Color Line: Identity, Hybridity, and Singularity in African-American Narrative* (Stanford: Stanford University Press, 1997), 124. In her analysis of the photographs in *The Health and Physique of the Negro American*, Evelynn Hammonds similarly argues: "Along with sociological data Du Bois used the then new technology, photography, to make visible the evidence of race mixing that white society denied. Du Bois' photographic evidence, rendered in the style of turn-of-the-century ethnographic studies of race, was deployed to show that race mixing was a fact of American life and that the dependence upon visual evidence to determine who was 'black' or 'white' was specious at best." Evelynn M. Hammonds, "New Technologies of Race," in *Processed Lives: Gender and Technology in Everyday Life*, ed. Jennifer Terry and Melodie Calvert (New York: Routledge, 1997), 107–21, 110. W. E. B. Du Bois, ed., *The Health and Physique of the Negro American*, Atlanta University Publication Number 11 (Atlanta: Atlanta University Press, 1906).

18. Robert J. C. Young, *Colonial Desire: Hybridity in Theory, Culture and Race* (New York: Routledge, 1995), 180–81.

19. Hazel V. Carby, *Reconstructing Womanhood*, 89.

20. Du Bois's photographs work toward reinscribing what Kaja Silverman has called a cultural "screen," and what Maurice O. Wallace has called "spectragraphia," "a chronic syndrome of inscripted misrepresentation." Kaja Silverman, *The Threshold of the Visible World* (New York: Routledge, 1996). Maurice O. Wallace, *Constructing the Black Masculine*, 30–31.

21. In her analysis of Du Bois's use of photographs in the *Crisis*, Daylanne English suggests that the middle-class African American man functioned for Du Bois as "visual confirmation" of racial uplift. Daylanne English, "W. E. B. Du Bois's Family *Crisis*," *American Literature* 72, no. 2 (June 2000): 291–319, 303–4, and 297, 308.

22. The photograph can be identified by comparing it to a slightly different view of the family and home in *The Negro American Family* (1908), ed. W. E. Burghardt Du Bois, reprint (New York: Negro Universities Press, 1969). Here the photograph is identified as "No. 37—Residence of a Negro lawyer, Atlanta (photo by Askew)," 80. The photograph of a house identified as "No. 36—Residence of a Negro minister, Decatur (photo. by Askew)" in *The Negro American Family*, 80, is also included in Du Bois's *Negro Life in Georgia, U.S.A.* As several other photographs in Du Bois's 1900 collection closely resemble these two images, I think it is quite likely that Askew made many of the photographs of well-to-do homes and family portraits included in the 1900 albums.

23. W. E. B. Du Bois, *The Philadelphia Negro: A Social Study* (1899), intro. Elijah Anderson, Centennial Edition (Philadelphia: University of Pennsylvania Press, 1996), 310–11.

24. W. E. Burghardt Du Bois, ed., *The Negro American Family*, 37. Du Bois proclaims: "The truth remains: sexual immorality is probably the greatest single plague spot among Negro Americans, and its greatest cause is slavery and the present utter disregard of a black woman's virtue and self-respect, both in law court and custom in the South." *The Negro American Family*, 41.

25. Mia Bay, " 'The World Was Thinking Wrong About Race': *The Philadelphia Negro* and Nineteenth-Century Science," in *W. E. B. Du Bois, Race, and the City: The Philadelphia Negro and Its Legacy*, ed. Michael B. Katz and Thomas J. Sugrue (Philadelphia: University of Pennsylvania Press, 1998), 41–59, 52.

26. As Mia Bay has suggested of *The Philadelphia Negro*, "Some of the book's most striking internal contradictions arise from its author's unsuccessful struggle to blend his study's empirical results with his own Victorian outlook and elitism." Mia Bay, "'The World Was Thinking Wrong About Race,'" 53.

27. W. E. Burghardt Du Bois, ed., *The Negro American Family*, 37.

28. W. E. B. Du Bois, *The Philadelphia Negro*, 72 note 5.

29. Ibid., 67–71, 72 note 5.

30. Ibid., 70. In *The Negro American Family*, Du Bois quotes Kelly Miller's discussion of the disproportionate number of African American women to men in the cities as a factor leading to sexual immorality. W. E. Burghardt Du Bois, ed., *The Negro American Family*, 36–37.

31. As Kevin Gaines has said of Du Bois's early work, his image of a black middle class is fundamentally patriarchal— "Patriarchal authority remained the crucial criterion of black bourgeois stability." Kevin K. Gaines, *Uplifting the Race: Black Leadership, Politics, and Culture in the Twentieth Century* (Chapel Hill: University of North Carolina Press, 1996), 169.

32. W. E. B. Du Bois, *The Philadelphia Negro*, 72 note 5.

33. Ibid., 195–96.

34. W. E. Burghardt Du Bois, *The Negro American Family*, 38.

# 12

## Pageantry, Maternity, and World History

■ *Susan Gillman*

The habit of self-quotation that is central to W. E. B. Du Bois's writing poses a special challenge to the historically inclined reader attentive to issues of gender and sexuality. It was common for Du Bois to incorporate into his autobiographies passages from his own speeches, or from essays and other writing he'd done for various magazines and journals, and to re-cite, in the later autobiographies, his own earlier recollections. For instance, everyone associates Du Bois with the famous color line aphorism, "the problem of the twentieth century is the problem of the color-line," but few question either the fact or the effect of the reiteration.[1] Similarly, who could forget the story of his origins ("by a golden river and in the shadow of two great hills") in Great Barrington—especially "the case of exchanging visiting cards" from his childhood, the moment of dawning realization of his own difference, "of being a problem," when one girl refused his card—but who accounts for the number of versions in which he tells it? As all the critical citations to the account in *Souls* attest, the gendered piece is most fully present in the initial version, but after that, it falls away, separated off from the main story as though an isolated, or isolable, element. Du Bois himself thus raises the question of what happens when "woman" and "color" "combine into one"—or not. (For more on the issue of "combine," see the Introduction to this volume.)

In this essay I will address the questions posed by Du Bois's use of self-citation by turning to *Darkwater,* a text that, along with *Dark Princess,* is fast becoming essential to the emerging feminist canon of Du Bois's work. There, concentrated in the well-known, frequently excerpted chapter in which he documents and celebrates historical black womanhood, "The Damnation of Women," and radiating out through the rest of the text, we find Du Bois, again, quoting himself, only in this case, it is some of his very least-known work, his experiments with the genre of the historical pageant that are cited. So this is a unique kind of citation, an unrecognized adaptation. The parade of black women at the structural heart of "The Damnation of Women," starting with the memory of "four women of my boyhood" and ending with a series of mythical and actual female figures representing the history of the black diaspora, is an adaptation, largely unrecognized either by the text or its readers, of Du Bois's pageant, *The Star of Ethiopia,* staged in the years immediately preceding the publication of Du Bois's second autobiography.

This essay will focus on the relation of that unrecognized matrix of women and pageantry, which is invoked in *Darkwater* through Du Bois's self-citation, to his longstanding interest in world race-history. We shall see that as Du Bois cites and adapts his own texts, and the historical contexts in which they are produced, he unveils the gendered substratum of his racial thinking and what he calls "racial feeling." Relocated within the maternal lineage of *Darkwater's* "Damnation," *The Star of Ethiopia,* which nominally dramatizes the monumental gifts to civilization of great race-men, unveils an unrecognized, gendered history of the color line, a transformed world history, structured as a maternal genealogy, and constructed within and through a meditation on black womanhood.

It would be difficult to arrive at an understanding of how gender underwrites Du Bois's racial–historical thinking without reading "The Damnation of Women," not simply as one of the few essays that is broadly about gender, but specifically as a feminist adaptation of the historical pageantry of *The Star of Ethiopia.* One difficulty, however, with the practice of adaptation through self-citation is that Du Bois doesn't always, or equally, acknowledge his sources. It is well known that Du Bois used, without attribution, the words of Anna Julia Cooper as a touchstone in "The Damnation of Women." Cooper's words are embedded within Du Bois's, largely in the form of quotations of the modern women speaking for "the world of today" (569). "As one of our women writes," writes Du Bois, "Only the black woman can say 'when and I where I enter, in the quiet, undisputed dignity of my woman-hood, . . . then and there the whole Negro race enters with me'" (569–70). This transparent ventriloquism works simultaneously to acknowledge and deny the provenance of the citation and the debt of the author. Du Bois, Joy James notes, advocated women's rights but "veiled" the achievements of individual women such as Cooper.[2] In so doing, Du Bois navigates between the particular and the universal in summoning through "one of our women" the collective voice of "the whole Negro race." The "one" and the possessive "our" of Du Bois's own words are, perhaps, even more problematic than the "I" and "the whole" of the words he quotes but does not attribute.

As if this weren't enough to produce the paradoxes of *Darkwater*'s "profeminist ideology," Du Bois also fails to acknowledge himself, the uses of his own pageantry, in the provenance of his text's mother-centered vision. Yet these are not quite parallel failures, for he is not only electing not to acknowledge himself, *per se*, but also to obscure the entire cultural context of pageantry. Just as with the notoriously long shadow cast by the unnamed Anna Julia Cooper, however, all of Du Bois's unrecognized adaptations draw attention to the very texts and contexts they allude to only imperfectly. And, in that regard, the historical context of pageantry itself raises one more, revealing diffi-culty. Although a "pageant woman," representing the "idealized Spirit of the Community," typically presided over many historical pageants of the period, the category of gender as an analytic is generally omit-ted in the manifestoes and histories of pageantry. Instead, dramatists then and historians now often simply celebrate the role of women, along with other ordinary Americans, as actors in and producers of the pageants.[3] As a result, in working though the pageant material, it is necessary to take at face value its democratic *donnée* and the cul-tural work accomplished by foregrounding the role of women (along with that of immigrants and various U.S. minorities), but minimizing their specificity. So while I outline the broad, seemingly ungendered context of pageantry, this essay will likewise appear to have forgotten the issue of gender that, as we'll see, is central to, yet submerged in, the feminist world race-history of *Darkwater.*

## The Culture of Pageantry

*Darkwater*'s meditation on woman and color is recontextualized when it is located in the cultural constellation of political and historical pageantry, of national and internationalist race history that emerges through the ambivalent aegis of the text itself. Du Bois's penchant for citation, recognized and unrecognized, produces a palimpsest of adaptations, also recognized and unrecognized, of contemporary texts and contexts. One of the few literary forms that is not generally associated with the polymath Du Bois—despite the fact that the W. E. B. Du Bois Papers at the University of Massachusetts, Amherst includes a whole archive of pageants—the pageant provided him with a popular mode of historical and political intervention that was highly visible in contemporary public culture.[4] Key to *Darkwater*'s representation of a female-centered, global black history, this contemporary cultural context is, however, not explicitly present in the text. Instead, Du Bois's pageant *The Star of Ethiopia* works its way into the autobiographical *Darkwater* in a more indirect type of self-citation. But there is no doubt that *Darkwater* as a whole is striking for what Eric Sundquist calls a "theatricality," in which a series of "pageant-like scenes" lift the veil, "like a stage curtain," to reveal the African past and diaspora history.[5] Both a dramatic form and a historical content, the pageants "cited" in the autobiography as a whole include both Du Bois's own text and the larger context of the culture of pageantry in the *Darkwater* years. This is relatively small window of time: the pageant phenomenon in which Du Bois participated had a short but intense period of flowering, concentrated during the early 1900s through the end of the political and social movements of the Progressive Era.[6]

Historians identify the short-lived popularity of this specific form with the many civic celebrations held across the United States, acting out, in "the characteristic genre of American ceremony," dramatic episodes from local and national history, and including a variety of parades ("allegorical," "street," and "ethnic") on behalf of various political causes and social movements.[7] The "American Pageantry Movement" is dated in part through the brief institutional life of the American Pageant Association (APA), a national organization founded in 1913 to oversee the development of pageants through sponsoring conferences, publications, and training programs (Prevots, 9). From 1913 to 1919, the APA issued monthly bulletins on such subjects as "Problems of Color and Costume in Pageantry," "The Spoken Word in Pageantry," "Graphic Time Analysis of Three Typical Pageants," and "Pageantry in Americanization Work" (Prevots, 206–7). In the December 1914 APA *Bulletin,* the first president of the APA (and a "pageant-master" himself), William Chauncey Langdon, issued one of the manifestoes for which the organization became best known, and later, most controversial, in the context of a suffrage pageant commissioned by the National Women's Party on Susan B. Anthony. "The Pageant is the drama of the history and life of a community," wrote Langdon, "and the development of the community is the plot" (quoted in Prevots, 96). Embracing both an aesthetics and a politics, the "pageantry craze," so "pervasive, yet so ephemeral," of the early twentieth century provided a locus for Du Bois's interest in the historical and political possibilities of pageantry to dramatize both a personal and global race-history (Glassberg, 1, 281). And, by the same token, historians and contemporary commentators characterize the political complexities of the era of pageantry in gendered and raced terms. In so doing they shed light on the limits and possibilities of Du Bois's own experimentation, his production of a woman-centered world history through adaptation of his own texts and of the larger contexts.

If we read *Darkwater's* womanist historicism back into and through the pageant-era that it evokes but does not name, then we must also do the same for the textual ensemble in which it was written. As the best-known of Du Bois's texts from this period that tell "the history of the development of the race concept," *Darkwater* points to two other, less familiar, historical works, not only *The Star of Ethiopia* but also *The Negro* (1915), a "history of the Negro peoples" tracking the diasporic histories of the Negro from ancient Africa

(Egypt and Ethiopia) to contemporary New World black cultures of the Caribbean, Latin America, and the United States.[8] Intended for a general audience, *The Negro* was part of a remarkable popularization of black history in which mass culture and consumption played a central role. Major milestones included the founding of Negro Society for Historical Research (by John E. Bruce and Arthur Schomburg) in 1911, the Association for the Study of Negro Life and History (by Carter Woodson) in 1915, and the *Journal of Negro History* (again, by Woodson) in 1916, and the inauguration of Negro History Week in 1926. Finally, *The Negro* shares with *Darkwater* a set of critical citations that outline Du Bois's lyric anticolonialism, ranging from a short poem praising Egypt, "the motherland of human culture" as "that starr'd Ethiop queen," to the Latin line (italicized in *Darkwater*, where it is attributed as a quotation from the Roman proconsul, but not in *The Negro*) that also opens and closes his famous essay "The African Roots of War" (1915), "*Semper novi quid ex Africa!*" (*The Negro*, 46, 242; *Darkwater*, 511, 520).

*The Star of Ethiopia* clearly complements and extends Du Bois's commitment in *The Negro* and *Darkwater* to producing a world race-history and making it accessible to a broad audience. According to the pageant program, *Star* portrays "the history of the Negro race and its work and sufferings and triumphs in the world" by combining "historic accuracy and symbolic truth." It was, Du Bois says, one of two projects of the 1920s (the other was the *Brownie's Book,* "a little magazine for Negro children") that he recalls with "infinite satisfaction," "most especially my single-handed production of the pageant 'The Star of Ethiopia' . . . , an attempt to put into dramatic form for the benefit of large masses of people, a history of the Negro race."[9] *The Star of Ethiopia* stages *The Negro*'s unconventional pan-racial history of the peoples on the worldwide color line as a spectacle divided into six "episodes," each featuring a parade of historical figures dramatizing a different "gift of the Negro to the world." A three-hour extravaganza, Du Bois's "pageant of Negro history," including (according to the ads in *The Crisis*) "1000 actors, 53 musical numbers, scenery and costumes," staged the history of blacks in Africa and the Americas on the steps of a papier-mâché Egyptian temple in a series of performances, starting in New York in 1913 as part of the

The Horizon Guild

in conjunction with a committee of citizens announces the presentation of

## A Pageant

illustrating the history of religious faith in the Negro race, and commemorating the 100th anniversary of the meeting of the General Conference of the African Methodist Episcopal Church, entitled

## The Star of Ethiopia

In the City of Philadelphia

## May 15, 17 and 19, 1916

One Thousand Actors——Fifty-three Musical Numbers——Scenery and Costumes

W. E. BURGHARDT DU BOIS, Master of the Pageant, 70 Fifth Avenue, New York City.

This pageant, which has already been given in New York City and Washington, D. C., will be repeated in Boston, Baltimore, and other cities South and West.

Mention THE CRISIS

FIGURE 12.1 "The Star of Ethiopia," The Crisis, *April 1915, n.p. Courtesy of The Crisis Publishing Co., Inc., the magazine of the National Association for the Advancement of Colored People.*

384

city's commemoration of the fiftieth anniversary of the Emancipation Proclamation, and then traveling to Washington, D.C. (1915), Philadelphia (1916), and Los Angeles (1925).

Du Bois wrote enthusiastically of his "signal contribution to the fine art of pageantry," stressing particularly the staggering numbers, first in the December 1915 Christmas *Crisis*, where he noted that the performance of the pageant in Washington "attracted audiences aggregating 14,000," and later, in *Dusk of Dawn*, where he quoted himself, and waxed lyrical, as well as analytical and quantitative, about the potential— dramatic, didactic, and political—of his pageant, "with masses of costumed colored folk and a dramatic theme carried out chiefly by movement, dancing, and music": "Six thousand human faces, shifting blaze of lights, shimmering streams of color . . . It was no mere picture: it was reality" (272–73).

The arts of pageantry, autobiography, and self-citation merge suggestively here, as Du Bois incorporates his 1915 review essay into the 1940 *Dusk of Dawn*. In addition to the performances themselves, then, the texts of *The Star of Ethiopia* also include a variety of related pieces published in *The Crisis*. During the same period in which pageantry was so popular, Du Bois covered *The Star of Ethiopia* and, more broadly, wrote on issues of black drama in a variety of *Crisis* columns and notices: from a full prose version, "People of Peoples and Their Gift to Men," in the November 1913 issue; to *The Star of Ethiopia*, in the December 1915 issue, featuring pageant photographs and a report on the trials and triumphs of the first performance at the Emancipation Exposition in New York; to "The Drama among the Black Folk" in the August 1916 issue, a position paper (frequently anthologized) on the social efficacy of "Negro drama." Studded throughout with passages from *The Star of Ethiopia* (another classic case of Du Boisean self-citation), the latter argues for the development of Negro drama "to teach on the one hand the colored people themselves the meaning of their history . . . , and on the other, to reveal the Negro to the white world as a human, feeling thing."[10] In this, he gives voice to his "dream" as well as his belief that "pageantry among colored people" is already a fact and can be made "a means of uplift and education and the beginning of a folk drama" (173)—ideas that clearly echo mainstream views of the wider world of pageantry, which saw itself as producing a theater "of, by and for the people." But he also sounds a tellingly skeptical note, saying that "on the other hand, the white public has shown little or no interest in the movement," and, further, that "the American Pageant Association has been silent, if not actually contemptuous" (173). This is only one of the many ways in which Du Bois, a producer and theorist of historical pageantry, adapts the cultural context while also tapping its contradictions.

Du Bois was not alone in recognizing the racial divisions that undermined the democratic aspirations of the pageant movement. He also saw that public tension was generated by extending to women and feminist issues the historical and political, as opposed to simply the aesthetic, possibilities of the pageant. Most strikingly in this regard, the December 1915 issue, titled *The Christmas Crisis: Pageant Number,* features a woodcut of a female figure holding aloft a banner emblazoned with "The Star of Ethiopia" on the cover, an image used repeatedly in announcements of the pageant, in photographs of and the article on the pageant, as well as in advertisements for Du Bois's *The Negro*.

The explicit commitment to race history is clearly the common denominator linking "The Star of Ethiopia" to *The Negro* and *Darkwater.* But more pointedly, *The Christmas Crisis* marks the middle of the decade in which Du Bois returned to his pageant and other *Crisis* texts, citing, incorporating and ultimately refashioning them into the historical consciousness, gendered female, of *Darkwater.*

To read all three as companion texts accentuates the pageantry of *The Negro,* the popular and scholarly ambitions of *Star,* and the gendered historicism of *Darkwater* that culminates in the chapter "The Damnation of Women." This textual ensemble, and its expression of an anti-imperialist internationalism, comes into view through what Alys Weinbaum and I call, in the introduction to this volume, Du Bois's "politics of juxtaposition." It is a critical practice, we note, with limits and possibilities, both of which are apparent in the examples that follow. Reflecting the combined aesthetic and political interrelations of this textual cluster, a full-page advertisement for *The Negro* that ran for several issues of *The Crisis* in 1915 calls it "the authentic romance of the black man, . . . a history of him at once scholarly and eloquent" (see Figure 12.3). At the very same time, Du Bois was not only taking his own show of black history on the road but also touting the advantages

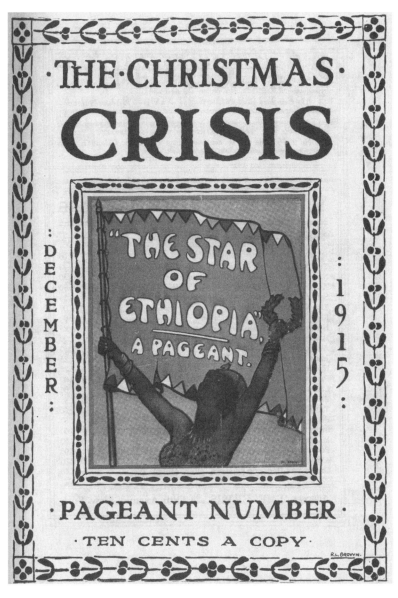

F<small>IGURE</small> 12.2  *"The Christmas* Crisis. *Pageant Number,"* The Crisis, *December 1915, front cover. Courtesy of The Crisis Publishing Co., Inc., the magazine of the National Association for the Advancement of Colored People.*

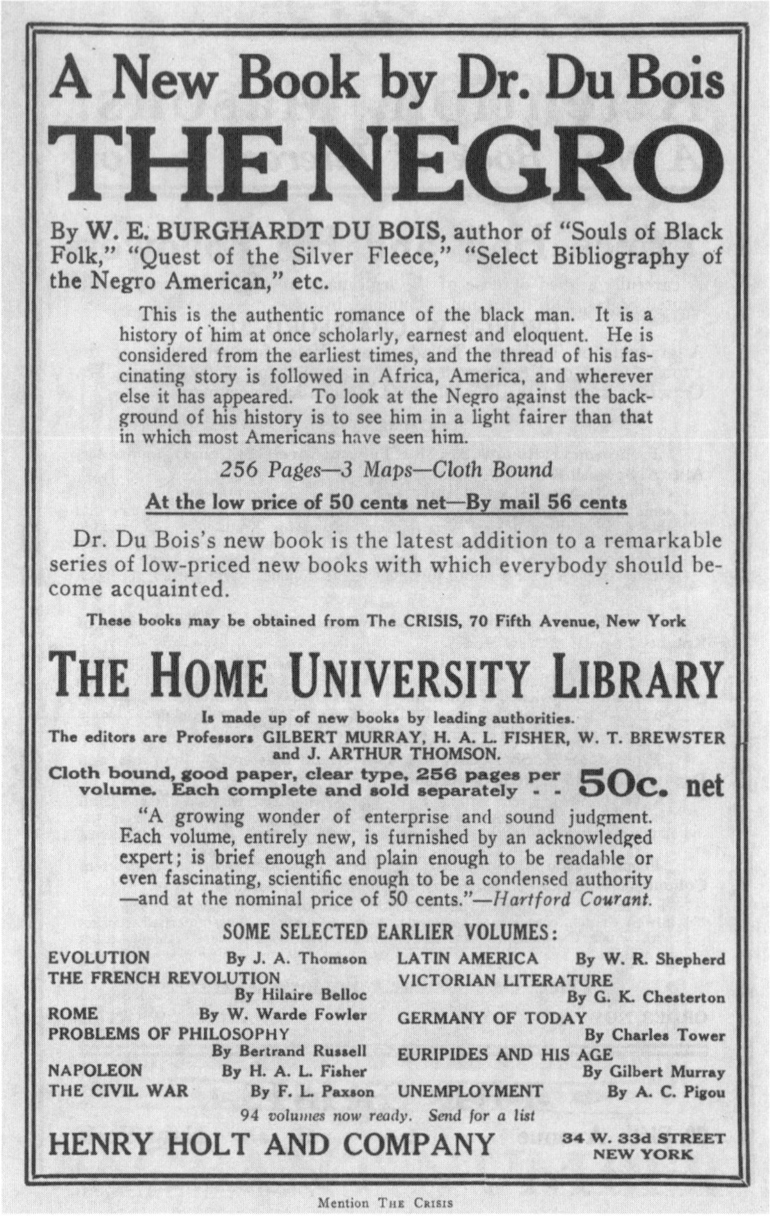

FIGURE 12.3 *"A New Book by Dr. Du Bois.* THE NEGRO," The Crisis, *November 1915, n.p. Courtesy of The Crisis Publishing Co., Inc., the magazine of the National Association for the Advancement of Colored People.*

of the dramatic arts for historical representation. "The Pageant is the thing," Du Bois exulted in *The Christmas Crisis: Pageant Number*, and concludes, "This is the gown and paraphernalia in which the message of education and reasonable race pride can deck itself."[11] In the "fabulous dramaturgy" of Du Bois's pageant, David Levering Lewis sees "the basics of an Afrocentric aesthetics and historiography—the sweeping interpretive claims [Du Bois] was just then inserting into the scholarship on which the forthcoming book *The Negro* . . . [was] . . . based."[12]

Beyond this textual cluster, there is more evidence for how pageantry combines, sometimes ambiguously, race and gender, aesthetics and politics. *Dark Princess*, Du Bois's 1928 historical romance, further develops the "historic accuracy and symbolic truth" of his pageantry with a messianic finale in the form of a pageant celebrating the birth of the "Messenger and Messiah to all the Darker Worlds."[13] Claudia Tate confirms the juxtaposition of these texts, saying that the "spectacular masque" at the novel's ending is reminiscent of the grand finale of Du Bois's pageant *The Star of Ethiopia*. For Tate, looking at the novel through the theoretical lens of psychoanalysis rather than the context of pageantry, however, the closing spectacle occludes the "polemical" message of the novel, opting for "fancy" rather than "fact": "the spectacle of pageantry seems a curious choice for a man whose prodigious scholarship was devoted to scrupulous factual detail" (see Tate's essay in this volume). Finally, the possibilities of pageantry as a historical form were not yet exhausted for Du Bois. He would later (in the year of his seventieth birthday) write yet another version of his own life in the form of a historical pageant, *A Pageant in Seven Decades, 1878–1938*. Later still, he would again yoke his dramatic muse to the narrative of his life and subtitle his final autobiography *A Soliloquy on Viewing My Life from the Last Decade of Its First Century*.[14]

Pageantry thus emerges as a key modality for Du Bois's theory and practice of history, both personal and political. But in both his own texts and the context from which he draws (and helped to shape), the gendered and sexualized elements tend to be unrecognized, or relegated to a brief mention, as an appendage to broader critical questions about national, racial, and class representations, for example. In part, we might attribute this to the aforementioned politics of juxtaposition, in which, as we've seen, woman is combined with but ultimately separated from color, creating a gap between gender and race politics that readers cannot help but see. Something of the same phenomenon, in which woman drops out of the equation, holds true for pageantry. So let me reiterate my earlier caveat that, although gender appears to fall away while I discuss the broad outlines of pageantry as cultural context, I will return (in the next section) to reinsert the gendered and sexualized elements that are so often unrecognized.

Key to the mobility of the pageant form is the way Du Bois taps into its complex context of popular history and political activism, revealing how national, ethnic, and sexual politics coalesced around the practice of pageantry in the Progressive era. This coincides with the *Darkwater* years, roughly 1910–1920, when Du Bois was working simultaneously on *The Negro* and *The Star of Ethiopia,* committed to the practice of pageantry as producer and commentator, and solidifying his position on anticolonialism. The culture of pageantry embraced a range of cultural, social, historical, and political practices, including processional, parade, and street theater, mobilized around the United States, but especially in urban settings such as New York City, in support of a variety of causes, from chronicling local community development to dramatizing national history and advocating for international social and political movements. The term "pageant" was used loosely and liberally, even "promiscuously," some feared, to include the Bryn Mawr College May Day fête, the IWW reenactment in Madison Square Garden in June 1913 of the Paterson strike, the "Pageant of Darkness and Light," produced in Chicago in 1913 to promote foreign missionary work, and the many patriotic Fourth-of-July observances.[15] What's striking about the perceived danger of watering down the aesthetic purity of the pageant is its perhaps unintended negative consequence: the sidelining both of women's causes and of the pageants that place those causes on center stage. The official history of pageantry favors brotherhood as the reigning metaphor for national solidarity.

Similarly, the parade as a display of fraternal and political solidarity took its place alongside the public oratory and pageantry of the spectacles at Madison Square Garden and other major urban venues. Historians document the broad uses during this period of pageantry, processional, parade, and spectacle, to educate or intimidate the public, and to advance a variety of political causes. Most prominent of these popular–cultural vectors is the vogue, among political groups outside the mainstream, for public performance as a mode of political intervention and popular historiography. In Greenwich Village, Socialists and others of the "Lyrical Left" staged plays and pageants to dramatize class struggle, the most famous of which was the 1913 Paterson Pageant. "Street historians" and "step-ladder radicals" invented another kind of public theater in the street corner oratory that reflected syncretic African American and Caribbean traditions.[16] Marcus Garvey's spectacular UNIA rallies adapted the "West Indian parade complex" to produce an effective, transculturated performance that represented the Caribbean immigrant ethos of the New York Garvey movement. Garvey built his movement as an amalgam of political theater, public pageantry, and race history, with ancient Egypt providing the symbolic, ceremonial icons for the Garveyite regalia.[17] Claude McKay's 1940 study *Harlem: Negro Metropolis* singles out the "gorgeous show" of the first Universal Negro Convention "staged" in 1920 by Garvey: "This was the dramatic occasion that made the City of New York fully aware of the movement in Harlem. The convention went over with theatrical éclat. . . . Harlem adores colorful, colossal demonstrations. Garvey borrowed generously from cult manifestations and fraternal rituals in painting his political mission in gay colors."[18] Du Bois reluctantly recognized Garvey as a fellow "master of propaganda," staging his own "comic opera," the parades of uniformed troops and Black Cross nurses in Harlem, and the rallies at Madison Square Garden.

Although Du Bois may be no "step-ladder radical," like Garvey (who spoke on a specially built platform—a stepladder—at "speaker's corner" at Lenox Ave. and 135th St.), or street corner historian, like John E. Bruce (a.k.a. pen name "Bruce Grit"), militant black journalist, Garveyite, and close friend of Arthur Schomburg, Du Bois, too, ventured into political theater. Du Bois's famous sense of competition with Garvey underscores the significance of pageantry, and its perhaps overcrowded uses, for political purposes at this moment. All the pageantry, parades, and mass meetings, as well as the street theater and oratory, represent the historically specific uses of spectacle in the early decades of the twentieth century to promote fraternal and race-based, national and internationalist, social and political movements of the era.

Not only do all these events and figures share what Sundquist calls a "penchant for dramatic form" (*Oxford Reader*, 304), but also they underscore the intertwined historicism, internationalism, and activism of early twentieth-century pageantry. The variety of feminist causes on display during these decades, in the popular performative modes of pageant and parade, causes associated both with political reform and reproductive rights (birth control as a major issue) and often compromised by racial and class divisions, provides another explanatory context for the aims of and the compromises in Du Bois's own feminist politics. Indeed, *Darkwater*'s feminist vision was made possible by the conjunction of these particular forces at this particular moment. Du Bois's own penchant for dramatic form, his "operatic" sense and "fabulous dramaturgy," converged with the many uses, historical, political, and cultural, of pageantry at the time.[19] He was invested in the educational possibilities of the pageant for popularizing black history, the political possibilities of increasing black solidarity, and the organizational potential to underwrite and build social movements. (He initially hoped that the staging of a pageant to commemorate the various fifty-year civil-rights anniversaries of the decade would help to finance the NAACP.) In all of this, Du Bois was in line with the ways that others used the pageant and its variants, the parade and street-corner oratory, to publicize social and political movements, including labor and feminism.

More to the point, in citing within the *Darkwater* context his own *The Star of Ethiopia*, Du Bois brings into view the gendered substratum of the broad culture of pageantry, itself fractured and contested, pulled in multiple directions by competing figures of motherhood, womanhood, and feminism, mobilized for a range of social and political movements. Du Bois transforms his own texts and adapts their contexts, while citing, incorporating, and ultimately refashioning them into the historical consciousness, gendered female, of *Darkwater*.

## Adapting the Texts of Pageantry

It goes without saying that, in the context of the pageant movement at the time, *The Star of Ethiopia* was an anomaly, representing a transnational history of diasporic Negro peoples in contrast to the nationally focused, community-oriented pageants that were so popular.[20] But Du Bois went beyond adapting to an Africanist content the formal structures of the pageant—the epic-scale performance, divided into episodes covering a span of 200–2000 years, introduced by a spoken prologue and accompanied by vocal and orchestral music, dance, and group pantomime—all of which he used liberally in *Star*. The six episodes of the pageant, dramatizing the history of blacks in Africa and the Americas, culminated in a finale, which portrays African American history from Reconstruction to the present with groups of "symbolic figures" representing various kinds of work, from teachers and ministers, to businessmen, doctors and nurses. Onstage, among them, Du Bois includes "the All-Mother, formerly the Veiled Woman, now unveiled in her chariot with her dancing brood, and the bust of Lincoln at her side" (*Star*, 310). To bring this figure of the past, "Ethiopia, Mother of Men," as Du Bois calls her elsewhere, up into the present was not uncommon in progressive pageantry, which typically emphasized historical continuities, nor was it unusual to foreground a pageant woman in classical garb, who reappears throughout the pageant and symbolizes the community. But it was not the norm to depict women either in scenes of historical turning points or of work outside the home. Not until later, however, when he re-presents the same figure of "the primal black All-Mother of men" at the head of "the ghostly throng of mighty womanhood" that dominates the opening of "The Damnation of Women," does the significance of Du Bois's transformation of the mother into a public figure, individuated in the world of work, emerge (*Darkwater*, 565)—and then, only in the form of an unrecognized adaptation.

*Darkwater* begins, as does *Souls*, with the standard acknowledgment by the author of prior publications: "Many of my words appear here transformed from other publications and I thank the *Atlantic* . . . [etc.] . . . for letting me use them again" (*Darkwater*, 483–84). Half of the nine chapters of *Darkwater* devoted to social criticism and fiction had appeared in shorter versions in a variety of publications; following each chapter are shorter interludes of poetry and allegorical vignettes, several of which had previously been published; and the autobiographical sketch at the opening ("I was born by a golden river and in the shadow of two great hills . . .") was derived, we know, from the account in *Souls*. In addition to the familiar, Du Boisean palimpsest of previously published work, *Darkwater* features a more elusive form of self-citation that clusters around the uses of pageantry in the text. Harder to pin down, more of an echo or aura, these sites of historical consciousness are less visible without some familiarity with the larger pattern of self-citation in Du Bois.

Even more specifically, the key chapter "The Damnation of Women," Du Bois's most extended experiment in pageantry, represents a mode of self-citation radically different from any of the recognized practices. It is different both in its formal structure and its women-centered content. No passages from Du Bois's own writings are quoted wholesale, nor does Du Bois acknowledge *The Star of Ethiopia*, but nonetheless Du Bois's penchant for pageantry, specifically *as* a mode of feminist history, suffuses the entire chapter. The procession of the stages of history in *Star*, central to which is the idea of "gifts," reappears, transformed we'll see, in the parade of historical black women that forms the centerpiece of "The Damnation of Women." As a mode of spatial and temporal organization, the pageant form structures both Du Bois's opening account of the four women of his boyhood ("they represented the problem of the widow, the wife, the maiden, and the outcast") and, especially, the ensuing staging of "the great black race in passing up the steps of human culture," through a procession of black female figures, mythical, historical, and little-known (*Darkwater*, 564, 566). The parade of *dramatis personae* draws, in spirit, form, and content, on Du Bois's own *Star*. Yet, typical of Du Bois's self-citation, when *Star* is adapted through *Darkwater*'s historical consciousness, in this case explicitly gendered female, the source-text is transformed, as though the pageant had been rewritten to unveil its own latent, female-centered history.

Although "Damnation" is at the epicenter of the book's feminist history, my reading of the historical pageantry central to that chapter would not have been possible without the theatricalized figuration of black womanhood that underlies the text as a whole. So a brief summary of the interrelations, and self-citations, among the various pieces will avoid the problem of "critical isolationism" (as Alys Weinbaum and I call it in the introduction) that plagues many readings of that frequently excerpted and anthologized essay, by instead placing the chapter back within the larger context of *Darkwater*.

The chain of re-citation starts with the poem entitled "The Riddle of the Sphinx," originally published in the November 1907 *Horizon* as "The Burden of Black Women," and reprinted under the same title in the November 1914 *Crisis,* where it followed an editorial, "World War and the Color Line." That editorial, which identifies "the wild quest for Imperial expansion" as the larger cause of the war in Europe,[21] is a rehearsal for the influential analysis that Du Bois would offer a year later in his May 1915 *Atlantic Monthly* essay about the global competition of colonialism, "The African Roots of War." Finally, when Du Bois incorporated the 1915 essay into *Darkwater,* he used much of it for a new piece, "The Hands of Ethiopia" (chapter 3), as well as for "The Souls of White Folk" (chapter 2), actually an amalgam of three essays, one of the same name first published in 1910, a second, "Of the Culture of White Folk," published in 1917, and a third, "On Being Black," published in 1920.[22] These revised chapters, linked by the crying voices of the dark daughter and black mother in the poem, now titled "The Riddle of the Sphinx" and functioning as an interlude between chapters, present the maelstrom of a world war of the races as an expository call-and-response generated in relation to the poem's riddle.

As an avatar of the black woman invoked at the end of "Hands of Ethiopia," weeping and waiting, beyond the awful sea, the black mother of "The Riddle of the Sphinx" is also a harbinger of the historical pageant of black women in "The Damnation of Women." The earlier group of pieces that cluster around "The Hands of Ethiopia" provides a preview of Du Bois's full-blown pageantry in "Damnation," both of its temporal form, a procession, "down," "from," "through," and "to" history, and its historical content, the figures of black women, "darker sisters," "daughters of sorrow," who dramatize their own history (*Darkwater,* 565). In "The Damnation of Women," the parade of female figures, mythic and historical, takes place in time and space, both actual and imaginary. Du Bois tracks this procession "from the primal black All-Mother of Men down through the ghostly throng of mighty womanhood, who walked in the mysterious dawn of Asia and Africa, . . . from black Neith down to 'That starr'd Ethiop queen . . ', through dusky Cleopatras, dark Candaces, and darker, fiercer Zinghas, to our own day and our own land,—in gentle Phillis; . . . the sybil, Sojourner Truth; and the martyr, Louise De Mortie" (*Darkwater,* 565–66). Not only is Queen Nefertari of "The Hands of Ethiopia" a harbinger of the "starr'd Ethiop queen" of both *The Negro* and "The Damnation of Women," but the earlier chapter, focused on world war, also prefigures the pattern of time in the pageant proper in "Damnation," where Du Bois unfolds the chronology of world history as a spatial movement "down-from-through-to." Similarly, the historical locations, ranging from "the mysterious dawn of Asia and Africa" to "our own day and our own land," conflate the categories of time and space. These spatiotemporal relations are key to the female-centered, historical consciousness with which Du Bois experiments.

The historical pageant of black women in "Damnation" reiterates the geo-temporal structure of *Star*, but differently. First, in the pageant proper we hear no individual voices, only the intermittent intonations of the four heralds, described in the prose version entitled "The People of Peoples and Their Gifts to Men" as "black and of gigantic stature, . . . with silver trumpets and standing at the four corners of the temple of beauty" (*Star*, 305). Second, the cast, in the 1913 New York performances, of 350 black schoolchildren, teachers and amateur dancers and actors, is dominated by groups of representative figures ("savages," "slaves," "Mohammedans," "Maroons," "Haytians," "Indians") of both sexes, with only a few actual historical figures, virtually all of them male.[23] Announced by trumpet blasts, the heralds' proclamations introduce the six episodes of *Star*, each associated with a different Gift, starting with "Iron" out of Africa, moving through the rise of African civilization ("Gift of the Nile") in ancient Egypt, and the kingdoms of Central Africa before European contact ("Gift of Faith"), shifting to the slave trade ("Gift of Humiliation") and the Middle Passage ("the Dance of the Ocean, showing the transplantation of the Negro race over seas"), and ending in "the Americas," with national revolution, slave revolt and the Haitian Revolution figured through Toussaint L'Ouverture, Nat Turner, and Denmark Vesey ("Gift of Struggle"). These representative figures, mostly exceptional men, stand for the monumental gifts and events that periodize Du Bois's alternative history.

The finale concludes with the All-Mother of Ethiopia unveiled as civilization's originator and defender, accompanying John Brown, Harriet Beecher Stowe, Frederick Douglass, and Sojourner Truth, as they give the "Gift of Freedom," in modern-day America. The gender distribution of the cast in relation to the implied audience underscores the default masculinism of the pageant. Although Du Bois picked activist Mary Church Terrell to play Harriet Beecher Stowe and featured other prominent female members of the local community as the Queen of Sheba and Candace of Meroë, nevertheless the pageant was addressed by the heralds to an audience called throughout "Men of All the Americas." As the pageant ends, "with burst of music and blast of trumpets," the heralds repeat, "Hear ye, hear ye, men of all the Americas, . . . and forget not the gift of black men to this world," reiterating each of the gifts that have been dramatized (*Star*, 310). The net effect is history dramatized, like all progressive pageants, of, by and for the people. Almost by definition, this presents itself as ungendered history that does not acknowledge its assumed masculine perspective.

Thus *The Star of Ethiopia* does not recognize the womanist history embedded silently within it. And so, in *Darkwater*, by silently citing the language and figures of the pageant—the stages of history, and, especially, the All-Mother—Du Bois transforms "the gifts of black men" into "The Damnation of Women." What are the elements and the process of this transformation? The key is Du Bois's repetition and adaptation. At the opening of his chapter, Du Bois recites, and adapts, his own civilizational metaphor for the stages of history, of "passing up the steps of human culture." It is "as if," he remarks, in "Damnation," "the great black race . . . gave the world not only the Iron Age, . . . but also, in peculiar emphasis, the mother-idea" (566). To stage world history through and as a maternal genealogy fundamentally revises the monumental, masculinist history of *Star*. Most of the predominantly male figures of black history dramatized in the six Episodes of the pageant, from Ra and Mohammed, to Crispus Attucks and Frederick Douglass, to Toussaint and Turner, fade away in "Damnation," and instead the female figures, only a few of which are present in the cast of characters of *Star*, come to the fore.

Not only does "the ghostly throng of mighty womanhood" in "The Damnation of Women" vastly outnumber its sisters in *Star*, but also black women take center-stage in the chapter far more than they do anywhere else in *Darkwater* as a whole. In *Star* the Queen of Sheba and Candace of Ethiopia merely "join the procession at intervals," while Ra is crowned "Priest and King." In "Damnation," these figures, renamed

"dusky Cleopatras, dark Candaces, and darker, fiercer Zinghas" define
the great middle period of woman-history in "Damnation"—the
"through" of the down-from-through-to (*Star*, 307; *Darkwater*, 566).
Sojourner Truth plays a part in both works, even speaking the same
line in the same setting, an abolitionist meeting where Frederick Douglass is featured, and she is among those assembled to listen. In both
texts she asks, in implicit rebuke to his message of violent rebellion,
"Frederick, is God dead?" (*Star*, 309–10; *Darkwater*, 571). But while in
*Star* other voices take up the cry and repeat her question, in "Damnation," hers is the lone voice, and she occupies the place of honor (rather
than entering and passing from one side of the stage as specified in
*Star*). She "was sitting tall and dark, on the very front seat facing the
platform," and "she spoke out in her deep peculiar voice, heard all over
the hall," asking her question (571–72). While in *Star* he thunders back
an answer that is reiterated by the heralds of the pageant ("No, and
therefore slavery must end in blood!" [310]), in "Damnation" she
has the last word. Left unanswered, her question, "Is God dead?" concludes the scene as Du Bois cites and transforms it, adapting the pageant to fit "The Damnation of Women" (*Star*, 309–10; *Darkwater*, 572).
Finally, the "Veiled Woman," dimly present in the second scene of the
pageant, is not "unveiled in her chariot" until the end, when she is
revealed as Ethiopia, "the All-Mother, formerly the Veiled Woman." In
contrast, she functions far more visibly in "Damnation," where she is
placed center-stage as "the primal black All-Mother," heading the procession from the very beginning of time (*Star*, 310; *Darkwater*, 565).

The All-Mother of "The Damnation of Women" presides over her
"daughters of sorrow," the "darker sisters" of the world that "worships
womankind" but "studiously forgets" them, who "typify that veiled
Melancholy" (565). To unveil their forgotten history, not simply a history of famous black women, but an explicitly gendered race-history of
womanhood, is the fundamental project driving "The Damnation of
Women." It is a "history of insult and degradation," but one, Du Bois
emphasizes, with results "both fearful and glorious" (569). Dramatized
in stages that parallel but revise the chronology and geography of
*Star*, the history of "the black motherhood of this race" is traced
from the "African mother-idea," down through the "crushing weight"
of the westward slave trade and American slavery, to five million

granddaughters "of Negro descent" in 1910, "an efficient womanhood, whose strength lies in its freedom" (568–69). Unlike the monumental events narrated in the six episodes of *Star*, this is a hidden, unrecognized history: "the outward numerical fact of social dislocation"— measured by such statistics as the ratio of males to females in the American black population—tells little of "the hell beneath the system," where "within lay polygamy, polyandry, concubinage, and moral degradation" (567). To unveil, and to dramatize on the textual stage, such a specific social and economic history of reproduction, "The Damnation of Women" combines pageantry with sociology, statistics with passion, and scholarly sources with the voices of ordinary women.

The cast of characters shifts dramatically from the roll call of the mythical and famous of *The Star of Ethiopia*. The Cleopatras and Candaces play bit parts, subordinated to the real stars of the pageantry of "The Damnation of Women"—the largely unknown and unsung black women of everyday life in the modern race history of the Americas. Among these, announced by the unattributed Anna Julia Cooper quotation, "Mum Bett," a runaway in Great Barrington, "scarred for life by a blow received in defense of a sister," and one of the first slaves to be freed under the Bill of Rights of 1780; Kate Ferguson, born in New York long before the Declaration of Independence, who established the first modern Sunday School in Manhattan; Mary Shadd, "out of Delaware," teacher, editor, lecturer, and recruiting agent for black soldiers in the West; and Louise De Mortie, "a free-born Virginia girl" and "a woman of feeling and intellect," who worked with "the orphaned colored children of New Orleans,—out of freedom into insult and oppression and into the teeth of the yellow fever" (*Darkwater*, 569–73). Unlike the mostly mute, largely symbolic figures of *The Star of Ethiopia*, these ordinary black women live in the concrete detail of local histories and speak, where evidence is available to Du Bois, in their own voices. So doing necessitates citation, where possible, and thus embroils Du Bois in another exercise of attribution, or lack thereof.

On the "strong women that laid the foundations of the great Negro church of today," for example, Du Bois quotes a long passage from "one of the early mothers of the church, Mary Still." He editorializes as he attributes the passage, introducing Still, whom, he says, writes

"thus quaintly, in the forties" (*Darkwater*, 570). Still's words provide
a transition from the early history of the church and establish the
"spiritual ancestry" of the female tradition that Du Bois is constructing. Still is presented as the progenitor of "two striking figures of
wartime," Harriet Tubman and Sojourner Truth. With such well-
known, exceptional women as these, Du Bois is able to give detailed
biographical information, including dates, names and places. Yet he
also gives or invents for both extended speeches of their own, incorporating them into his own prose but setting them off as citations
without attribution. The effect is that of an oral history, actual or
imaginary. On Harriet Tubman: "She was born a slave in Maryland,
in 1820. . . . A standing reward of $10,000 was offered for her, but as
she said: 'The whites cannot catch us for I was born with the charm,
and the Lord has given me the power.' She was one of John Brown's
closest advisors . . ." (571). Omitting his source, Du Bois gains the
immediacy of the voice and authenticity of the words he quotes. On
Phillis Wheatley, who is the subject of one of Du Bois's little-known
pageants: he belittles her as a poet whose "muse was slight" by today's
measure, and her poetry as a "trite and halting strain." Yet, he insists,
"we call to her still in her own words" and then sets off a single line of
quotation from one of her poems, " 'Through thickest glooms look
back, immortal shade' " (570–72).

Strikingly, the individuated voices here resonate clearly, differentiating both their personal histories and the "chapters in their history"
that Du Bois narrates. These female figures are at once representatives and individuals, ordinary and exceptional. In this, Du Bois has
come closer, perhaps, than anywhere else in *Darkwater* to resolving
the problem of the universal and the particular that we raise in the
introduction. Although it was difficult for him to acknowledge black
women in the plural, here he does so. Rather than turning these figures either into historical representatives of blackness or mythical
abstractions of womanhood, they are both black and women: black
women, taken as a collectivity, as a vocal, plural category.

Layered onto the ethnographic incorporation of women's voices is
statistical evidence from sociological studies of the kind that Du Bois
had conducted—measuring literacy rates, employment, and "death,
divorce, [and] desertion"—in urban and rural black communities. In

this section of "Damnation," Du Bois shifts to the sociological idiom in order to ground the chapter's passionate affirmations ("These women are passing through, not only a moral, but an economic revolution" [573]), and equally impassioned laments ("Down in such mire has the black motherhood of this race struggled . . ." [569]). He is especially scrupulous about providing statistics of black women as workers, to buttress his argument that "these women are passing through, not only a moral, but an economic revolution" (573). As a group of workers, they number "a million farm laborers, 80,000 farmers, 22,000 teachers, 600,000 servants and washerwomen, and 50,000 in trades and merchandizing" (573). Not only does this list resonate backward, as a female adaptation of the groups of workers onstage in the final episode of *Star*, but also it allows Du Bois to address debates over "this new economic equality within a great laboring class," "the new economic freedom of women" (574). Whether citing a line from a Wheatley poem, or incorporating fugitive-slave bills, or quoting the son of the judge who freed Mum Bett (as well as "a sister of a president of the United States" and George Washington himself), or referring to the scholarly authorities on African tribal life (Mungo Park, Schweinfurth, Ratzel), Du Bois draws on all the available sources—historical, social scientific, literary—to give imaginative life as well as ethnographic authority to his pageant of the "mother-idea" as a key to race-history.

Those sources include his own family history recounted in his several autobiographies. In "The Damnation of Women," Du Bois takes a long, global view of the maternal line of descent, going back to *Souls,* that he repeats in tracing his personal history in each subsequent autobiography. Here, the sorrow song of "the little, far-off mother of my grandmothers" has a complex lineage, a nonlinear provenance, traced both backward to previous autobiographical texts and forward to those not yet written. The little song, cited in the "Bantu" lyrics of "Do bana coba," in the first chapter of *Darkwater,* just as it had been in *Souls* and would be later in *Dusk of Dawn,* provides a conception of history in which multiple temporalities coexist simultaneously. Thus the song does not represent simply the Du Bois family heritage but rather taps incantatory memories of world-mothers: "All the way back in these dim distances it is mothers and mothers of mothers who seem to count, while fathers are shadowy

memories" (*Darkwater*, 567). But mothers count only in the absence
of translation, through a code imperfectly transmitted. The song of
the mother responds to a diasporic history of uneven communica-
tion, both incomplete and excessive; the song is thus a form of
"genealogical counternarrative" that circumvents what Alys Weinbaum calls the "race/reproduction bind," just as Fred Moten argues
that it corresponds to a "broken matrilinearity," given in "a resistant,
forceful materiality that emerges most clearly after the fact of a deprivation," the partial loss of the mother and of meaning, that Du Bois
both reveals and represses.[24] Dramatizing race-conscious history
means making visible the occult history of the African mother-idea,
but not, Du Bois says in "Damnation," solely as "a survival of the historic matriarchate through which all nations pass,—it appears to be
more than this" (566). The more-than-this is the excess of meaning,
untranslatable, in the song of the mother, or simply what Du Bois
calls the mother-idea. Maternity is thus defined not as an identity, a
static state of "motherhood," but rather as a genealogical process, a
malleable mode of transmitting, within and across time, nonbiologi-
cal, diasporic heritages.

In so doing, Du Bois breaks away from contemporary debates over
whether the black mother is a positive or negative force, pure or
impure, by mythologizing and historicizing the "mother-idea." As a
mythic abstraction and a historical conception, the "mother-idea" is,
for better or worse, uncoupled from the materiality of the "black
mother." Some of the longstanding problems that have been recognized by so many readers and critics in Du Bois's representation of
womanhood are thus fundamental to the mother-idea: his reliance
on a mythic orientalism, the idealizing of the victimized black
mother, the insistence on the sexual purity of black women—all
means of countering racist stereotypes.[25] But the "damnation of
women" is historically structured and narrated, counterbalancing the
mythologizing of black womanhood through the series of vocal, local
figures from specific national histories. So, too, the Black All-Mother
of "Damnation" is both a static, mythologized figure and the source
of an active, genealogical process, the mobilizer of a narrative of
matrilineal descent for a global race-history that includes both individual women and collective womanhood. In the process of citing,

adapting and transforming this figure from *The Star of Ethiopia* to "The Damnation of Women," Du Bois brings together the competing registers of motherhood discourse, the mystical and the social scientific, the racist and the antiracist.

That the figures of black women, and the particular, hidden history they dramatize, had always been a constitutive component, partially unrecognized, of Du Bois's historical consciousness becomes apparent when we read backward to *Star* from the *Darkwater* perspective. In the advertising imagery and *Crisis* coverage of *Star*, visual images of women—what Levering Lewis calls the pageant's display of "the flower of Talented Tenth pulchritude"—dominate those of the men by at least two to one.[26] The December 1915 *Crisis* features photographs of Miss Adella Parks in costume as the Queen of Sheba, Miss Eleanor Curtis as Ethiopia, and Miss Gregoria Fraser as Candace of Meroë, as well as a photograph of Mrs. Dora Cole Norman, Director of Dancing. (Du Bois appears only in the photograph taken of the local pageant committee.)[27] And accompanying Du Bois's long essay in the

THE QUEEN OF SHEBA
(Miss Adella Parks)

ETHIOPIA
(Miss Eleanor Curtis)

CANDACE OF MEROE
(Miss Gregoria Fraser)

From the Pageant: "The Star of Ethiopia"

FIGURE 12.4   *"From the Pageant:* The Star of Ethiopia," The Crisis, *December 1915, 90. Courtesy of The Crisis Publishing Co., Inc., the magazine of the National Association for the Advancement of Colored People.*

FIGURE 12.5 *"THE PAGEANT, STAR OF ETHIOPIA, IN PHILADELPHIA. Leading characters, and Temple built and decorated by Richard Brown and Lenwood Morris," The Crisis, August 1916, 172. Courtesy of The Crisis Publishing Co., Inc., the magazine of the National Association for the Advancement of Colored People.*

August 1916 *Crisis*, "The Drama Among Black Folk," in which he incorporates passages from *The Star of Ethiopia*, are group photographs that place the white-robed female participants in the pageant front-and-center.

In the essay Du Bois also adds the figure of the mother, not present in the 1913 version, when he cites the opening and closing cry of "the dark and crimson-turbaned Herald" at the pageant. "Hear ye, hear ye!," the herald begins, "learn the ancient Glory of Ethiopia, All-Mother of men, whose wonders men forgot," concluding with the injunction: "And remember forever and one day the Star of Ethiopia, All-Mother of Men, who gave the world the Iron Gift and Gift of Faith . . ." ("Drama among Black Folk," 169, 173). At the very headwaters of black history and the source of race-gifts, the maternal presence stands, both forgotten and remembered. The female-only pageantry of "The Damnation of Women" confirms, and compensates for, what this imagery from *The Star of Ethiopia* suggests, the problem that the absence or silence of black motherhood from and in most accounts of race-history haunts them, nevertheless.

## Adapting the Contexts of Pageantry

Rereading backward to *Star,* from the perspective of its adaptation in "Damnation," brings out another, small, but significant, transformation in the earlier work: the many black female figures onstage at the end of the pageant, the teachers, nurses and, finally, the Mother of Men, all of whom come together in modern America, may be Du Bois's way of swimming against the current of the conflicted female role in pageantry. In placing his own allegorical All-Mother, incongruously and anachronistically, within the circle of modernity, Du Bois recognizes, or allows us to recognize, both the gendered limits and the racial-historical possibilities of the culture of pageantry. Especially in both his dramatic portrayal and his economic analysis of black women as workers of the world, Du Bois taps the contradictions that underlie the progressive pageantry movement. As revealed in his adaptations, it's a fractured cultural context, with competing crosscurrents generated largely around and by race and gender.

This is a view confirmed only by a minority of historians of pageantry, those who foreground the many contradictions within the inclusive, democratic theory and the exclusive, hierarchical practices of pageantry. Cultural historian David Glassberg argues that while women were incorporated in striking numbers as actors, their roles, even when depicted in the world of work, were relegated largely either to allegorical or domestic spheres.[28] In the arena of production, women also played leading roles as writers, directors, producers, and heads of civic committees but, in at least one, well-documented episode, the staging in 1915 of a controversial suffrage pageant, Hazel MacKaye's "The Pageant of Susan B. Anthony," led to an attempt at official censure by the American Pageant Association. Nominally an issue of whether a pageant based on the life of an individual, rather than "a drama expressing the character of a community," could be included in the annual APA bulletin list of pageants, the terms of the controversy say it all: adjudicating the relation between the individual

and the collective, one which we know also plagues Du Bois's representation of black womanhood, MacKaye's defense redefined community expression to mean "some form of community participation
with some civic or community purpose in view." The activist imperative in "community participation" locates precisely the unrecognized
reason for the controversy over this suffrage pageant, commissioned
by the National Women's Party "in order to impress upon the con-
gressmen the imperativeness of our demand for the vote."[29] The
episode sums up many of the tensions within the pageantry movement, divided between progressive and antimodern impulses and
producing an inclusive, homogeneous national collectivity based on
exclusivity.[30] In contrast to this fragmented mainstream, lacking
the capacity for self-consciousness or self-criticism, Du Bois's experiments in historical pageantry, the adaptation of Star in "Damnation,"
produce both his own transformed, gendered race-history and a critique of the prevailing cultural and political uses of the form.

Closer to home for Du Bois, another indicator of the conflicts,
both of race and gender, over both the presence and significance of
women in the culture of pageantry, is a series of photographs of
Marcus Garvey's UNIA parades in the 1920s. Historian Robert A. Hill
analyzes, as a record of the gender and race politics of the Garvey
movement, the famous photograph of Garvey, dressed in a field mar-
shal's uniform and riding in an open car, in the August 1922 parade
that inaugurated the third convention of the Universal Negro
Improvement Association (UNIA). While he reads the photograph as
an "ethnic adaptation" of the "American ceremony" of the street
parade, a version of the "West Indian parade complex" that represented the continuity of Caribbean cultural life in New York, he also
notes the absence of Amy Jacques Garvey, whom Garvey had married
only a few days earlier. Hill concludes that by refusing to take the
photograph at face value and looking instead for what it omits, it
reveals the implicit contradiction between power and gender in the
UNIA. Although female contingents marched prominently in all
UNIA parades, which represented its organization in ranks with such
uniformed auxiliaries as the Black Cross Nurses, the Ladies' Motor
Corps, and the Boys' and Girls' Juvenile Corps, nevertheless, Hill
concludes, "it is now apparent that the procession was, fundamentally,

a celebration of black manhood—a depiction of New Negro manhood."[31] More broadly, if we see the parade as a species of civic pageantry, then Hill's analysis not only exposes the contradictions in the pageantry movement but also suggests some reasons why historians might fail to recognize both the raced and gendered complexities.

Du Bois's mother-idea represents an adaptation of the cultural context in which motherhood played a critical and contradictory role. Du Bois's work on black womanhood, we know, is sometimes read as defensive, a response to counteract prevailing stereotypes of the immoral black woman. But placing the mother-idea in the largely unrecognized context of pageantry reveals a group of multiple interlocutors in the discourse and debates over motherhood at this period, going beyond such usual suspects as Madison Grant (author of *The Passing of the Great Race*, 1916) and Lothrop Stoddard (author of *The Rising Tide of Color*, 1920). Although there's no question that Du Bois wrote on black motherhood in and against the powerful collaboration of eugenics and white supremacy, the context for his mother-idea is broader. It extends from the occult sphere of spiritualists such as Madame Blavatsky (founder of the Theosophical Society and author of *Isis Unveiled* [1878]), to the suffrage and labor movements and, of course, to the use of maternal figures in pageantry.

The occultist mother-idea, in Du Bois's adaptation, originates with the invention of Egypt in *Darkwater*, which is instrumental both to the gendering of Du Bois's text and its contexts. One of those signature sites, Egypt, serves as a refrain throughout Du Bois's writings, but nowhere is it as thoroughly both gendered and historicized as in *Darkwater*. "Egypt" is invoked by Du Bois in a variety of ways: mystically and spiritually, as an ancient civilization in *Souls*; historically, as in *The Negro*, where it is treated as a body of evidence and interpretation produced by secondary sources; archaeologically and ethnographically, as in the *Encyclopedia Africana*, a multivolume "history of the Negro race."[32] Yet the Egypt citations in *Darkwater* are as difficult to locate as they are critical to the text's female-gendered pageant of world history on the color line. As such, the uses of Egypt, especially in "Damnation," perplexingly fits with the contradictions characteristic of Du Bois's thinking on gender.[33]

If the idea of Egypt lends itself to universal metaphors with an unac-knowledged female presence (e.g., the riddle of the sphinx), Egypt is also a specific place in time and space, representing the prehistory of Du Bois's Pan Africa, what Sundquist describes as a nation consisting of "a transhistorical consciousness" rather than a particular geography or racial body.[34] Yet at the same time Egypt is explicitly identified as female, associated by Du Bois (and others), drawing on Egyptological occult discourses, with the moon-goddess Isis and with the Egyptian queen Nefertiti. Du Bois specifically invokes both female figures in *Darkwater*, naming these twin sources as "Isis, the mother," (in "The Damnation of Women," *Darkwater*, 566) and (in his variant of Nefer-titi) "Queen Nefertari, 'the most venerated figure in Egyptian history'" (in "The Hands of Ethiopia," *Darkwater*, 520). The source of the latter quotation is not identified, nor is the association of Isis with what he calls "the mother-idea"—a gift to the world from the civilization of Africa ("the land of the mother," 566)—itself placed in historical or intellectual context. This is a significant omission. For Du Bois is hardly alone in using what turns out to be a protean phenomenon that appears in a wide variety of venues, from occultist tracts to domestic advice manuals, to the "Mothers' Meetings and Conferences" instituted by the black women's club movement.[35]

As a syncretic figure, Du Bois's Isis, "the mother," "still titular god-dess, in thought if not in name, of the dark continent," brings together the cult of the "Great Mother" in the Egyptian occultism of Madame Blavatsky's *Isis Unveiled* (1878) with interest in Africanist myth and ritual as well as the uses of Egyptological symbology in Masonic and black popular history (*Darkwater*, 566). This is hardly a politically homogenous context. For under the umbrella of Theosophy, we find the white supremacist cast of Blavatsky's "root races" in *The Secret Doctrine* (1888), most prominently the "Aryan race," that brings together both a *Volk*-ish nationalism, dedicated to racial purity, and an internationalism, visible in the support for the Indian independence movement of Blavatsky and Annie Besant, both of whom were sympa-thizers with the Indian National Congress.[36] This only serves to com-plicate further the racial politics of the popularizers of the Isis myth.

Du Bois's use of Isis as symbol for "the land of the mother" and "the spell of the African mother" also adapts Masonic icons of the

Bible and ancient Egypt. (Notably, Solomon's Temple and the pyramids are standard Masonic emblems.) In the traditional account narrated by the Order of the Eastern Star, the Masonic women's auxiliary, the five-point star on which the Eastern Star degree is based consists of five biblical figures, "eminent female characters," according to Grimshaw's *Official History of Freemasonry*, symbolizing the five roles of woman's life—daughter, widow, wife, sister, and mother—as well as the virtues they embody (Ruth represents devotion, Esther represents fidelity, and so on). As such, the Eastern Star points, first, to Du Bois's own boyhood history, with the four women who represented the "problem" of the widow, the wife, the maiden, and the outcast, and, second, to the collective history of global black sisterhood dramatized in *Darkwater*. Just as the Eastern Star joins with the Star of Ethiopia to produce "The Damnation of Woman" in *Darkwater*, so, too, does the discourse of occult mysticism, with its valence of racial and familial imagery, organize the feminist historiography and pageantry of "Damnation."[37]

The history of Masonic women's auxiliaries also reveals another set of contradictions underlying the use of familial, often maternal or sororal, imagery in the rhetoric of social movements. Despite the rhetoric of Masonic equality, based on revolutionary *fraternité*, women were not permitted as members, and even the establishment of the ladies' auxiliaries in the late nineteenth century, best known of which is, in fact, the Daughters of the Eastern Star, meant in practice little more than a set of "various female orders attached to" the chief secret societies, as Du Bois says of them in *Philadelphia Negro* (224). But contemporary Masonic historian Charles Wesley notes that as a "man of vision," Prince Hall, the first black Mason, would have black women attain similar goals to male Masonry, "and they heard his message in the Eastern Star, the Daughters of Isis, . . . and the women at home, school, and abroad, all of whom have constituted a unity of purpose under the leadership of the life and spirit of Prince Hall. . . ." The Eastern Stars produced historiographical accounts (for example, Mrs. S. Joe Brown's *The History of the Order of the Eastern Star Among Colored People* [1925]) that mirror the Prince Hall Masonic histories. Feminist historians read these histories of black female Masonry, calling to separate women's history from that of "Colored Men" and of "white Americans," as essential to the historical record of black women's activism. Women's auxiliaries, which seemed to represent an acceptance of male dominance, may thus also be viewed as the products of women's struggles and the targets of masculine resistance.[38]

The same kind of fractured environment, divided unevenly along lines of race, gender and class, is revealed by the incorporation of female and familial roles in the parades and pageants associated with the labor and suffrage movements. Although unlike Du Bois, most pageant directors rarely depicted modern women in economic or political roles, they consistently relied on a "pageant woman" to represent the social cohesiveness and emotional essence of the community. This idealized female image, according to historian Glassberg, was explicitly tied to "images of both maternity and maturity," with the women commonly cast in this role being "both middle-aged and married" (*American Historical Pageantry*, 136–37). Yet the large, 5,000-member woman suffrage pageant, more accurately a massive demonstration, held in Washington, D.C. on the day before Woodrow Wilson's inauguration in March 1913, included a prominent scene of women workers in the procession. So when Du Bois links motherhood and work, as he does in *Star* and "Damnation," he is tapping into a fraught conjunction (*Darkwater*, 573, 576). Hazel MacKaye, author of the 1913 pageant as well as of the "Pageant of Susan B. Anthony," summed up the threat posed by a public discourse of women and work. "Women are becoming more and more alive to the fact that the working-world is man-made, and that women will have to put up a good fight to get a fair share as bread-winners. . . .Through pageantry, we women can set forth our ideals and aspirations more graphically than in any other way" (quoted in Glassberg, 135). MacKaye makes clear the appeal for Du Bois of pageantry as a mode of gendered performance that disrupts the separate spheres of private and public. When the mother-idea enters the public sphere of the parade and street theater, when mothers are aligned with workers in agitating for the vote or in narrating Du Bois's history of black people, then we see the "combination" of the movements of woman and color that for Du Bois, during the era of *Darkwater*, has such "deep meaning."

## The Uses of Adaptation

Having begun with the challenge of reading Du Bois's self-citation, I shall end by suggesting how and why a theory of self-citation and, more broadly, of adaptation is a key to reading Du Bois's gender politics: each of his texts, as we've seen, is a palimpsest of adaptations, recognized and unrecognized, of both texts and contexts. The unacknowledged Anna Julia Cooper was a touchstone for the first-wave feminist readings of Du Bois, just as establishing the provenance of "Damnation" and "Riddle," partially recognized in the text of *Darkwater*, has produced a genealogy of Du Bois's writings on women. Some might say that Du Bois's citation, without attribution, of Cooper's "when and where I enter," inserted right in the middle of "The Damnation of Women," marks one unmistakable limit of the text's recognition of black women. Yet it is clear that the articulation of *Darkwater*'s feminist politics could not have been achieved without Du Bois's many uses of citation.

Nowhere, then, are the paradoxes of Du Bois's citational practices as starkly, or as symptomatically, displayed as in *Darkwater*. Although Du Bois tends to be scrupulously accurate when citing himself, he is sometimes castigated for a lack of scholarly generosity in his relations with other black historians, especially Arthur Schomburg, from whose collection of books and manuscripts it is well known that Du Bois borrowed freely, often without acknowledging the favor. Yet *Darkwater*'s reliance on self-quotation, not consistently noted, is such that scholars have had to reconstruct painstakingly all of the interrelations among both earlier and later uses of various pieces of the text. Moreover, as we've seen in the context of the historical pageantry of "Damnation," Du Bois both reverses and intensifies his usual pattern of attribution: while Du Bois does not cite himself as a source for the global pageant of women's race-history in "Damnation," he names some (masculine) sources for the quotations spoken in female voices but fails to name other (female) sources for the lines he quotes in his own voice. At the same time, the chapter is punctuated by many passages of quotation, incorporating while also setting off women's voices without actually crediting their sources.

One unmistakable result is to sidestep the whole problem of authentication, mixing ethnographic and fictional reportage without distinguishing between the two modes. Another effect is to bring the reader into intimate contact with the individual voices and lives of the ordinary, or representative, black women Du Bois commemorates, as well as with the lives of the rich and famous. He thus, perhaps paradoxically, bridges the gap between the individual and the collective by playing fast and loose with questions of provenance, which might otherwise privilege those whose words may be fully documented as their voices and texts are adapted. Finally, though, reading Du Bois with a critical awareness of his penchant for adaptations, both recognized and unrecognized, both of himself and others, both of texts and contexts, provides a sure way of excavating his race-history of and by black women. Thinking through adaptation gives access to the layers of forgetting and remembering, the collaboration between the individual and the collectivity, the backwards and forward movement of historical consciousness, all of which are central to Du Bois's gendered history of the color line.

## Notes

1. While the 1900 Pan-African Conference is generally attributed as the first moment of citation (See "Address to the Nations of the World," in Philip S. Foner, ed. *Speeches and Addresses of Du Bois, 1890–1919* [New York: Pathfinder, 1979], 125), Du Bois invoked the color line most famously in *The Souls of Black Folk* (1903), where it is repeated three times by the end of only the second chapter. From these generative moments, Du Bois went on, in other texts and venues throughout his career, to numerous reformulations, restatements, and replayings of both phrases, "the color-line" and "the Negro Problem." Thomas Holt has discussed at some length Du Bois's various uses and revisions of his most "axiomatic" text, the passage on double-consciousness, first presented in a speech to the American Negro Academy, then reformulated and published in the August 1897 *Atlantic Monthly,* and finally appearing in "Of Our Spiritual Strivings," the lead essay of *Souls.* "The Political Uses of Alienation: Du Bois on Politics, Race, and Culture, 1903–1940," *American Quarterly 42* (June 1990): 301–23.

2. For that sin of omission, James continues further to castigate Du Bois for "reproducing gender dominance" through "his selective memory for the agency of his contemporaries," including Ida B. Wells-Barnett as well as Anna Julia Cooper. See "Profeminism and Gender Elites: W. E. B. Du Bois, Anna Julia Cooper, and Ida B. Wells-Barnett," reprinted in this volume; hereafter all citations will be to the reprint.

3. On the "pageant woman" as "idealized Spirit of the Community," see David Glassberg, *American Historical Pageantry: The Uses of Tradition in the Early Twentieth Century* (Chapel Hill: The University of North Carolina Press, 1990), 136–37.

4. For Du Bois's pageants (years 1913–1941 and undated frames 1390–1545), see *W. E. B. Du Bois Papers*, Special Collections and Archives, W. E. B. Du Bois Library, University of Massachusetts Amherst, Series 12, Reel 87.

5. On the "pageant-like scenes," see Sundquist, *Oxford Du Bois Reader*, 303; on the interrelations of the theatricality of the black history pageant and the lifting of the veil over the African past, see Sundquist, *To Wake the Nations: Race in the Making of American Literature* (Cambridge, Mass.: Harvard University Press, 1993), 579–80.

6. On the phenomenon of pageantry during this period, see Glassberg, *American Historical Pageantry*; David Krasner, *A Beautiful Pageant: African American Theatre, Drama, and Performance in the Harlem Renaissance, 1910–1927* (New York: Palgrave Macmillan, 2002); Alessandra Lorini, *Rituals of Race: American Public Culture and the Search for Racial Democracy* (Charlottesville: University Press of Virginia, 1999); Naima Prevots, *American Pageantry: A Movement for Art and Democracy* (Ann Arbor: UMI Research Press, 1990). For specific discussions of Du Bois in the context of the pageantry movement, see Sundquist, *To Wake the Nations*, 578–81.

7. See Mary Ryan, "The American Parade: Representations of the Nineteenth-Century Social Order," in ed. Lynn Hunt, *The New Cultural History* (Los Angeles and Berkeley: University of California Press, 1989), 132.

8. W. E. B. Du Bois, *The Negro* (1915; reprint, Millwood, N.Y.: Kraus-Thomson, 1975), Preface, vi (hereafter page numbers cited parenthetically in the text).

9. W. E. B. Du Bois, *The Autobiography of W. E. B. Du Bois: A Soliloquy on Viewing My Life from the Last Decade of Its First Century*, ed. Herbert Aptheker (New York: International, 1968), 270 (hereafter page numbers cited parenthetically in the text).

10. W. E. B. Du Bois, "The Drama Among Black Folk," *The Crisis*, August 1916, 169–73, 171 (hereafter page numbers cited parenthetically in the text).

11. *The Christmas Crisis*, December 1915, 91.

12. David Levering Lewis, *W. E. B. Du Bois: Biography of a Race, 1868–1919* (New York: Henry Holt, 1993), 461.

13. *Dark Princess: A Romance* (1928; reprint, Jackson: University Press of Mississippi, 1995), 310–11. Claudia Tate's comment that *Dark Princess* could be seen as a consolidation of the opening "Credo" of *Darkwater* and the 1915 pageant deepens the textual connections and extends the temporal horizons of the context I want to construct. See Tate's "Introduction" to *Dark Princess*, xx–xxi.

14. Reflecting yet another set of autobiographical and dramatic intertextualities, Levering Lewis comments that *A Pageant in Seven Decades* is the "skeleton" for *Dusk of Dawn*, with *The Souls of Black Folk* and *Darkwater* "the flesh." David Levering Lewis, *W. E. B. Du Bois: The Fight for Equality and the American Century, 1919–1963* (New York: Henry Holt, 2000), 472.

15. On how the term was "stretched" by local promoters to cover many different kinds of festivities, see Glassberg, 105; on the fear of "promiscuity," see Mary Porter Beegle, who wrote in the APA Bulletin No. 7 (September 1914), "The promiscuous use of the word 'Pageant' has caused a great deal of confusion in the minds of the general public" (quoted in Prevots, 95). This view represents the general consensus of the pageant organization that "mere parades" ought to be eliminated and community drama furthered only in the form of pageants, masques and festivals (Prevots, 95).

16.  On Greenwich Village and the "Lyrical Left," see Edward Abrahams, *The Lyrical Left: Randolph Bourne, Alfred Stieglitz and the Origins of Cultural Radicalism in America* (Charlottesville: University Press of Virginia, 1986), 1–11; on "street historians," see Ralph L. Crowder, *John Edward Bruce: Politician, Journalist, and Self-Trained Historian of the African Diaspora* (New York: New York University Press, 2004).

17.  On Garvey's pageantry, see Du Bois, "Marcus Garvey," *Century Magazine* 105 (February 1923), reprint in Sundquist, ed., *Du Bois Reader*, 265–76; Robert A. Hill, "Making Noise: Marcus Garvey *Dada*, August 1922, in Deborah Willis, ed., *Picturing Us: African American Identity in Photography* (New York: New Press, 1994), 181–205).

18.  Claude McKay, *Harlem: Negro Metropolis* (New York: E. P. Dutton, 1940), 155. On Du Bois's role, see Manning Marable, *W. E. B. Du Bois: Black Radical Democrat* (Boston: G. K. Hall & Co., 1986), 83–91.

19.  In addition to the historical pageants and stage plays produced by black and leftist political activists, these would include the chief forms of Masonic symbolic activity (the traditions of masking, costuming and symbolic regalia, the initiation rites and parades). See Mary Anne Clawson, *Constructing Brotherhood: Class, Gender, and Fraternalism* (Princeton, N.J.: Princeton University Press, 1989), 42–45, 228–31.

20.  No one could possibly fail to notice the contrast, and virtually all historians comment on it. See Krasner on Du Bois's concept of pluralism and the African difference (84); Glassberg on how, in contrast to Du Bois, most community historical pageants depicted "local class, ethnic and race relations as a stable cohesive hierarchy" (133); and Lorini on the absence in "most pageants produced during the period 1905–1917 of African, Native and Asian-Americans," other than as exotic characters (224).

21.  "World War and the Color Line," *The Crisis*, November 1914, 28–30, 28.

22.  For the best, most detailed and extensive account of the strategy by which Du Bois revised and replaced these pieces in *Darkwater*, see Sundquist, *To Wake the Nations*, 582–84; for general comments on the changes in the various versions of these texts, see Levering Lewis, *W. E. B. Du Bois* (2000), 11–19.

23.  Du Bois, we know, was especially enthusiastic about providing statistics for all the performances of *Star*, estimating that the total attendance of the New York audience amounted to 30,000 and that he planned to use 1250 actors and singers in Philadelphia (*The Crisis*, May 1916, Editorial: "The Pageant," 28–29).

24.  See Alys Eve Weinbaum, "The Sexual Politics of Black Internationalism: W. E. B. Du Bois and the Reproduction of Racial Globality," *Wayward Reproductions: Genealogies of Race and Nation in Transatlantic Modern Thought* (Durham, N.C.: Duke University Press, 2004), 222–23, and Moten's essay in this volume.

25.  See Bettina Aptheker, *Woman's Legacy: Essays on Race, Sex, and Class in American History* (Amherst: The University of Massachusetts Press, 1982); Angela Davis, *Women, Race and Class* (New York: Vintage Books/Random House, 1983); Patricia Morton, *Disfigured Images: The Historical Assault on Afro-American Women* (New York: Greenwood Press, 1991).

26.  Levering Lewis, *W. E. B. Du Bois* (1993), 460.

27.  *The Christmas Crisis: Pageant Number*, December 1915, 94.

28.  Glassberg further comments, "Women, like labor and recent immigrants, were left out of scenes depicting crucial turning points in local economic or political history." See *American Historical Pageantry*, 135–36.

29. On the Hazel MacKaye controversy, see Prevots, *American Pageantry*, 96–98. I have drawn all of my citations from this source.

30. For an extended discussion of these tensions, see Glassberg, *American Historical Pageantry*, 284–86.

31. Hill, "Making Noise," 189–94. Hill quotes historian Mary Ryan on "American ceremony" (189); on "West Indian parade complex," see 194; on the procession as celebration of black manhood, see 192–93.

32. Du Bois says in his Woodson sketch that the English ethnographer William Mathew Flinders-Petrie and the American anthropologist Franz Boas were among those with whom he originally wanted in 1909 to collaborate on the idea of an *Encyclopedia Africana*; see Sundquist, *Du Bois Reader*, 281.

33. Nellie McKay argues that Du Bois's three autobiographies demonstrate how central black women have been to the development of his intellectual thought. See "W. E. B. Du Bois: The Black Women in His Writings—Selected Fictional and Autobiographical Portraits," in *Critical Essays on W. E. B. Du Bois*, ed. William L. Andrews (Boston: G. K. Hall, 1985), 230–31; "The Souls of Black Women Folk in the Writings of W. E. B. Du Bois," in *Reading Black, Reading Feminist: A Critical Anthology*, ed. Henry Louis Gates, Jr. (New York: Meridian, 1990).

34. See Sundquist, *To Wake the Nations*, 559. On "Ethiopia as an uncolonized territory of the spirit," see ibid.

35. On the discourse and iconography of true black womanhood, see Anne Stavney, "'Mothers of Tomorrow': The New Negro Renaissance and the Politics of maternal Representation," *African American Review* 32.4 (1998): 533–61.

36. On the racial and sexual politics of the occult, see Peter Washington, *Madame Blavatsky's Baboon: Theosophy and the Emergence of the Western Guru* (London: Secker & Warburg, 1993); K. Paul Johnson, *The Masters Revealed: Madame Blavatsky and the Myth of the Great White Lodge* (Albany: State University of New York Press, 1994); Bruce F. Campbell, *Ancient Wisdom Revealed: A History of the Theosophical Movement* (Berkeley: University of California Press, 1980); Howard Kerr and Charles L. Crow, eds., *The Occult in America: New Historical Perspectives* (Urbana and Chicago: University of Illinois Press, 1983).

37. See Clawson, *Reconstructing Brotherhood*, 192–99; William H. Grimshaw, *Official History of Freemasonry Among the Colored People in North America* (1903; reprint, New York: Negro Universities Press, 1969), 359–60, and *Order of the Eastern Star, An Instructive Manual on the Organization of Chapters of the Order with Ritual and Ceremonies* (Chicago: Ezra A. Cook, 1923); Mrs. S. Joe Brown, *The History of the Order of the Eastern Star Among Colored People* (1925; reprint, New York: G. K. Hall, 1997).

38. Charles Wesley, *Prince Hall Life and Legacy* (Washington, D.C.: The United Supreme Council Southern Jurisdiction, Prince Hall Affiliation; Philadelphia, Pa.: The Afro-American Historical and Cultural Museum, 1977), 180; Sheila Smith McKoy, Introduction to *African-American Women Writers, 1910–1940*, ed. Henry Louis Gates, Jr. (New York: G. K. Hall, 1997), xvi, xxi. This series includes these texts: Elizabeth Lindsay Davis, *The Story of the Illinois Federation of Colored Women's Clubs*, and Mrs. S. Joe Brown, *The History of the Order of the Eastern Star Among Colored People*.

# Contributors

Hazel V. Carby is Charles C. and Dorathea S. Dilley Professor of African American Studies and Professor of American Studies at Yale University. Her books include *Reconstructing Womanhood, Race Men,* and *Cultures in Babylon: Black Britain and African America.* Her current work in progress is tentatively titled "Child of Empire: Racializing Subjects in Post–World War II Britain."

Vilashini Cooppan is assistant professor of literature at the University of California, Santa Cruz. Her essays and articles on postcolonial theory, comparative and world literature, psychoanalysis, and nationalism have appeared in *symploke, Comparative Literature Studies, Public Culture, Gramma,* and several edited volumes. Her book, *Inner Territories: Fictions and Fantasms of the Nation,* is forthcoming in 2008.

Brent Hayes Edwards teaches in the English department at Rutgers University in New Brunswick, New Jersey. He is author of *The Practice of Diaspora: Literature, Translation, and the Rise of Black Internationalism.* With Robert O'Meally and Farah Griffin he co-edited *Uptown Conversation: The New Jazz Studies.* He is coeditor of the journal *Social Text* and also serves on the editorial boards of *Transition* and *Callaloo.*

Michele Elam is Director of Undergraduate Studies and associate professor in the Department of English and the Research Institute at the Center for Comparative Studies in Race and Ethnicity at Stanford University. She is author of *Race, Work, and Desire in American Literature, 1860–1930* and *Mixtries: Mixed Race in the New Millennium.*

Roderick A. Ferguson is associate professor of race and critical theory in the Department of American Studies at the University of Minnesota, Twin Cities. He is the author of *Aberrations in Black: Toward a Queer of Color Critique* (Minnesota, 2004).

**Susan Gillman** is professor of literature at the University of California, Santa Cruz. She is author of *Dark Twins: Imposture and Identity in Mark Twain's America* and *Blood Talk: American Race, Melodrama, and the Culture of the Occult*, and she is coeditor of *Mark Twain's "Pudd'head Wilson": Race, Conflict, and Culture.*

**Joy James** is the author of *Transcending the Talented Tenth: Black Leaders and American Intellectuals, Resisting State Violence* (Minnesota, 1998), and *Shadow Boxing: Representations of Black Feminist Politics*. She is John B. and John T. McCoy Presidential Professor in Africana Studies and College Professor in Political Science at Williams College.

**Fred Moten** teaches English and American studies at the University of Southern California. He is the author of *In the Break: The Aesthetics of the Black Radical Tradition* (Minnesota, 2003) and of two books of poetry, *Arkansas* and (with Jim Behrle) *Poems*. He is completing a manuscript on philosophical, aesthetic, and political criminality in black culture.

**Shawn Michelle Smith** is associate professor of visual and critical studies at the School of the Art Institute of Chicago. She is the author of *American Archives: Gender, Race, and Class in Visual Culture* and *Photography on the Color Line: W. E. B. Du Bois, Race, and Visual Culture*. She is also a visual artist whose recent projects include "Maintaining a Life" and "Economies of Happiness."

**Mason Stokes** is associate professor of English at Skidmore College, where he teaches African American literature and the history of sexuality. He is author of *The Color of Sex: Whiteness, Heterosexuality, and the Fictions of White Supremacy*, as well as essays in *American Quarterly, Callaloo, Transition*, and *American Literary History.*

**Claudia Tate** was, at the time of her death in 2002, professor of English and African-American studies at Princeton University. Her books include *Black Women Writers at Work, Domestic Allegories of Political Desire: The Black Heroine's Text at the Turn of the Century*, and *Psychoanalysis and Black Novels: Desire and the Protocols of Race.*

**Paul C. Taylor** is a fellow of the Jamestown Project at Yale Law School and an associate professor of philosophy at Temple University, where he has served as department chair and as the Associate Director of the Institute for the Study of Race and Social Thought. He writes on aesthetics, race theory, Africana philosophy, and social philosophy, and is author of *Race: A Philosophical Introduction*. He is working on his second book titled *Black is Beautiful: A Philosophy of Africana Aesthetics.*

**Alys Eve Weinbaum** is associate professor of English at the University of Washington, Seattle. She is author of *Wayward Reproductions: Genealogies of Race and Nation in Transatlantic Modern Thought* and coeditor, with the Modern Girl Around the World Research Collaborative, of *The Modern Girl Around the World*. Her current book project is tentatively titled "The New Biologic: Reproductive Labor in Transnationalism."

# Publication History

A brief portion of Chapter 1 appeared in "The Double Politics of Double Consciousness: Reading Nationalism and Globalism in *The Souls of Black Folk*," *Public Culture* 17, no. 2 (Spring 2005). Reprinted by permission.

Chapter 2 appeared in Joy James, *Transcending the Talented Tenth: Black Leaders and American Intellectuals* (New York: Routledge, 1997). Copyright 1997 Joy James. Reprinted with permission; all rights reserved.

Parts of the third section of Chapter 3 appeared in *Wayward Reproductions: Genealogies of Race and Nation in Transatlantic Modern Thought* (Durham: Duke University Press, 2004), and in "Reproducing Racial Globality: W. E. B. Du Bois and the Sexual Politics of Black Internationalism," *Social Text* 67 (Summer 2001): 15–41.

Chapter 5 was previously published in Claudia Tate, *Psychoanalysis and Black Novels: Desire and the Protocols of Race* (New York: Oxford University Press, 1998). Copyright 1998 by Claudia Tate. Used by permission of Oxford University Press, Inc.

Portions of Chapter 7 appeared in "The Souls of Black Men," from Hazel V. Carby, *Race Men* (Cambridge: Harvard University Press, 1998), 9–41. Copyright 1998 by the President and Fellows of Harvard College. Reprinted by permission of the publisher.

Portions of Chapter 9 appeared in a different form as Mason Stokes, "Strange Fruits: Rethinking the Gay Twenties," *Transition* 92: 56–79. Also available online at www.transitionmagazine.com/online/strangefruits.htm. Special thanks to Michael Vazquez for permission to reprint.

Portions of Chapter 11 appeared in Shawn Michelle Smith, *Photography on the Color Line: W. E. B. Du Bois, Race, and Visual Culture* (Durham: Duke University Press, 2004). Copyright 2004 Duke University Press. Reprinted with permission of the publisher.

# Index